fountains Splash and Spectacle

fountains
Splash
and Spectacle

Water and Design from the Renaissance to the Present

Edited by Marilyn Symmes

Kenneth Breisch

Maria Ann Conelli

Naomi Miller

Marilyn Symmes

Marc Treib

Features by

Stephen Astley

Bart Barlow

Paula Deitz

Andrew S. Dolkart

Katherine W. Rinne

Stephen Van Dyk

With 302 illustrations, 140 in colour

Thames and Hudson
in association with
Cooper-Hewitt
National Design Museum
Smithsonian Institution

Frontispiece: Night view of the
Trevi Fountain, Rome.
Designed by Nicola Salvi,
completed 1762.

This edition published on the
occasion of the exhibition
Fountains: Splash and Spectacle
at Cooper-Hewitt,
National Design Museum,
Smithsonian Institution,
9 June – 11 October 1998.

Design by Avril Broadley

British Library Cataloguing-in Publication Data
A catalogue record for this book is
available from the British Library

ISBN 0-500-23758-1
Printed in Singapore

contents

foreword

Fountains unite the physical and inspirational aspects of water to play a fundamental role in enhancing the human environment. Fountain designers and hydraulic expertise often push the limits of water's physical properties. When creating fountains, designers consider how the water should move—with gentle insistence or raging force; how the water should sound—as a soothing trickle or as a surging splash; and how the water should look—clear and smooth or frothy and white. Some of the world's greatest cities—Rome, Paris, Madrid, London, New York, Los Angeles, Chicago, Dallas, and Washington D.C.—as well as some of its smallest towns are distinctive because of fountains. This book discusses the design, function and meaning of fountains from the Renaissance to the present, with examples selected from the many glorious public fountains in western Europe and the United States. Rather than approach the subject in a strictly chronological or geographical manner, the chapters are treated thematically. The first chapter introduces some of the history and ways fountain designers consider the qualities of water and manipulate its movement. The following chapters present fountains as refreshment, as metaphor, as propaganda, as spectacle at international expositions, as commemoration, as entertainment and pleasure, and finally, fountains as urban oases.

The goal of the National Design Museum in undertaking this book and the associated 1998 exhibition is to underscore the value of fountain design as a vital element in our built environment. We want to increase people's understanding and appreciation of the circumstances and characteristics that make fountains successful in enlivening public spaces. It is our hope that readers will be prompted to look anew at the fountains they encounter in their own communities or on their travels, and thus help promote interest in preserving existing fountains or developing new ones.

The decision to embark on a major book and an exhibition exploring aspects of the fountain in western Europe and America was due in part to the many beautiful and fascinating fountain drawings and prints in the museum's collection. The sheer number and variety of wonderful fountains throughout the world elicited some basic questions. Why has water, nature's most abundant resource, become such an important design element in the creation of gardens and public spaces? How have designers harmonized water with static materials to create compositions with texture, color, pattern, movement and spatial dimension? What stylistic and iconographic traditions have developed over the centuries to make fountains such distinctive sources of aesthetic and sensory delight, as well as generators of symbolic and social meaning? It is our hope that *Fountains: Splash and Spectacle* will provide some answers, prompt further inquiry and spur design innovation.

The museum is indebted to the generous donors who have helped to make this important fountains publication and the 1998 *Fountains: Splash and Spectacle* exhibition a reality. Our deepest gratitude goes to the Florence Gould Foundation for making the exhibition possible. The publication was funded in large part by The Andrew W. Mellon Foundation Endowment Fund. Additional major support for the exhibition and publication was provided by the Arthur Ross Foundation; the Colbert Foundation, and the Comité Colbert; the Graham Foundation for Advanced Study in the Fine Arts; Furthermore, the publication program of The J. M. Kaplan Fund; the Lisa Taylor Fund; the New York State Council on the Arts; the Fleming Charitable Trust; Ms. Sheridan Brown; and the Smithsonian Institution Special Exhibition Fund.

I wish to take this opportunity to express gratitude to the Cooper-Hewitt, National Design Museum Department of Drawings and Prints staff, Gail Davidson, Samantha Finch, Elizabeth Marcus, John Randall, Susan Vicinelli and other museum colleagues, for their efforts on behalf of this book and the coinciding exhibition. As always, the many people who assisted in realizing these projects are too numerous to list. Nevertheless, I would like to single out several individuals who are particularly important. My deep appreciation is extended to Marilyn Symmes, curator of Drawings and Prints, Cooper-Hewitt, National Design Museum, who has been involved in this project since its inception in 1994. She has enthusiastically carried much of the responsibility for the publication and exhibition, involving herself in every aspect of its organization. I applaud her dedication and determination in planning and nurturing this book through many stages to its realization. Others also deserve very special recognition and our gratitude. Jeannette Redensek, research associate for the *Fountains: Splash and Spectacle* project, provided collaborative insight, scholarly knowledge and the logistical efficiency necessary for the challenge of producing this book and exhibition. I especially thank all the authors who thoughtfully enriched the text: Kenneth Breisch, professor, Department of History and Theory, Southern California Institute of Architecture, Los Angeles; Maria Ann Conelli, chair, Masters Program in the History of Decorative Arts, Cooper-Hewitt, National Design Museum, Smithsonian Institution/Parsons School of Design, New York; Naomi Miller, professor of art history, Boston University; and Marc Treib, professor of architecture, University

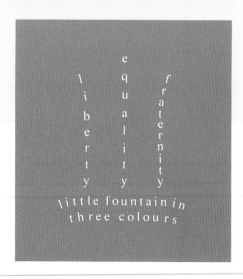

of California at Berkeley; along with Marilyn Symmes, who wrote the chapters. I would also like to thank those who contributed lively and informative features on selected topics: Stephen Astley, assistant curator [drawings], Sir John Soane's Museum, London; Bart Barlow, a photographer and writer based in Ohio and New York; Paula Deitz, editor of *The Hudson Review* and a New York cultural critic; Andrew S. Dolkart, adjunct associate professor, Columbia University School of Architecture, Planning, and Preservation; Katherine W. Rinne, associate fellow, Institute for Advanced Technology in the Humanities and visiting research faculty, School of Architecture, University of Virginia, Charlottesville; and Stephen Van Dyk, librarian, Cooper-Hewitt, National Design Museum, Smithsonian Institution Libraries. My appreciation is also extended to the editors of this publication: Lorraine Karafel, project editor; Serena Totman, assistant editor; and Caroline Mortimer, the museum's editor. And finally, I extend my warm thanks to all the designers and colleagues cited in the acknowledgments for kindly contributing their expertise and support.

This book is dedicated to the countless fountain designers and hydraulic engineers throughout the world and to the enlightened patrons who make fountains possible. Through their vision and innovative ideas, fountains have increasingly come to grace and enhance the designed environment, and our public spaces have become more enjoyable places to visit.

Dianne H. Pilgrim
Director
Cooper-Hewitt, National Design Museum
Smithsonian Institution

∧ 2 Prometheus Fountain, dramatically lit at night, and the soaring tower of the G. E. Building, Rockefeller Center, New York. Designed by Paul Manship, 1934; fountain effects updated by WET Design, 1988.

< 3 *Little Fountain in Three Colours*, 1987. Caligramme print by Ian Hamilton Finlay.

Note to the Reader
Information about fountains and their designers is given in full in the Chronology on p. 183.

chapter 1

the rise and fall of Water

Fountains harmonize water and design to fulfill both practical and aesthetic purposes. In the past, public fountains served as places to meet while collecting water for drinking or washing, but they were also landmarks designed to impress as they refreshed. Then, as now, fountains embody symbolic, artistic and social ideas as they enliven places and reinvigorate people. As ensembles of stone, metal or concrete, the success of a fountain design is ultimately determined by its aesthetic mastery of light and water. While water is a familiar substance, understanding its versatile qualities and how best to use them in fountains requires sustained observation of nature, knowledge of technical hydraulics and artistic sensibility. Many glorious fountains attest to the ingenious ability of designers to transform a dry, solid monument into a vibrantly wet and changeable work of art. The existence of fountains as amenities for people's use and pleasure, however, depends upon the expert integration of rising and falling water, design elements and hydraulic technology.

< 4 *The Great Fountain, Enville, Staffordshire*. Chromolithograph by E. Adveno Brooke from *The Gardens of England* (London, 1857).

Water

Water permeates the natural world and every aspect of our being. It covers about two-thirds of the earth's surface, but only a small percentage is available as fresh water. Its cyclical presence in the earth's atmosphere influences our daily weather. It constitutes a major component in the cells of our bodies. We physically need its refreshment to live. We crave seeing, hearing or touching it for sensual pleasure, spiritual solace or experiences of enchanting wonder. Myths, legends, symbols, poetry, music and art all extoll water's power and versatility. Civilizations exploit its forces for both simple and complex purposes. It has affected the political and economic course of history; villages and cities first developed near sources of water and trade and exploration depended on waterways. Water continually shapes our world, and people constantly devise ways to capture and control it to fulfill their daily needs and desires.

When in repose, the surface of water, a transparent and colorless liquid, can be luminous, crystalline or reflective. When large amounts move rapidly or turbulently, however, water then becomes an undulating, churning mass of frothy

whiteness. Its movement can be invitingly gentle or frighteningly destructive. The ancient Chinese philosopher Lao-Tze once said: "Nothing in the world is as soft and yielding as water. Yet for dissolving the hard and inflexible, nothing can surpass it."[1] Water is most prevalent in its liquid state, but it also exists in other physical states. When water freezes, it is transformed into flakes of snow or masses of solid ice; in its gaseous state, it becomes billowing vapor, steam, fog or mist eluding containment.

Nature provides the most awesome spectacles of rising and falling water. The Old Faithful Geyser in Wyoming's Yellowstone National Park [5] shoots colossal columns of hot spring water and steam skyward in periodic eruptions that occur almost hourly. Reaching heights ranging from 100 to 180 feet, each dazzling performance lasts only a few minutes. The majestic beauty and unceasing power of the mighty cataracts of Niagara Falls, one of the most celebrated natural landmarks in North America, impress all who behold them [6].

No two water jets and no two waterfalls are exactly alike since moving water produces an infinite range of changing forms and sounds. Designers deliberately

∧ 5 *Old Faithful*, 1870. Albumen print by William Henry Jackson.

> 6 *Niagara in summer, from below*, c. 1888. Photograph (combination print) by George Barker.

exploit water's unique liquid properties. For instance, it can separate into variously sized drops that sparkle like diamonds [13]; conversely, drops can seamlessly join together as they flow and fall to form undulating shapes [12]. Because of water's viscosity, smaller, individual drops disappear completely when they merge with larger volumes.

Capturing and coaxing precise performance from water has been a significant part of fountain design, particularly since the Renaissance. The dramatic water effects found in nature have inspired the form of many monumental fountains. In 1857, the English artist E. Adveno Brooke described his memorable experience of the Great Fountain [4] in the gardens of Enville in Staffordshire, England:

As we stood admiring the beauty and tranquillity of the scene, a bubbling sound of water, at first gentle and gathering force by degrees, broke out and we beheld the commencement of one of the most beautiful aquatic displays it is possible to conceive. This, the large fountain, is on a level with the surface of the lake, and composed of five jets, the central one throwing a column of water 150 feet high; the supply being obtained from a large reservoir on the hill, to which it is first pumped by the united action of two engines, each of thirty-horse power. The day was one of the most favorable, as the slightest breeze spoils the regularity of the display, and the clear blue sky, into which towered the conical head of the massive cloud, with the crystal stream darting across it, brought distinctly out the most beautiful and effective features of the fountain. In the course of a few minutes it had reached its culminating point, leaping like a bright and joyous thing of life high into the air, and falling around in absolute clouds of the most brilliant and variegated color. We stood watching the superb spectacle till, at a given signal, it gradually sunk as if tired with its exertions; the bosom of the lake caught its last murmuring ripple, and all was still.[2]

Like a gigantic geyser, the Jet d'Eau in Geneva, Switzerland, vigorously soars, controlled yet free, to a height of over four hundred feet [8]. The water jet only temporarily defies gravity, however, and eventually collapses back into Lake Geneva. Sunlight refracting through the spray and gusts of wind alter the jet's effects; during inclement weather, the Jet d'Eau is turned off. This singular fountain, which the Geneva Water Board claims is the tallest such fountain in the world, originated in 1886, as a result of an industrial safety measure at the city's power plant. In order to relieve accumulating water and steam pressure, water was regularly discharged upward over the plant's roofs. The Jet d'Eau soon became an appealing tourist attraction and, in 1891, it was moved to a more prominent location in Geneva's harbor on the Eaux-Vives Jetty. A major feat of engineering upgraded the jet in 1951. Powerful electric pumps now propel 130 gallons of water each second so that seven tons of water are suspended in the air at any given time. The towering plume of water has become this Swiss city's symbol of the triumph of man's mastery over nature. The Jet d'Eau also serves as an emblem of Geneva, especially in the tourism industry, where it graces everything from travel brochures to luggage labels [7].

∨ 7 An early 20th-century luggage label from the Hotel Richemond, depicting the Jet d'Eau against the skyline and mountain backdrop of Geneva, Switzerland.

∨ 8 Jet d'Eau, Geneva, Switzerland, 1886; upgraded 1951.

Elsewhere in Europe and America, tall jet fountains serve as captivating focal points for formal gardens and landscaped settings. In the baroque gardens of Herrenhausen, near Hanover in Germany [10], a water jet punctuates the vista of a long avenue at its cross-axis. In the grounds of the White House in Washington, D.C., a single jet in a circular pool, modeled after the fountains of French formal gardens, accents the official residence of the American president. In the parklike setting of the General Motors Technical Center outside Detroit, Michigan, Alexander Calder's rising and falling water jet fountains enliven an artificial lake set amid starkly modernist buildings [9]. Dubbed "GM's Industrial Versailles," Calder's jets perform a beautiful water ballet. At the Trocadéro (Palais de Chaillot), opposite the Eiffel Tower in Paris, fountains devised for the 1937 Paris exposition periodically shoot massive jets horizontally, like cannons, to form bridgelike arcs [194]. In Chicago, the Nicholas J. Melas Centennial Fountain and Water Arc (1989), designed by Lohan Associates, periodically fires an eighty-foot-

∧ 9 "GM's Industrial Versailles," General Motors Technical Center, Warren, Michigan. Fountains designed by Alexander Calder, completed 1956.

∧ 10 Great Fountain in the gardens of Herrenhausen, near Hanover, Germany, 1682–1720s.

high water arc across the 222-foot-wide Chicago River from May through October. It marks the point where the waters of the Chicago region flow east through the Great Lakes and the St. Lawrence River to the Atlantic Ocean, and just south-west of Chicago, where the waters flow into the Mississippi and the Gulf of Mexico.[3]

Picturesque wild cascades, like those at Terni near Tivoli in Italy, exemplify the exciting ways gravity makes water fall, tumble and splash over a gradual, sloping rocky terrain or drop suddenly down a steep cliff. The cascade was popular in Italian Renaissance villa gardens, usually taking the form of water stairs, such as those at the Villa Lante and the Villa Aldobrandini [133]. Water stairs and cascades need only a thin layer of water to provide the maximum visual and sound effects, and they are prominent architectural features in many formal gardens, including Saint-Cloud in France [147], Chatsworth in England [264], Caserta in Italy [148], and quite grandiosely, at Peterhof in Russia [146]. Contemporary waterfall fountains mimic nature more closely, creating informal oases in the heart

of the city, as in New York's Greenacre Park [11], Portland's Ira C. Keller Fountain [285], or Fort Worth's canyonlike Water Gardens [287]. The mountainlike streams of these fountain cascades splash turbulently down manmade terraces and boulders providing temporary visual and aural distraction from urban cares and noise. Fountain designers carefully orchestrate a cascade's descent, so that in some places the flowing water glistens as it smoothly hugs the surface beneath (laminar flow), while in other places the slightest disturbance causes it to mix with the air and become frothy white splashes (turbulent flow).

Fountains

Originally, the word "fountain" referred to a natural spring or source, but it has come to mean an artificial structure designed to contain and move water, providing people with refreshment, aesthetic pleasure, or both. The solid sculptural or architectural structure is designed to manipulate and shape the fluidity of water into delicate or grand jets and sprays, or to channel it into refined or thundering flows and falls.

Since antiquity, artists and architects have strived to work with and imitate nature. Leon Battista Alberti, the fifteenth-century humanist and architect, wrote in his treatise on architecture: "We consider a building to be a body which, like other bodies, consists of design and of matter of which one is produced by the mind and the other by nature."[4] In fountains, water serves as an additional natural material that the designer can mold and transform into art and ornament. In a letter dated 26 July 1543, the Renaissance humanist Claudio Tolomei wrote enthusiastically about the sensual pleasures and the then-novel visual marvels of Roman garden fountains: "But what pleases me more in these new fountains is the variety of ways with which they guide, divide, turn, lead, break, and at one movement cause water to descend and at another time to rise." He also remarked on "the ingenious skill newly rediscovered to

< 11 Greenacre Park, New York. Designed by Sasaki, Dawson, De May Associates, 1971.

∧ 12 Falling water (detail) at California Plaza Watercourt, Los Angeles. Designed by WET Design, 1992.

∧ 13 Jet spray from the Avenue of the Hundred Fountains, Villa d'Este, Tivoli, Italy. Garden design by Pirro Ligorio, 1550–72.

make fountains, in which mixing art with nature, one can't judge if it [the fountain] is the work of the former or the latter; thus, one appears a natural artefact and another, man-made nature. Thus they strive nowadays to assemble a fountain that appears to be made by nature, not by accident but with masterful art."[5] What Tolomei perceived about fountain design is still true today.

A fountain is comprised of two basic components: the source or genesis of the water flow or trajectory; and the receiver, basin, or pool capturing and containing the water. Contemporary artist Bruce Nauman's *Self-portrait as a Fountain* perfectly illustrates the concept of fountain genesis, as he spouts water from his mouth [15]. Art often mimics nature, and throughout the world one finds many fountains with human, animal or imaginary grotesque heads, whose mouths serve as fountain spouts or faucets [16]. Marcel Duchamp's readymade *Fountain* (1917) transcended its original functional purpose as a urinal to illustrate the concept of a fountain basin as a receiver and container of water.[6]

Fountains can be divided into two categories: those where the structure dominates, and those where water is the primary feature. In fountains where the architectural or sculptural framework is foremost, the water plays a supporting decorative role, animating and enhancing the central structure. The majority of European fountains since the Renaissance, and many American ones harking back to the European model, showcase sculpture or architectural mastery. Classic examples include the Fountain of Neptune in Florence [130], the Trevi Fountain in Rome [128, 271], the Bassin d'Apollon at Versailles [142], the fountain at London's Piccadilly Circus [208], and the Prometheus

< 14 Dragon spouting ice, Fontaine Saint-Michel, Paris. Designed by Gabriel Davioud, 1858–60. Late 19th-century photograph on albumen paper by Amédée Denisse.

< 15 *Self-portrait as a Fountain*, 1966. Photograph by Bruce Nauman.

< 16 Fontana del Mascherone, Via Giulia, Rome, *c.* 1626.

Fountain in New York City's Rockefeller Center [161]. Such fountains can still be understood and admired for their aesthetic qualities even without the water running. When flowing water is present, however, the fountains gain added vitality from the constantly changing kinetic motion, sparkling effects and splashing sounds. In other fountains, the aesthetic impact depends chiefly, if not exclusively, on the rise and fall of water, either as a singular feature (as in Geneva's Jet d'Eau) or as the sequential choreography of various water movements. Islamic fountains (where figurative sculpture is forbidden) and Western ones such as those at the Trocadéro in Paris, at Lincoln Center in New York [254], and at Fountain Place in Dallas [42–44, 295] comprise kinetic sculptures of rising and falling jets. Fountains which rely on falling water for dramatic effect, such as the cascades at Caserta, Chatsworth, or in Portland, are far less enthralling when dry. Without the water, there is only a still pool, or an unsightly puddled or dry fountain bed revealing its arrangement of pipes and outlets. Some contemporary fountains are designed with jets recessed into the pavement, or as stepped terraces, so that even without moving water, their artistic substance is not noticeably compromised. In winter, particularly in regions with freezing climates, fountain water is usually turned off to protect the fountain structure from ice damage. Some traditional fountains hibernate gracefully, reverting to their role as sculptural works of art or architecture. Occasionally, when a cold spell occurs before the water is turned off, magical transformations can occur, as when a dragon appears to be snorting ice in the Fontaine Saint-Michel in Paris [14]. Some contemporary fountains, such as the Northland Fountain in Kansas City, Missouri, are designed to operate throughout the winter to take advantage of ice effects that create impromptu sculpture.

In addition to concerns about water flow and the underlying sculptural or architectural structure, fountain designers must also consider the placement of a fountain on its site. If the fountain is to be viewable and accessible from all sides, then it must be placed in the center of its space, as are many fountains in city plazas and at intersections of garden pathways. Other fountains are placed against a building, creating monumental and theatrical settings, such as the Trevi Fountain [1] or the Fontaine des Quatre Saisons (Fountain of the Four Seasons) in Paris [68], and are best viewed in their entirety from a frontal and central position. Practical drinking fountains are often inset into building walls at street level for the convenience of pedestrians [70, 71].

The role of drawing in fountain design

Fountains, like architecture and works of art, originate as abstract ideas in the designer's mind. These ideas usually first assume visual shape, however tentatively, as conceptual drawings. Since the Renaissance, artists, architects and other designers have often used speculative sketching as a way to explore and develop design possibilities. Although computer-aided design is used increasingly today, many contemporary artists, architects and designers continue to work out initial ideas by drawing, employing the medium to elaborate an idea from first concept to final realization. Such drawings are the tangible traces of creative thought. While drawings have long been recognized and appreciated as a traditional part of artistic and architectural practice, design drawings for fountains are rarely singled out as a discrete genre, although quite a large and distinctive body of them exists. Surviving drawings for some of the world's most famous fountains provide important insights into the fountain design process. Those for Siena's Fonte Gaia (completed 1491 [56, 57]), for Rome's Trevi Fountain (completed 1762 [149, 150]), and for Paris's Place de la Concorde (completed 1840 [157, 158]) reveal some of the complexities behind the making of these fountains. It is rare, however, for all the documents of a fountain's design process to be preserved so that one can track the process step by step from start to final realization. Occasionally, in later stages of design development, the designer may also choose to employ three-dimensional models or scale maquettes to work out the fountain's precise details or overall proportions and structural relationships.

∧ 17 Triton Fountain, Piazza Barberini, Rome. Designed by Gian Lorenzo Bernini, 1642–43.

< 18 *Study for a Triton*, 1642–43. Red chalk and tinted wash drawing by Gian Lorenzo Bernini.

Sometimes fountain design drawings astonish viewers with their utter simplicity. For example, from a few rippling red chalk outlines and a bit of well-placed shading, one can sense the powerful torso Gian Lorenzo Bernini was envisioning for the Triton Fountain in Piazza Barberini, Rome [18]. This sole surviving study from 1642–43, firmly attributable to Bernini's own hand, is a vital clue to the artist's original intentions for what was to revolutionize Italian fountain design. In fact, this drawing and the extant Triton Fountain rank among the most spectacular examples of the genesis and conclusion of an important fountain design. He created sculptural forms that suggest a liberating sense of movement, so that instead of the statues being static in their solidity, they seem to interact with the water. Built for his patron Pope Urban VIII (Maffeo Barberini), Bernini's Triton Fountain transforms what had been a quotidian type of fountain in a Roman square into the eloquent glorification of a sea god and of papal rule. While tritons are often ornamental features of fountains, Bernini's Triton Fountain infuses a convincing vigor into the mythological creature who was summoned by Neptune to blow the conch shell mightily so that even the most distant turbulent waves would hear the command

to restore calm. Perched on a scallop shell held aloft by the tails of four dolphins, the kneeling Triton blows a forceful jet upward, a hydraulic visualization of colossal sound [17]. For its day, the Triton Fountain's jet was the highest in Rome. Fed by the waters of the nearby Acqua Felice, the jetted water cascades back down on the Triton's magnificent torso, drenching the papal tiara and Barberini bee emblem nestled between the dolphins.

In addition to preparatory drawings for existing fountains, the legacy of fountain design also includes drawings which document proposed works that were never built and were purely imaginary conceptions. Some fountain drawings serve as tests of inventive ideas. They hint at the concerns of the designer. How will the fountain appear in a specific setting? How will the fountain structure interact with various water effects? How best can the fountain achieve its symbolic form, its festive spectacle or its utilitarian function? What are the design ramifications of certain technical considerations? Without question fountain designers have always looked to historical precedents as sources for ideas and inventive forms. The powerful originality of Bernini's Triton Fountain has inspired many artists, designers and architects through the years. The French architect Gilles-Marie Oppenord began his career in the 1690s studying in Rome, where he found a wealth of ornamental ideas amid the city's examples of antique and baroque art and architecture. Aspects of Bernini's ingenuity probably sparked a playful, imaginary fountain design by Oppenord in which two engaging dogs stand to reach the rim of a shell supported by the tails of two dolphins, each snorting water, recalling the base of Bernini's Triton Fountain [20]. Instead of a triton, however, Oppenord has his jet rising from a central arrangement of crown and orb, which is further enlivened by water branching from the sticks offered up by the dogs. Oppenord preserved this drawing in an album which he referred to throughout his life whenever he needed a spark of inspiration to trigger a new decorative idea.

Carlo Marchionni, a Roman architect, engineer and designer of figurative and other ornamental decoration for churches, palaces and monuments, also used drawings to develop his fountain designs. In 1746, Marchionni received a commission for his first grand-scale project, the design of a villa and garden embellishments for his patron Cardinal Alessandro Albani. The Villa Albani was intended as a showcase for the cardinal's splendid collection of classical antiquities. Among Marchionni's accomplished designs for the villa is a drawing for a Pegasus fountain simulating a naturalistic landscape with a statue of the mythic horse tapping its hoof on a rocky arch over a stream [19]. The sculptural allusion to the origins of the first fountain in classical mythology would have been much appreciated by Marchionni's learned patron.

Marchionni's contemporary, the eighteenth-century Roman architect Giuseppe Barberi, who received few actual commissions, unleashed his restless artistic energy in fluid, yet sure, applications of pen and ink, producing a large corpus of drawings.[7] Among his many fountain designs are ideas for enhancing plazas with urban landmarks featuring river gods and jetting water [21], a traditional fountain form that may have been prompted by Bernini's Fountain of the Four Rivers [122] or by antique statues of river gods.

In this century, designers have sought to update past styles with a modern architectural sensibility. The French garden designers André and Paul Vera revived French classical garden design, exemplified by André Le Nôtre, but simplified it by introducing a modest scale and new materials, defining spaces, for example, with concrete walls. Among their initial concept drawings is a proposal for a secluded *salon* (or outdoor room) where people could enjoy tranquillity in the midst of a larger public garden [22]. The central focus is a figurative fountain, a personification of a water source, with water falling from the urn on her shoulder, and two symmetrical trellises house columnar fountains for drinking or handwashing.

Many contemporary designers continue the practice of drawing regularly in personal sketchbooks to record observations from nature and to jot down ideas for fountain designs. For decades the American designer Lawrence Halprin has sketched moving water in mountain streams [281] and on coastal shores. Jim Garland, fountain designer for the Los Angeles firm of WET Design which specializes in creating fountains using the latest engineering and computer technology, always starts his design process with sketchbook drawings. While many of Garland's drawings show plans for different playful water effects, some show the designer working out how to use the technological devices that create the desired water action, such as leaping arcs of water. Other studies show Garland resolving the "iris" wave action in a pool, in which turbulent water moves concentrically toward and away from the center, similar to

∨ 21 *Elevation of a Fountain*, *c*. 1790. Pen, ink, brush and sepia drawing by Giuseppe Barberi.

> 22 *Studies for an Ornamental Garden with Fountain and Statue*, *c*. 1912–14. Pen and black ink, watercolor, white gouache and black crayon drawing by André and Paul Vera.

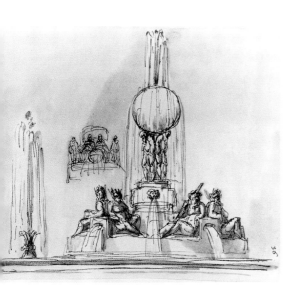

Hydraulics: how water moves from there to here (or here to there)

Water, the simple chemical compound of hydrogen and oxygen (H_2O), is complex in its myriad fluid movements, which range from gentle and controlled to torrentially powerful and wildly unpredictable. Thus, when designing fountains, designers consider all the possible nuances of water's appearance, sound and motion. Hydraulics, a branch of physics and engineering, deals with the properties and practical applications of water in motion—that is, velocities, pressures and flow patterns associated with water's fluidity.[8] The art of fountain design flourishes as hydraulic technology advances. Increasingly spectacular fountain effects are possible as technology perfects the ability to manipulate water in various ways, either by gravity, mechanical methods, pressurized pumps, electrically powered equipment or, most recently, with the aid of computers. In order to design particular fountain effects, designers have to understand what factors affect the volume and flow of water. Lessons in fountain design are learned by observing how water fluctuates in nature or in manmade situations: how it glides smoothly down narrow, straight channels; how the surface ripples when hit by rain drops or objects; how it shimmies and shivers around rocks or other obstacles in its path; how it tumbles and whirls creating agitated white water; how it can delicately spray like dewy mist; how it changes momentum as it courses through wide or narrow openings; or how it vigorously splashes and crashes. What situations cause water to make noises such as plops, gurgles, trickles, and rushing roars? Knowing how to use the pull of gravity and familiarity with artificial ways to move water upward are part of the repertoire of hydraulics.

From the sixteenth to the late eighteenth century, fountain designers were multitalented individuals, often serving as architect, artist, artisan, engineer and cultivated scholar all in one. Leonardo

The movement of an eye or a camera iris. The designer then uses hydraulic and computer technology to translate these visions into actual fountains.

Habit de Fontainier,

A Paris, Chez N. de Larmessin, Rüe St. Iacq, à la Pôme d'Or.   Auec. Priuil. du Roy.

da Vinci exemplified the Renaissance artist as creative genius, inventor and scientific expert. His immense curiosity about the forces of nature led him to investigate the properties and movement of water, and he methodically recorded his observations in his now-celebrated notebooks. Early Italian fountain designers coupled imagination with hydraulic and gardening expertise to transform private villa settings with ingenious water displays full of symbolic meaning and natural beauty. Renowned for his virtuosity in archeology, architecture and garden design, the humanist Pirro Ligorio provided the vision behind the splendors of the Villa d'Este in Tivoli (1550–72 [229–36]). Bernardo Buontalenti, well versed in humanistic subjects and classical scientific texts, masterminded the extraordinary water marvels, automata and water jokes for the Medici Villa, Pratolino, near Florence (1569–89).[9] Roman architect-

∧ 23 *The Fountain Maker's Costume*. Engraving by Nicolas de Larmessin from *Habit des métiers et professions* (Paris, 1690). With a tasteful jet and tier as a hat, the fountain maker's torso is charmingly clad in two broad basins adorned with tritons. His legs sport reeded columns topped by stout *gnudi*.

> 24 *Another Way to Augment the Strength of a Fountain*, from Book One, Problem XV, *Les Raisons des forces mouvantes* by Salomon de Caus (Frankfurt, 1615).

> 25 *Design of a Mount Parnassus, Inside of Which One Could Make Grottoes*, from Book Two, Problem XIII, *Les Raisons des forces mouvantes* by Salomon de Caus (Frankfurt, 1615).

engineers Domenico and Giovanni Fontana were responsible for designing Rome's first major public fountains since antiquity, the outlets for the Acqua Felice (1585–88 [58]) and the Acqua Paola (1610–12 [90]).

A broad range of skills, often diplomatic as well as technical, were required to devise ways to obtain water for fountains from distant sources. The creation of sixteenth-century Italian fountains needed two particular kinds of specialized expertise in addition to that of the designer: the architect-engineer, today called the hydraulic engineer, who was concerned with the logistics of getting the gross water supply to a garden or public city fountain; and the artisan (*fontaniere* in Italian or *fontainier* in French), who crafted the fountain structure and the plumbing [23].[10] The technical demands of fountain design projects were such that they were almost always the result of collaboration, and this team approach has survived to our own day. The bigger and more complicated the project, the more people trained in diverse specialized skills are necessary. Yet public recognition of those responsible for realizing the feats of fountain design and construction is traditionally reserved for those who masterminded the project, and

the names of the accomplished builders, craftsmen, plumbers and technicians who worked to execute the fountain are often deeply buried, surfacing only occasionally in contracts and financial records.

Although the names of early European *fontanieri* are rarely known, a few have been singled out for recognition. The talented services of the Italian Curzio Maccarone were highly prized by several wealthy patrons in the 1550s and 1560s. He is credited with executing two notable masterpieces at the Villa d'Este, the Fountain of Tivoli [234] and the Fountain of Rome, or Rometta [232].[11] Because the Villa d'Este included so many elaborate waterworks, numerous *fontanieri* were involved in their construction. Some artisans focused on the task of fashioning the fountain structure, while others took care of maintaining and repairing those that were completed. Still others specialized in water-powered automata, such as the French *fontainiers* Luc Le Clerc and his nephew Claude Venard, who were employed to create the Villa d'Este's Water Organ [230].[12]

Major hydraulic expertise migrated to France from Italy in 1598 when Tommaso and Alessandro Francini, who had worked with Buontalenti on Pratolino's impressive waterworks, were summoned by Henri IV and his Italian wife Marie de' Medici to design a great Italianate garden for the château of St. Germain-en-Laye, west of Paris. In France, they were known as the Francine brothers, and their innovations greatly influenced French garden and fountain design. Their expertise trickled down to their descendants who continued the family tradition of employing the latest technology when devising inventive waterworks for later royal gardens, including those at Versailles.

The primary means of transmitting practical hydraulic information and fountain design ideas throughout Europe and abroad, however, was via published treatises and illustrated books which contributed to the evolution of scientific technology. Salomon de Caus (1576–1626), born in Normandy, France, was an internationally renowned pioneer in hydraulics. He began his career working with Buontalenti at Pratolino, and his pre-eminent expertise in designing gardens, grottoes and ingenious water features brought him royal commissions in Brussels, London and Heidelberg. Toward the end of his life, back in France, de Caus

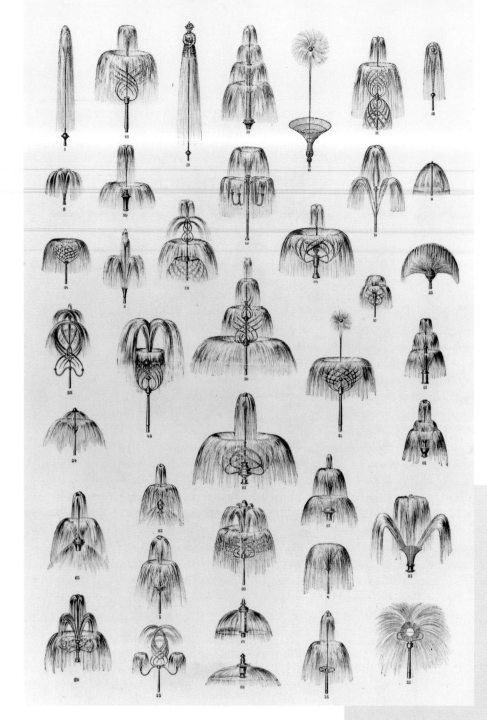

wrote *Les Raisons des forces mouvantes*
(The Principles of Moving Forces), 1615,
a fundamental text on hydraulic mechanics
and engineering. The book updated
the key hydraulic discoveries of classical
antiquity, particularly the work of
Archimedes, inventor of the water screw as
a mechanical means to move water [259],
the *Pneumatica* (*Pneumatics*) of Hero of
Alexandria, and the architectural and
engineering treatises of Vitruvius.
In addition, *Les Raisons* functioned as an
illustrated manual demonstrating various
ways to make water rise (either through
conduits or as a water jet) and showing the
behavior of steam or air pressure interacting
with water. One illustration shows sunlight
heating water in two vessels hidden in a
room adjacent to an ornamental fountain.
As the heated water expands, it rises and
flows up the pipes leading to the fountain,
thereby activating it [24]. De Caus also
included designs for pumps, waterwheels,
water automata (including artificial singing
birds inspired by Hero's ancient text),
organs, grottoes and fountains.

Les Raisons also documents one of de
Caus's masterpieces, a marvelous Mount
Parnassus grotto fountain he designed in
1609 as a prominent feature for the garden
of Somerset House, the London palace of
Anne of Denmark [25].[13] In a pool about
eighty feet in diameter, de Caus designed
an artificial mountain made of boulders, sea
stones and mussel and snail shells, with
shrubs, herbs and flowers tucked into
various crannies. Statues of Apollo and the
Muses, each playing a musical instrument,
sit near the top. The winged horse Pegasus
crowns the peak of Mount Parnassus, from
which spring several graceful arcs of
water—a reference to the mythological
origins of the first fountain caused by
Pegasus's tapping his hoof and thereby
uncovering a hidden spring which spurted
forth. Fed by an elaborate waterworks
running from the nearby River Thames,
the Mount Parnassus fountain must have
enchanted visitors as Apollo and the Muses
celebrated the virtues of peace, harmonious
beauty, and nature. The etching in *Les
Raisons* is all that remains of de Caus's
Mount Parnassus since, by the eighteenth
century, all traces of this wondrous creation
were obliterated by the later redesign of the
garden. After Salomon de Caus's death in

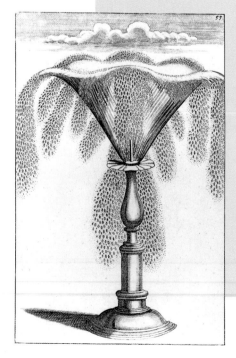

∧ 26 Fountain jets from *Illustrated
Catalogue of Statuary, Fountains,
Vases, Settees, etc., for Parks,
Gardens and Conservatories,
Manufactured by the J. L. Mott Iron
Works* (New York, 1873). Amidst
their inventory of cast-iron fountains
featuring classical figures, twining
acanthus leaves, and putti wrestling
with dolphins, the Mott Iron Works
also offered customers this diverse
selection of fountain jets, in which
the water shot from sinuously
twisting pipes becomes pure
decorative form.

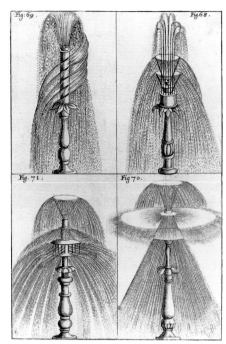

< > 27–31 Fountain designs from *Architectura Curiosa Nova, Die Lustreiche Bau- und Wasserkunst* by Georg Andreas Böckler (Nuremberg, 1664).

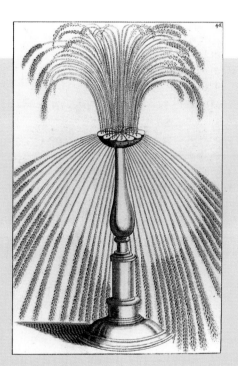

∨ 32–35 "With the advent of flower fountains it is now possible for gardeners without green thumbs to have a dazzling display in the backyard—or by simply lowering the pressure to have a year round 'water garden' in the living room." On 4 May 1962 the *Better Living* section of *Life* magazine advised American home owners that without elaborate plumbing installation, they could enjoy these German-made fountains whose rotating jets created petunia or lily designs, some as high as thirty feet.

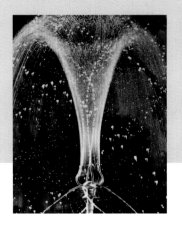

1626, his equally talented brother Isaac dominated the garden design field in England. In the 1630s, Isaac created his masterwork for Philip Herbert, fourth earl of Pembroke, the fountains and formal gardens of Wilton House in Wiltshire. In 1644 Isaac published *Nouvelle invention de lever l'eau* (translated as *New and Rare Inventions of Water-works*, 1659), based on his brother's text and twenty-six of the earlier illustrations, thus reinforcing the importance of the de Caus contribution to fountain and garden design. The publication was one of the major sources of information transmitting what was known about hydraulics in the Renaissance to later generations of fountain designers and engineers.[14]

Georg Andreas Böckler (active *c.* 1644–98), a German architect and engineer, also wrote on the fundamentals of hydraulics. His book *Architectura Curiosa Nova, Die Lustreiche Bau- und Wasserkunst* (1664) was illustrated with more than two hundred captivating prints, which served as a valuable visual compendium documenting inventive fountains ideas, playful water effects, and many fountains known at the time [27–31]. Since Böckler did not know the fountain marvels in Italy and France first-hand, he relied on prints gathered from all over Europe for information about possible decorative water displays. Many images show various pipe and nozzle systems that spin, jet or spout like ornamental sprinklers on columnar pedestals. There are also prints depicting niche and grotto fountains, and those with water complementing figurative statuary,

often with water spouting from every possible orifice. Inspiring his contemporaries and later fountain designers, Böckler's book delights with its pictures of pinwheels, sunbursts, flowerlike shapes and other patterns of aquatic choreography. Almost two centuries after Böckler, with the advent of the Industrial Revolution, cast-iron companies, such as the Coalbrookdale Company in England and the J. L. Mott Iron Works in the United States, mass-produced affordable decorative fountains based on traditional fountain styles. The 1873 J. L. Mott trade catalog offered a selection of readymade nozzles capable of producing jetting sprays and twirling patterns [26] similar to those that had first appeared in Böckler's book. Böckler's legacy even continues to modern times. A 1962 issue of *Life* magazine featured photographs of affordable flower fountains, with petunia or lily shapes created by rapidly rotating fountain heads, looking like those that appeared in *Architectura Curiosa Nova* [32–35].

The Italian architect and engineer Carlo Fontana (1638–1714), who worked with Bernini redesigning the plaza in front of St. Peter's and who designed the fountain pool for Rome's Fontanone (the Fountain for the Acqua Paola) in 1690 [90], also published an important treatise on hydraulics. Fontana's *Utilissimo trattato dell'acque correnti* (The Most Useful Treatise on Moving Waters), 1696, was based on an ancient text about Roman aqueducts by Frontinus, but it also incorporated explanations of the most

recent scientific discoveries.[15] In his treatise Fontana describes the properties of water in its natural state and how it behaves when artificially contained, as well as how it moves through conduits, and runs from far away lakes and springs via aqueducts across hilly terrain to city fountains. Fontana also discusses theories pertaining to the speed of falling water flowing out of a hole in the side of a container, a principle discovered by physicist and mathematician Evangelista Torricelli in the early seventeenth century. Fontana's book includes prints showing fanciful urn-shaped fountains with assorted jets, whose trajectories vary in shape and flow depending on the position of the aperture on the urn in relation to water level and pressure [36].

Fontana's text on aqueducts is a reminder that pipes are an essential component of the hardware that makes fountains work. While pipes often suffer from the "out of sight, out of mind" syndrome, since they are usually hidden underground or within a fountain structure, water could not reach the fountain outlet without them. Whenever fountains are constructed, the design of the internal plumbing system is as important as the structure's external appearance. Many European and American community water systems depended on wooden pipes fashioned from logs before lead and other metal pipes were more widely manufactured and used. A print in Salomon de Caus's *Les Raisons* shows a waterwheel being used to turn the boring machinery so that one man, unaided, could hollow out an

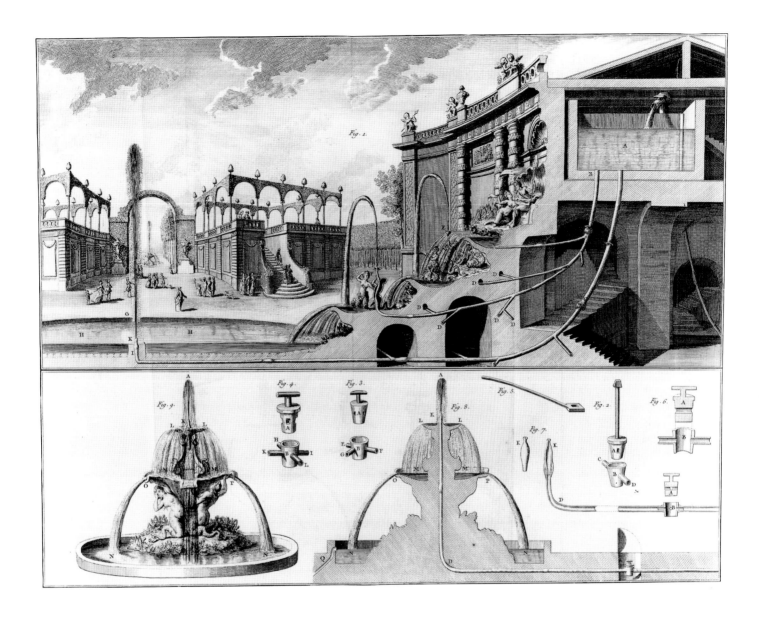

< 36 *Capitolo XI, Nel fine del precipizio dell Acque incondottate, hanno esse Acque doppia velocita di quella, che è a mezz'altezza.* Etching from *Utilissimo trattato dell'acque correnti* by Carlo Fontana (Rome, 1696).

< 37 *Hand-drilling Wooden Pipes, Nuremberg,* late eighteenth century. Etching by Nikolaus Gabler.

∧ 38 *Cross-section of a Reservoir which Feeds a Cascade and a Series of Water Jets, Elevation and Cross-section of a Fountain,* along with *Various Types of Pipes, Nozzles, Taps, and Spigots.* Etching from *L'Art du plombier et fontainier* attributed to Claude Mathieu Delagardette (Paris, 1773).

entire log to make a length of pipe. A German eighteenth-century print, set in Nuremberg with the 1687 copy of Bernini's Triton Fountain in the background, shows pipemaking as a more time-consuming hand-drilling process involving two men [37]. The late eighteenth-century French book, *L'Art du plombier et fontainier* (The Art of Working in Lead and Fountain Making), 1773, attributed to Claude Mathieu Delagardette, is an informative guide to forging lead, as well as to making pipes, joints, drains, gutters and other fountain fixtures. It also covers the installation methods necessary for utilitarian and ornamental fountains. One of its plates shows how gravity moves water from a reservoir through a network of pipes to supply various fountain outlets [38]. Depending on the water pressure and the type of nozzle, spout or basin rim,

the resulting fountain display is a jet or a cascading spray. Other fountain designs, such as the 1866 drawing by English architect Philip Webb [82], detail the placement and shape of the pipes planned to feed the faucets of a public London fountain.

Two important eighteenth-century French publications contributed greatly to fountain design. Bernard Forest de Bélidor (1693–1761), a military civil engineer, wrote a major four-volume opus *Architecture hydraulique, ou l'art de conduire, d'élever, et de ménager les eaux pour les différens besoins de la vie* (Hydraulic Architecture, or the Art of Conducting, Raising, and Managing Water for the Different Needs of Life), 1737–53, which addresses not only theories of hydraulics, the designs of fortifications, canal waterways, water reservoirs, watermills and pumps, but also the design of ornamental fountains. Bélidor's encyclopedic approach and authoritative grasp of the technical issues influenced subsequent generations of designers. In a chapter about decorating gardens, Bélidor provides a lexicon of the basic water forms possible in fountain design: *jets d'eau* (vertical jets where water is shot upward from a horizontal surface); *berceaux* (tilted water-stream trajectories or water arcs varied by increasing or decreasing water pressure and direction); *nappes* (flowing water sheets smoothly hugging surfaces like tablecloths); cascades (agitated, splashing, foamy water falling in stages, as over steps, or in a single major plunge, as in waterfalls or waterwalls); *bassins* (basins or pools to collect and contain water from jets, *nappes* or cascades). Bélidor also describes a panoply of more imaginative water effects: *gerbes* (pyramids of water formed by arranging small jets of different heights to form this geometric shape); *arbres d'eau* (fountain forms with branches and leaves of water, as in Chatsworth's Willow Tree Fountain [262], or the modern dandelion fountain [46]); *grilles* (rows of little downward flows of water, like grills); *champignons* (low jets sprouting like mushrooms, as in the fountains in the Place de la Concorde in Paris [159]); and *buffets, montagnes d'eau* or

Parterre de Compartiment

théâtres d'eau (buffets, water mountains and water theaters) which are grand compositions in which different water effects are combined in multilevel displays or in triumphant spectacles presented as if on a stage [230, 244].[16] As Bélidor advises, the manner in which one uses water in gardens requires considerable taste, art and industry in order to distribute the water effects agreeably.[17]

Antoine-Joseph Dézallier d'Argenville's (1680–1765) *La Théorie et la pratique du jardinage* (*The Theory and Practice of Gardening*), first published in 1709 and eventually appearing in eleven editions in three languages, was the first major guide to French formal garden design. Based upon the aesthetic doctrines of André Le Nôtre, the great seventeenth-century garden designer celebrated for his work at Vaux-le-Vicomte and Versailles, Dézallier d'Argenville's book describes ways to order and integrate nature and ornament by using flower beds, parterres, hedges, groves of trees and fountains. Of the ten chapters, the ninth is devoted to tips on how to locate sources of water and channel them to the garden. The tenth chapter discusses fountains, which Dézallier d'Argenville regarded as the "soul" of the garden. He advises on the various types of fountains, their construction, placement and proportion, as well as how to contrast lively water play with "sleeping" pools. For parterres that juxtapose elegant symmetry and asymmetry with designs incorporating volutes, scrolls, tendrils and knots, Dézallier d'Argenville proposes using elegantly simple, rather than overly decorated, fountains. In one passage, he remarks: "'especial care then should be taken in the choice of ground, that water may be had without difficulty: the necessity of it is as visible as the beauty 'twill add, in making *jets d'eau*, canals, and cascades, which are in truth, the noblest ornaments of a garden."[18] One of the book's etched plates shows a parterre pattern, looking like embroidery, accented by a single water jet in a circular pool [39]. Dézallier d'Argenville's proposed design is very similar to that realized in 1760–61 in the handsome formal gardens for the Augustusburg Palace (now called Brühl Castle) near Cologne, Germany [41].

Since the Industrial Revolution, hydraulic technology has developed extensively, and the cumulative body of specialized writings on the subject is vast. Since the mid-nineteenth century, advances in the newest technologies have been showcased at international expositions, and the waterworks in fountains have become increasingly large and spectacular, in order to show off industrial prowess while providing entertainment for the crowd. With improved industrial and engineering knowledge and skill, mass-produced fountain structures, equipment, and hardware have proliferated, as indicated by the abundance of trade catalogs for prefabricated fountain hardware (pumps, valves, tubing), decorative nozzles, basins and even statuary. Creating imaginative visual and aural water effects on a grand scale requires a daunting labyrinth of plumbing and electrical hardware. The complex technical demands of modern fountain design are such that fountain designers must work with hydraulics consultants.

The collaboration of fountain design expertise

Every fountain is the result of harmonizing aesthetic goals with technical design considerations while working with water's natural properties. Public fountains, like every major building, are still realized through the collaborative talents and efforts of a team of individuals. The designer is responsible for envisioning the aesthetic appearance of the fountain structure as complemented by the effects of moving water; the engineer coordinates the mechanics and physics of the structural design so that the desired water effects are achieved. Often, the services of a lighting designer, an artist or a landscape architect may also be called upon. After the fountain structure has been built with all the plumbing equipment in place, the design team conducts trial tests with running water to adjust and modulate volumes and pressures, with and without lighting. Once a fountain is working correctly, it is officially "turned on" and the constant movement of water brings the static, inanimate structure to life. After the construction process has been completed, all fountains require regular maintenance of their water systems to ensure they constantly perform as they should. When a fountain fails to operate properly, or when its structure deteriorates, the vitality of its setting also declines. Without the enlivening movement of water, fountains become inert and lose their sense of magic. When a fountain is dead, people no longer congregate to enjoy the sights and sounds of splashing water.

In the twentieth century, a new field of hydraulics expertise has evolved, combining the traditional methods of de Caus, Fontana and Bélidor with new digital and micro-processor technologies. Who are some of the hydraulic experts who ensure the vibrant performance of today's fountains? Several contemporary ones, such as the Ira C. Keller Fountain in Portland, Oregon [285] designed by Lawrence Halprin & Associates and the Dodge Memorial Fountain in Detroit designed by Isamu Noguchi [270], were done in consultation with engineer Richard Chaix. Chaix describes his job as translating the subjective descriptions of desired water effects, such as "smooth water skin," or "a great deal of white, frothy water," or "a trickling spray," into calculations to determine water volume and flow rate requirements. The engineer must also address the practical considerations of feasibility and budget.[19] Chaix has many counterparts throughout the world, most of whom are unknown outside professional circles. Although technical expertise often serves a creative aesthetic vision, it is the fountain designer whose name traditionally remains the most prominent among those associated with a fountain project. For example, New York architect Philip Johnson envisioned the Houston Transco Waterwall as a modern-day nymphaeum celebrating water, by providing people with an experience of being almost surrounded by a waterfall surging with eleven thousand gallons of water streaming down the walls every minute. Johnson and his design team imagined the Transco Waterwall, and Johnson proudly posed in front of it shortly after its completion in 1985 [291], but fine-tuning the water effects depended upon the skills of the fountain consultants, CMS Collaborative and Richard Chaix. In admiring the waterworks of any fountain, we should pay silent tribute to the designers and engineers, even if we do not know their names.

< 39 Design for a *parterre de broderie* (embroidered parterre) from *La Théorie et la pratique du jardinage* by Antoine-Joseph Dézallier d'Argenville (The Hague, 1711; first published Paris, 1709).

∧ 40 *Grotto in a Salon in the Royal Orangerie, the Zwinger, Dresden.* Etching by Lorenz Zucchi after Matthäus Daniel Pöppelmann from *Das Kupferstichwerk über den Zwinger* (Dresden, 1721–29).

∨ 41 Parterre and fountains, Brühl Castle, Germany. Designed by Dominique Girard, a student of Le Nôtre, begun 1717.

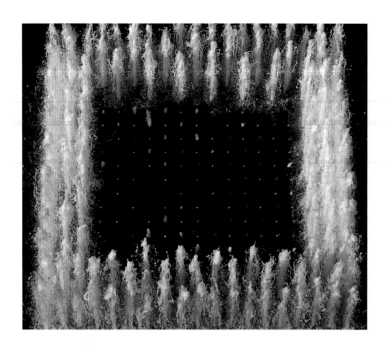
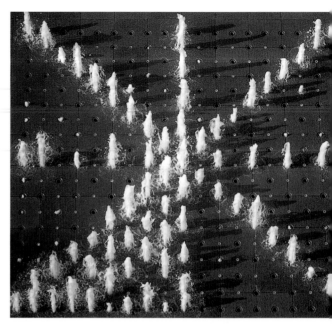

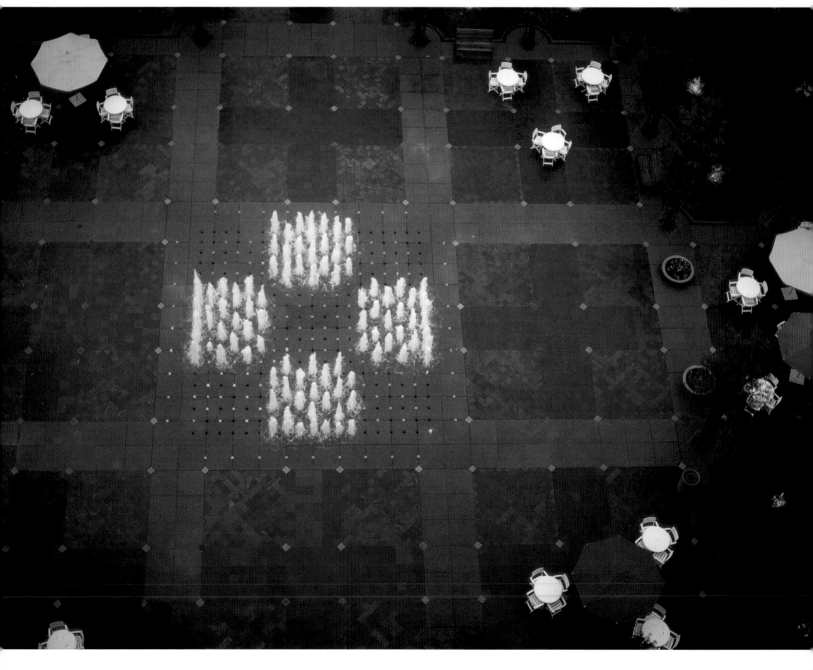

Fountain patterns and shapes

Fountains which use the precision of technology to enliven and define space have a legacy harking back to the Renaissance. The German architect Mattäus Daniel Pöppelmann became familiar with the ingenious waterworks of his age through his travels in Italy and in France. He applied his knowledge in his design for the Zwinger, the royal palace of Augustus the Strong of Saxony, in Dresden, with moving water forming part of the design throughout. A print, dated 1721, documents the innovative grotto he designed [40]. This view shows court visitors being temporarily trapped within walls of vertical water jets, which appear to be thin bars that move up and down at intervals to permit people to pass by without getting wet. Sadly this marvelous fountain feature no longer survives, and few records detail how the enchanting effects were achieved. Over two centuries later, WET Design unites a similar kinetic water design with the latest precision engineering technology to create equally captivating, innovative effects of rising and falling water jets. Fountain Place in Dallas, completed in 1986, presents a popular water feature that recalls the earlier version in Dresden: a grid of 160 jets (the aerated water comes from nozzles recessed in small holes) flush with the ground's surface, with no fountain pool or other barrier, so people have immediate access to the water. Each jet is individually controlled by computer to create various linear or geometric pattern sequences, which, when viewed from above [42–44], recall those found in traditional cross-stitch embroidery or the contemporary minimalist art of Sol LeWitt. Viewed at plaza level [295], as a constantly changing three-dimensional water sculpture, the playful choreography of jets rise and fall within seconds, enthralling people with their

unpredictable sequences. WET Design has repeated this formula in other plaza fountains in Los Angeles [247, 248] and at the Universal CityWalk Fountain in California [249], while throughout the world other designers have created similar banks of water jets in Paris [300], San Jose, Atlanta, West Palm Beach [299], and elsewhere. With water jets functioning as defining points in fountain compositions, devising any shape on one or several levels is possible. More and more public fountains of this type feature jets in rows, angles, squares, circles, spirals, or any shape the space permits.

Tree-like fountains, originating in Islamic gardens and Renaissance villa water joke fountains, are also popular and today's version, the dandelion fountain, has sprouted up in cities around the world, including Sydney, Minneapolis, New York [46], and Paris. Australian architect and fountain designer Robert Woodward is credited with the first modern reincarnation of the dandelion fountain. When he designed the El Alamein Memorial Fountain (1959–61) in Sydney, its structure was to be a spherical arrangement of 211 bronze pipes diverging from a central core. At the tips of the pipes are specially designed nozzles which project fine radiating sprays, so that the resulting fountain looks

like a huge fuzzy dandelion. Since then, the design, which Woodward did not patent, is now a staple of many fountain manufacturers who provide prefabricated parts. Woodward believes that if architects and designers do their jobs well, their work should stimulate others to do good designs, even if the latter are close imitations of a concept first realized elsewhere. Like dandelion seeds blown in the wind, this spherical fountain type is taking root in many places around the world. With geometry and nature as models and enough innovative designers, the potential for using water to form points, lines or sculptural forms is boundless.

Fountains of ice and steam

Some artists and designers deliberately exploit water in its non-aqueous states to create unique structures that expand the traditional notion of a fountain that surprises and fascinates viewers. Buffalo, New York, is notorious for its harsh, snowy winters. There, in 1983, the Norwegian artist Carl Nesjar completed the Butler Ice Fountain for Buffalo State College [45].[20] In the mid-1960s, inspired by the natural beauty of the craggy rocks, water seepage, snowbanks and ice in his homeland, Nesjar, who had studied art in New York, Oslo and Paris, began to design fountains that would function in every season, particularly

in northern climates. In the early 1970s, he received grants to investigate the effects of freezing temperatures on fountains at the Norwegian Institute of Technology at Trondheim and at the Center for Advanced Studies at the Massachusetts Institute of Technology. Nesjar was enthralled not by the fluid transitoriness of water but by the changing sculptural qualities of solid ice, which gradually thaws and refreezes before it melts completely in warmer temperatures. For the 1980 Winter Olympics at Lake Placid, Nesjar created his first ice fountain in the United States as a memorial to the Norwegian ice-skating champion, Sonja Henie. He made other innovative ice fountains in Norway, Sweden, and the French Alps. For the Butler Ice Fountain, Nesjar devised a nine-armed stainless-steel sculpture, forty feet long and with nozzles creating fan-shaped sprays, in a reflecting pool with twenty-five jets. The fountain is most remarkable in winter when it is shrouded in a mass of icicles and abstract ice forms.

Stuart Wrede, a contemporary American environmental artist and architect born in Finland, has designed fountains that use two states of water simultaneously in all weathers. Some feature geometric shapes of ice that seem to float on a calm expanse of water, while others present square pools with water flowing into a central abyss from which vapor emerges. The water movement is subtle, changing slowly in response to the environmental conditions. He has also designed minimalist fountains with two rectangular symmetrical waterfalls falling as water sheets toward each other.

There are also fountains relying on water's most volatile state as a gas. The Tanner Fountain at Harvard University in Cambridge, Massachusetts [47, 48], designed by Peter Walker with the SWA Group, steam artist Joan Brigham and fountain consultant Richard Chaix of CMS Collaborative, releases ethereal steam in winter, and a misty spray in the warmer seasons. Dispensing with any traditional structure, the fountain area, about sixty feet in diameter, is defined by a circle of 159 granite fieldstones embedded in the ground at a level so that they can serve as comfortable seating. Sited at a busy campus pedestrian intersection, it offers a relaxing oasis for adults and a place for children and pets to climb and explore. Recalling the Stonehengelike installations by ancient cults, yet also exemplifying contemporary minimalism and earth art, the fountain contrasts the hard immutability of stone with water vapor that assumes a soft, spatial dimension. A fine mist, caused by five concentric rings of jets flush with the ground's surface, hovers over a twenty-foot area at the fountain's center. The stones are

"The wisp of water rises, wavers, reappears: a white bouquet whose flowers sway until the moon releases showers of bright tears."

Charles Baudelaire, "The Fountain" in *Les Fleurs du Mal*, translated by Richard Howard

spaced so that people can walk between them, into and through the shimmering mist, which makes rainbows in the sunlight. When the temperature freezes, the water is turned off, and a steam cloud from the university's central heating system camouflages the stones, before it drifts off and dissipates. When the stones are snow-covered, it offers a contrast between water's two states of white—frozen and steamy. In northern cities, one regularly sees steam escaping from manhole covers, vents or chimneys, but rarely is it channeled to a fountain to produce foglike effects, like magical, silent clouds close to the earth. At night, lighting makes the vapor glow mysteriously.

Throughout history, fountains have refreshed, cleansed, satisfied, spiritually nourished, soothed, inspired, impressed and entertained people while enhancing places. Symbols associated with fountains convey ideas and messages about human imagination, aspirations or triumphs over nature. For any combination of these reasons, people often seek out fountains as destinations when celebrating memorable occasions. Whether as sites for weddings, family gatherings, festive holidays or civic events, fountains often serve as settings for important human affairs. And it is often the presence of fountains, or their surrogate images—whether drawings, prints, photographs, films, souvenir postcards or snapshots—that remind us of the promise of renewal, since water is always the source of new beginnings.

Marilyn Symmes

< 46 Dandelion Fountain,
Alliance Capital Building, Avenue
of the Americas, New York.

∧ > 47, 48 Tanner Fountain,
Harvard University, Cambridge,
Massachusetts. Designed by
Peter Walker and the SWA Group
with Joan Brigham, 1984.

chapter 2
fountains
as
Refreshment

Cool, refreshing and thirst-quenching water is not simply a necessity, but one of life's great pleasures. Throughout history, in countless public places worldwide, drinking fountains have been designed to provide abundant pure water, which can taste and feel wonderful [50, 52]. Nothing compares to its restorative powers, and children—or the young at heart—show playful relish in gleefully splashing (their own and other people's) faces, hands, feet and clothes when the opportunity arises [54].

Water possesses almost magical qualities. A spraying fire hydrant can transform a sweltering city street into a temporary oasis, offering neighborhood children a showery playground as welcome relief from the dry, hard pavement [302]. Their delight is comparable to what the unsuspecting visitor must have felt when suddenly surprised by squirts from a hidden water joke fountain in a Renaissance or baroque garden [235]. The sound of moving water—sometimes a roar, at other times a whisper—breaks the stillness and can provide aural refreshment on a warm day. Even the slightest trajectory of water can transform a place into a watery paradise, as in the Moorish gardens of the Generalife in Granada, Spain. The thirteenth-century summer palace, built for Nazar dynasty sultans and enlarged in the Renaissance, has a series of delicate, arched water jets that gently splash into a narrow, rectangular pool, offering both a pleasing vista and a natural music similar to falling rain [297].

The novelty that once delighted sultans is almost lost upon the contemporary consumer as water readily flows at the turn of a faucet whenever desired. Before water was widely available within private homes, places of work and public buildings for every domestic, hygienic, practical or recreational use, people had to collect water daily for their drinking, cooking, bathing and other washing needs [53]. Besides natural sources of water, there were often wells and public fountains strategically situated in town squares and marketplaces. Fountains were not only places to get water, but also places to meet and exchange information or gossip, thereby contributing to a sense of community. Or, in exchange for a few coins, water sellers provided a cup of water for those in need of a drink. There were also water carriers who transported barrels to homes far from a source. Their role was such a vital one for a community, that they were occasionally immortalized, as in Rome's Fontana del Facchino, or Water Porter Fountain [51], from the late sixteenth century, showing a burly man holding a barrel with a hole spouting water.

< 49 View of the Fontaine des Quatre Saisons, Rue de Grenelle, Paris. Designed by Edme Bouchardon, completed 1745.

> 50 A young girl enjoys a drink of water in the streets of Rome.

31

He represents the type of porter who would have drawn his water from the pre-eighteenth-century Trevi fountain (which until the 1580s was the sole source of water for the city), and then transported his barrels to residences further away.[1]

Just as all living things need water to grow, cities cannot develop beyond the reaches of their water supply. For example, medieval Roman inhabitants crowded into the small area served by the water of the Acqua Vergine. After the 1580s, Rome was among the first cities to develop a sophisticated system for distributing drinking water to a much wider area, allowing the city to grow. Today, running water comes to us, and we rarely have to seek it out. Water journeys from a source, via a largely out-of-sight, complex, subterranean network of channels and pipes, until summoned for its transitory appearance from a faucet, before exiting through another system of pipes to be recycled. People barely consider the centuries of technological progress and design development that have enabled people to live almost anywhere, confident that their various needs for water will be adequately served. Taken for granted, it is only when minor or major disasters stop or foul the water supply that people become aware of their dependence on the public utilities infrastructure. As Benjamin

Franklin wrote in 1746, "When the well is dry, we know the worth of water."[2]

From the Renaissance to our own day, public drinking fountains—some monumental in design, and some more modest—have played a significant role in the well-being of European and American cities, while providing easy access to life's essential source. In Renaissance Europe, many fountains functioned primarily as reservoirs to collect potable water, but their sculptural or architectural form and decoration also reinforced their importance as civic monuments designed to impress while they served utilitarian needs. The Fonte Gaia (1408–19 [55]) in Siena, Italy, was the city's first reliable public water supply. Named the Fountain of Joy (or Gay Fountain) on account of the great celebrations that welcomed water's arrival into the center of the hilltop city, it was prominently placed opposite the Palazzo Pubblico, the principal government building, in the Piazza del Campo, the main public square. Designed by Jacopo della Quercia, a Sienese sculptor and contemporary of Lorenzo Ghiberti and Donatello, the Fonte Gaia was a large rectangular basin into which water poured from a row of spigots located at the base of the surrounding balustrade, decorated with relief sculpture. The fountain design was adapted to the slightly sloping site. Enclosed on three sides, the fourth side

△ 51 *Fontana del Facchino (Water Porter Fountain), Rome*, late 16th century. Etching by Domenico Parasacchi from *Raccolta della Principali Fontana inclitta Città di Roma* (Rome, 1647).

< 52 Pausing for a refreshing drink at a public fountain. Anonymous family snapshot, 1930s.

∨ 53 *Collecting Water from the Fountain at the Foot of the Capitoline Hill (Campidoglio), Rome*. Etching (detail) by Giovanni Battista Falda from *Le Fontane di Roma* (Rome, 1691).

∧ 54 Audrey Hepburn cools her
feet in the waters of the Barcaccia
Fountain, Piazza di Spagna, Rome.
From the film *Roman Holiday*
(directed by William Wyler, 1953).

"[Water] quenches the excessive heat
which would destroy this life. Thus water can
be called the only everlasting source
of continuous being." Nicola Salvi, *c.* 1732

∧ 55 Fonte Gaia, Piazza del Campo, Siena, Italy. Original fountain designed by Jacopo della Quercia, completed 1419; replaced in 1868 with a copy by Tito Sarrocchi.

< ∧ 56, 57 Two studies for the Fonte Gaia, Siena, showing the left and right sides of the fountain, probably 1409. Pen and brown ink, brown wash on vellum attributed to Jacopo della Quercia.

was low to allow people access to the water, with the elegant sculptural reliefs adorning the interior walls of the basin in full view. In the central place of honor was the Virgin and Child, flanked by angels, and personifications of Wisdom, Hope, Fortitude, Prudence, Justice, Charity, Temperance and Faith. In early Renaissance Siena, it was understood that the Virgin, the city's protector, was synonymous with good government.[3] The fountain also included two figure groups alluding to the legendary founding of Siena. Atop each side pier was a sculpture of a woman with two children, one representing Acca Larentia (clad in goatskin), and the other being Rhea Silvia (wearing a crown), who were, respectively, the foster mother and regal mother of the twins Romulus and Remus—Remus being the father of Senus, who founded Siena. The bringing of an ample supply of water for community use was a most visible demonstration of good government, and the Fonte Gaia fulfilled this prime civic duty, uniting the religious, political and practical agendas of Siena's leaders.

When Jacopo della Quercia received the commission in December 1408, the contract specified that he was to design a functional *and* elaborately decorated fountain.[4] The Fonte Gaia, after all, was to be the monumental terminus to a system that brought, for the first time, abundant fresh water from a considerable distance to Siena. Early designs pertaining to fountains rarely survive, yet two pieces of an ink drawing on vellum, thought to date to 1409, reveal della Quercia's second version of the Fonte Gaia decoration, and these are important documents for both early Italian art and fountain design. While scholars have debated whether these drawings are copies after della Quercia's design or by his own hand, they do agree that one shows the left side of the Fonte Gaia (The Metropolitan Museum of Art, New York [56]), while its companion shows the right side (Victoria and Albert Museum, London [57]).[5] The central portion of the design is missing. Each drawing shows four seated figures in ogival niches (changed to rounded arches in the executed fountain), two in the back wall and two in each wing. The left section

shows, from left to right, the angel Gabriel, and the personified Virtues, Temperance, Fortitude and Faith. The right section shows Justice, Humility, Prudence and the Virgin of the Annunciation. The drawings show Acca Larentia and Rhea Silvia with Romulus and Remus. Later, della Quercia enlarged and again altered the fountain before its completion in 1419. For example, the seated monkey in the New York drawing, and the seated dog in the London drawing, symbolizing, respectively, faithlessness and watchful loyalty, do not appear on the completed fountain. There were additional alterations: the positions of the Virtues changed; other figures (Wisdom, Hope and Charity) were added; and the scenes from the Creation of Adam and the Expulsion from Paradise replaced Gabriel and the Virgin. The scenes from Genesis alluded to the Virgin's role in man's salvation as the Mother of Christ. Thus, the decoration evolved to integrate further a strong spiritual message with civic symbolism, so that when the Fonte Gaia was finally realized, those who collected its waters would be refreshed in physical ways, while also receiving spiritual and moral sustenance. The fountain itself enhanced the beauty of the city and all this was possible because of Siena's enlightened municipal government. By the nineteenth century, the fountain had deteriorated; it was replaced with a copy created by Tito Sarrochi (constructed 1858–68), which is what one sees in the plaza today. What remains of the original Fonte Gaia is now preserved in the Palazzo Pubblico.

In Renaissance Rome there was a severe water shortage. While ancient Rome had boasted eleven aqueducts delivering water to over twelve hundred fountains, as well as to hundreds of public baths,[6] sixteenth-century Rome was comparatively dry. Pliny the Elder wrote of the marvels of the hydraulic technology of the ancient empire: "If we take into careful consideration the abundant supplies of water in public buildings, baths, pools, open channels, private houses, gardens, and country estates near the city, if we consider the distances traversed by the water before it arrives: the raising of arches, the tunneling of mountains, and the building of level routes across deep valleys, we shall

readily admit that there has never been anything more remarkable in the whole world."[7] Centuries after Pliny, amid the ruins of the great imperial aqueducts, only one, the Acqua Vergine, had been regularly maintained, and was the sole water source for the city until the papacy of Sixtus V. Succeeding what was once the civic duty of emperors, the pope assumed the responsibility of getting Roman fountains to flow profusely again. It was part of an ambitious urban program to improve the city and its waterworks in order to proclaim papal power and the universal supremacy of the Church by reestablishing Rome as the center of spiritual and political life.

During his five years as pope, Sixtus V (born Felice Peretti) undertook many urban renovations, including the restoration of the Aqua Alexandrina (which he renamed the Acqua Felice after himself) and the construction of twenty-two miles of new conduits.[8] Under his auspices, the *mostra terminale* (display fountain at the terminus) of the Acqua Felice (1585–88) was erected on the Quirinal Hill.[9] The Acqua Felice, or Fountain of Moses [58], was the first new monumental wall fountain since antiquity. Obviously, having a capable hydraulic engineer to oversee this important venture was crucial to its success.

Unfortunately, Matteo Bartolani, the first assigned to the task, badly miscalculated the incline of the channel to accommodate the water volume, so only a trickle flowed from the Acqua Felice. As this was inadequate to supply the daily needs of the neighborhood (not to mention a poor display of papal power) Sixtus then appointed the architect-engineer Domenico Fontana, who was also highly skilled in hydraulics.[10] Fontana designed a *mostra* that recalled architecturally the great triumphal arches of antiquity, thus the fountain's form visibly celebrated the successful arrival of water in the city. As emperors had done centuries before to note their achievements on their aqueducts, an inscription honoring Sixtus as the provider of water was prominently displayed beneath angels supporting the papal coat of arms of Sixtus V (with Montalto *monti* and obelisks). Sculpture inspired by Old Testament subjects is placed within each of the three arches. A colossal statue of Moses (sculpted

by Leonardo Sormani and Prospero da Brescia in 1588) occupies the central niche, hence the name Fountain of Moses. In each side niche is a relief alluding to other biblical associations with water: *Aaron Leading the Israelites to Water* (on the left) by Giovanni Battista della Porta, and *Gideon Leading his People across the River Jordan* (on the right) by Flaminio Vacca and Pietro Paolo Olivieri. Water pours from beneath each niche into basins, into which four Egyptian lions also spout water. While the sculpture of Moses was derided at the time for being ungainly and out of proportion with the architecture, it fulfilled the goals of Sixtus V to have a fountain that strongly asserted the Church's Counter Reformation message, as the Acqua Felice reinvigorated

the Quirinal district. The fountain was instrumental in developing what was then a rustic, suburban site for villas into a viable urban residential area, providing ample water to sustain inhabitants who wished an alternative to living in the overcrowded city center. Although the modern city has somewhat encroached on the space where the fountain once impressively presided, the structure remains a prominent landmark.

The monumental design of the Acqua Felice fountain and the ambitious example set by Sixtus V inspired Pope Paul V Borghese to repair the aqueduct originally built by Emperor Trajan (the Aqua

∧ 58 The Acqua Felice (also called Fountain of Moses), Rome. Designed by Domenico Fontana, 1585–88.

> 59 *View of the Fountain for the Acqua Paola*, 1756–57. Etching by Giovanni Battista Piranesi.

Traiana), to build a new aqueduct (the Acqua Paola), and to commission an imposing *mostra* for the Janiculum Hill, near the church of San Pietro in Montorio.[11] The idea to create a monumental fountain on the Janiculum dated to 1607, but funds had to be raised. One of the most lucrative methods was initiating a tax on wine, to be paid by inn and tavern keepers. An *avviso* (notice) dated 22 August 1607 documents and broadcasts the complaint about taxing wine to bring water.[12] With funding secured, the pope could pay the Orsini family for the rights to a spring on their land near Lake Bracciano, a short distance from Rome, which then carried water to the Janiculum.

Designed by Giovanni Fontana (who had also worked with his brother on the Acqua Felice) and Flaminio Ponzio, the Fountain of the Acqua Paola (1610–12, also called Il Fontanone [59, 90]) was the first major fountain on the left bank of the River Tiber, and from its site there is a magnificent panoramic view of the city. Using white marble plundered from the ancient Roman Temple of Minerva in the Forum of Nerva, the *mostra*'s triumphal arch structure expands to an impressive five arches. Rather than using religious subjects for a spiritual message like the Acqua Felice had done, the grandiose architectural form and scale, embellished by the dynastic

papal emblems of Paul V, are enlivened by flowing water. Angels support the Borghese family coat of arms of an eagle and a dragon, which is surmounted by the papal tiara and keys. The inscription on the entablature presents elegant Roman lettering announcing Paul V as the bringer of the precious water. Whereas the Acqua Felice had been initially criticized for its inharmonious integration of architecture, sculpture, inscription and water, the Fontanone beautifully harmonizes all aspects of its design. Here, then, is architecture serving as a glorious, monumental screen—or water gate—for the sumptuous display of water. From the five arches, there were five vigorous streams rushing into small marble basins giving direct access to the cascades. Whereas local residents had previously gathered water from brackish springs or the less-than-pure Tiber, now they had plenty of fresh water. In 1690, Carlo Fontana designed a large, semicircular pool as a reservoir for the water that overflowed from the basins. Low marble posts prevented animals from using the pool as a trough. However, the pool proved so tempting to local inhabitants who used it for bathing and other washing needs that a 1707 ordinance was issued to prohibit such ablutions.[13] The flourishing waters from the Fontanone remain, as they have done for centuries, one of the most impressive sights of Rome. The

monumental architecture of both the Acqua Felice and the more harmonious Fontanone, enframing structures which emphasize the aural and tactile qualities of moving water while exalting its unique power to refresh and cleanse, anticipated the awesome effects of Nicola Salvi's later design for the Trevi Fountain [128].

Unlike the monumental fountains of Rome, where the presence and display of water was a pronounced, visible element in the urban landscape, early fountains in Paris, constrained by chronic water shortages and insufficient distribution, emphasized architecture and sculptural decoration. The display of water was, by necessity, minimal—usually confined to discreet spurts from mascaron-headed taps or faucets. The Fontaine des Innocents, or Fountain of the Innocents, was designed in the sixteenth century to be a commemorative monument that happened to supply a bit of water to inhabitants of the *quartier*. Yet through subsequent alterations and a resiting of the fountain in the eighteenth century, it was resurrected so that its primary purpose was to provide water in a market square, serving a variety of refreshment needs.

Originally located on the former site of the Church and Cemetery of the Innocents, at the corner of Rue aux Fers (now Rue Berger) and Rue St. Denis, the Fontaine des Innocents was erected in 1549 to grace the royal processional route of Henri II's triumphal entry into Paris.[14] Designed by sculptor Jean Goujon and architect Pierre Lescot, the Fontaine des Innocents was an impressive structure, recalling both a loggia and a triumphal arch, elegantly decorated as befitting an edifice honoring a sovereign [61].[15] The waterworks were secondary. The only tangible evidence of the structure's utilitarian function were the lion-headed spouts at street level, giving local inhabitants easy access to the water. The fountain building had three sides, with the fourth backing directly onto the church. Raised on a high base, one bay of the loggia opened on to the Rue St. Denis, while two arches faced on to the Rue aux Fers. The fountain integrated finely proportioned architecture with graceful sculptural decoration. Goujon's elegant sculptural

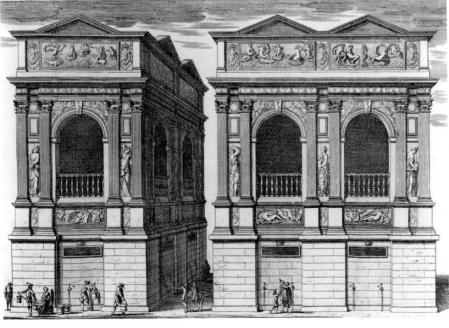

∧ 60 *A Market Scene with the*
Fontaine des Innocents, Paris,
c. 1800. Oil on canvas by
Jean-Charles Tardieu.

< 61 Fontaine des Innocents, Paris.
Designed by Pierre Lescot and
Jean Goujon, completed 1549.
Etching by Gabriel Perelle from
Vues des belles maisons de France
(1650) showing two views of the
fountain, the facade facing on to the
Rue St. Denis (left) and that facing on
to the Rue aux Fers (right).

> 62 View of the Fontaine des
Innocents just prior to its renovation,
mid-1850s. Photograph by Charles
Marville, who is shown leaning
against the base of the fountain.

> 63 Fontaine des Innocents, Paris.

reliefs symbolically evoked water as compensation for the meagerness of its actual presence. Five nymphs between Corinthian pilasters hold urns eternally pouring water, alluding to a nymph's power to generate life and creative forces, as well as providing purifying refreshment [118].[16] Their clinging drapery, as if wet, recalls Hellenistic prototypes. Other reliefs filled with sea nymphs, tritons and other marine images completed the decoration. Latin verses by Jean-Baptiste Santeuil inscribed on the fountain in 1689 proclaim: "The waters rendered here in marble imitate nature to such a high degree that the nymphs therein depicted are mistaken for those of the actual spring."[17]

In 1785–87, the Church of the Innocents and the adjacent cemetery were demolished, and the fountain was also threatened with destruction. However, public outcry championed Goujon's reliefs as masterpieces of French Renaissance sculpture, so the fountain was saved and adapted as an elevated, freestanding structure in the midst of the new Marché des Innocents, sited on the former cemetery.[18] Architects Jacques-Guillaume Legrand and Jacques Molinos carried out the reconstruction; Augustin Pajou created the sculptural decoration on the newly added fourth side.[19] At this time, the architects redesigned the fountain to accommodate a flow of water falling into a large square basin. The fountain became an icon for the city after the French Revolution, as leaders radically sought to integrate hygiene, commodity, beauty, order and monumentality.[20] Jean-Charles Tardieu's painting conveys the fountain's stately presence in a lively marketplace [60] and two rare photographs by Charles Marville show the fountain as it looked without running water in the mid-1850s [62, 118].

In the 1860s, Gabriel Davioud, an architect to the City of Paris during the Second Empire and designer of the Fontaine Saint-Michel [100], supervised the disassembling and relocation of the Fontaine des Innocents to another site, a garden square east of the market of Les Halles.[21] There, the fountain assumed its present-day form. Unlike its original design, water abundantly flows from the font in the temple structure at the top, and

then, on each side, it cascades exuberantly over newly designed steps to a circular pool at street level. In the twentieth century, some have praised it as "a pearl among Paris's oldest fountains" and "a precious reliquary from the Renaissance."[22] Today, within the urban renewal surrounding the Centre Georges Pompidou, in an area filled with shops and cafés, the Fontaine des Innocents resonates with the refreshing sights and sounds of water [63]. Those who pause for respite from urban cares also experience a restorative connection with ageless nymphs and the mythic origins of fountains.

While some monumental fountains were major city landmarks, many public fountains in Paris and elsewhere in Europe were, in fact, smaller, more modest decorative structures with practical functions. Often placed in the vicinity of churches, city halls or in market squares, such fountains assumed a standard form of a functional basin with water coming from a central column or pedestal, decorated with a statuette of either a religious, civic or allegorical figure. Such fountains usually exemplified local pride, and their decoration had special meaning readily understood by those using the fountain. A popular type of fountain in medieval times, especially prevalent in Germany and Switzerland, is exemplified by the Fontaine de Sainte Anne in Fribourg, Switzerland, which still supplies local residents with potable water [64]. Nuremberg, a great

Fribourg
Fontaine de Sainte-Anne

German artistic center in the late medieval and Renaissance periods, boasts several fine sixteenth-century fountains. One of the smallest is the delightful Gänsemännchenbrunnen (Geesebearer Fountain, *c.* 1540) by Pankraz Labenwolf [102, 103]. The tiny figure carries a goose under each arm, water streaming from their beaks and from two spouts on the pedestal to the basin below. An ornamental ironwork grill encloses the fountain, probably intended to keep animals from partaking, and thus tainting, its water. Now situated just south of the Rathaus (town hall), it originally stood in the Obstmarkt (fruit market), where poultry was also sold. Instead of an image of a poor, shabby peasant, the statue is an icon of a well-dressed, honest, hard-working farmer, bringing two fat geese to market, who will undoubtedly be rewarded in town for his labors. His rural economic interest is allied to the mercantile city's peaceful prosperity. He symbolizes the virtue of interdependent cooperation between country and urban dwellers.[23]

Numerous fountains also dot the Swiss city of Bern. A startling subject for a fountain is the sixteenth-century Kindlifresserbrunnen (Ogre Fountain) attributed to Hans Gieng, a sculptor from Fribourg.[24] Perched atop an ornate, fluted column is a polychromed figure of an ogre,

possibly in carnival disguise. He is devouring a small child, while others, stuffed into his sack, try to escape the same fate [65, 101]. A group of amusing, armed, marching bears encircles the base of the column, bears being the symbol of Bern and the heraldic emblem of the Zähringen founders of the city. Below are four lion-headed masks from which pipes spouting water emerge into an octagonal basin. While fairytalelike cannibalism is hardly a pleasant sight to behold when fetching water, the Ogre Fountain is, curiously, still one of the most beloved in the city. It has been regularly maintained and restored through the centuries.

In the south of France, Aix-en-Provence calls itself the "city of a thousand fountains." On the tree-lined Cours Mirabeau, the main avenue in the heart of the old city, intervals are marked by several fountains, among them the Fontaine d'Eau Chaude (Hot Springs Fountain), which dispenses thermal waters from a supply dating back to the city's Roman origins in 105 B.C. [66].[25] The fountain was originally erected in 1667 with a triton sculpture by Jacques Fossé, but was destroyed shortly thereafter by seventeenth-century vandals, who were reportedly "young imbeciles drunk from wine."[26] Fossé received a second commission to replace the fountain with a sculpture of putti holding the city's coat of arms, a basin and a jet of water. This sculpture, too, no longer survives. However, the fountain remains in place, and it provides local residents with heated water—ideal for a healthful drink, bathing or washing laundry. Today the fountain is a dense, moss-covered mound (with four spouts and a small jet) looking more like a large, soft sponge dribbling water, and is commonly known as the Font Moussu or Mossy Fountain.

New water distribution networks and fountains sprouted throughout Europe during the seventeenth and eighteenth centuries to provide sufficient drinking water for daily use. With every fountain, there had to be regular maintenance by supervisors and workmen to assure regular flow no matter the season. In Paris,

following the construction of the Hôtel des Invalides (1680–1708) under the auspices of Louis XIV, the westward development of the Left Bank of Paris was rapid. In the early eighteenth century, the Rue de Varenne and the Rue de Grenelle were fashionable addresses for the nobility. Their mansions were set within gardens, separated from the streets, and surrounded by tall walls and a porte cochère, providing a sense of dignified privacy. In such a setting, another exceptional, monumental Parisian fountain was built.

In 1739, Edme Bouchardon received the important commission from the City of Paris to design the Fontaine des Quatre Saisons (Fountain of the Four Seasons [49]) on the Rue de Grenelle, in order to introduce a water supply to that section of the city.[27] As water supplies were still unreliable, Bouchardon had to design around the limitations of unpredictable water volume and pressure. He adopted the standard, practical solution of making water accessible via faucets at street level, so that water porters serving the local population could easily fill their containers. However, even though the fountain's *raison d'être* was the provision of water, the contract also called for an elaborate iconographic program. Bouchardon was to create a grandiose fountain worthy of a monarch proclaiming

to his citizens that he had contributed to the city's embellishment. It had to be both a supreme expression of art and a political symbol. Designing such a monument on the narrow street proved difficult, and Bouchardon expended considerable effort, even though he was no stranger to fountain design. While in Rome, he had studied the fountains and even participated in the 1730 competition to design the Trevi fountain.[28] Throughout his career he made many red chalk drawings documenting his fertile ideas for elegant fountains. For the Fontaine des Quatre Saisons, he began with academic studies of nude models in various poses to seek the best solution for the allegorical sculpture, before making three-dimensional terracotta maquettes.[29] Before work began on the actual execution of the fountain, the artist made more studies, directly from nature, in order to refine details.

Finally completed in 1745, the fountain's classical architectural facade features a personification of the City of Paris presiding over two recumbent figures symbolizing the Rivers Seine and Marne [68, 69]. Statues of the four seasons, with reliefs below showing activities appropriate to the time of year, are paired on each side. At the base of the principal group, in the center, are four bronze, mascaron-headed faucets. After the fountain's inauguration, many celebrated the elegant interplay of sculpture and architecture which provides a distinguished landmark for the neighborhood. The edifice successfully proclaims the glory of Paris which thrived and benefitted from the abundant provisions of nature during the reign of Louis XV.[30] Yet there were pragmatists who complained that while the fountain's theatrical presentation was about water and nature, the water itself was too inconspicuous. Even Voltaire is said to have commented: "A great deal of stone for very little water."[31] In spite of the criticism, the fountain adequately served the comfort and hygiene needs of its populace, as befitting an enlightened city. Today, the splendid fountain ranks among the great masterpieces of the eighteenth century, still *in situ* as Bouchardon originally designed it.

< 64 Fontaine de Sainte Anne, Fribourg, Switzerland. Postcard, 1890s.

< 65 Kindlifresserbrunnen (Ogre Fountain), Kornhausplatz, Bern, Switzerland. Sculpted by Hans Gieng, 1542–46. Albumen print, late 19th century.

∨ 66 Fontaine d'Eau Chaude, Cours Mirabeau, Aix-en-Provence, France, originally erected 1667. Postcard, early 20th century.

∨ 67 *Fontaine de la Porte St. Denis, Fontaine de la Charité, and the Fontaine des Petits-Pères Noirs, Paris.* Etching by Adam Perelle from *Vues des plus beaux bâtiments de France* (1693).

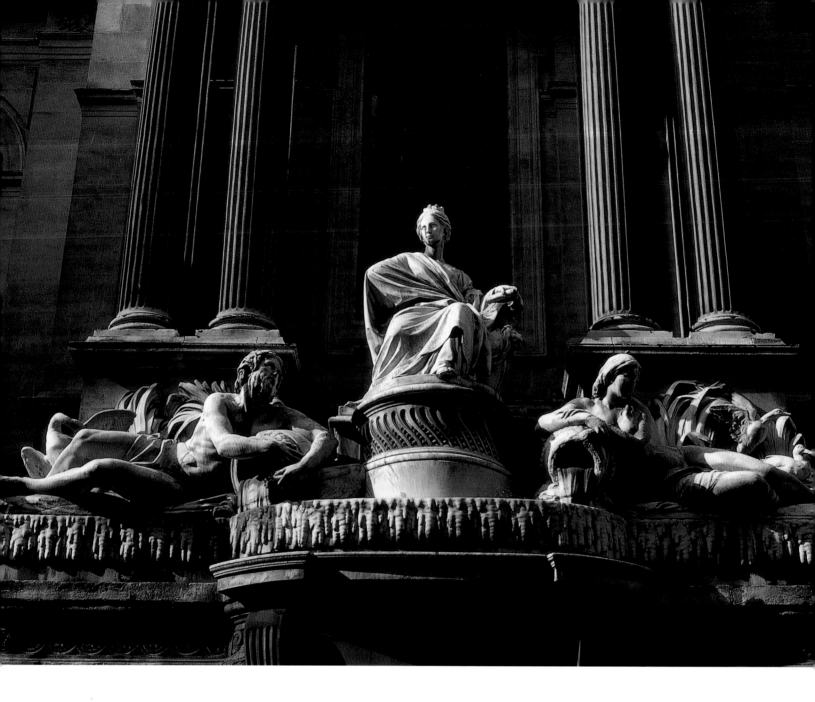

∧ 68 The City of Paris flanked by the Rivers Seine and Marne, Fontaine des Quatre Saisons, Paris. Designed by Edme Bouchardon, completed 1745.

< 69 Elevation of the Fontaine des Quatre Saisons. Ink and wash drawing by an anonymous draftsman, June 1777.

> 70 Fontaine de la Croix-du-Trahoir, Paris. Originally erected in the 16th century; rebuilt 1606; dismantled 1636; reconstructed 1775 by Jacques-Germain Soufflot.

> 71 A workman drinking from a wall fountain, Rue de l'Estrapade, Paris. Postcard, early 1900s.

As Paris grew, royal (and, later, Napoleonic) decrees ordered the installation of smaller, utilitarian fountains to be freestanding in public spaces, on street corners or as niches in walls aligning the street. Officials and engineers worked to improve the city's pump and conduit systems while architects and artists designed the small structures housing the pipes and faucets as urban furniture. A seventeenth-century print by Adam Perelle documents the sober appearance of classically styled stone fountain houses typical of those installed throughout the city during the long tenure of Jean Beausire, supervisor of public buildings from 1684 to 1743 [67].[32] Some early wall drinking fountains survive to this day, such as the Fontaine de la Croix-du-Trahoir (Fountain of the Cross of Trahoir), constructed in 1775 on the Rue de l'Arbre Sec, at the corner of Rue Saint-Honoré, and designed by neoclassical architect Jacques-Germain Soufflot in his capacity as superintendent of buildings. A scowling mascaron, sculpted by Simon-Louis de Boizot, spits water into a shell basin beneath the coat of arms of Louis XVI and a Latin inscription announcing the monarch's role in providing this fountain for public benefit [70]. An early twentieth-century postcard depicts a Parisian drinking at an early wall fountain beneath the city's coat of arms, located on the Rue de l'Estrapade near the Panthéon [71]. Napoleon's campaigns in Egypt inspired architect Louis-Simon Bralle to design the Fontaine du Fellah or Egyptian Fountain (1806–08) on the Rue de Sèvres, where it backs on to the wall of a hospital [73].[33] As one can still see today, the fountain shows an Egyptian temple doorway with a water carrier holding two pitchers, from which water flows into the basin. Instead of a river god, an Egyptian figure evokes the Nile, the original life-giving river.

With improved technology and a guaranteed steady flow of water, fountains emphasizing water bursts and chutes as a primary element of civic embellishments came into vogue. Throughout the nineteenth century, French designers conceived a variety of impressive fountains, some exceedingly grand in concept and scope with spectacular displays of water. One remarkable but unrealized project was for a fountain tower, designed several decades before the Eiffel Tower to mark an artesian well at Passy. While the concept originated with Jean Darcel (an engineer of bridges and roads) and Adolphe Alphand (also an engineer), Émile Reiber rendered the design in a handsome 1857 watercolor [74].[34] Darcel and Alphand were working with Baron Haussmann to upgrade Paris's promenades, public gardens and parks, as well as to drill the Passy artesian well as a new water source for the city. Their scheme shows a distinctive landmark designed to exploit the water extracted from deep under the ground. Upon arrival, visitors would behold a profuse display of water in a *château d'eau*. At the base is a neoclassical facade, flanked by staircases. Water streams from a trio of circular openings in the facade, as well as from above, from two figures pouring water standing between two spouting chimeras. On the second level, water descends over a rusticated wall and then dramatically cascades over large boulders. Higher still, water flows from urns and arcs in trajectories on to a tier of small jets. Those who desired a view of the surrounding panorama could climb the spiral staircase to the top of the tower, which also contains the water tank. With the water source nearby, the volume and pressure would ensure constant running water, and this would be part of the recreational attraction that would make the tower an adventurous destination. However, accessing water on this site proved difficult, so the project did not proceed as envisaged.

In the south of France, in the port of Marseilles, the ostentatious and theatrical presentation of abundant fresh water became a reality in 1869. Designed by Henry Espérandieu, the monumental Château d'Eau at the Palais Longchamp signaled the terminus of the canal supplying the city and symbolized the city's renewed prosperity [72].[35] It was the glorious culmination of a project that took decades to realize. In the 1830s, Marseilles's inhabitants had suffered the consequences of a severe drought followed by a devastating cholera epidemic. Although the idea for a canal system linking the River Durance to the city dated back to the eighteenth century, it was in 1839 that officials prioritized the project as a way to

solve the problems of their increasingly inadequate water supply.[36] Years later, as the canal neared completion, and as part of an overall urban plan to beautify the city with gracious boulevards and dramatic buildings, designs were sought for elaborate waterworks and a grand cascade as the focal point of a museum complex. At the invitation of the mayor in 1859, the sculptor Frédéric Auguste Bartholdi (famous for his later colossal Statue of Liberty in New York's harbor) proposed several versions. While Bartholdi's grandiose plans helped to define the architectural program, he was not awarded the Palais Longchamp project because city leaders felt they needed the expertise of an experienced architect.[37] Espérandieu was already overseeing the building of the neo-Byzantine basilica of Notre-Dame-de-la-Garde, and he was well known in Marseilles. City leaders were thus more confident that he could best orchestrate the ambitious Palais Longchamp project that was to address both civic refreshment needs and cultural aspirations.

The architecture and waterworks of Palais Longchamp are today regarded among the masterpieces of the Second Empire. In the center of an elegant

∧ 72 Château d'Eau, Palais Longchamp, Marseilles. Designed by Henry Espérandieu, 1869.

> 73 Fontaine du Fellah, Rue de Sèvres, Paris. Designed by Louis-Simon Bralle, 1806–08; statue by Jean-François-Théodore Gechter, 1844. Photograph by Eugène Atget, early 20th century.

> 74 *Project for a Tower and Fountains Marking the Artesian Well at Passy, Paris,* 1857. Watercolor heightened with white gouache by Émile Reiber. Tower and fountain design by Adolphe Alphand and Jean Darcel.

> 75 *Fountain at City Hall Park, New York,* 1843. Engraving by John Rolph, printed by Burton.

colonnade is the ornate triumphal arch announcing the arrival of water from the canal. Emerging from the arch is a majestic sculpture by Jules Cavelier showing the River Durance, accompanied by her entourage, Vineyard and Wheat, on a chariot pulled by four Carmargue bulls. They present a paradigm of Mediterranean abundance and fertility. The water chute begins its dramatic fall here, and then descends to become a "hymn of water," a great cascade flanked by a voluted balustrade surmounted by small bronze basins from which shoot tiny water jets.[38] The undulating water comes to rest in a circular pool at street level. There, on special days, large water jets are turned on to cavort and explode as a grand finale. Embracing this marvelous celebration of water and nature, are the Musée des Beaux-Arts and the Museum d'Histoire Naturelle with twin staircases, from which people can view the fountain as they ascend the colonnade in order to enter the public gardens and zoo on the Longchamp plateau behind. With its spectacular mastery of water married with architecture, sculpture, art and science, the Palais Longchamp reinvigorated Marseilles as monumental fountains had previously enlivened Rome.[39]

Across the Atlantic Ocean, fountains and festivities heralded the official introduction of pure water into American cities in the 1840s, although these fountains feature the soaring power of water jets as a promising symbol of future abundance, without the accompaniment of decorative architecture and sculpture [75]. New York and Boston were among the first American cities to develop reliable water distribution systems for their citizens. For decades, New Yorkers had been dependent on water of unpredictable quality and quantity, and like the inhabitants of Marseilles, they had suffered repeated scourges of epidemics due to impure water. To rectify the problem, the city turned to the private Manhattan Company, founded in 1799 by Aaron Burr, ostensibly to devise a water distribution system for the city, but actually the project became an excuse to create the city's second bank.[40] From 1800 to 1840, the Manhattan Company's convoluted network of wooden pipes serviced a small percentage of homes in the growing city.

Fires were usually doused with water from city-owned tanks and it was the inadequacy of that supply to control the Great Conflagration of 16 December 1835, which destroyed much of New York, that forced city leaders to pursue getting water from the Croton River, about forty miles away. For its day, the Croton Dam, aqueduct and reservoir system was the most major undertaking of its kind in America.[41] On 14 October 1842, New Yorkers celebrated the completion of the Croton system and eagerly anticipated the first drops of the abundantly available, safe, drinkable water. Union Square and City Hall Park showcased spectacular fountains jetting Croton water skyward; marching bands, politicians, soldiers, firemen, engineers, and other notables paraded throughout the city. At the official ceremony at City Hall, while the fountain danced in the background, a choir sang:

Water leaps as if delighted
While her conquered foes retire:
Pale Contagion flies affrighted
With the baffled demon Fire
Water shouts a glad hosanna
Bubbles up the earth to bless:
Cheers it like the precious manna
In the barren wilderness.[42]

In 1859, news of New York's water generated interest elsewhere, even in England, where an issue of the London journal *The Builder* reported that the New York City Council had just passed a resolution requiring the Croton Aqueduct

Department to report to them regarding plans and estimates for placing five hundred drinking fountains and hydrants on city streets and squares.[43] While the major Union Square and City Hall fountains, along with these streetside drinking fountains, no longer exist, many descendants of those nineteenth-century hydrants remain.

Boston held its great citywide water celebration on 25 October 1848. A colorful lithograph documents the public rejoicing on the momentous occasion which marked the official completion of the aqueduct from Lake Cochituate (some twenty miles distant) and the fountain jet on Boston Common burst into the air for the first time [76].[44] After a large parade and a one-hundred-gun salute, throngs of Bostonians poured on to the Common for the official ceremony of speeches, special prayers and hymns. School children sang an eight-stanza ode written by James Russell Lowell especially for the occasion. It began:

My name is Water: I have sped
through strange dark ways untried before,
By pure desire of friendship led,
Cochituate's Ambassador;
He sends four gifts by me,
Long life, health, peace, and purity.[45]

As the print shows, amid the citizens dressed up in their best attire to witness the event were notable dignitaries, such as the statesman and orator Daniel Webster, then a United States senator (lower left), and the poet Henry Wadsworth Longfellow (lower right foreground). The fountain jet towers in the background. According to a contemporary report, the water rose dramatically to a height of about eighty feet, exhibiting a powerful beauty that few had seen before, which elicited shouts of surprise and delight from the crowd.[46] After jetting for a while, the fountain engineer changed the fixtures to produce different spectacular spraying effects. Successive displays impressed the audience well into twilight. After this grand beginning, other traditional, sculptural fountains adorned the Boston Common and other sites in the city.

In the 1850s, private citizens, particularly in England and the United States, campaigned for the installation of more public drinking fountains freely dispensing fresh water to serve a growing urban population. It was a crusade that combined evangelical zeal, temperance,

activism and sanitary reform. Philanthropists concerned about addressing the social needs of their day, helped to spawn a proliferation of public drinking fountains, some of which survive today in capital cities, such as London, Paris, and Washington, D.C.

London had appalling water conditions, especially in its overcrowded working-class neighborhoods, during the early reign of Queen Victoria and even into the 1850s. Though industrialization made all sorts of technological wonders possible, a reliable supply of uncontaminated water was still hard to obtain. In commenting on the Great Exhibition of 1851, the magazine *Punch* quipped, "Whoever can produce in London a glass of water fit to drink will contribute the rarest and most universally useful article in the whole exhibition."[47] For most of the poor, who could ill afford the luxuries of coffee and tea, obtaining decent drinking water was more difficult than finding refreshment from beer and spirits in public houses. Incidents from water-borne diseases and alcoholism affected much of the populace.[48] Although temperance

societies existed, they did not offer a practical alternative to the evils of alcohol until the drinking fountain movement provided a means to do so. In 1859, Samuel Gurney founded the Metropolitan Free Drinking Fountain Association dedicated to erecting fountains to benefit all social classes.[49] Many early ones were placed in deliberate proximity to churches and pubs, as an overt moralistic statement. Fountains exhibiting religious associations, for example, with statues of Rebecca at the well or in the form of a baptismal font, accompanied by biblical quotations, were common. Others featured allegorical depictions of Temperance and Charity. Some fountains had inscriptions reflecting Victorian sentiments such as "Drink, friend, drink, and take your fill,/ Do not use my fountain ill," or, more simply, "Try, Try," and "Water is Best."[50] Philanthropists felt that the deep spiritual associations accompanying the pure fountain water along with its promotion of good health, was the best remedy for improving and uplifting people's lives.

Under Mr. Gurney's auspices, the association erected, with much fanfare, its first fountain on the boundary fence of St. Sepulcre's Church on Snow Hill, near Smithfield, on 21 April 1859.[51] Soon after, it was being used by over seven thousand people per day. While there was praise for making drinking water more widely available, the designs of the fountains were scrutinized by those in the architecture and building professions. An article in *The Civil Engineer and Architect's Journal* stated: "We cannot but express much regret that the major portion of the drinking fountains recently erected are, with reference to their design and the material employed, of the most unsatisfactory description.… Great credit is due to the promotors of the Drinking Fountain Association for its establishment and the vigour of its operations; but it is very desirable that the committee should obtain superior talent for the production of designs, and employ a more suitable class of materials."[52] The journal *The Builder* regularly reported on newly erected fountains appearing throughout England, and illustrated selections from fountain design competitions. The association maintained its own pattern book of possible drinking fountain designs, publishing from time to time a sampling, as it did in the 6 August 1859 issue of *The Builder* [78]. The following week an article in the same journal complained that the structures looked like funerary monuments and implored the association

not to convert city thoroughfares into cemeteries. Some subsequent designs were straightforward, unornamented utilitarian structures, while others were laden with the eclectic decorative styles of the day— either classically simple or elaborately ostentatious, depending on the vanity and means of the donor. Not popular in England were fountains adorned with animal or figurative heads spouting water from their mouths, since the design seemingly contradicted the fountain's sanitary purpose. Instead, the architectural profession campaigned for fountains in the Gothic Revival style, with its associations of moral reform. *The Builder* published two drinking fountain design ideas [77] by Henry Godwin, who, as the text proclaims had "striven to throw a little more ornamentation into them than is usually done.… In one of the designs, proposed to be of Bath stone, the voussoirs to the arches are alternately of red and white marble; the basin which stands in the arched recess is of white marble; as also are the brackets on either side for the cups; the back of the recess [is] to be faced with tile having a pattern of some water plant in blue upon a white ground. Two recesses for dogs below are proposed.… Above is a panel for the erector's name, or an inscription. Bullrushes in metal are introduced as a termination to the stone work, with an octagon lamp surmounting the whole, supported by the same plant symbolical of fresh water."[53]

< 76 *View of the Water Celebration on Boston Common, October 25, 1848*, 1849. Tinted lithograph with additional hand-coloring by S. Rowse after Benjamin Franklin Smith, Jr., printed by Tappan & Bradford's Lithography, Boston.

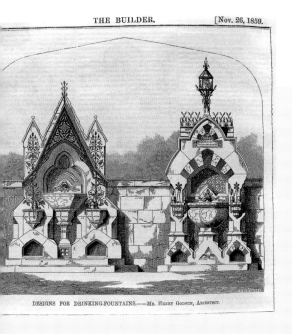

THE BUILDER. [Nov. 26, 1859.

DESIGNS FOR DRINKING-FOUNTAINS.—Mr. Henry Godwin, Architect.

∧ 77 Designs for drinking fountains by architect Henry Godwin, from *The Builder*, 26 November 1859.

> 78 Designs for drinking fountains selected by the Metropolitan Free Drinking Fountain Association, from *The Builder*, 6 August 1859.

Like Godwin's mural fountain designs, William Dyce's two fountain designs also exemplify the nineteenth-century preference for the Gothic and medieval style popularized by Augustus Welby Northmore Pugin and the Pre-Raphaelites. Originally from Aberdeen, where he had obtained degrees in medicine and theology, Dyce later studied art and design in London, and then in Rome with the Nazarenes. By mid-career, Dyce was in London pursuing ecclesiastical and decorative mural commissions. In 1856 he moved to Streatham, where, being an exceedingly devout man, he was also actively involved with the local church of St. Leonards.[54] In 1862, the parishioners of St. Leonards raised enough money to commission Dyce to design a fountain for their community, partly as a public acknowledgment of his services to the parish. Dyce offered a choice of two

designs [79, 80]. One is Italianate, with a fontlike basin and a central, twisted baluster column supporting a figure of Christ with outstretched arms. At the base of the column are lion masks spouting water into an octagonal basin. Mosaic patterns on the outside of the basin are similar to those in the artist's frescoes in the Palace of Westminster and his stained glass at St. Paul's in Alnwick, Northumberland. Beneath the rim of the basin is the inscription: "He that drinketh of this water shall never thirst." However, the parishioners chose the second design for the fountain [81], which is a polychromatic Gothic design, with alternating layers of red brick and white stone. Two buttresses frame a blind gabled wall with a basin shaped like half of a font. Above is a round arch containing the upper half of a quatrefoil in relief. The arch is lettered in Gothic script: "For I will pour water on him that is thirsty." In offering refreshment, the fountain also encourages piety, and the

church is nearby for those in need of further solace. Drinking fountains, like this one, forge a bond between the church and the local community it serves.[55]

Instead of alluding to piety, Philip Webb's working drawings for a fountain intended for London's Battersea Park deliberately emphasize functionality [82]. Known for his first major commission, the Red House in Kent, the home of William Morris, and for other country houses, Webb rejected symbolic and historicist designs in favor of those which thoughtfully combined technology, fine craftsmanship and practicality. The 1866 fountain design clearly reveals the detail and exactitude that accompanied plans for even the plainest fountain structure. The inscriptions show attention to materials: the paving and steps are to be of York stone, the basin of pink granite, the exposed metalwork to be of cast and polished gun metal. They also document the considerable care that went into designing the interior pipes connecting to the main water supply and their relation to the surface covering.

During the 1860s, over one hundred drinking fountains were installed throughout London. Some, like Dyce's fountain, were humbler structures relating to church architecture. Others, however, were grand structures placed in new urban parks designed in such a way that space, fresh air and water would relieve the dank congestion of London's poorer neighborhoods. Among these was the "Queen" of London's drinking fountains, the Victoria Fountain (1862) presented "for the love of God and country" through the immense generosity of Baroness Burdett-Coutts [83]. Over ten thousand people attended the dedication of the Venetian-Moorish "water temple," designed by Henry Darbishire as the glorious crowning centerpiece in the new Victoria Park. Functional accoutrements of clocks and a weathervane adorn the slate cupola, and the interior is more Italian Renaissance in style with putti in niches pouring water from urns. Borrowing from art and architectural styles traditionally found abroad, the Victoria Fountain ennobled the previously impoverished area.

The English belief in public fountains as beneficial amenities was carried abroad, even to remote areas of the British colonial empire, such as to Kandy, Ceylon (now Sri Lanka), where a European-style fountain looked out of place [84]. However, in Paris, among the attractive features still scattered about the city are the distinctive drinking fountains given in 1872 by Sir Richard Wallace, an Englishman who had inherited a fortune, a taste for art and a fondness for the city of Paris.[56] Wallace had lived there during the siege of the Franco-Prussian War and the Commune of Paris, so he had witnessed the suffering of Parisians during that period. At the end of the hostilities, Wallace wanted to make a gift to the city, so he offered to pay for fifty drinking fountains to be placed wherever they would be most useful to quench the thirst of those passing by.[57] The city readily accepted this generous offer. There were three fountain types designed by Charles-Auguste Lebourg, a sculptor from Nantes who had previously created portrait busts of Sir Richard and Lady Wallace. The cast-iron fountains were subsequently produced at the Berbezat foundry. What we now call a Wallace Fountain is a small, elegant monument on an octagonal base, only just over the height of a standing adult [85]. It presents four classical caryatids supporting a graceful cupola; the water tap is inside. Nicknamed by some as "the temple of the four goddesses," the figures symbolize Simplicity, Temperance, Charity and Goodness.[58] The first was installed on the Boulevard de la Villette. They became so popular that soon eighty fountains were scattered throughout the city. In 1876, one writer remarked on the constant use of the beloved fountains, saying that all sorts of people lined up for a drink: small children, their mothers, the elderly, anyone in the neighborhood, and these gatherings prompted spontaneous fraternizing and fellowship similar to that which had occurred at public fountains in the past. In addition, he continued, these fountains supplied water for meals, as people brought carafes to be filled. The writer urged the installation of other such fountains since the present number could not keep up with the public's thirst and the temptation of wine remained.[59] In 1898, twelve more fountains were added. As one was damaged or displaced, Wallace had stipulated that another one should replace it in the same vicinity.

∨ 82 Design for a conduit for Battersea Park, London: plan, elevation, and section, 1866. Pen and ink drawing, partly tinted, by Philip Webb.

< 79 *Design for a Drinking Fountain*, 1862. Pencil, pen and ink, watercolor, and Chinese white by William Dyce.

< 80 *Design for a Gothic Revival Drinking Fountain*, 1862. Pencil, pen and ink, watercolor, and Chinese white by William Dyce.

∨ 81 Gothic Revival fountain, Streatham Green, London. Designed by William Dyce, 1862.

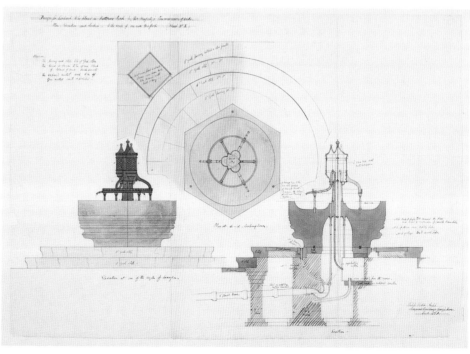

∧ 83 Victoria Fountain, Victoria Park, Hackney, London. Designed by Henry Darbishire, 1862.

∨ 84 Fountain in a public square in Kandy, Ceylon (now Sri Lanka). Albumen print, 1880s.

Sir Richard Wallace's gift to Paris was a gesture of true philanthropic altruism, and people have gladly perpetuated his name in association with the drinking fountains he donated. The same cannot be said for the American drinking fountains provided by Henry D. Cogswell, whose zeal for temperance was twisted with misguided self-promotion. Cogswell made his vast fortune in dentistry, mining investments and real estate in the wake of the California Gold Rush. His success permitted him to retire in San Francisco. After 1856, he crusaded to distribute fountains and statues of his own devising to cities and towns throughout the United States.[60] A maverick unaffiliated with any official organization, he waged a personal reform campaign to promote sobriety as the best foundation for society. His monuments reflect a variety of historic styles, dependent on standardized architectural, decorative, and figurative types available from manufacturers of iron- and stonework. Moralizing slogans, such as "Indefatigable Perseverance, with Patience, Industry, Leads to Fortune; Idleness and Dissipation, to Poverty," broadcast his convictions.[61] Typically, a Cogswell Fountain is a thirteen-foot-high granite baldachin supported by four Doric columns. The words "Faith," "Hope," "Charity," and "Temperance" are inscribed on the entablature. Crowning figures include

standardized cranes, the figure of Hebe (the water carrier) or a statue of Cogswell himself. Usually, beneath the canopy stands a sculpture of entwined dolphins whose mouths spout water [86].

Cogswell's offer of "free" drinking fountains came with certain conditions. Before any fountain could be erected, Cogswell required a commitment to pay for four lanterns to light each corner of the fountain, for all shipping and assembly costs, as well as for the future water supply and maintenance. In transactions after 1880, Cogswell insisted that his fountains be adorned with a statue or relief portraying himself as the exemplar of "non-alcoholic manhood."[62] While the erection of a personalized statue as part of the public fountain caused consternation in some communities, other towns were so in need of a communal drinking facility that they tried to "swallow" the unwanted likeness. Even the American Capitol became entangled in Cogswell's vanity.

In 1882, Washington, D.C. commissioners prompted Congress to approve Cogswell's offer before viewing the design. When the picture of the proposed fountain (with the statue portraying Cogswell) arrived, government leaders quickly perceived its unsuitability for a city adorned only by statues commemorating those who had

> 85 Wallace Fountain, Paris.
Designed by Charles-Auguste
Lebourg, 1872.

> 86 The Cogswell Fountain
on Boston Common in winter.
Photograph by Baldwin Coolidge,
c. 1884–90.

demonstrated noble service to the nation. Rather than rescind an Act of Congress, a statue of a crane was substituted so the plans could proceed.[63] In 1884, the fountain was erected in the market area at Seventh Street and Pennsylvania Avenue; just over a century later, it was restored and relocated to a spot approximately 150 feet from its original site. Similar Cogswell Fountains were also installed in 1884 on the Boston Common (albeit with a cylix) and in New York City's Tompkins Square in 1888 (with a statue of Hebe).[64] While the Washington, D.C. and New York City Cogswell Fountains are the most notable ones to survive to the present day, most were removed in the face of public objections. Boston's Cogswell Fountain was dismantled in 1894 when opponents derided it as an affront to good taste. Shortly thereafter, Boston formed an arts commission to approve all future public art and monuments.[65]

Even Cogswell's own city complained about his statues. A *San Francisco Examiner* article of 1894 commented on a recent attack: "For years it [the fountain] has caused runaways, turned good milk sour and dried up the artistic fountains of the soul…. But to Cogswell it was a source of pride. It showed his solemn proportions to all the world and advertised abroad that he had never taken a cup that cheers."[66] Still, there were some grateful communities, such as St. Joseph, Missouri, and Pawtucket, Rhode Island. While Americans usually applaud the results of independent spirit and enterprise, public reaction to Cogswell Fountains was mixed. Today, in the East Village of New York City, a rehabilitated Tompkins Square (which in the 1980s and early 1990s had been inhabited by vagrants) is a pleasant park setting where young and old eagerly partake of the Cogswell Fountain water, unaware of the controversy that once surrounded the donor.

The western city of Portland is distinctive for its beautiful parks and fountains which enhance its highly livable city center. The free-flowing fountains, symbols of Portland's hospitality and Oregon's wilderness abundance, are the source of tremendous civic pride. Three of the earliest drinking fountains are the legacy of citizens who had emigrated there, and with pioneering initiative and hard work, prospered as the city grew. As gestures of gratitude to the community that had nurtured their success, Portland received its first public fountains: the Skidmore Fountain (1888); "Benson Bubblers" (1912); and the Shemanski Fountain (1926).

A poor young man who had arrived in Portland in a covered wagon, Stephen Skidmore eventually developed his own pharmaceutical business. Inspired by fountains he had seen during a trip to Europe as the city's representative at the 1878 Paris Universal Exposition, he bequeathed funds so Portland could erect its first public fountain.[67] Those executing

∨ 87 Skidmore Fountain, Portland, Oregon. Designed by Olin L. Warner, completed 1888.

> 88 Three women pause for a drink at one of the cast-bronze "Benson Bubblers" in Portland, designed by A. E. Doyle. Photograph, c. 1915.

Skidmore's wishes had the foresight to approach one of the best American sculptors to realize the project—Paris-trained Olin L. Warner, who would later design two of the massive, ornamental bronze doors for the entrance of the Library of Congress in Washington, D.C. Located in what was then Portland's fashionable shopping and entertainment district, the Skidmore Fountain [87], which rises to a height of almost eleven feet, presents a large bronze basin held aloft by two classically draped caryatid nymphs, resembling those on the Wallace Fountains. Water, which originally emerged from a central jet (a spray today), flows over the edge to fall into an octagonal granite pool, twenty feet in diameter. Four metal cups were once attached by chains to the sides of the pool. Four horse troughs, fed by spouts from the pool above, are placed at street level. Shortly after the fountain's unveiling in 1888, national journals of the day applauded the aesthetic merits of the fountain. In 1889, *Century Magazine* noted: "To come on work like this in a new western town must prove a charming surprise, for there is nothing so beautiful in statuary westward from Chicago."[68] The critic W. C. Brownell, writing in *Scribner's* in 1896, remarked: "The fact that Warner's figures look calmly down upon buggies and buck-boards, and shirtsleeves and slouch-hats in Oregon, instead of decorating [New York City's] Central Park is grotesquely significant."[69] While Portlanders resented the patronizing East Coast attitude about their general lack of culture, they were proud to have one of the most beautiful fountains in the country.[70]

Of all Portland's fountains, "Benson Bubblers" are the most frequently used and are a design unique to the city. Simon Benson, a Norwegian emigrant who arrived in Oregon via Wisconsin, made his fortune in the lumber business. Although unsubstantiated, the origin of these fountains is attributed to Benson's observation that on weekends his company loggers could only obtain a drink of water in Portland saloons, and then only after ordering other refreshment. This led to disastrous working days. In 1912, Benson commissioned twenty fountains to be placed on Portland's sidewalks, so people could quench their thirst without having to enter a saloon. Looking somewhat like graceful, large-scale candelabra, the four-branched, cast-bronze drinking fountains were designed by A. E. Doyle, a local architect. Constantly bubbling and gurgling with pure water piped from Oregon's mountain cascades, Doyle's utilitarian design is so simple—people just have to bend over to imbibe the fresh water [88]. Benson donated ten thousand dollars for the fabrication and installation of the first fountains at strategic street locations. Today the Portland Water Bureau tends to seventy-four such fountains; the newer models produced by students in a technical school also funded by Benson. Except for during a drought in 1992, when the fountains had to be turned off, they have been running copiously, day and night, to serve a thirsty multitude. While Benson's name is prominent in the community for his other philanthropic activities, he modestly provided the water fountains without requesting any recognition. Long after, his daughter claimed that her father felt the fountains were the best investment he ever made, since they contributed greatly to the quality of Portland life and the vitality of its citizens.[71]

Almost fifty years after the Skidmore Fountain first flowed, Joseph Shemanski, a Jewish immigrant from Poland, donated a fountain to Portland as an expression of gratitude to his adopted city. Shemanski had prospered in his clothing business by allowing poor people to pay by installment, a novelty at the time. Unveiled in 1926, the fountain was a small monument, inspired by traditional European styles. Designed by Carl L. Linde, it is a three-sided, cast-stone canopy temple, sheltering a statue of Rebecca at the well, by the local artist Oliver L. Barrett. It provided drinking water for people from its basins, and for dogs at sidewalk level. Restored in 1987 by Shemanski's grandchildren and great-grandchildren, the fountain serves as a focal point in one of Portland's parks linking the commercial areas to the city's cultural institutions and university.

Today, countless cities and towns are able to provide citizens with plentiful, pure water whenever it is desired. Historic and recent fountains abound exploiting water's benefits for people's health, spirits and refreshing pleasure. Most people seldom worry about having enough water for drinking or washing even though

environmentalists broadcast concerns that the world's pure water supply is a finite resource threatened by pollution and the needs of a growing global population. Taken for granted in numerous countries, water is only newsworthy when it is over abundant—in the case of floods, hurricanes or blizzards—exceedingly scarce—as in droughts—or when governments are dealing with issues of water quality. In many parts of the world, however, where people still obtain clean water with great difficulty, replenishing the household supply is an essential task of daily life. What had not been envisioned by the ancient Romans, Renaissance rulers or even by Simon Benson, is that bottled water, still a necessity in some communities, could also be merchandized as a chic commodity and status symbol, especially in metropolitan areas where potable water is bountiful at every tap. What is essential, natural and almost as free as air, is even more valued by today's materialistic society when it is in a package saying, "Drink Me." When supply

is not an issue, consumers can instead assess the nuances of differing tastes and qualities of waters derived from diverse geographical sources. In areas where publicly provided water may not be the tastiest or purest, people can choose to filter what is available or to purchase bottled varieties. Today, a booming $4 billion-a-year market for bottled water showcases time-honored favorites, such as Perrier, Evian and San Pellegrino, which compete with tantalizingly named recent brands, such as Crystal Geyser and Glaceau. Many water suppliers are tapping into this lucrative business, including those in Houston and Kansas City who plan to bottle and market proudly their own excellent municipal supply, while still making it available to area residents at a fraction of the cost.[72] Yet while a burgeoning water industry strives to meet the needs and whims of an increasingly mobile and thirsty public, profusely flowing fountains continue to satisfy our ever-present cravings for fresh water.

Marilyn Symmes with Maria Ann Conelli

The Fall and Rise of the Waters of Rome

The fountain systems of baroque Rome, perhaps the best known in the world, are in principle no different from those in other pre-industrial cities that rely on gravity to distribute water. In Rome, aqueducts channel water from various sources and deliver it to *mostre*, or display fountains, within the city walls. From each *mostra*, water flows to where needed in conduits beneath the city's streets. It is made easily accessible through smaller fountains to people, animals and industries within its own watershed, outside of which it cannot flow. Like a family tree, each fountain system branches out from a single *materfamilias* to form numerous offspring. Hence, each fountain has its own personality, but shares a kind of genetic structure as well as a topographic relationship with others in its system. The elevation of the *mostra* in relation to subsequent fountain sites determines whether the water falls or rises, gushes or drips as it makes its way through the city. Typically, with less pressure available as water flows farther from its source, fountain size diminishes correspondingly.

The three aqueduct and fountain systems developed in Rome from 1570 to 1612 clearly demonstrate these principles. Each was based on an existing ancient Roman aqueduct that had deteriorated through sabotage or neglect during the previous thousand years. The first, and lowest in elevation, was the Acqua Vergine. Restored several times during the medieval period, and again in 1570, it arrived near the Piazza di Spagna at only sixty-seven feet above sea level (fasl). Next, the Acqua Felice completed in 1587 arrived on the Quirinal Hill at 194 fasl. Last was the Acqua Paola completed in 1612 on the Janiculum Hill at 266 fasl. Ultimately, each would have its own elaborate *mostra* with cascading water: the Trevi, the Moses and the Fontanone that respectively display Vergine, Felice and Paola water.

Serving the low-lying, densely populated Campus Martius area, the Vergine had the smallest distribution range. The twenty-three-foot fall over the entire system allowed little pressure for water display. With one exception, the fall, not the rise, of water defined Vergine fountains including the Trevi, the Barcaccia, the Pantheon and those in the Piazza Navona. Due to the minimal elevation change within the system, each fountain struggled to carry the water as high as possible for the most impressive display. Sites were often regraded or fountains submerged below street level to create enough room to manipulate the water. This meant that once released, Vergine water did not rise in jets and sprays but typically fell or trickled. For example, the dazzling subterranean display at the Trevi fountain is only possible because a clever manipulation of the sloping ground plane allows room for the waterfalls, cascades and pools.

Felice topography was more varied with hills and valleys, densely and sparsely populated areas, and political and ceremonial centers including the Quirinal and Capitoline Hills and the Roman Forum. With over 130 feet of elevation difference in this system, the water shot or fell depending upon the fountain's location and purpose. On hilltops the water usually fell as at the Moses, Quattro Fontane and Campidoglio fountains. In the valleys, such as at the Piazza Barberini, the water flaunted itself a full sixteen feet above the conch of Bernini's Triton Fountain. Neighborhood fountains such as the Madonna dei Monti, Aracoeli and Giudea sent modest jets of water upward for pleasure and downward for service. Like the Vergine, Felice water was inviting, approachable and intended for drinking.

Lofty and versatile, the Paola system could go anywhere and do anything it wanted. It shot a jet of water some twenty feet above the fountains at St. Peter's, allowed the slightest whisper of water to trickle from the Mascherone, and activated a spectrum of jets, sprays and cascades in other fountains around the city. This water though was insalubrious and it served primarily for display, irrigation and industry. Unlike the Vergine and Felice, it rarely fed humble drinking fountains. There was typically a distance between the water jet and the thirsty person, as seen at the twin Farnese fountains; this distance implied, "Look, but don't drink."

Today the Roman water system includes both gravity and pumped systems. In some instances waters from various aqueducts are mixed together and even sent outside their original watersheds. The beauty of the former system, however, is that it allowed the true nature of water to be revealed. Unlike with mechanized pumps that force water into unnatural contortions, a gravitational system nurtures and enhances natural abilities.

Katherine Wentworth Rinne

< 89 Triton Fountain, Rome.
Etching by Giovanni Battista Falda from
Le Fontane di Roma (Rome, 1691).

> 90 Fountain of the Acqua Paola, Rome. Designed by Giovanni Fontana and Flaminio Ponzio, 1610–12; pool by Carlo Fontana, 1690. Albumen print, 1870s.

fountains as Metaphor

"For with thee is the
fountain of life;
in thy light do we
see light." Psalms 36:9

"The teaching of the
wise is a fountain of life,
That one may avoid
the snares of death."

Proverbs 13:14

< 91 Fountain of the Lions,
The Alhambra, Granada, Spain,
11th century; basin added 14th
century.

From the beginning, fountains have been rife with symbolic connotations. All cultures associate water with sources of spiritual blessing, whether as part of the ritual of cleansing, purification, ablution or baptism. In the Bible, God is equated with the fountain of living waters and with light. Thus, fountains are the source of life, goodness and wisdom.

"Of all things water is best." So said the Greek poet Pindar and his praise of the primary element has persisted throughout all ages and civilizations. Whereas in antiquity water sources had often been confined to springs and guarded by nymphs or numinous beings, under the aegis of Christianity, figures allied with the Church took their place, and the provision of water was deemed an act of God. In the Renaissance, alongside the sacred personages, classical gods appeared in new guises.

Certain commonalities are inherent in the properties of water, but provisions for its distribution and display are subject to the vicissitudes of circumstance, whether historical, cultural or technological. By focusing on selected fountains and fountain designs from the Renaissance to the present, an attempt will be made to provide a rationale for the choice of imagery. Some fountains incorporate themes of life, wisdom, justice, poetry, inspiration, love and youth;[1] others show the transformation of classical and Christian motifs in their iconography.

Knowledge of God is a fountain of life. The citation from Psalms opening this chapter, identifying the fountain as the source of life, resonates throughout the Scriptures. Endowed with cosmological significance, the fountain is rarely isolated. Rather it is a theme emanating from Paradise, with early ties to baptism, as witness illuminations in prologues to manuscripts of the gospels, and a mosaic in San Giovanni in Laterano (1290), which depicts the Heavenly Jerusalem beneath the Fountain of Life. Symbolic of salvation and grace, the Fountain of Life, that "pure river of water of life, clear as crystal, proceeding out of the throne of God and the Lamb" (Revelations 22:1), is perhaps most familiar to us at the very center of Jan van Eyck's Ghent altarpiece, *The Adoration of the Lamb* (1432). In the sixteenth-century panels of the *Fountain of Life* (now in Oberlin, Ohio [93] and Madrid) attributed to a follower of Jan van Eyck, salvation is attained through sacred waters. The triumph of the Church over the Synagogue depicted here has been interpreted as signifying the spiritual purification of baptism and the ritual of the Eucharist.[2]

Similarly, elaborate tabernacle fountains equated with the Fountain of Life appear in the form of cathedral lanterns and liturgical objects in fifteenth-century Franco-Flemish manuscripts, such as the one symbolizing Paradise in the *Très Riches Heures* (1411–16) by the Limbourg Brothers [92]. In Jean Fouquet's illumination, The

"A river flowed out of Eden to water the garden, and there it divided and became four rivers." Genesis 2:10

Meeting of the Apostles from the *Hours of Étienne Chevalier* (Chantilly, Musée Condé, 1452–60), the fountain serves as a gathering place for the faithful to affirm the unity of the apostolic ministry. Jets of water symbolizing universal baptism bless the kneeling worshipers.[3]

A universal symbol of water and personifications of mythological deities, the four rivers in gardens east and west, including those inspired by Islam, represent a microcosm of the four parts of the world. In the Koran, the image of Paradise abounds "with gushing fountains and rivers flowing beneath." In few places are these more in evidence than in the waters and gardens of the Alhambra in Granada, Spain. Situated at the intersection of two water channels in the Court of the Lions, the eleventh-century Fountain of the Lions [91] features a basin (of later date), some ten feet in circumference, supported by twelve marble lions. A small jet rises from the center, while an Arabic inscription on the basin praises the beauty of the palace and the abundance of the water supply, alluding to the fountain as the ruler supporting the Lions of the Holy War. Ibn Gabirol, a Jewish poet in the eleventh century, compares the fountain to the molten sea in Solomon's Temple, a huge tank which stood upon twelve oxen (I Kings 7:23–26), rife with connotations of fertility and power, set according to the four points of the compass,

and recalling Solomon's palace and gardens. A fourteenth-century poem cites the horticultural aspects of the paradisal garden, the rich vegetation clearly visible in the Patio de la Acequia [297].[4] In the gardens of the Alhambra and the Generalife, we find that the advanced technology required to display water is necessitated by its scarcity in an arid land. Maximum aesthetic effects are achieved with the minimum of means.

Survivals of the baptismal font appear in the basins of monastic gardens and are often converted to purely secular purposes in scenes depicting the *hortus conclusus* (enclosed garden) and the Garden of Love. An example of the former, richly endowed with both Christian and pagan imagery, was the early sixteenth-century twenty-two-foot-high Italian fountain [94] that once adorned the court at Gaillon in France, a château near Rouen that was destroyed in 1798. This grand fountain, with John the Baptist presiding at its summit, paid homage to its patron Cardinal Georges I d'Amboise, prime minister and advisor to Louis XII. The fountain's style was similar to those found in the sketchbooks of the Venetian painter Jacopo Bellini (Paris, Musée du Louvre, 1440–60). The fountain was shipped from Genoa in Italy to Honfleur in 1508, and an inscription *Perpetui fontis* (everflowing fountain), once on the base, may contain a reference to the recently concluded peace between French and Italian allies as well as to the cardinal's spiritual mission.[5]

In canto XXV of *Paradiso*, Dante equates the *fons vitae* (fountain of life) with baptism and with poetic inspiration and, further, is cognizant of the miraculous nature of the source of water. Endowed with the power of transformation, the fountain becomes the site of pure innocence where remission for all sins may be granted. Revival of Neoplatonic thought perpetuated the belief that the fountain as an everflowing source is a symbol of the One or God, and this was consonant with the belief that the fountain, the origin of all knowledge, is God.[6]

To renew one's vigor, to render one immortal: these ancient precepts originally drawn from Oriental sources were translated in the West as a belief in earthly paradise, free from the destruction wrought by time. Hesiod's description of a Golden Age reflects this state where disease and old age are unknown: "The deathless gods who dwell on Olympus made a golden race of mortal men.... And they lived like gods without sorrow of heart, remote and free from toil and grief; miserable age rested not on them; but with legs and arms never failing they made merry with feasting."[7]

Because of its inherent moral thrust, latent mysticism and the coexistence of satirical writings, such as Sebastian Brant's *Ship of Fools* (1494), the Fountain of Youth became a popular subject north of the Alps in the sixteenth century. At that time, the fountain was viewed as a symbol of regenerative forces, allied to the healing power of water, and also considered capable of alchemical transformations. In 1513 when the Spanish explorer Ponce de León discovered Florida while seeking the spring that would ensure eternal youth, known too for its healing powers, the Swiss physician Paracelsus was documenting the properties of medicinal plants as elixirs of rejuvenation, and as the means of inducing mystical and spiritual states.

Albrecht Altdorfer's painting *Rest on the Flight to Egypt* (Berlin, Gemäldegalerie, 1501) bears witness to Paracelsus's thought as well as to the artist's own cosmic visions. One historian identifies the fountain's crowning figure as Saturn, who presides over a Golden Age, reminiscent of Christian Paradise, the fountain emblematic of the justice bestowed by Christian doctrine.[8] In a woodcut [95], Altdorfer depicts the same subject with an imposing fountain which occupies almost the entire space of a church vault. Based on Italian Renaissance models, and inspired by Mantegnesque prints, by those of Zoan Andrea and by the Tarocchi Master, the four diminishing cycloid tiers are crowned by a seated figure bearing a lantern. The whole fountain overshadows the Holy Family hovering about the lowest basin.[9]

The magical properties of water are most vividly expressed in the theme of rejuvenation, hence in the concept of the Fountain of Youth, and consequently in the forces of love. Fountain and pool become the inevitable loci for illustrations of this theme, from fourteenth-century manuscripts and ivories to Hans Sebald Beham's enormous *Fountain of Youth* woodcut (*c.* 1536 [96]), where fountain and bathhouse are joined by a single jet aimed

< 92 *The Garden of Eden* from the *Très Riches Heures du Duc de Berry*, 1411–16. Manuscript illumination by the Limbourg Brothers.

< 93 *Fountain of Life*, 16th century. Oil on panel by a follower of Jan van Eyck.

∨ 94 Fountain in the court at Gaillon near Rouen, France. Etching by Jacques Androuet Du Cerceau from *Les Plus excellents bâtiments de France* (Paris, 1576).

"A poet I will return, and at my baptismal Font I will take the laurel crown."

Dante, *Paradiso*, XXV, 1–9, trans. A. Vivante

by a bather at an alluring nude. The metamorphosis of the old and infirm into young and healthy athletes disporting on the basins of the Renaissance fountain culminates in the lovemaking scenes of the colonnaded bathhouse, incorporating the erotic components of the *fons amoris* (fountain of love) that was popular in fifteenth-century prints such as those by the Master of the Banderolles (1460). A cautionary element appears in the presence of a fool, pinpointing the folly of the search for youth and eternal love. Like Brant's verses or Hieronymus Bosch's satirical paintings, Beham's print might have been intended as a moralizing sermon, an ironic comment on the quest for eternal youth, but this does not preclude the pleasurable response of the viewer.[10]

Another Eden, the *hortus conclusus*, with its resonances of the Song of Solomon (4:12), becomes the symbol of Marian virginity as the "flawless mirror" of the book of wisdom. This enclosed garden is linked to the Garden of Love, evident in the Christianization of the biblical theme found in depictions of the Madonna in a rose garden.

"A garden locked, a fountain sealed… a garden fountain, a well of living water and flowing streams from Lebanon."

Song of Solomon 4:12

∧ 95 *Rest on the Flight into Egypt at a Fountain*, c. 1512–15. Woodcut by Albrecht Altdorfer.

> 96 *Fountain of Youth*, c. 1536. Woodcut on four sheets by Hans Sebald Beham.

Fountains are frequently at the center of merrymaking and music in the garden, the *mise-en-scène* of the thirteenth-century allegory *Le Roman de la rose*. Throughout this romance by Guillaume de Lorris and Jean de Meun, telling of the search for a terrestrial paradise, the fountain appears as a mirror of God, a metaphor for light and a symbol of love. Whereas the Fountain of Narcissus is compared to a fountain that deceives by making the reflected image seem real, the Fountain of Paradise is a source of the light divine recalling the Eden of Genesis and the *fons vitae* of Revelation (7:17, 21:7, 22:1).[11]

In the Garden of Love, the domain of Cupid, the baptismal font and the secular civic fountain merge—the sacred and the profane, the *Civitas Dei* (City of God) and pagan abandonment. Giovanni Boccaccio too considers the fountain as the principal attribute of gardens in the allegorical *Amorosa visione* and his *Teseida*, both written in the early 1340s. Figural sculpture

replaces the well, often a symbol of purity, as young Florentines escape the plague-stricken city in the *Decameron* (1348–53). In early prints and manuscripts, garden villas often depict musical angels mingling with lovers in feasts that gravitate about the fountain. A miniature of a Garden of Delights [98] in an astrological tract, *De Sphaera*, features male and female youths bathing in a gilded Fountain of Love. Others chant and play flutes, viols and tambourines while servants distribute food and wine and a couple embrace in the foreground of the flowered meadow; beyond the walled garden, a city rises.[12] The legacy of the *fons amoris* is also perpetuated in festival fountains for weddings, aquatic displays and court ceremonies.

Some medieval fountains dramatically express the conflation of the classical and the Christian. Like the great Gothic cathedrals, with their complex iconographical programs, the Fontana Maggiore [99] in the center of Perugia, Italy, may be likened to an encyclopedia in stone. It was designed by Nicola Pisano as part of a scheme of civic improvements and was inaugurated in 1278 to celebrate the autonomy of the free

comune. A tribute to the city's political power and ideals, and combining themes both sacred and profane, the fountain is a summation of the municipality's activities. Propitiously sited in the heart of the city, between the cathedral and the Palazzo dei Priori, it assumes propagandistic and didactic roles, proclaiming the town's economic and urban revival. On this twenty-five-sided polygon, pagan and religious motifs fuse to represent prophets and saints, allegories of the arts, labors of the months, signs of the zodiac, scenes from Genesis and reliefs of Roman history. In its totality, the fountain celebrates Perugia's prosperity and freedom, its closed form echoing that of the city, a protected entity.[13]

Similarly, the sixty-foot-high Schöner Brunnen (Beautiful Fountain [97]) in the market place in Nuremberg, Germany, begun in 1386 probably by Heinrich Parler, is a combination of pagan, Christian and civic glory. Its configuration in tabernacle form bespeaks the aesthetic of the goldsmith, so closely associated with the

< 97 Schöner Brunnen,
Nuremberg, Germany, begun 1386.

∨ 98 *Hortus Delicarum with the Fountain of Love*, 15th century. Illuminated manuscript from *De Sphaera*.

> 99 Fontana Maggiore, Perugia, Italy. Sculpted by Nicola and Giovanni Pisano, 1277–78.

> 100 Fontaine Saint-Michel, Paris. Designed by architect Gabriel Davioud, 1858–1860; restored 1872 and 1893. Albumen print, 1870s.

fountains in medieval manuscripts and with those designed as table ornaments. Destroyed in World War II, this fountain once celebrating Emperor Charles IV has since been resurrected. Here too is a panoply of past history and contemporary society, which includes the seven imperial electors, the nine Christian, Jewish and pagan heroes, the four church fathers, the four evangelists, the seven liberal arts, Moses and seven Old Testament prophets, and figures of philosophy and science with their bands of identification and attributes. The legacy of the fountain as a *speculum majus* (mirror of the world) is inherited by the Renaissance and, with infinite variations, by modern society.[14]

The Fonte Gaia [55] in the Piazza del Campo in Siena, by Jacopo della Quercia (1408–19) marks the advent of an abundant supply of water for public use. Part of a political and ideological mandate of the Sienese republic, it may be equated with good government, whose benefits are demonstrated in the 1338–39 frescoes in the Palazzo Pubblico. On the fountain, reliefs depict the Creation of Adam and the Expulsion from Paradise, symbolic of original sin, redeemed by baptism, along with allusions to the founding of Siena. As the city's patron, the Virgin occupies the prominent central niche, flanked by personifications of eight virtues.

Themes drawn from biblical texts find justification in the grand fountains of baroque Rome, where the opening of new water channels is proclaimed to be bestowed by God. Following the restoration of aqueducts in the Renaissance, Rome witnessed a boom in fountain building not seen since the time of Agrippa. Once the responsibility of Roman emperors, fountains were now under papal domain, testaments to the grandeur and beneficence of the Church. Nowhere is this more visible than in the *mostre* of aqueducts, where each pope tried to surpass the achievement of his predecessors. The Acqua Felice, or Fountain of Moses (1585–88), is adorned with reliefs depicting the miracles performed by Moses [58], such as the bringing forth of water by striking the rock (Numbers 20:10–12). Its portrayal of the prophet, who bears a copy of the Ten Commandments, described as "the most

water conduit, which rises from a simple basin. Their sculptural ornament comprises narratives pertaining to local history, legends and events. The heraldic bears of Bern appear frequently, as do references to the Duke of Zahringen who founded the city in 1191 as a military outpost and who appears on the Zahringen Fountain armed as a lansquenet. The Anna Seiler Fountain, dedicated to the patron of the Island Hospital, shows women mixing wine and water in a display of temperance. Other fountains are dedicated to an archer; to a musketeer waving the banner of his company and supported by a bear at his feet; and to the free brotherhood of minstrels with children dancing about a column. The butchers' guild is represented by the Samson Fountain, where the giant opens the jaws of the lion to reveal the water spout; the town courier appears in full Bernoise regalia on another. None is more provocative than the Kindlifresserbrunnen, the so-called Ogre Fountain (1542–46 [101]), its protagonist devouring a child, bearing a sack of children in reserve, and wearing a Jew's cap. Though perhaps related to "Saturn Devouring his Children" from Ovid's *Fasti*, Swiss contemporaries interpreted the fountain as part of anti-semitic folklore; today, tourist guides may

shameful parody of Michelangelismo in Rome," elicited much criticism: "One could hardly imagine a more unhappy *mostra* for the Acqua Felice." Still, the fountain has always provided much delight, as witnesses the account of John Evelyn in 1644, in which he observes the many details accompanying the main theme of the camels and people drinking: "the design and vastness truly magnificent. The water is conveyed no less than twenty-two miles in an aqueduct by Sixtus V… as the inscription testifies. It gushes into three ample lavers raised about with stone before which are placed two lions of a strange black stone." The latter is a reference to the four Egyptian lions that have since been replaced.[15]

Not unexpectedly, religious subjects are relatively rare in modern fountains. An exception is the Fontaine Saint-Michel in Paris, designed by Gabriel Davioud in 1860 as part of Baron Haussmann's program of urban embellishments [100]. An architectural wall fountain, this monument in alignment with the Pont Saint-Michel offers a fine prospect of the Latin quarter in the manner of a seventeenth-century portal. Four allegorical statues above the Corinthian columns depict the cardinal

virtues—Prudence, Force, Justice and Temperance—while the curved pediment bears Napoleon III's arms between personifications of Power and Moderation. Michael, venerated in the Old Testament as guardian of the Hebrew nation, was adopted as a Christian saint of the Church Militant. His apparition in France *c.* 700 led to the abbey at the summit of Mont Saint-Michel bearing his name. In the central arch of the Parisian fountain, he is seen astride the devil on a rocky mound from which water cascades; he brandishes a sword to represent the triumph of good over evil. The entire fountain evokes a triumphal gateway similar to Napoleon's Arc du Carrousel (1806–08).[16]

Practical considerations dictate the erection of fountains in civic centers and marketplaces as sources of water for man and beast, and consequently they provide opportunities for meeting. In different countries and regions, the local vernacular often determines style and content. For example, Bern, the Swiss capital, has many fountains illustrating the city's cultural history. Here, a series of mid-sixteenth-century fountains, most of them by Hans Gieng, are formed by a shaft, serving as a

prefer to cite the ogre as a carnival mask. Most renowned in Switzerland is the Fountain of Justice (1543), where a blindfolded Justice bearing an upright sword and scales is surrounded by an emperor, sultan, pope and magistrate.[17] Fountains of a similar type, often crowned by local saints or heroes are commonplace in the towns of Alsace and in cities throughout central Europe. Fountains in the North frequently indulge in rustic, peasant subjects, as seen in the Geesebearer Fountain [102, 103] in Nuremberg.

Italy, too, has her share of local types, such as the Fontana del Facchino [51] in Rome, a sixteenth-century figure of a water porter, who would have hawked water drawn from the River Tiber or the Trevi Fountain. Identified by the dress of the medieval guild and the casket he bears, the fountain was once one of Rome's "talking statues," the site of pasquinades,[18] where notices of a satirical nature were posted. Usually in the form of a dialogue, these were often political and critical of current regimes. Genre was sometimes translated into the bizarre, as seen in Il Bacco (Bacchus, 1561–68), a fountain in the Boboli Gardens, Florence, by Valerio Cioli, which represents Pietro Barbino, a favored court dwarf of Cosimo I, astride a tortoise.

Known as the oldest inhabitant of Brussels, the Manneken-Pis [105, 106], sculpted by Jérôme Duquesnoy in 1618,

depicts a little boy emitting an arched jet stream, supposedly based on legends dating back to the late fourteenth century. Though it may be difficult to believe that this fountain records a lad extinguishing a local fire and thereby saving the city from destruction, we can appreciate the statue's many adventures—it has been hidden, stolen, captured, and honored—and wine or beer is often substituted for the fountain's water on festive occasions. For special events, the boy is costumed from his wardrobe of sundry outfits. Many replicas exist, since the original statue is kept in a vault, and there is a sizable industry in cast effigies as souvenirs. The Belgian Tourist Office tells us that the sculpture "represents the irreverent spirit and humor of the Brussels people… to the Belgians, the very spirit of freedom." Not uncommon, the theme of a micturating boy appears in earlier woodcuts such as that by Erhard Schon, *c.* 1535, where the fool atop the fountain is a precursor of the Brussels version.[19] A variation of this type of fountain also appears in *Architectura Curiosa Nova* by Georg Böckler [107].

Few cities are as graciously adorned with fountains portraying aspects of local culture as Aix-en-Provence in southern France. From the seventeenth century on, the shady promenade of the Cours Mirabeau was interspersed with fountains celebrating its provincial heroes (Fountain of Roi René), its events (Fountain of the Nine Canons) or its topography (Hot Springs Fountain [66]). The tradition is perpetuated in the Grand Fountain built in 1860, crowned by personifications of Agriculture, the Beaux-Arts and Justice. Situated at the intersection of three routes, the fountain's figures locate the axes of their respective cities, namely, Marseilles, Avignon and Aix.[20]

Local traditions continued to serve as inspiration for fountains, as exemplified by William Burges's drawing for the Sabrina fountain in the city of Gloucester [104]. Encapsulating the Gothic revival in nineteenth-century England, the fountain was inspired by a medieval legend related by Geoffrey of Monmouth and celebrated in John Milton's masque *Comus*; the unfortunate heroine Sabrina, daughter of King Locrine, was thrown into the River

△ 101 Kindlifresserbrunnen (detail of the Ogre Fountain), Bern, Switzerland. Sculpted by Hans Gieng, 1542–46.

△ 102 *View of the Geesebearer Fountain (Gänsemännchenbrunnen), Nuremberg*, mid-19th century. Engraving by Johann Falkner and Friedrich Geissler.

▷ 103 Gänsemännchenbrunnen, Nuremberg, Germany. Sculpture by Pankraz Labenwolf, *c.* 1540.

Severn, which runs through Gloucester. The protagonists of the fountain are accompanied by aquatic beings and paraphernalia, and the whole is topped by an otter displaying a shield with the arms of the city. Burges sets the fountain within an imaginary view of the thirteenth-century town, depicting its town hall, belfry tower, armorers' shop, and pillory. Although the fountain was never executed, contemporaries recognized in the drawing the portrait of Gloucester, and furthermore, the very spirit of the Middle Ages.[21]

In the Renaissance, the revival of the classics in literature and art spawned a revolution in fountain design and content. Humanists brought to light the ancient texts of Homer, Ovid and Virgil, while artists studied the remains of Roman sculpture and architecture. Fountains constituted the perfect vehicle for virtuoso sculptural displays, and by the end of the sixteenth century they became part of an elaborate scenography. Gods and goddesses drawn from antiquity now mingled with Christian saints, living monarchs and local heroes, in programs that were often devised by scholars for garden villas or town squares. The imagery of fountains could draw on a

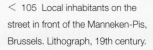

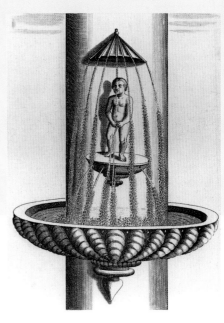

< 105 Local inhabitants on the street in front of the Manneken-Pis, Brussels. Lithograph, 19th century.

∨ 106 Manneken-Pis, Brussels. Designed by Jérôme Duquesnoy, 1618.

∨ 107 *A Beautiful Fountain with a Naked Child*, etching from Georg Böckler, *Architectura Curiosa Nova, Die Lustreiche Bau- und Wasserkunst* (1704 edition).

∨ 104 *Design for a Fountain to be Erected in the City of Gloucester, Illustrating the Story of Estrilda and Sabrina, as Told by Geoffrey of Monmouth (c. 1100–1154), c. 1856.* Pen and ink and watercolor over preliminary pencil drawing by William Burges. This unrealized fountain exemplifies a Victorian revival of interest in the Middle Ages.

great range of literary sources—Neoplatonic tracts, emblem books, mythographies and manuals for festival decor—which often served to create personal or civic iconography.

Of all mythological beings, it is Neptune, identified with Poseidon, the Greek god of the sea, who constitutes the ideal figure to reinforce maritime associations. Statues of the Roman god proliferated on fountains from the fifteenth to nineteenth centuries. Renaissance humanists would have been familiar with the passage in Virgil's *Aeneid*, where Neptune used his power to calm "the troubled waves" of the storm unleashed by Juno on behalf of the Greeks.

Meanwhile Neptune saw the sea in a turmoil of wild uproar, the storm let loose and the still waters upheaved from their lowest depths. Greatly troubled was he, and gazing out over the deep he raised his serene face above the water's surface.... "Do ye now dare, O winds, without command of mine, to mingle earth and sky, and raise confusion thus? Whom I—! But better is it to calm the troubled waves: hereafter with no like penalty shall ye atone me your trespasses. Speed your flight and bear this word to your king: Not to him, but to me were given by lot the lordship of the sea, and the dread trident."... Thus he speaks, and swifter than his word he calms the swollen seas, puts to flight the gathered clouds, and brings back the sun... even so, all the roar of ocean sank, soon as the Sire, looking forth upon the waters and driving under a clear sky, guides his steeds and, flying onward, gives reign to his willing car.
Virgil, *The Aeneid*, I, 124–56.[22]

Although no longer worshiped as the creator of waters, Neptune was an appropriate figure to mark the building of new aqueducts or to direct new courses of water. Bearing a trident, he rides over the waters, often accompanied by attributes such as dolphins or a chariot drawn by sea horses. A timely symbol for harbor fountains, we see the colossus towering over Giovanni Angelo Montorsoli's fountain in Messina, Italy (*c.* 1554–57), where he is depicted calming the straits and ruling over sea monsters Scylla and Charybdis below him. Situated as a gateway to the sea, this Fountain of Neptune [108] denotes a great maritime power. Montorsoli's earlier Fountain of Orion (1547–53) in the city's cathedral square features Neptune's son, the legendary founder of Messina. His power to walk over land and sea made him an ideal subject to pay tribute to Hapsburg munificence, which had benefitted the town's water supply, while celebrating Charles V's triumphal entry into the city. Giovan Paolo Lomazzo, in his *Trattato dell'arte della pittura* (1584) which discusses possible subject matter for fountains and gardens, cites the Fountain of Orion and its representation of mythological episodes, nymphs, river gods and marine monsters, as ornament in accord with the rules of decorum.[23]

In few fountains does Neptune exercise greater command than in Giambologna's Fountain of Neptune in the Piazza Nettuno in Bologna (1563 [109]), a paradigm of commemoration and celebration. Poised on an island in the midst of the piazza, the fountain represents the god between earth and sea. Not only did the fountain mark the opening of the city's improved water supply, but it also pays homage to Pope Pius IV, whose arms are prominently displayed. Inscriptions on the base state that this public fountain was the gift of the pope, cardinal and papal legate. Virgil's epic poem solemnizing an Augustan peace is recreated in a new Christian order. Neptune is a paean to Pius IV who, with the establishment of the Tridentine decrees, following the conclusion of the Council of Trent, brought order out of chaos and calmed papal seas.[24]

We find Neptune, sculpted by Bartolomeo Ammannati, to be an allegorical representation of Medici Duke Cosimo I, presiding over the waters of the enormous basin in the Piazza della Signoria in Florence (*c.* 1560–75 [130]). A gigantic but awkward figure, this white marble Neptune stands on a sea chariot with astrological symbols referring to the alliance of Cosimo and Charles V. Known as Il Biancone (big, white fellow), he dominates the bevy of bronze naiads, fawns and satyrs cavorting at the fountain's rim. With its seventy original jets, the fountain was proof of Cosimo's campaign to increase the citizens' water supply, and moreover, a reflection of his intention to make Florence a great naval power.[25] Across the River Arno, near the rear of the amphitheater in the Boboli Gardens, Stoldo Lorenzi's statue of Neptune (1568) digs his trident into a rustic mound at the center of a fish pond surrounded by tritons and sirens.

Neptune fountains are ubiquitous; in fact, the sea god is inextricably associated with fountains in city and country. He also looms large in temporary fountains and designs for festivals, as is visible in the engraving after Joannes Stradanus for a Florentine fountain on the Via Tournabuoni, dated 1575. Apparently intended for a Medici celebration [110], its inscription may be translated as follows: "It is golden Florence over here [which] rises on its high hills/ Over there the meadows shine gem-like with green color/ And the fountain surges more lifelike;/ Naiads, and Dryades, and Oreads and Napee pour down their

streams." Neptune also found a home in local marketplaces, such as the Neptune Fountain (1660–68 [111]) in Nuremberg by Georg Schweigger. Like other fountains in the city, this Neptune shows a marked affinity with the designs of ornamental table fountains by Albrecht Dürer, Hans Holbein and their contemporaries.

The great château and gardens of Versailles in France, so famous for their fountains, pay tribute to Apollo. Notwithstanding, the Bassin de Neptune [112] occupies a prominent site north of the cross-axis of the château. Begun by André Le Nôtre in 1679, the huge hemicycle is dominated by a dense group, from which rise Neptune and his bride Amphitrite, each with a large retinue in tow—a chariot drawn by dolphins, tritons, nereids, sea monsters and cupids. But it is the architecture of the water that dazzles, especially the vertical jet spouting from a dragon's mouth that reaches a height of nearly ninety feet.[26] Such was the renown of Versailles that authoritarian monarchs and princes used it as a model for their own gardens and fountains, thereby perpetuating the glory of gravity-defying jets and powerful waterwalls, subjecting nature to the will of man. Imitations abound throughout Europe, from Drottningholm near Stockholm (1680s) to Schönbrunn in Vienna (1690) and from Wilhelmshöhe near Kassel (1701) to La Granja de San Ildefonso in Spain (1720s [145]). Few, however, attain the spectacular scale of those built for Peter the Great at Peterhof (1714–25), such as the Neptune Fountain and the Grand Cascade [146] with its centerpiece of Samson rending the lion's jaws (1734) to commemorate the Russian victory over the Swedes in 1709.

One of the most beautiful urban spaces in France, the Place Royale in Nancy [114] honoring Louis XV (now Place Stanislas) was designed in 1751–55 by architect

< 108 Fountain of Neptune, Messina, Italy. Sculpted by Giovanni Angelo Montorsoli, *c.* 1554–57. Local legend holds that, with his mighty trident, Neptune cut Sicily from the Italian peninsula and that Scylla and Charybdis haunted the treacherous straits between the island and the mainland.

< 109 Fountain of Neptune, Piazza Nettuno, Bologna, Italy. Sculpted by Giambologna, commissioned 1563.

∨ 110 *A Fountain of Neptune in Florence*, 1575. Engraving after Joannes Stradanus, also called Jan van der Straet.

∨ 111 Neptune Fountain, Nuremberg, Germany. Sculpted by Georg Schweigger, 1660–68.

∧ 112 Bassin de Neptune, Versailles, France, begun 1679. Neptune and Amphitrite sculpted by Lambert Sigisbert Adam in 1741.

< 113 Court of Neptune Fountain, Library of Congress Main Building, Washington, D.C. Designed by J. L. Smithmeyer and others, with sculptor Roland Hinton Perry, 1897–98.

∨ 114 Fountain of Neptune, Place Stanislas, Nancy, France. Designed by Emmanuel Héré with sculpture by Barthélémy Guibal, 1751–55.

Emmanuel Héré to join the old and new town. In the voids at the corners of the gilded grilles of triumphal arches cast in wrought iron, Barthélémy Guibal sculpted lead statues of Neptune and Amphitrite with their cortèges; both are poised on massive rocks amid luxuriant verdure and framed by minor arches, reinforcing the maritime theme.[27]

Classical revivals, including the so-called American Renaissance in the United States, called for classical themes. Hence, Neptune continued to be incorporated in fountain designs, and the spirit of this powerful pagan god and his equestrian entourage seemed especially appropriate for fountains which adorned public buildings or civic monuments. See, for example, the Court of Neptune Fountain (1897–98 [113]) in its grottolike setting adjoining the Library of Congress in Washington, D.C.[28]

Symbol of worldly power and physical prowess, of health and well-being, Hercules appears on fountains in various allegorical guises. At the Villa Medici in Castello outside Florence, the Fountain of Hercules and Antaeus designed by Niccolò Tribolo and completed by Bartolomeo Ammannati (1550s) is surmounted by a bronze statue; water springs in great quantities from the mouth of the god in his struggle with Antaeus. Fountains and grottoes in the villa are part of an elaborate program to honor the house of Medici and to mark the extension of aqueducts to the rivers and mountains around Florence.[29]

Humanist advisors, such as antiquarian Pirro Ligorio, who devised the program of the gardens in the Villa d'Este in Tivoli (1550–72) for the Cardinal Ippolito II d'Este, rendered obeisance to the dynastic ties of the Este. The patron traced his family back to the mythical deity Hippolyte (slain by Hercules), after whom he is named. Hercules then appears to be the paradigm of virtue overcoming vice, for example, in the episode depicting the Choice of Hercules, laid out between the grottoes of Diana (virtue) and Venus (voluptuousness).[30] L'Hercule chrestien, considered an analogue of Christ (with Hercules's mace comparable to the cross, his labors prefiguring the works of Christ) as interpreted by humanist Guillaume Budé, would be appropriate in this cleric's villa.[31]

At the Villa Farnese in Caprarola, Hercules's labors symbolize the four elements, water being represented by the god and the hydra. Vincenzo de' Rossi's preparatory drawing for a fountain (1560s) also represents the Labors of Hercules [115], in a design probably projected for Cosimo I, rendering homage to his bravery and his virtue. In the sixteenth and seventeenth centuries, Hercules is often depicted bearing Atlas; this pairing is transformed into an allegory of Astronomy, with Hercules receiving the weight of learning from Atlas as at the Villa Aldobrandini in Frascati [132]. Charles Le Brun, director of the Académie Royale de Peinture in France and chief painter under Louis XIV, proposed a series of inventions for the fountains of Versailles. In the *Recueil de divers desseins de fontaines et de frises maritimes*, the Fontaine d'Atlas et d'Hercule shows the protagonists upholding the sphere, while an infinity of jets creates a finely wrought curtain of falling water [116].

Among the gods who descend to adorn the fountains of Francis I's favorite château at Fontainebleau, none is more prominent than Hercules, who personified the king in the image of *Hercule gaulois*. A white marble Hercules, now lost, attributed to Michelangelo (1541), was designed for the Cour de la Fontaine overlooking the fish pond, to celebrate the virtues and deeds of the king. In a similar vein, Benvenuto Cellini's projected Fountain of Mars (1543), a colossal fifty-four-foot statue was to be accompanied by personifications of "those arts and sciences in which your majesty takes pleasure, and which you so generously patronize… for you are truly a god Mars, the only brave upon this globe."[32] Could flattery to the king be less disguised, especially considering the arcane program associated with the Gallery of Francis I?

If Pius IV is personified as Neptune in Bologna's fountain, it is the ruler as Hercules who dominates the monumental Augustus Fountain, designed by Hubert Gerhard, formerly in Augsburg, Germany (1589–94). In the same genre as Giambologna's Fountain of Neptune, it was built to honor the city's putative Roman founder, who looms over personifications of the region's four rivers.

Another Netherlandish sculptor, Adrian de Vries, designed a monumental Fountain of Hercules (1596–1602) in Augsburg. An engraving by Jan Muller (1602 [117]) depicts Hercules poised to slay the hydra, on an elaborate shaft adorned with four figures and a panoply of shells and garlands. Its inscription reads: *Fons ex marmore et aurichalco cum imaginibus Herculis et charitum Augustae vindel. in foro vinario opus stupendum* (Fountain from marble and gilded bronze with the image of Hercules and the charity of Augusta Vindelicorum [the Roman camp founded by the tribe named here] in the wine market— stupendous work). These fountains on the Maximilianstrasse are adapted from Florentine mannerist prototypes in both their typology and their iconographical programs.

Quite naturally, nymphs—naiads and nereids—as minor divinities dwelling in springs and rivers are commonplace motifs for fountains. Generators of life, nymphs are often endowed with healing powers and act as guardians of poetic inspiration. Symbolizing their primacy in a most elegant style are the nymphs which adorn the Fontaine des Innocents (Fountain of the Innocents) in Paris [62, 63, 118]. The fountain, built in 1549 to mark the triumphal entry of Henri II, originally stood on the border of the Cemetery of the Innocents and the processional route on Rue St. Denis. Designed by sculptor Jean Goujon and architect Pierre Lescot, the fountain heralded a new classicism in

∧ 115 *Fountain with the Labors of Hercules, c.* 1560. Black chalk drawing by Vincenzo di Raffaello de' Rossi.

∧ 116 *Fountain of Atlas and Hercules.* Etching after Charles Le Brun from *Recueil de divers desseins de fontaines et de frises maritimes* (Paris, 1684–87).

∧ 117 *Fountain of Hercules in Augsburg,* 1602. Engraving by Jan Muller after Adrian de Vries.

France. It was a combination of tribune and temple, altar and tomb, open loggia and triumphal arch. But water is minimal in this monument to aquatic glory. Rather it is the five urn-bearing nymphs, seemingly emerging from the sea, who embody the allegory of water. The meaning of the fountain is further explicated by the attic reliefs of tritons, nereids and dolphins. Symbolic of resurrection and salvation, the dolphin representing the just among fish—in Neoplatonism, the ascent of the soul—is fitting in a monument honoring the dauphin Henri II. Monarch of France and God's viceroy on earth, it is he who provided the gift of water embodied in the fountain, wherein the city of Paris becomes the metaphorical ship of state.[33]

Nymphs are also associated with the Muses as sources of inspiration. Fountains, like the Castalian spring on Mount Parnassus, are often conceived to be personifications of poetry, as noted in engravings by the Tarocchi Master [119] or on the title page of the Paris *Iliad*, 1545, where Homer is represented as the Fountain of Poetry. The idea that water inspires those who drink from certain sources with the genius of poetry reverts to the ancients who sought inspiration at the Boeotian springs.

Allied to nymphs are the Charities and Graces, known from antiquity as attendants of Venus, who, according to Seneca, symbolize the threefold aspect of generosity, and, in humanist thought, the threefold aspect of love. Also associated with the theological Virtues and accompanied by cornucopias, the figures

119 *Poetry, c.* 1465. Engraving with traces of gilding by the Master of the E- Series Tarocchi. This muse, seated beside a sacred spring, personifies a source of inspiration for poetic creativity as boundless as freely flowing water.

118 Fontaine des Innocents, Paris. The man posed between two of Jean Goujon's nymphs provides a sense of scale. Albumen print by Charles Marville, *c.* 1855–57. This photograph was taken just before the fountain was renovated.

< 120 *A Grand Fountain,* woodcut from *Hypnerotomachia Poliphili* (Venice, 1499).

> 121 The Nile, Fountain of the Four Rivers, Piazza Navona, Rome. Designed by Gian Lorenzo Bernini, 1648–51. Sculpture by Jacopo Antonio Fancelli.

> 122 Fountain of the Four Rivers. The figures are carved in marble which contrasts markedly with the rough travertine on which they rest. The Ganges, sculpted by Claude Poussin, reclines beneath a swaying palm, while beneath a serpent winds around his oar.

become emblematic of earthly charity. Such beings appear in fanciful fountain designs, replete with obscure symbolism, in *Hypnerotomachia Poliphili* (*The Dream of Poliphilus*), an early romance written by Francesco Colonna, a Dominican monk. Printed in Venice in 1499, it was translated into French in 1546, and into English at the end of the century. In France, the dreamlike setting was familiar to readers of the courtly medieval *Roman de la rose*, in which Christian and pagan rites are intertwined as the language of alchemy is set against a pastoral landscape. Regeneration, once associated with baptism, is now a part of the tradition set within the Garden of Love. Among the illustrations is the Grand Fountain [120], composed of three gilded nymphlike figures in the pose of the classical modest Venus, with water streaming from their breasts. A conflation of the Graces and the Charities, they bear three cornucopias which merge into an urn overflowing with fruit. Delicate jets of water create a linear architecture in the fountain of precious stones rising from a porphyry plinth and supported by a basin decorated with gilded harpies. The surfeit of rare materials recalls the "Fantastic Fountain in the Temple" described by Rabelais in *Gargantua and Pantagruel* (v. 42), its three Graces armed with cornucopias and jetting water from every orifice. Comparable, too, is the fountain with the three marble nudes that Boccaccio places in the garden of his *Amorosa visione*.[34]

In the Middle Ages, Paradise was located at the nexus of four rivers—the Pison, Gehon, Tigris and Euphrates— which became symbols of the Gospels. Rivers remain a stock feature of later fountain designs, but their names and meanings have altered to accommodate changing circumstances.

Undoubtedly, Gian Lorenzo Bernini bears the palm for the art of fountains. In 1644 he designed a statue depicting Neptune calming the waters (now in the Victoria & Albert Museum, London) as the climactic set piece of a fish pond in Cardinal Montalto's Roman villa. Fearful and angry, the powerful sea god may have inspired Urban VIII's command to Bernini to set in motion the rebuilding of the Trevi in Rome. Although never completed, Bernini's idea may have been realized in Nicola Salvi's final version, in which Neptune appears under the guise of Oceanus (the ancient river of the world which bounds earth and sea, and whose genealogy is entirely different from that of Neptune). Other Roman fountains, unequaled anywhere in their enhancement of the urban fabric, certainly drew on Bernini's design. Perhaps Rome's ultimate city fountain is the Triton in the Piazza Barberini (1642 [17]). The sea god, half-man, half-fish, is the son of Neptune at whose bidding he blows on his conch to calm or rouse the sea. Described as an apotheosis of water, Bernini's poetic conceit is based on Ovid's account of the cessation of the Flood (*Metamorphoses*, I, 327–48): "Then too the anger of the sea subsides, when the sea's great ruler lays by his three-pronged spear and calms the waves; and calling the sea-hued Triton, showing forth above the deep... he bids him blow into his loud-resounding conch, and by that signal to recall the floods and streams." The emblem of the Barberini family bees adorns the dolphin-carved base of the fountain and sings the praises of Urban VIII's literary talents.[35]

Fountains enhance the magnificence of the Piazza Navona. Memories of antiquity survive in the form of Domitian's circus, reinforced by the three fountains along the central axis. The terminal fountains are by Jacopo della Porta. At the north, the Neptune Fountain (1575) shows the god sparing an octopus, with tritons, sea horses and mermaids at the base. At the southern end, the fountain known as Il Moro (1575) may be another version of Neptune; astride a fish on a conch shell, the violent torsion of the figure's pose recalls the work of Bernini. The Fountain of the Four Rivers (1648–51 [122]) at the center is a scenographic *tour de force*. Bernini, supplanting Francesco

Borromini as the result of a competition, reflects temporary festival designs in this fountain. Upon completion the entire plaza was the site of mock naval battles and aquatic displays on hot summer evenings, as Giovanni Paolo Pannini's painting of 1756 (Landesgalerie Niedersächsisches Landesmuseum, Hanover) and numerous eighteenth-century engravings testify.[36] In the fountain, the rivers of Paradise are transformed into rivers representing the four great continents, the Nile [121], Danube, Plata and Ganges. Each bears appropriate emblems and gestures, revealing the rivalry between the two artists: the Nile, veiled, alluding to its unknown source (or more popularly identified as refusing to view the defects of the adjacent church, Borromini's Sant'Agnese, completed in 1666); and the Plata, whose raised hand could be seen to implore or withstand the fall of the church facade. Artifice vies with nature in the arched travertine rockscape in which the marble river gods support a fifty-four-foot-high granite Egyptian obelisk, crowned by a cross bearing the arms of the Pamphili dove. Designed under the aegis of Pope Innocent X (Giambattista Pamphili), whose family palace was located in the piazza, the fountain manifests the power of the Church triumphant over paganism.

In the eighteenth and nineteenth centuries, many of the earlier themes are combined and recycled. Edme Bouchardon's Fontaine des Quatre Saisons on the Rue de Grenelle (1739–45 [68]) is an allegory of the City of Paris between the Rivers Seine and Marne, while statues and reliefs depicting children at play represent the seasons. Subject to political vicissitudes, the arms of France in the pediment were replaced after the Revolution with a crown of laurels.

If French public plazas were often designed as places for new statues, urban schemes combined statuary with fountains. None are more effective than the fountains built under Jacques Ignace Hittorff's aegis in the Place de la Concorde (1840) in Paris [159]. Consciously echoing the axis of the fountains and obelisk in St. Peter's Square in Rome and reflecting Hittorff's admiration for the Renaissance fountains in Messina, Italy, the figures on the north fountain represent the Rivers Rhône and Rhine. They are accompanied by personifications of Harvest and Abundance, and the three genii symbolic of rivers, Navigation, Agriculture and Industry. Figures on the south fountain represent Maritime Navigation, Astronomy and Commerce. On the site of the infamous guillotine of the French Revolution, the waters of these fountains may help to obliterate the memory of the blood which once flowed there, replacing it with technological splendors. The wonder of water and the transport and erection of the obelisk, surrounded by statues of eight cities of France pay tribute to modern French industry and agriculture.[37]

The paradigm of the nineteenth-century city fountain and a product of the Renaissance revival stands in a square opposite the Bibliothèque Nationale in Paris. Composed of four nymphs upholding a basin, the Fontaine de la Place Louvois represents the four main "female" rivers of France—the Seine, Loire, Saône and Garonne [123]. Hierarchically oriented, it is the Seine who faces the prestigious Rue de Richelieu. Naiads are seated at the base, together with masks of the seasons and signs of the zodiac. Designed by Ludovico

> 125 The Meeting of the Waters,
St. Louis, Missouri. Designed by
Carl Milles, 1940.

Visconti in 1836–39 to embellish the city
of Paris in collaboration with sculptor Jean-
Baptiste-Jules Klagmann, it refers to
sixteenth-century predecessors; the vase
at the summit echoes the funerary urns
sculpted by Pilon, and the nymphs recall
those of Goujon on the Fontaine des
Innocents. The whole structure is animated
by a thin veil of water, creating a transparent
counterpoint to the horizontal basins.[38]

Both Neptune and the four rivers
continue to be incorporated in civic
fountains, for example, the Fountain of
Neptune by Reinhold Begas (1891) in the
Alexanderplatz in Berlin, Germany, a site
it also shares with the grand nineteenth-
century town hall and a Gothic church.
Here Neptune rules over an allegory of
four rivers—the Elbe, Weichsel, Oder and
Rhine—reflecting both the rule of Prussian
lands and the naval policies of Wilhelm II.

In the United States, the phenomenal
urban development of the nineteenth
century stimulated City Beautiful
movements and programs to improve
the water supply and to embellish civic
centers and city parks.

New York City's Central Park, the most
renowned of Frederick Law Olmsted's
great works, features the Bethesda
Fountain (1873 [126, 127]) as part of the
scenic perspective between the formal
axis of the mall and the more romantic
surrounding landscape. The centerpiece of
this recently restored sandstone fountain is
composed of ornamental representations of
the four seasons in the guise of birds, berries,
fruit and foliage. Four youths, personifications
of Health, Purity, Temperance and Peace,
support an Angel of the Waters (John 5:2–4).

Frédéric Auguste Bartholdi, author of
the colossal Statue of Liberty Enlightening
the World adds the symbolism of light to
that of water in the cast-iron fountain he
sent to the United States Centennial
Exhibition in Philadelphia in 1876 [178].
Here the quintessential classical fountain
is adorned with gas lamps, befitting the
idea of progress, emblematic of the
modern city.[39]

Fountain Square, today the hub of
Cincinnati, Ohio, has been cited by author
and urban enthusiast William H. Whyte as
"the finest square in the country." At its
center stands the Tyler Davidson Fountain,
a gift from Henry Probasco, who wished
to honor his business partner and friend.
Crowning the fountain, the Genius of the
Water, arms outstretched, bestows blessings
upon the city [124]. Its dedication in 1871
declares: "Water is not only beautiful in
nature and useful in art, but it is rich with
meaning in the teachings of religion. It is…
a symbol of purity and life in the soul."[40]
Cast from an old bronze cannon by a
sculptor from Nuremberg, the fountain
includes reliefs depicting the uses of water
for navigation, fishing, milling, and power,
with children at play suggesting the
pleasures of water.

In St. Louis, Missouri, Carl Milles
created The Meeting of the Waters (1940
[125]) opposite the former Union Station,
which has recently been adapted as a hotel.
A panoply of fourteen bronze figures
presenting mythological creatures, naiads,
tritons, leaping fish and water jets, all join
in celebrating the union of the Mississippi
and Missouri Rivers north of St. Louis. A
male figure, the mighty Mississippi, astride

a catfish offers a flower to the Missouri, a
young woman. Comprising a vocabulary
derived from classical, primitive and
historical sources, the fountain bespeaks
the diverse heritage of the United States.

Figures drawn from mythology, the
Bible and local history once constituted the
principal symbolism of fountains, at a time
when sculptural forms dominated. The use
of classical myths and biblical references, so
prevalent in art and literature during the
Renaissance, gradually declined as the
allusions became more remote. Who still
hears "old Triton blow his wreathed horn"
(Wordsworth) or wonders that the "shore
beats back the envious siege/ Of watery
Neptune" (Shakespeare, *Richard III*)?
Today, fountains are often part of urban
development schemes and the shift is from
scenographic displays to improvisational
theater and participatory performance with
water as the protagonist. The metaphor
has become nature—the seas, mountain
streams, rivers, cascades and falls, and the
underlying motion inherent in the flow of
water. The stress now lies on the dynamic
properties of water in accordance with the
words of Heraclitus: "All is flux, nothing
stays still." As ever, the Greeks had the
words for it—*Panta re* (everything flows).

Naomi Miller

The Bethesda Fountain in New York City

In 1858 Frederick Law Olmsted and Calvert Vaux conceived New York City's Central Park as an almost wholly artificial environment, creating the illusion of a natural landscape. The naturalistic park was to be an antidote to the built-up city, a place where urban dwellers could experience the reinvigorating power of nature while consciously or unconsciously communing with God's natural world. The Bethesda Fountain, one of the most important American fountains of the nineteenth century, is the symbolic heart of Central Park and the physical embodiment of Olmsted and Vaux's vision [126, 127].

One formal element was planned in the park—a mall with rows of elm trees culminating in a richly sculpted terrace with views over a lake toward the forested ramble. At the base of the terrace would be a large fountain basin with a single jet of water; it would be flanked by smaller fountains set atop the terrace. These stone basins were part of the initial construction phase of the park, but in 1863, the Board of Commissioners of Central Park decided to commission a monumental fountain for the central basin, set on an axis with the center of the mall.

The fountain project was given to the relatively unknown American sculptor Emma Stebbins, who happened to be the sister of the board's president.[1] Stebbins was a New Yorker who had gone to Rome in 1857 to study painting but instead turned to sculpture. She became part of a small group of artists that centered around her companion, actress Charlotte Cushman. For the Central Park project, Stebbins interpreted a popular verse from the New Testament's Gospel of Saint John in which an angel touched, or "troubled," the waters of the Bethesda pool in Jerusalem, giving it curative power.[2] Ironically, in 1885, when an official revision of the Bible was completed, this verse was dropped because it was deemed to be inauthentic.

With its biblical source, the fountain is an allegorical representation of the rejuvenating power of Central Park's natural landscape. Stebbins designed a bronze angel, known as the Angel of the Waters, whose feet touch rocks from which water spouts. Its left hand holds lilies symbolizing purity and its right arm reaches out, extending the water's healing powers toward viewers on the terrace. The curative waters flow over the lip of a bronze basin, creating a veil around allegorical figures representing the blessings of Temperance, Purity, Health, and Peace, four attributes that the fresh air and healthy environment of the park could provide. The water pours into an octagonal granite bowl, designed by Vaux and his assistant Jacob Wrey Mould, before flowing into the earlier round basin.

For New Yorkers, the display of cascading water at the Bethesda Fountain was more tangibly associated with the blessing of clean water, provided by the Croton Aqueduct. Emma Stebbins noted in her description of the fountain, that "we have no less healing, comfort and purification, freely sent to us through the blessed gift of pure, wholesome water, which to all the countless homes of this great city, comes like an angel visitant."[3]

The fountain, dedicated in 1873, was not greeted with universal acclaim. While the *New York Herald* proclaimed it "the chief attraction of the Park," the *New York Times* found it a "feebly-pretty idealess thing."[4] Today the fountain is considered one of Central Park's most significant features, and its symbolism continues to resonate, as is evident in the epilogue of *Perestroika* (1992), the second part of Tony Kushner's award-winning drama *Angels in America*, where the characters, in need of physical or mental healing, meet beneath the angel, and are reinvigorated.[5]

Andrew Scott Dolkart

< 126 View of the Bethesda Fountain with weekend strollers, Central Park, New York. Designed by Emma Stebbins, Calvert Vaux and Jacob Wrey Mould, 1873. Albumen print, late 19th century.

> 127 *The Fountain, Central Park (View of Bethesda Fountain with the New York City skyline)*, 1933. Etching by Albert Flanagan.

chapter 4
fountains
as
Propaganda

Many European and American fountains serve as potent instruments of propaganda.* Over the centuries, the nobility and the papacy as well as governments and corporations have commissioned these works as images of strength, power, prosperity, and glory. To fulfill such aspirations, designers use their ingenuity to capture water, then control and mold it into impressive sprays, jets, flows, and cascades, often complementing symbolic sculpture or architecture. Classical myths frequently provide sources of inspiration for subjects and themes. Situated in city centers, gardens or parks, the prominent locations of fountains effectively convey the desired message.

Fountains not only reflect an aesthetic sensibility but also the technological advances in hydraulics and engineering, often resulting from the need to bring water from a distance. The labor and money necessary for such an undertaking can bring as much honor to the patron as the completed fountain. Some designs for extraordinary fountains exist only as drawings and prints on paper, their colossal scale and ambitious message are a testament to the glory of the patron. Other designs, pure fantasy and beyond the practical means of execution, celebrate the designer's own power of invention.

The role of fountains as vehicles for propaganda has its roots in the ancient world, but it was not until the Renaissance, as various ruling families vied for control, that this idea was fully explored and exploited. In antiquity, the Romans undertook the enormous expense of building aqueducts to provide water for an urban population. Since the primary objective was to offer potable water for consumption, water was distributed throughout the city and collected in simple basins. Beginning in the Renaissance, rulers rebuilt or constructed aqueducts, and fountains were added to act as both a terminus and a monument for their patrons. Fountains could convey, through symbol or metaphor, political, dynastic or civic propaganda. The combination of water and sculpture became a symbol of power and identity. Fountains possess an aesthetic and an aural appeal, but the subjects of the sculptures, the dedicatory or commemorative inscriptions, and the location of these works often suggest a more complex history.

In 1537, Alessandro de' Medici was murdered and Cosimo I de' Medici, from another branch of the family, became duke of Florence at age seventeen. Anxious to legitimize his right to the title, he launched an ambitious program of dynastic propaganda intended to forge a stronger Medici succession through both civic and private commissions.[1] Through these projects, Cosimo sought to create a lineage that would rival, if not surpass, that of the oldest Italian noble families.

< 128 Trevi Fountain, Rome.
Designed by Nicola Salvi, 1732–62.

Among Cosimo's first major commissions was Bartolomeo Ammannati's Fountain of Neptune (c. 1560–75) prominently situated in the Piazza della Signoria, the political center of Florence [130]. Ammannati, both a renowned sculptor and an architect, had been summoned in 1555 from Rome, where he had been in the service of Pope Julius III, to work for the Medici in Florence. Within five years he had created a number of private fountains to adorn the Medici villas, but the public Fountain of Neptune, his best-known work, not only revolutionized fountain design in Florence, but held a special significance for its patron, Cosimo I. Previously, water for the few existing Florentine fountains had come from wells or from rain water collected in reservoirs, resulting in a fountain type that relied on sculpture for its display, in contrast to Roman fountains which had featured cascading water, pools and jets.[2] Ammannati's fountain celebrated Cosimo's achievement of increasing the city's water supply through the creation of an aqueduct which provided water not only for consumption, but a sufficient amount to permit, for the first time, the luxury of a continuously flowing fountain.

∧ 129 Fountain of Oceanus, Boboli Gardens, Florence. Sculpted by Giambologna, 1567.

> 130 Fountain of Neptune, Piazza della Signoria, Florence. Sculpted by Bartolomeo Ammannati, c. 1560–75.

The early eighteenth-century art biographer, Filippo Baldinucci, wrote of Ammannati's fountain: "In the midst of a great basin full of the most limpid water, gushing from many jets, rises the great Colossus of Neptune… standing on a chariot drawn by four sea-horses… between his legs three figures of Tritons which stand with him upon a great sea shell…. The four sides [of the basin] are low enough to permit everyone to enjoy the limpidity of the water, which, gushing forth, is received by some beautiful shells… everything is so well planned, and arranged with so much grandeur, that it is truly a marvel."[3] This novel play of water is integral to the design as numerous small jets envelop the great white marble figure, and through their spray and mist transform the nude statue of Neptune into the commanding god of the sea, as sleek bronze sea figures, wet and glistening atop the basin, pay homage.

Water fed not only this prominent public fountain, but also flowed to the Pitti Palace and Boboli Gardens to supply the private fountains there. Cosimo and his wife, Eleanora of Toledo, had purchased this palace and its surrounding lands from the Pitti family in 1549. Over the next decade, Cosimo's favorite architect, Niccolò

Tribolo, and later Ammannati, transformed the vineyards and orchards located behind the palace into formal gardens adorned by statues, grottoes and fountains.[4]

The extraordinary Fountain of Oceanus (1567) by Giovanni Bologna, called Giambologna, was originally located in the amphitheater behind the Pitti Palace [129].[5] This powerful standing figure of the personified ocean holds a baton in one hand and rests his right foot on the head of a dolphin. Oceanus is surrounded by three crouching river gods, the Nile, Ganges and Euphrates, representative of the great ocean tributaries, and this entire group is supported by an oversized granite basin.[6] The play of water is minimal and the fountain is dominated by the colossal central figure.

Giambologna's Oceanus, not accidentally, bears a striking resemblance to Ammannati's Neptune, as both were commissioned to celebrate Cosimo's building of the aqueduct.[7] These two sculptures were so strongly associated with Cosimo that they were later recalled by Pietro Francavilla in his 1594 portrait statue of the duke who stands in precisely the same pose as Oceanus with his right foot resting on a dolphin. Oceanus, considered

△ 131 *Fountain Design with Oceanus and the River Gods Arno and Tiber*, 1570. Black chalk, pen and brown ink, brown wash drawing by Jacopo Zucchi.

▽ 132 Water Theater, Villa Aldobrandini, Frascati, Italy. Designed by Carlo Maderno, begun 1602, with later additions by Giacomo della Porta and Giovanni Fontana.

in the Renaissance to represent the universal power of water, was a fitting image for Francavilla's Cosimo which stood in the Piazza dei Cavalieri in Pisa before the headquarters of the Knights of Santo Stefano, a naval order founded by Cosimo in 1561 to police the waters of the Mediterranean against the Turkish corsairs.

Neptune was also a relevant image to evoke and, in fact, Cosimo's founding of a naval order provided the impetus for a fountain in the Boboli Gardens. Situated in a small formal garden to the left of the palace, Stoldo Lorenzi executed the Fountain of Neptune between 1565 and 1568. Originally atop a cylix fountain and surrounded by sea deities, the menacing bronze figure of Neptune is poised to spring forward, with trident raised as if ready to plunge into the sea.[8] This assertive stance distinguishes it from the more passive Neptunes by Ammannati (*c.* 1560–75) and by Giambologna in the Piazza Nettuno in Bologna (1563–67) who possess a quiet dignity.[9] Instead, Lorenzi's Neptune is more tempestuous, a vivid reference to Cosimo's diligent role in actively protecting the Mediterranean from the enemy who sought to control her.

The fountains in the Boboli Gardens are formally distinct from other contemporary Florentine works which tend to be shaped like candelabra, surmounted by sculptures, and characterized by a minimal play of water as, for example, Niccolò Tribolo's Fountain of Hercules and Antaeus at Castello or his Fountain of the Labyrinth at Petraia, both Medici villas.[10] The monumental scale and the dominant single central figure that distinguish the Boboli fountains likened them to civic works and thus continued Cosimo's political message within a private setting.[11]

Cosimo died in 1574 and his son, Francesco, succeeded him as grand duke of Tuscany. Francesco focused his interests on his two loves, alchemy and Bianca Capello, leaving him little time to continue his father's political pretensions. His brother, Cardinal Ferdinando de' Medici, however, shared the Medici ideology as demonstrated by Jacopo Zucchi's unexecuted *Fountain Design with Oceanus and the River Gods Arno and Tiber* [131], thought to have been made for the cardinal.[12] The design shows the principal rivers of Florence and Rome dominated by Oceanus, a less than subtle allusion to Ferdinando's papal aspirations. The cardinal's ecclesiastical plans were

thwarted by his brother's death. He returned to Florence, became grand duke in 1587 and continued the Medici legacy of propaganda from there.

At the Villa Aldobrandini at Frascati, Cardinal Pietro Aldobrandini, nephew of Pope Clement VIII, boldly followed Cosimo's example of using fountains as a vehicle for his political and dynastic agenda. The *casino* was situated halfway up the hillside, offering a panoramic view over the Roman countryside. In 1602, the cardinal commissioned an extraordinary water theater [132] from Carlo Maderno, best known as the architect of the facade of St. Peter's in Rome. Giacomo della Porta and Giovanni Fontana, who had worked on the Acqua Felice and would later contribute to the Acqua Paola in Rome, provided the hydraulics expertise. The theater is unique for its dominant axial position behind the unusually wide and shallow palace and for its message which professes spiritual over temporal rule.[13] Set into the hillside, this curved structure or exedra, articulated by pilasters and caryatids, contains a large central niche flanked by four smaller lateral ones, each with statues and gurgling fountains.[14] In the center, a figure of Hercules reaches up to take the globe from the shoulders of Atlas, in order to complete another labor that will lead ultimately to his

immortality. The Herculean imagery continues above the theater where a small and narrow cascade of water flows down the *scaletta d'acqua*, or water stairs [133]. Situated atop a hill are two twisted columns symbolizing the legendary Pillars of Hercules, said to be where the waters of the Mediterranean Sea and Atlantic Ocean meet. Once thought to represent the limits of the known world, the pillars, by the mid-sixteenth century, were synonymous with unlimited expansion of power.[15]

Visitors do not need to speculate on the meaning of the water theater because there is an inscription explaining how the cardinal both restored peace to Christendom through the absolution of Henri IV of France in 1595 and reacquired the duchy of Ferrara for the Papal States. In doing so, like Hercules, the cardinal shouldered the weight of his uncle's burden, taking upon himself the arduous tasks of government and diplomacy. When his work was done, the inscription continues, he erected this villa as a retreat and brought the water from Mount Algido. This last part might seem incongruous given the political bias of the inscription, but its inclusion was anything but bucolic. The villa, dominating the hillside above Rome, was a manifestation

of the owner's political and dynastic ambitions. The cardinal also prided himself on having brought water via a five-mile-long aqueduct.[16] Although Frascati had served as a retreat for popes and cardinals throughout the sixteenth century, it suffered from a shortage of water. Cardinal Aldobrandini, therefore, undertook the tremendous expense to remedy this situation, in part so his fountains and waterworks would rival those at the Palazzo Farnese at Caprarola and the Villa Lante at Bagnaia. Indeed, the new features of the Villa Aldobrandini not only surpassed those of the sixteenth-century villas, but laid the groundwork for the transformations that would characterize gardens and fountains throughout Europe in the following century.

In the seventeenth century, as land became synonymous with wealth, gardens grew larger and more lavish. The money needed to manipulate the landscape, to bring water where it was lacking, could only be provided by the richest and most powerful patrons, and nowhere is this better exemplified than at Versailles in France. Originally a modest hunting lodge for Louis XIII, the château was enlarged in the 1660s by the architect Louis Le Vau.[17]

< 133 *The Water Stairs (Scaletta d'Acqua) and Pillars of Hercules at Villa Aldobrandini, Frascati, Italy.* Etching by Giovanni Battista Falda from *Le Fontane delle ville di Frascati* (Rome, 1691).

> 134 *Versailles: Large Plan of the Château, Town, Gardens and Surroundings*, 1687. Pen and black and red ink, black chalk, gray, green, and blue wash drawing by an unknown draftsman.

> 135 *Fountain of Fame*. Etching after Charles Le Brun from *Recueil de divers desseins de fontaines et de frises maritimes* (Paris, 1684–87).

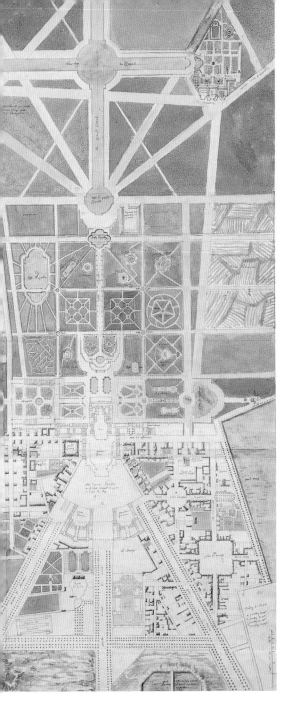

In 1661, following the death of Cardinal Mazarin, Louis's first minister, the young king abolished the post, consolidated his own authority, took the reins of government into his hands and for the next half century was the absolute ruler of France. Louis XIV was determined that Versailles should surpass the splendors of Vaux-le-Vicomte. The gardens were magnificently designed to mirror the monarch's control. The dominant central axis bisecting the garden with symmetrical parterres on either side, the ordered progression of descending terraces, the orchestration of dramatic views, and the creation of artificial canals, pools and fountains, all display man's dominance over nature. Abandoning the Arcadian ideal of man living in harmony with nature, Versailles's landscape and iconography promote man's supremacy over nature, and the harnessing of water proved to be the greatest challenge. Water was an essential consideration in the development of châteaux and verdant gardens, and the expense of bringing it to the site was enormous. At one point, Louis XIV even considered abandoning Versailles for a place with a more adequate water supply.[19]

In the 1660s, major reshaping of the park, earth moving, dredging and excavating for the Grand Canal began. Le Nôtre wanted water to be used in pools and canals to mirror the surrounding gardens and the grand château so that their space would seem limitless. Spectacular jetting fountains were also necessary to reflect the king's absolute power. At Versailles, the exorbitant cost of the hydraulics projects exceeded all other artistic expenditures, especially since some ventures failed. Elaborate horse-driven pumps, windmills, networks of channels and ditches were all laboriously devised over the course of decades in order to supply enough water to Versailles's reservoirs. In 1684, one such ambitious undertaking was suggested by Sébastien le Prestre, Seigneur de Vauban, a fortifications architect who sought to divert the River Eure, a tributary of the Seine, from a point near Chartres, some forty miles

away.[20] The king, agreeing to Vauban's plan, dispatched thirty thousand troops to construct the necessary aqueduct that would carry the water to Versailles. Just when the project appeared as if it would succeed, in 1688, disease and military demands led to suspension of the work.[21] Other costly hydraulic schemes also failed. The vision of Versailles filled with continuously flowing fountains seemed as if it would never be realized, until a more modest and carefully controlled system of canals and aqueducts was eventually devised to supply the required water. The most sophisticated engineering achievement of its day was the Machine de Marly. Constructed at a fantastic cost in the 1680s, it consisted of fourteen waterwheels and 253 pumps that raised the water three hundred feet from the River Seine by purely mechanical means.[22]

While the question of hydraulics occupied the king and his engineers throughout the 1670s, work proceeded on the construction of the château. In 1678 Jules Hardouin-Mansart was named the architect-in-charge. Destroying Le Vau's Italian-style open terrace that overlooked the garden, Mansart created an enclosed gallery, known as the Hall of Mirrors, flanked by salons at either end.[23] Mirrors were both a novelty and a luxury and their inclusion here was an expression of

From 1662, the innovative garden designer André Le Nôtre closely collaborated with Le Vau on transforming the garden. From the beginning, Le Nôtre designed the park to take priority over the palace, surpassing what he had earlier done so successfully at Vaux-le-Vicomte, also just outside Paris and completed in 1661, for Louis's financial minister Nicolas Fouquet.[18] It was Fouquet who first brought together Le Vau, the painter Charles Le Brun, and Le Nôtre. This château demonstrates the unity between house and garden that would subsequently distinguish Versailles, while its gardens harbor the features of its grand successor. The balance of the varied parts—moat, parterres, pools, allées, fountains, grottoes and canal—reveals why Vaux-le-Vicomte epitomizes the classic French formal garden.

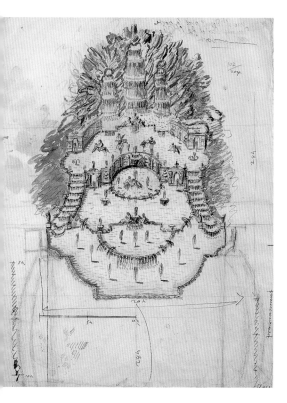

∨ 136 *Project for a Giant Cascade, Versailles*, 1684–87. Pen and black ink, red chalk, blue and gray wash drawing by André Le Nôtre.

∨ 137 *Fountain of Apollo and Daphne*. Etching after Charles Le Brun from *Recueil de divers desseins de fontaines et de frises maritimes* (Paris, 1684–87).

unparalleled magnificence. In order to link iconographically the various aspects of kingly splendor, Charles Le Brun conceived of adapting the myth of the Sun God Apollo to unify the decorative imagery of the château with the fountains in the park.[24] Apollo, who carried the sun across the heavens, brought light and enlightenment, truth and peace. He inspired and protected the arts and sciences. Louis XIV, the exalted Sun King, brought order and peace to his kingdom, while his palace set the standard for artistic and technical achievement.

Within the grand gallery, under Le Brun's artistic direction, the decorative cycle mixed allegory and history, combining the mythical deeds of Apollo with Louis's current rule. With Le Brun's paintings overhead, the sun streaming through the windows of the hall, captured and reflected in the mirrors and silver furnishings, it was an optimum expression of the Sun King. When Louis XIV emerged from his bed chamber and looked out of the central window, he saw an impressive landscape that further epitomized his power and image. After almost twenty-five years of

planning, designing and construction, the palace with its vast gardens were nearing completion, as shown in the plan of 1687 [134].

Many prints show the extraordinary effects created by the fountains as they looked during the reign of Louis XIV. These drawings and prints are often the only record of the ambitious designs envisioned for Versailles, and some provide a glimpse into the design process. Others document the designer's concept, such as a print based on Le Brun's drawing for the Fontaine de la Renommée, or the Fountain of Fame, as the central feature in the Bosquet de la Renommée, later called the Bosquet des Dômes [135]. Drawings and maquettes relating the design development for the principal fountains are rare. Instead, there seems to be a preponderance of drawings and prints showing ideas for unrealized fountains, revealing the rich imagination of Versailles's designers, excited by the possibility of a royal commission. An exceptional drawing attributed to Le Nôtre, renowned for the precise, restrained, formal symmetry of his gardens, shows an unrealized project

for an exuberant cascade inspired by Italian villa design [136]. Meant to highlight Versailles's water prowess, this energetically drawn design is thought to be among the first fountain proposals for the park.[25] An engraving for the unrealized Fontaine des Arts, or Fountain of the Arts, has the winged horse Pegasus poised upon the crest of a rocky arch signifying Mount Parnassus, surrounded by the Muses, who preside over springs and streams, as sources of inspiration [138]. Le Brun's fountain, which would have been centered in a pool, features a water jet reaching skyward, symbolizing the soaring power of artistic inspiration, while below the arch, descending water creates a veil showering reclining river gods. On the other side of the arch, not depicted here, Le Brun intended a figure of Apollo, who officiated over Mount Parnassus. Another fountain design by Le Brun was inspired by Ovid's *Metamorphoses*, and by Bernini's sculpture of *Apollo and Daphne* (1624–25) in the Villa Borghese in Rome. In the print, water jets sprout from Daphne's fingers as she is transformed into a laurel tree [137].

Exploration of the palace and gardens of Versailles reveals its exceptional qualities of art and design. The first garden terrace presented two large pools of water rimmed by water nymphs and allegorical figures of France's four great rivers. From this vantage point, the full extent of the garden was not visible; one had to move through the

garden to experience fully the enchanting delights it offered, including its one thousand fountains of which about three hundred remain. Then, as now, off the central axis, visitors could explore a variety of fountains and smaller gardens that accented the secondary axes. The principal fountains were placed as centerpieces on the dominant axes. The first one on the central axis, located on the second lower level, reached by gentle horseshoe slopes designed by Le Nôtre in 1666, was the Fontaine de Latone (1668–70), sculpted by Gaspard and Balthazar Marsy [139].[26] The marble statue of Latona with her children Apollo and Diana forms the apex of this fountain. Surrounding her are figures in various stages of transformation into frogs and lizards. Taunted by the Lycian peasants, the myth relates, Latona called upon the gods to punish those who failed to show the mother of Apollo respect. Their punishment was metamorphosis into amphibians and reptiles. The story with its semiaquatic figures was easily adapted for the Versailles fountain design, and it held great significance for the king and queen mother, Anne of Austria, who was regent during Louis's minority, and had suffered a similar indignation during the civil uprising known as the Fronde in the 1650s.

An engraving by Adam Perelle shows an early stage of the fountain with frogs and other creatures adorning the basin, an arrangement devised specifically for a fête

< 138 *Fountain of the Arts.* Etching after Charles Le Brun from *Recueil de divers desseins de fontaines et de frises maritimes* (Paris, 1684–87).

∧ 139 *Fontaine de Latone,* Versailles. Sculpted by Gaspard and Balthazar Marsy, 1668–70.

> 140 *The Latona Fountain, Looking Toward the Fountain of Apollo and the Grand Canal, Versailles.* Etching by Adam Perelle from *Vues des belles maisons de France* (Paris, 1693).

on 18 July 1668 [140]. Between 1687 and 1689, after the death of the Marsy brothers, the statuary was elevated on to graduated tiers in a pyramidal form, and further frogs were added.[27] Without the play of water, the sculpture sits serenely in its pool, and the focus is on its iconography and the sweeping vista toward the Bassin d'Apollon and the Grand Canal beyond [141]. However, when the fountain jets are activated, the resulting display of great sprays suggests Latona's vengeance raining down on the peasants who abused her and their frenzy in the discovery of their own transformation.[28]

The grand allée stretching from the Fontaine de Latone and the Bassin d'Apollon reflected the king's absolute order, authority and control. The expanse of *tapis vert*, or green lawn, is flanked by a straight wall of trees that are cultivated, pruned and, when necessary, replaced, to achieve this highly groomed effect. The crowning centerpiece of this prominent axis is Jean-Baptiste Tuby's fountain showing Apollo rising from the sea (1668–71), based upon Le Brun's design, and similar to his painted decoration in the palace's Hall of Mirrors.[29] The chariot of Apollo seems to emerge from an expanse of water, his arrival announced by tritons with conch-shell horns. Without the play of water, the Sun God shines in perpetual brilliant glory [142]. As with the decoration inside the palace, Apollo reigns as an exalted symbol of Louis XIV. Late seventeenth- and early eighteenth-century paintings, drawings and prints show the waterworks spectacle of the Bassin d'Apollon which regularly attracted the curious aristocracy who came by coach, on horseback, or on foot to view it. Today, when the fountain is switched on, frothing white jets of water burst into the air and splash vigorously, suggesting the powerful force needed to propel the chariot of Apollo from the sea at daybreak to begin his journey across the heavens [143]. Designed for dramatic effect, and to flatter the king, the fountain is oriented so that the Sun God rises from the west and travels east toward the château, in contradiction to nature. So when the sun sets behind the fountain, a dazzling aura of sunlight is created, a wondrous scene best viewed from the palace.

∧ 141 Fontaine de Latone, looking toward the Grand Canal, Versailles.

∨ 142 Bassin d'Apollon, Versailles. Sculpted by Jean-Baptiste Tuby, 1671. Photograph by Michael Kenna, 1988.

> 143 Bassin d'Apollon, Versailles.

> 144 *Fountain of the Wolf and the Stork in the Labyrinth at Versailles*. Etching by Sébastien Le Clerc from *Labyrinte de Versailles* (Paris, 1679). A bone has caught in the Wolf's throat, and he asks the Stork to dislodge it with his long beak. The task done, the Stork asks for payment, to which the Wolf replies, "What ingratitude, why you're lucky I didn't eat you!"

The myth of Apollo and other classical subjects did not, however, permeate the entire garden. Before the unified program had been adopted, Jean de La Fontaine's immensely popular fables inspired a charming, light-hearted series of thirty-nine animal fountains situated throughout the labyrinth, begun in 1672 to a design by Le Nôtre.[30] The idea for a labyrinth originated with Charles Perrault, best known for his own story *Puss in Boots*, who had a keen interest in science, natural history and animals. Both Perrault and La Fontaine were inspired by the royal menagerie, as were other court sculptors and painters including the Marsy brothers who studied the amphibians and reptiles in preparation for their Fontaine de Latone. La Fontaine, a well-known writer who had been encouraged by the king to use his talents to celebrate Versailles, had recently translated Aesop's tales into French, transforming these moralizing fables into miniature dramas and comedies that discreetly satirize

human foibles. The maze with its animal fountains reveals a playfulness and childlike quality; it was in fact created for Louis's heir, the dauphin.[31] A small book, *Labyrinte de Versailles* (1679) with etchings by Sébastien Le Clerc, is one of the few surviving documents of this maze. The realistically painted lead fountains, sculpted by Étienne Le Hongre, Jacques Houzeau, Pierre Mazeline, Étienne and Jacques Blanchard, Jean-Baptiste Tuby and the Marsy brothers, in addition to fourteen others, faithfully followed the fables.[32] Each fountain featured the animals involved in a particular story, such as "The Cock and the Fox," "The Peacock and the Nightingale," and "The Monkey King." Each sculptural ensemble was placed in a small basin, animated by small jets of murmuring water. Many were tucked into the corners of the maze, while others, featuring dramatic vertical jets, punctuated the pathways, such as "The Wolf and the Stork [144]." The labyrinth was eventually replaced in 1775 with the Bosquet de la Reine, reflecting the changes the garden underwent later in the seventeenth and

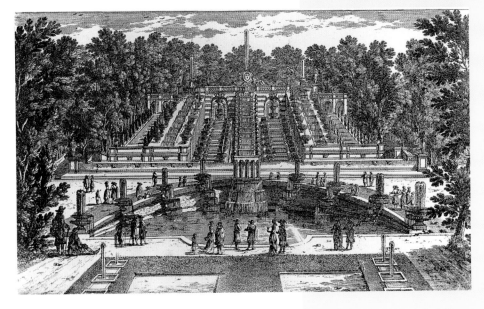

eighteenth centuries from an emphasis on mythology in favor of a classical style that expressed the dignity of the king.

It was the spectacular fountains and gardens of seventeenth-century Versailles, as well as those of other French royal châteaux, that inspired Tsar Peter the Great's summer residence of Peterhof,[33] begun in 1709 and located some ten miles west of St. Petersburg in Russia. The tsar, having acquainted himself with French garden innovations through books, models and the importation of French architects,[34] may have imitated the approach and grand vistas of Versailles, but water played an even greater role at Peterhof. Unlike the scarcity of water on Louis XIV's site, the Gulf of Finland was at the disposal of the Russian residence. This abundance of water at Peterhof allowed for spectacular displays, including not only canals, cascades and basins as at Versailles, but numerous jets of water, bursting like fireworks—the whole appearing more like a waterpark than a formal French garden.

As in its French predecessor, a central axis dominates the plan of Peterhof. The approach begins at the Gulf of Finland and continues to the Grand Canal, which is some 650 yards long and lined with fountains. The focus of this progression is the famous Grand Cascade and the palace behind [146]. The cascade is comprised of seventy-five fountains and framed by the Great Grotto, smaller grottoes and three cascading stairways. When activated, over

< 145 Fountain of Neptune, La Granja, San Ildefonso, Spain. Sculpted by René Frémin, Jean Thierry and others, 1721–28. Photograph by Charles Clifford, probably late 1850s.

∧ 146 The Grand Cascade, Peterhof, Russia. Designed by Jean-Baptiste-Alexandre Le Blond, Niccolò Michetti, and others, begun 1709.

∧ 147 View of the Cascades of St. Cloud. Etching by Gabriel Perelle after Israel Silvestre from Vues des belles maisons de France (Paris, 1693).

> 148 Cascade with sculptural tableaux of Diana and Acteon in the foreground, Palazzo Reale, Caserta, Italy. Designed by Luigi Vanvitelli and Martin Biancour, with sculpture by Paolo Persico, Angelo Brunelli, and Pietro Solari, 1752–72.

2600 gallons of water run through the complex hydraulic system. Jean-Baptiste-Alexandre Le Blond, a pupil and follower of Le Nôtre, and the Italian architect Niccolò Michetti, created this masterwork whose obvious influence is not Versailles but Le Nôtre's cascade at Louis XIV's château of Saint-Cloud [147].

The compositional centerpiece of the Grand Cascade is the monumental sculpture by Bartolomeo Carlo Rastrelli depicting Samson rending the lion's jaws, (1734) that emits a seventy-foot jet of water. This odd juxtaposition of subject and fountain is the result of a commission to commemorate the twenty-fifth anniversary of 27 June 1709, St. Sampsonius's Day, when the Russians defeated the troops of Charles XII of Sweden at the Battle of Poltava in the Ukraine.[35] This reference to a historical event is not unique at Peterhof as the military and political triumphs of Peter permeate the garden. For example, the central axis terminates in the upper garden with the Neptune Fountain where the god is synonymous with Peter the Great, and with Russia's dominance over the sea.

Versailles also influenced the design of the gardens and fountains of La Granja (1720–39), or The Grange, at San Ildefonso, near Segovia, in Spain.[36] Created for the first Spanish Bourbon monarch, Philip V, they are the only gardens in Spain based on the French formal model, known to Philip from his youth when he visited the court of Louis XIV. Located to the east of the royal palace created in 1726 by the Italian artist Andrea Procaccini,[37] the design of the formal gardens was the collaborative work of the sculptor René Carlier, the gardener Esteban Boutelou, and the military engineer Esteban Marchand. As in its French forerunner, a central axis bisects the park with parterres on either side. Further from the palace, strict geometric control gives way to the more natural setting of the bosquets. A team of sculptors, including René Frémin and Jean Thierry, was imported from Louis XIV's court to create the twenty-six fountains and numerous statues that form the complex iconographic program based on classical mythology [145].[38] Some of the fountains at La Granja are specific quotations from those at Versailles such as the Fuente de las Ranas or Fountain of the Frogs (based on the Fontaine de Latone), the Plazuela de los Ocho Calles (recalling Hardouin-Mansart's Colonnade), and the well-known Fuente de la Fama, or Fountain of Fame (inspired by the Bosquet des Dômes), which is renowned for its enormous jet, at that time the highest in Europe. Water was plentiful, supplied by nearby mountain streams. The objective at La Granja was to create a larger and more magnificent version of its French counterpart.

The most spectacular fountain at La Granja, designed by Frémin and surrounded by lead statues by Jacques Bousseau, is the Bath of Diana, a popular subject because of its watery setting. The same subject serves as the centerpiece for another Versailles-inspired Bourbon garden, created for King Charles VII of Naples (later King Charles III of Spain) for the royal residence at Caserta in Italy.

Luigi Vanvitelli designed the palace at Caserta between 1752 and 1772, while the formal gardens were laid out in accordance with Le Nôtre's model by Martin Biancour under Vanvitelli's supervision. A canal almost two miles long, flanked by carriage paths, divides the garden. The deceptively wide stretch of water, punctuated by sculptural fountains, leads to the Bath of Diana and the grand cascade at the foot of the hillside [148]. The central waterfall separates the sculptural groups: on the left is the transformation of Acteon into a stag surrounded by his hunting dogs; at the right, Diana and her female companions. The cold white figure of Diana seems unmoved by the violence awaiting Acteon who spied on the goddess while she bathed. It is the forceful rush of the falling water with its thunderous roar, like a musical score, that enhances the drama of the scene, as the hunting dogs prepare to attack the master they no longer recognize.

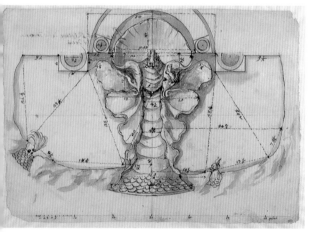

∧ < 149, 150 *Designs for the Trevi Fountain, Rome: Section through the Central Niche and Cascade* and *Plan of the Central Niche and Cascade*, c. 1741. Pen, brown ink, brown wash and black chalk drawings by Nicola Salvi. The lower drawing shows the form of the central niche (indicating the position of Oceanus's feet) and the irregularly shaped cascade channel—so designed to encourage a spirited flow of water to fall over the precipice into the basin.

The hydraulic system at Caserta proved to be one of the great technical achievements of the eighteenth century. The twenty-six-mile aqueduct, the Archi della Valle, did as much to enhance the glory of the king as the garden itself. Only a great monarch could afford the manpower, materials and money that its construction demanded.

Private garden fountains provided a haven in which to indulge in self-promotion, but the role of fountains as urban monuments was quite different. While the Fountain of Neptune in Florence was a testament to Cosimo I de' Medici's self-proclaimed magnanimity, its primary function was to provide water for the citizens. Likewise, Pope Sixtus V recognized the need for a sufficient water supply when he built the Acqua Felice in Rome (1585–88) to expand the habitable space of the city [58]. Paul V Borghese continued the practice of building public fountains with the restoration of the ancient Aqua Traiana and the creation of the Acqua Paola whose waters fed the Janiculum Hill and Trastevere [90]. The most well-known of these urban fountains, however, remains the Trevi. It has been the inspiration for songs, the setting for movies, and every tourist knows a coin must be tossed into it to ensure a return to Rome.

The history of the Trevi began in ancient Rome when in A.D. 19 Marcus Vipsanius Agrippa built the aqueduct that brought the Aqua Virgo to the undeveloped quarter known as the Campus Martius.[39] Exceptional in that its conduit was mostly underground, the aqueduct required less maintenance and decreased the chance of contamination, which led to ancient writers extolling the purity of its waters. The aqueduct fell into disrepair following the fall of the empire and was only restored in the Renaissance during the ambitious building and urban renewal projects initiated by Pope Nicholas V. Executed

< 151 *View of the Great Fountain of the Acqua Vergine called the Trevi, Rome, c.* 1773. Etching by Giovanni Battista Piranesi.

> 152 *Fuenta de Cibeles, Madrid.* Designed by Ventura Rodríguez, with sculptures by Francisco Gutierrez and Robert Michel, 1780–86.

by Leon Battista Alberti, the Trevi's design was simple. Its three water streams collected into a single basin and it was ornamented only by an inscription and the papal coat of arms. Its unpretentious appearance belied its importance as the sole aqueduct to supply Rome until the opening of Sixtus V's Acqua Felice in 1588.[40]

Over the next two centuries, the urban context of the Trevi continued to change with the construction of new palaces, but the appearance of the fountain remained the same. In 1640, at the request of Urban VIII, the fifteenth-century fountain was razed, along with many houses, to accommodate a new design by Gian Lorenzo Bernini. A critical feature of his project was the reorientation of the fountain, resulting in a greatly enlarged piazza on a less restricted site.[41] Ultimately, Bernini's project was abandoned, and the fountain remained for the next fifty years as only a semicircular basin.

During the pontificate of Clement XI Albani, a number of designs incorporating Roman antiquities were devised to complete the Trevi. Carlo Fontana, a student of Bernini, executed drawings that combined the fountain with an obelisk from the Villa Ludovisi and an ancient granite basin, or *tazza*, from the Campo Vaccino.[42] Water would flow from the *tazza*, while the obelisk would serve as the crowning central feature. Fontana's pupil Filippo Juvarra outlined his thoughts for the Trevi, combining the fountain and the antique Antonine Column before a semicircular exedra that recalled the water theater of the Villa Aldobrandini in Frascati. Ferdinando Fuga's 1723 design breaks with these earlier projects. Primarily architectonic, its ties are with ephemeral festival designs, characteristic of the seventeenth and early eighteenth centuries.[43]

Although there were numerous projects for the Trevi fountain, none were implemented until the election of Pope Clement XII Corsini in 1730 when a competition was held to complete the Trevi. Two years later, Nicola Salvi's design was selected.[44] The project had to incorporate the facade of the Palazzo Poli that the Trevi fronted. Two drawings reveal how Salvi succeeded in fusing the palace and fountain, and adeptly harmonized the architecture and sculpture with the rushing sound, sight and movement of water. Salvi

proposed Oceanus, who embodies "an impression of power which has no limit," as the centerpiece of the design. In one drawing, Oceanus, standing on a rocaille shell, presides over the cascade [149]. The other, a plan of the central niche, shows the arrangement of the shell-like basins and the pool below [150].

The triumphal arch that provides the centerpiece and framework for Salvi's design is flanked by the recessed wings of the Palazzo Poli [1]. The monumental Corinthian pilasters that articulate the palace become the columns that define the fountain on either side of the niche containing the statue of Oceanus. The basin is partially filled by hewed rock and marine figures that break forth from the central group. It is the predominately architectonic quality of the Trevi, however, that distinguishes it from earlier fountain designs, such as Bernini's Fountain of the Four Rivers for the Piazza Navona [122].[45] The art historian Howard Hibbard described this work as "a gigantic papier-mâché confection, an exuberant piece of stagecraft," reflecting the festive architecture of its day.[46] While Bernini's work informed Salvi's, particularly in the organic quality of the carved stone, it was to achieve a different effect. Bernini's mid-seventeenth-century fountain, commissioned by Pope Innocent X Pamphili, made both a papal and dynastic

statement. The rivers symbolized the expansion of the church into new territories throughout the world, but at the apex of the design, atop the obelisk, was the Pamphili dove. The Fountain of the Four Rivers reflects an era dominated by spiritual and temporal politics whereas the Trevi reflects the new interests and ideals of its age.

While the Corsini coat of arms supporting the papal stemma crowns the attic story and an inscription below celebrates Clement's role in the creation of the fountain, his successors are also commemorated. An inscription to Benedict XIV adorns the entablature and one to Clement XIII encircles the center niche, attesting to the work's thirty-year building history. The structure, however, is not about self-glorification, papal politics, or dynastic pretensions, it is about the role of water as the primary animator of nature.

The symbolic program of the Trevi is revealed by its central sculptural group. Oceanus, the personification of all water, stands in his oyster-shell chariot, pulled by winged sea horses and accompanied by tritons, amid marine flora and fauna. Salvi, in his explanation of the iconographic program of the Trevi,[47] called Oceanus "a Power superior to other Powers,... most powerful agents among natural phenomena." Tritons and sea nymphs,

Salvi continued, symbolize the Sea who has the power to "go forth to give necessary sustenance to living matter for the productivity and conservation of new forms of life." He called water "the only everlasting source of continuous being." It nurtures and gives life to new forms. Salvi's interest in nature reflects the growing preoccupation with the natural sciences in the eighteenth century. Giovanni Battista Piranesi's famous views were among the first to show the entire setting of Rome's largest and most spectacular fountain [151]. Piranesi had witnessed the start of construction in 1732, the death of its designer in 1751 and its 1762 completion by the architect Giuseppe Pannini and Pietro Bracci, who sculpted Oceanus and the other marine figures. The popularity of Piranesi's contemporary views attests to the immediate fame of the Trevi, the monumental terminus of the Acqua Vergine, the most celebrated fountain in Rome. On many levels, the Trevi altered the appearance, function and intent of fountains and was a watershed for future designs. Modern works like Paul Manship's 1934 Prometheus Fountain at Rockefeller Center [161] and particularly the Piazza d'Italia, designed in 1978 by Charles Moore [273], reveal a debt to the Trevi.

The Italian and French use of fountains as a dramatic way to embellish a setting *and* to reflect enlightened learning spread to Madrid after 1759 when Charles VII of Naples (and Caserta) left Italy to succeed his father as King Charles III of Spain. Among his many legacies still evident today in Madrid are the Museo del Prado (originally intended as a natural history museum) and the botanical garden along the elegant boulevard, the Paseo del Prado. From 1767 to 1782, architect-engineer José de Hermosilla designed the Paseo del Prado by planting trees and rerouting its stream underground to feed splendid fountains, designed by Ventura Rodríguez. There are three fountains marking the major intersection plazas: the celebrated Fuenta de Cibeles (Fountain of Cybele, 1780–86), personifying the Greek goddess of Nature (or Earth [152]), stands between the Fountain of Neptune and the Fountain of Apollo with the Four Seasons. Riding a chariot pulled by two lions, showing her dominion over wild beasts, Cybele

symbolizes the abundant fertility of the region. Regarded as one of the most famous landmarks in Madrid, the sculpture of the goddess and the chariot were created by Francisco Gutierrez, the lions by the French sculptor Robert Michel.

Charles III's vision transformed this previously undistinguished section of the city. On summer evenings, members of fashionable society would flock to the Paseo, not only to enjoy the cool and picturesque setting, but also to partake in a sophisticated promenade mingling with historians, philosophers, natural scientists, doctors and astronomers. The fountains were overt symbols of the city's increasing knowledge of nature and the sciences. Today, the still-regal Fuenta de Cibeles, ever the symbol of benevolent Nature, presides over a prominent transportation hub in a much-visited, thriving cultural and commercial area of Madrid.

∧ 153 *Project for a Public Monument to be Erected on a Paris Square*, 1799. Pen and gray ink, brown wash, pencil drawing by Jean-Pierre-Laurent Hoüel.

> 154 *Monumental Elephant Fountain for the Place de la Bastille, Paris*, 1813–14. Ink and watercolor, heightened with gold by Jean-Antoine Alavoine. In this version of the design, the elephant is richly harnessed and bedecked with a golden throne palanquin.

While personifications of Oceanus and Neptune proclaim a universal power linking water to all living things, and Cybele represents the bountiful rewards gleaned from nature, other propagandistic fountains attempt to evoke a global authority via other symbolic means. In France, several decades after the completion of the Trevi, the revolutionary fervor of the 1790s prompted designs for many monuments in the name of Liberty, Equality and Fraternity. Artist Jean-Pierre-Laurent Hoüel, known for his landscapes of Sicily, as well as for his scientific writings on geology and natural history, participated in furthering the French Republican agenda by organizing competitions for national festival decorations and monuments to Napoleon's military conquests. It was in this context that he conceived an idea for a huge globe-shaped monument almost forty feet in diameter, elevated a further sixteen feet or so above the ground. In his drawing *Project for a Public Monument to be Erected on a Paris Square* (1799), Hoüel shows the world suspended above a fountain of billowing clouds, caused by mist and evaporation from an abundance of water falling turbulently into a large circular pool [153]. The fountain spray, partially hiding some of the globe's countries and oceans, would provide a constantly changing tableau at street level mimicking the clouds in the skies above.

The spherical form of Hoüel's design refers to the neoclassical visions of his contemporaries, architects Étienne-Louis Boullée and Claude-Nicolas Ledoux. In the 1780s, while Boullée proposed an immense spherical cenotaph to Isaac Newton, Ledoux also explored ideal architecture based on pure, rational geometric volumes, including the sphere and pyramid, to convey utopian perfection. Hoüel's globe, as the most perfect of geometric shapes, not only represents the total mass of the earth and all its inhabitants, but also evokes universal equality. In the drawing one can see Europe, Africa, the Near East and part of the expanse of Asia. On top sits the triumphant Republic of France, as an emblem of permanent stability, next to a winged Liberty, who stands assertively to inspire victorious exploits. On Liberty's raised left hand a bird is poised to fly away bearing the message of freedom. Both ride in a chariot driven by the four gilded bronze horses of San Marco, which Napoleon had captured from Venice in 1797. In a pamphlet dated 1799, Hoüel wrote that the chariot bearing the Republic of France and Liberty had travelled a victorious course through Germany, Italy, Egypt and Holland.[48] The San Marco horses are the tangible evidence of conquest in an otherwise allegorical evocation. Hoüel believed that such a fountain monument would offer the public a means for understanding global geography,

while at the same time proclaiming France as a world power and triumphant ruler. The drawing's iconography, reflecting the zealous ambitions shared by the artist's compatriots, declares that France, the exemplar of Enlightenment and Freedom, is the rightful leader to spread her powerful message throughout Europe and the rest of the world. To encounter such a bold monument of the world—announcing universality, freedom and equality—would have been an extraordinary experience, but Hoüel's project was never realized.

A few years later, another politically charged idea for a fountain in Paris took the form of a colossal elephant. While Versailles had many fountains in the shapes of various animals, including those inspired by La Fontaine's fables [144], no previous fountain was as grandiose and extravagant as the Elephant Fountain for the Place de la Bastille.[49] Since 1789, when crowds had stormed and demolished the Bastille, the centuries-old fortress and prison, the site had remained empty and in need of a suitable patriotic monument. Ideas to create an elephant monument there can be traced back to 1795.[50] As part of his self-aggrandizing campaign as emperor, Napoleon authorized the construction of the larger-than-lifesize elephant fountain. He wanted this extraordinary pachyderm monument to conjure visions of heroic foreign campaigns, imperial splendor and glory, partly inspired by his own campaigns in Egypt and partly by the legendary conquests of Alexander the Great. As a conspicuous monument in the Bastille square, Napoleon believed it would overshadow any lingering memory of 1789 and the era of revolutionary chaos. The commission was given to the Dijon architect Jacques Célerier in 1810, with the mandate to design a fountain with an elephant standing on a circular base with smooth water sheets streaming into a large circular basin. Construction began in earnest on the Place de la Bastille in August 1811 and continued into the following year. Adjacent to the site was a hangar where the giant elephant was being modeled and cast in bronze (partly supplied by melting down enemy Spanish cannons). When Célerier died in 1812, architect Jean-Antoine Alavoine supervised the project, assisted by Pierre-Charles Bridan who created the

maquettes. As the foundation work proceeded, Alavoine made drawings and Bridan models, showing variant possibilities for the elephant fountain. The government allotted enough money so that Bridan could execute a full-scale, polychromed plaster model to stand in for the final version in bronze until further funds could be secured.

Four brilliant presentation watercolors and five drawings by Alavoine for the Elephant Fountain project are in an album in the Musée du Louvre.[51] The four watercolors, three of which are heightened with gold, show the monument from different vantage points, and with variants for the richly decorated thronelike palanquin on top of the elephant's back. They also present alternative ideas for the water play, with water shooting vigorously from the elephant's trunk [154]. In one of the designs, instead of the palanquin, a Roman warrior stands on top of the elephant poised to hurl his spear. One view of the Elephant Fountain was exhibited at the 1814 Salon, to show what was being planned for the Place de la Bastille. By 1820, Alavoine had designed eight different versions of the monument. Then, still

incomplete, the fountain project stalled. Once Napoleon was no longer in power, the driving impetus to commemorate his great glory evaporated. Although some officials argued for the great merits of the monument's ingenuity and grandeur, the prevailing opinion was to give up this costly monstrosity, especially since funds were insufficient. The large-scale plaster model for the elephant remained languishing on the site, slowly deteriorating, until 1848.[52] In 1833, another monument to honor the citizens who died during the 1830 July Revolution was proposed in its place, resulting in the July Column Monument which stands today in the center of Place de la Bastille.

During the 1830s, as the Elephant Fountain sank deeper into obscurity, Jacques Ignace Hittorff was redesigning the prominent Place de la Concorde, a Paris square also steeped in royal and revolutionary history.[53] Today, the square's two fountains, symmetrically flanking a central obelisk, express an iconography that

celebrates France's triumphs in industry, agriculture, commerce, transportation and engineering [156]. The Place de la Concorde also serves as a ceremonial urban hub for transportation routes, and as a conciliatory civic focal point balancing various forms of governance between monarchy, church and state. The site is strategically located between the Tuileries gardens (signifying royal power) on the east; the Champs Élysées leading to the Arc de Triomphe (a monument glorifying Napoleonic military power) on the west; the church of the Madeleine to the north; and, across the River Seine, the Assemblée Nationale (Chamber of Deputies, the branch of representative government in the Palais Bourbon) to the south.

While the Place de la Concorde and its fountains have a readily apparent iconographic program drawn from the lexicon of traditional sculptural allegory, much of the square's propagandistic resonance rests upon the site's unique history. From 1753 to 1772, when the square was known as Place Louis XV, architect Jacques-Ange Gabriel worked on its formal design around a central equestrian statue of the monarch. Gabriel's plan called for twin fountains to enhance the setting for the regal statue, but inadequate water supply prevented their execution. Two of Gabriel's large classical buildings, flanking the Rue Royale, still grace the Place de la Concorde today: the Ministère de la Marine and the building that now houses the Hôtel Crillon. Gabriel also designed pavilions, marking the periphery of the plaza, which remain today.

After 1789, when the square was named Place de la Revolution, the statue of Louis XV was removed, to be replaced by the guillotine and a plaster statue of Liberty, which witnessed the beheading of thousands in her name. In 1795, after the Reign of Terror, it was renamed Place de la Concorde and various projects were considered to embellish the square and to obliterate the memory of recent bloodshed. During Napoleon's rule, there was no

< 155 *Project for the Place Louis XVI, Paris, Competition of 1829: Perspective View.* Ink and watercolor drawing by Jacques Ignace Hittorff.

∨ 156 Maritime Fountain and the Obelisk of Luxor, Place de la Concorde, Paris. Designed by Jacques Ignace Hittorff, 1836–40. Albumen print, 1870s.

> 157 *Fountain Project for the Place de la Concorde, Paris*, 1833. Ink and watercolor by Jacques Ignace Hittorff.

building activity in the square. Instead, the emperor focused on other projects such as erecting the Arc de Triomphe, beginning the Canal d'Ourcq to supply central Paris with more abundant fresh water, and the Elephant Fountain. After 1816, during the restoration of the Bourbon monarchy under Louis XVIII, the square was renamed to honor the memory of Louis XVI, and plans commenced to adorn this public space with several equestrian statues of the monarch who had been executed there. The completion of the Canal d'Ourcq in 1824 brought more water to central Paris, so it was possible to build more public fountains. The idea arose to make the Place de la Concorde a park, closed to vehicular traffic, with lawns and plentiful fountains. In 1829, the city sponsored a competition, to which ten architects, including Hittorff, were invited to submit proposals for the square, incorporating a minimum of four fountains. Ultimately, some forty designers entered the competition. Hittorff, though German by birth, had established himself in Paris as a festival architect designing decorations for royal ceremonies, including baptisms, funerals, and the 1825 coronation of Charles X.[54] For the competition, Hittorff proposed, as shown in his perspective view [155], four quadrants, each containing a fountain and an equestrian statue of the king, around a circular intersection. Four additional fountains accent the strips of lawn bordering the Tuileries, an

arrangement symmetrically echoed on the Champs-Élysées side. Hittorff's design offered a festive stateliness for this prominent urban setting. Apart from a preponderance of lamps dotting the edges of each quadrant, his project closely followed the competition guidelines. However, he was not voted the winner.[55]

Following the change in government after the 1830 July Revolution, King Louis-Philippe rejected the competition results and delayed plans for the square, again renamed Place de la Concorde. The July Monarchy wished to resuscitate this vital square with a symbolic message untainted by revolutionary memories. When Mohammed Ali, viceroy of Egypt, offered Louis-Philippe a Ramses II obelisk from Luxor as a gift in 1831, the problem of how to distinguish this square as an important landmark was solved. In 1832, Hittorff was asked to design a full-scale model of the obelisk (still to arrive from Egypt) in time for the 1833 July Festival, commemorating the 1830 July Revolution, and for an industrial exposition taking place in the square. Shortly afterward, without any official competition, Hittorff received the prestigious civic commission to redesign the entire Place de la Concorde.[56] From 1833 until the dedication on 1 May 1840, Hittorff diligently developed his designs for this great public space. He sought to link and to unify the complex urban plan of Paris, but also to broadcast symbolically that, under the July Monarchy, France would prosper through prowess in industry and commerce.

△ 158 *Elevation of One of the Two Fountains in the Place de la Concorde, Paris, Executed under the Administration of Monsieur le Comte de Rambuteau, Prefect of the Seine,* 1839. Ink and watercolor by Jacques Ignace Hittorff.

△ 159 Maritime Fountain, Place de la Concorde, Paris. Designed by Jacques Ignace Hittorff, 1836–40.

▷ 160 Pulitzer Fountain (Pomona), Grand Army Plaza, New York. Designed by Thomas Hastings, with sculpture by Karl Bitter, 1913–16.

A watercolor shows one of Hittorff's preliminary fountain designs [157].[57] Modeled after the grand twin fountains in the square in front of St. Peter's in Rome, which notably accent one of the most prominent obelisks in the world,[58] and which Hittorff had seen during his travels in the early 1820s, this design shows the central feature of an unusual mushroom cap (similar to a rounded, inverted basin). Water jets from the top and cascades in curtains of water over two tiers of basins, to a larger decorated one below. This mushroom cap design would become the crowning element of the fountains finally executed for the Place de la Concorde.

As further designs for the Place de la Concorde were modified and improved in the mid-1830s, Hittorff entertained several ideas for how best to design fountains around the obelisk. After a government committee reported that four or more in the square would overburden the water supply, leaving less for reservoirs, drinking fountains and hydrants, Hittorff was asked to plan the square with just two fountains on either side of the obelisk.[59] A revised plan was approved by the appropriate officials in April 1835. Construction began a year later, followed by the dramatic erection of the obelisk on 25 October 1836, witnessed by immense crowds of people. The engineer Jean-Baptiste Lebas had been commissioned to devise the custom-designed ship and machinery necessary to transport the 240-ton monolith from Egypt and to install it. The French and Latin inscriptions on the obelisk's base celebrate this major feat of French engineering and navigational skill. Once in place, the obelisk became the pivotal monument punctuating the axis between the Musée du Louvre and the Arc de Triomphe, and the cross-axis between the church of the Madeleine and the Palais Bourbon.

Although it was Hittorff's idea to combine aspects of Gabriel's original plans for the square with the design of the fountains in front of St. Peter's, the iconography of the square was carefully orchestrated by Claude Philibert Barthelot Rambuteau, prefect of the Seine. Rambuteau was eager to promote a conspicuously impressive display of water in the most major urban fountain project occurring during his tenure. He, along with

Edouard Gatteaux, a friend of the painter Jean Auguste Dominique Ingres, suggested the fountain's allegorical themes: oceans, rivers, earth harvests, abundance and technological triumph.[60] A splendid presentation drawing of 1839, dedicated by Hittorff to Rambuteau who kept it until his death, shows the elevation of the Maritime Fountain, the one closest to the Seine, with water splashing exuberantly and frothily [158].

By May 1840, both fountains, with their carefully calculated plumbing systems, were completed.[61] In the Maritime Fountain, large semi-nude figures representing the Atlantic and the Mediterranean rest against the fountain pedestal, and are joined by other figures personifying aspects of the maritime fishing industry: Coral, Fish, Shells and Pearls [159]. Each is seated on a prow of a ship, the symbol of Paris, which are interspersed with dolphins snorting water through their nostrils. Above the main basin, genii symbolize the triumphs of Maritime Navigation, Astronomy and Commerce. Between them, swans spout water to the pool below at the edge of which tritons and nereids holding fish shoot water backward toward the main basin. All the figures, except for the bronze tritons and nereids, were made of cast iron, "florentined" with bronze and gold paint, as the presentation drawing reveals, although today one sees bronze-coated sculptures, dating to a 1862–63 restoration. On the north fountain, the large figures symbolize the two greatest rivers of France, the Rhône and the Rhine, which empty into the Mediterranean and Atlantic respectively, while the other figures personify harvests of Wheat and Grapes, Flowers and Fruit. The three genii above symbolize River Navigation, Agriculture and Industry. Hittorff worked carefully with a team of twelve sculptors to coordinate the relationships between each sculpture and to unify the final groupings.[62]

The ingenuity of Hittorff's elegant design for the Place de la Concorde rests in the way he balanced and integrated the earlier buildings, the spaciousness of the square, and the colossal Egyptian monument into a unified iconographical ensemble.[63] In addition to the fountains, the edges of the square are punctuated by eight statues personifying eight major French cities (Bordeaux, Brest, Lille, Lyon, Marseilles, Nantes, Rouen and Strasbourg) and handsome, fluted-column candelabra street lamps.

Today, the fountains of the Place de la Concorde still sparkle vividly in what has become their island domain, surrounded by seemingly ceaseless traffic that makes it difficult for pedestrians to cross the road for a closer experience of the sculpture and the splashing water. As a masterpiece of urban design that retains its rich patriotic symbolism, the square has become an important ceremonial site for national celebrations attracting vast crowds, whether political rallies, Bastille Day festivities, or the exhilarating final lap of the Tour de France bicycle race.

Many American architects trained in Europe saw that the great fountains in Paris, Rome and Florence help to make those cities memorable. In New York City today, between the luxurious Plaza Hotel and the F. A. O. Schwartz toy store, an Italianate sculpture of Pomona by Beaux-Arts sculptor Karl Bitter graces the top of the large Pulitzer Fountain (1913–16) as a benevolent symbol of abundance in a commercially affluent city [160]. In the 1890s, shortly after he emigrated from Vienna in Austria, Bitter suggested a fountain as an adorning feature to set off this Fifth Avenue site just outside the south-east corner of Central Park. Bitter was instrumental in many monumental public projects around the turn of the century, and he was especially gifted in sculptural allegory and architectural decoration, exemplified by his sculptures embellishing the main entrance of New York's Metropolitan Museum of Art.[64] Like other architects and artists of his day, he subscribed to the tenets of America's City Beautiful movement, which held that ennobling architecture and art, thoughtfully conceived and sited along major transportation routes, would enhance the urban environment and project an image of cultural well-being. Citing the Place de la Concorde as a model that brilliantly integrated urban redesign with inspiring iconography, Bitter's vision called for a grand plaza worthy of New York City's cosmopolitan status.

The 1911 bequest from newspaper publisher Joseph Pulitzer made it possible for city planners to proceed with reshaping the Fifth Avenue plaza.[65] A closed competition resulted in the commission being awarded to architect Thomas Hastings (of Carrère and Hastings) in collaboration with Bitter. While the plan of the square looked to nineteenth-century Paris, Hastings proposed a single large fountain inspired by Italian Renaissance models of a basin surmounted by an allegorical figure.

The Pulitzer Fountain features a series of five stone basins (the lower ones lobed, the two upper ones twelve-sided) rising like a pyramid to the freestanding, pedestal-supported, saucerlike basin on which stands the nude statue of Pomona. Similar to figures of Venus and to bathers by Florentine Renaissance sculptors such as Niccolò Tribolo and Giambologna, Bitter sculpted his goddess in a *contrapposto* stance holding a basket at her left while turning to her right.[66] Pomona overlooks a generous supply of water spilling from the uppermost basin to the lowest fountain pool. Two cornucopias with rams heads by sculptor Orazio Piccirilli top the elongated, three-tiered cascades flanking the lower basins.

The sculpture, in concert with the water, which flows in controlled vertical spills from pool to pool, conveys the theme of nurtured bounty and peaceful prosperity. Situated in a tree-shaded plaza, this traditional European-style fountain offers respite by conveying a sense of classic timelessness amid the modern-day bustle of a heavily trafficked area.

Several blocks away, another major New York fountain looks to the future, albeit via the inspiration of classical mythology. Symbolizing the heroic success made possible by the modern capitalist empire developed by John D. Rockefeller, Jr., Paul Manship's gilded bronze sculpture of Prometheus soars over fountain jets in the sunken plaza at the foot of the General Electric Building (formerly the Radio Corporation of America Building) in the heart of Rockefeller Center [161]. Completed in 1934, the Prometheus Fountain remains a grand symbol of society's empowerment. Manship depicted the great titan bringing the torch of

primordial fire down from the heavens to mankind, in defiance of the Olympic gods, who had left humanity defenseless in the process of creating the world.[67] An inscription from the writings of Aeschylus adorns the wall behind the fountain: "Prometheus, Teacher in Every Art, Brought The Fire that Hath Proved to Mortals a Means to Mighty Ends." Centuries after Louis XIV's Versailles proclaimed his royal authority through glorifying decorative symbolism and impressive waterworks, here was a modern-day financier recruiting other businessmen to join in a major building venture also to be decorated with powerful artistic metaphors, albeit to broadcast business vitality and global strength. In proclaiming the triumph of civilization's mythological origins, the Prometheus Fountain plays a key role in heralding the Rockefeller Center as a "brave new world" in midtown

Manhattan.[68] John D. Rockefeller, Jr. wanted Rockefeller Center to be a monument to skill, imagination and economic democracy, social ideals that would uplift a broad national and international audience while also promoting business.[69]

In 1929, after the collapse of the stock market left the national economy in ruins, Rockefeller launched his plan for a skyscraper city that would help revive New York City by creating new opportunities for commercial enterprise. Rockefeller called upon a strong team of some of the country's leading architects (Raymond Hood, Godley & Fouilhoux; Corbett, Harrison & MacMurray; and Reinhard & Hofmeister), engineers, interior designers and real estate development advisors. In 1930, Hood and Corbett proposed that the R. C. A. Building have a welcoming plaza and promenade, in addition to a lobby, to announce its entrance. Their idea developed into the creation of a grand public outdoor space.[70]

By January 1933, when Manship received the commission for the Prometheus Fountain, he was already admired in the United States and Europe for his figurative sculpture in a sleek, modernist style inspired by classical subjects. His reputation for businesslike reliability was a factor strongly favoring his selection by the Rockefeller board of directors, who wished to complete the fountain within a year.[71] Guided by architectural drawings of how the R. C. A. Building would look behind the fountain, Manship proceeded rapidly to design what would become the main feature of the Rockefeller Center's urban landscaping. He started by drawing several small-scale concept sketches on tracing paper, experimenting with various poses for a Prometheus in flight—tiny figures vaguely resemble athletes lunging for the finish line [162]. Usually Manship had ample time to develop his drawings, then make plaster models, before the final casting in bronze, but his tight schedule prevented this extended process. Dedicated in January 1934, the original Prometheus Fountain featured jets gently arcing from each side toward the central figure of the titan encircled by a ring of zodiac signs representing the heavens. Like a festive focal point in a town square, Prometheus rested on a mountainlike base (representing Earth), rooted in a rectangular, stepped basin, with water overflowing into a larger pool.[72] The silvery water provided a spectacular contrast to the gleaming gold Prometheus, exemplifying the electrifying potential of the universe. Visible from Fifth Avenue, the Prometheus Fountain anchored the end of the gently sloping promenade of the Channel Gardens, marked by six tiered pools and by horticultural displays that changed with the seasons.[73]

By 1938, Rockefeller Center, located between Fifth and Sixth Avenues, from Forty-eighth to Fifty-first Streets, included fourteen office buildings, theaters and multileveled pedestrian spaces lined with shops and restaurants. It was an immense urban complex unlike anything any city had built before. The building interiors, particularly the public lobbies and passageways, incorporated a sophisticated art-deco style with striking murals, lavish materials and tasteful furnishings. At the time, Frederick Lewis Allen, the social historian and critic, described Rockefeller Center for American radio listeners: "This is headquarters. This is the center of things, this is the mainspring of the metropolis of the Western World. And also this is the Future, or what these tourists hope will be the Future… in Rockefeller Center they see Paradise Regained."[74] Allen further described the experience of visiting Rockefeller Center: "Walk down the promenade from Fifth Avenue westward toward Rockefeller Plaza on a summer evening with the mighty floodlighted prow of the R. C. A. Building looming above you: look at the crowds gathered round the edges of the sunken plaza, watching the diners under the bright colored umbrellas, below in the café, and listening to the music while the wind tosses the trees and the fountains play… and you will feel the tingle of Metropolitan success in the very air."[75]

During the ensuing decades, the plaza and fountain, with its restaurant and ice-skating rink, continued to be a popular recreational destination, attracting New Yorkers and visitors from all over the world. In 1988, the Los Angeles firm WET Design renovated the fountain's water effects and added a row of jets in front of and behind Prometheus. The jets alternate in their display, looking like watery flag poles and producing a verticality that is echoed in the real flagpoles above and in the surrounding skyscrapers. At night, when the fountain is lit, the rising and falling water seems to mimic flickering flames, and the splashes sound like bursting sparks [2]. The experience of the fountain changes dramatically, depending on when one sees it. By day, it is a commanding theatrical stage beneath a fluttering array of flags; a constant flow of people, like improvisational actors, come, stop to rest and look around, and then move on. At night, the glowing Prometheus seems linked to the lofty heavens by the brilliant beams of light accenting the soaring tower of the G. E. Building, still one of the city's great skyscrapers. While the Bassin d'Apollon at Versailles and the Trevi Fountain in Rome both proclaim omnipotent authority, the Prometheus Fountain, and the entire Rockefeller Center iconographic program, instead inspire courageous optimism about the future and the rewarding promise of achievement.

In the decades following World War II, American corporate and civic fountain commissions shifted toward the abstract, the natural and the minimal. Rather than using water in a secondary role to complement and enliven traditional figurative sculpture, many major corporate fountains feature water as the primary display. Often set in landscaped parks or gardens, such fountains downplay overt propagandistic messages in favor of providing urban and suburban oases. At the General Motors Technical Center in Warren, Michigan (outside Detroit), Eero Saarinen and Associates planned the industrial headquarters in the midst of a spacious manmade landscape (1949–56). Saarinen's starkly modernist low-rise buildings face a picturesque lake, for which the sculptor Alexander Calder designed a fountain with giant water jets sequenced to shoot water vertically like a geyser ballet [9]. For New York City's Chase Manhattan Bank Plaza, designed by Skidmore, Owings & Merrill (1961–64), Japanese-American sculptor Isamu Noguchi created a sunken Zen meditation garden, recalling those in Kyoto. As microcosms of the world, such

< 161 Prometheus Fountain, Rockefeller Center, New York. Designed by Paul Manship, 1934; water jets added by WET Design, 1988.

∧ 162 *Prometheus Studies*, 1933. Pen and ink over pencil on tracing paper by Paul Manship.

> 166 Williams Square,
Las Colinas, Texas. Designed by
the SWA Group, with sculpture by
Robert Glen, 1980.

∧ > 163, 164 Views of Chase
Manhattan Bank Plaza sculpture
garden and fountains, New York.
Designed by Isamu Noguchi,
1961–64.

∨ 165 Levi's Plaza, San Francisco.
Designed by Lawrence Halprin,
1978–82.

gardens are intended to be viewed and
contemplated from outside, not entered.
In his circular, granite-paved garden,
Noguchi asymmetrically placed seven large,
uniquely eroded rocks, foraged from the Uji
River near Kyoto. On summer weekdays,
the garden is wet and active as recessed jets
spray water on the rocks and pools. Visitors
can choose to look down on the garden
from the pedestrian plaza level above [163],
or from inside the bank lobby on the lower
level, where one can walk around the
circular window enclosing the garden to see
the rocks and spraying water from different
vantage points [164]. In the heart of the
Lower Manhattan financial district filled
with towering office buildings, where time
is shaped by the dictates of work and
money, this minimalist public space
evokes timeless calm. Noguchi's precisely
positioned rocks and quiet splashes of
water summon up a sense of geological
permanence and continuity, evoking the
enduring qualities of water and stone.
The tiny garden subtly but effectively
communicates the message that this
powerful bank, founded in 1799 as an
outgrowth of its business supplying
water to New Yorkers, is declaring itself a
reliably solid business, capable of adapting
to change.

In San Francisco's Levi's Plaza
(1978–82), Californian landscape architect
Lawrence Halprin conjures an even more
dramatic evocation of nature and corporate
stability. For an open area before the
entrance to the Levi Strauss & Company's
headquarters, Halprin designed what he
called the "experiential equivalent"
of untamed mountain waterfalls and
meandering streams as part of the four-
acre urban campus. The executives of Levi
Strauss wanted low-rise buildings situated
in a landscape where employees could
work and interact informally in a relaxed
atmosphere that reflected the lifestyle of
the blue jeans it produces. The company's
landscaping would benefit the San
Francisco community by providing a new
park with a panoramic view of nearby
shipping docks and the bay. Although the
site was carved out of a former warehouse
district that had been converted to offices
and studios, Halprin's design offers an
escape from its urban setting, by offering
opportunities to stroll or sit in a park with
grassy knolls and a meadow stream. There
is also a plaza with a huge granite boulder
fountain, looking like a rough-hewed *tazza*

overflowing with water [165]. The setting recalls the mountainous Sierra Nevada terrain where the fortunes of Levi Strauss & Company began during the California Gold Rush, while also promoting the image of a caring, environmentally aware corporation.

Although abstraction predominates, the metaphorical use of figurative sculpture occasionally appears in contemporary fountains. Sculpted horses, vigorously churning water into turbulent action, have been important symbolic attributes in many of the world's greatest fountains. At the Trevi, wild sea horses bound across the roughly sculpted rocks before the figure of Oceanus. At Versailles, powerful steeds pull the Sun God Apollo's chariot from its resting place in the sea to the sky. As if to compete with or perhaps to resurrect these icons of mythological omnipotence, a different type of heroic fountain was designed in 1980 for Williams Square in Las Colinas, near Dallas, Texas. It features a bronze sculpture of untamed mustangs galloping across a prairie stream [166]. The developer Ben Carpenter wanted the focus of the Las Colinas public space, surrounded on three sides by high-rise office buildings, to evoke the rugged south-west frontier that gave rise to proudly independent, enterprising, ready-to-tackle-anything Texas communities. The SWA Group, landscape architects with James Reeves and Dan Mock as project designers from the Houston office, collaborated with the San Francisco-based office of Skidmore, Owings & Merrill, and sculptor Robert Glen to create a pedestrian plaza that would suggest the hot, dry terrain of that part of Texas. Shady trees and seating were confined to the edges so that the only interruption in the expanse of granite would be an abstract stream running diagonally across the square. In the center, nine realistically modeled wild horses stampede to cross the stream, their hooves creating a vibrant, splashing path. The designers had to study the water action caused by live animals running through water in order to mimic the effects. Though recalling horses from classical mythology, the fountain at Las Colinas draws on a distinctive regional mythology—mustangs are a part of the legend of the Wild West. They symbolize the spirit of mavericks who defy conventional authority, yet who survive and even prosper in the unforgiving climate of the south-western plains. While Texans may not readily identify with the foreign deities Oceanus or Apollo, they can relate to the independent character of the mustang. So amid the glass and steel of the urban plaza, nature and history reassert themselves, as the welcome presence of water in Las Colinas refreshes plaza visitors. The square also conveys the confident message of today's businessman, who, not unlike Cosimo I de' Medici and other European rulers, proclaims in his own way that he is helping to transform this part of the world into a thriving community. While the great fountains of Europe's past still reign supreme as inspiring symbols and design models, artistic imagination continually seeks new ways for fountains to broadcast messages of power and identity.

Maria Ann Conelli and Marilyn Symmes

Fountains as Globes

Symbols of the Universe and Democracy

Before Jean-Pierre-Laurent Hoüel's fountain monument project for Paris of the 1790s [153], globes had already been part of the symbolism of earlier fountains, such as those inspired by the legend of Hercules at the Villa Aldobrandini in Frascati [132]. Het Loo, the Dutch baroque country palace of Prince William of Orange (later King William III of England) and Princess Mary, had a handsome garden designed by Daniel Marot with regal Terrestrial and Celestial Sphere Fountains, each showering water from tiny holes [167]. They are colorful, medium-sized focal points at the ends of a cross-axis in the garden. A globe would later figure prominently in the Atlas Fountain (1850–53 [168]) designed by William Andrews Nesfield for the stately grounds of Castle Howard, near York in England. At one end of Paris's Luxembourg gardens, Jean-Baptiste Carpeaux's principal figurative sculpture, *The Four Parts of the World,* supports an armillary celestial sphere (containing the terrestrial world) as part of the Fontaine de l'Observatoire (1867–74 [170]), its overall design supervised by architect Gabriel Davioud, who worked with a team of other artists.[1] It was Eugène Legrain, a pupil of Carpeaux, who executed the celestial sphere encircled by signs of the zodiac. The symbolism of the sculpture refers to the nearby Observatory, erected in 1668–72 to Claude Perrault's symmetrical and exacting

architectural design. Each of its four walls face one of the four cardinal directions, while within its confines, scientists expanded world knowledge by studying the phenomena of astronomy.

It was not until the twentieth-century world's fairs, however, that colossal globes similar to Hoüel's project were actually constructed. The 1939 New York World's Fair featured a visionary design by architect Wallace K. Harrison. The enormous Trylon and Perisphere, as timeless architectural symbols, evoked the fair's message of Building the World of Tomorrow [196]. The Perisphere housed the major Democracity exhibit, an urban model for the future devised by designer Henry Dreyfuss. As the largest globe ever built and radical for its time, the Perisphere temporarily rivaled the great engineering feat of Paris's Eiffel Tower. The looming structure appeared to float above a reflecting pool on columns of water which disguised the actual structural supports.[2]

At the 1964–65 New York World's Fair, the Unisphere greeted visitors as a twelve-story centerpiece hovering above a double ring of vigorous water jets [169, 206, 207]. In a decade when space exploration was full of

potential, the Unisphere, designed by landscape architect Gilmore D. Clarke, looked like an enormous satellite with stainless-steel bands, depicting the entire earth as an integral unit bound together. The Unisphere symbolized America as a world leader promising a universe where every creature lives together harmoniously in peace and understanding.[3]

Ian Hamilton Finlay, a Scottish concrete poet-artist and a skilled gardener, used the idea of a fountain to evoke the French tenets of freedom that had been forged in Hoüel's day. In the 1980s Finlay devised many works inspired by the French Revolution and the Declaration of the Rights of Man, including a print entitled *Little Fountain in Three Colors* [3] that is very small in scale but heroic in impact. On a pale-blue background, merging motto with fountain image, are three ascending jet sprays, fashioned from the words "liberty," "equality," and "fraternity." The rallying cry of French revolutionaries silently explodes through a fountain metaphor for democracy, reverberating now as powerfully as it did in Hoüel's day.

Marilyn Symmes

< 167 Celestial Sphere Fountain in the gardens of Het Loo, The Netherlands. Designed by Daniel Marot, 1685–99; reconstructed 1979–84.

∨ 168 Atlas Fountain, Castle Howard, Yorkshire, England. Designed by William Andrews Nesfield, with sculpture by John Thomas, 1850–53.

> 169 Unisphere, also called Fountain of the Continents, World's Fair, New York. Designed by Gilmore D. Clarke with Hamel and Langer, 1964–65, it symbolized "Man's Achievements on a Shrinking Globe in an Expanding Universe." Photograph from *La Feria Mundial de New York* by F. Estrada Saladich (Barcelona, 1965).

∨ 170 Fontaine de l'Observatoire, Paris. Designed by Gabriel Davioud, 1867–74.

The Fountains in
Trafalgar
Square
London

Trafalgar Square's fountains have played a significant role in British national life, and, as countless souvenir postcards attest, they enliven a popular tourist destination. But they were not in the square's original plan. Approved by an Act of Parliament in 1826, Trafalgar Square was to be a dramatic open space linking the major streets of Pall Mall, Charing Cross Road, the Strand, Whitehall and the Mall. Commemorating the 1805 British victory over Napoleon's fleet in the decisive Battle of Trafalgar off the coast of Spain, the new monumental square was to proclaim the triumph of country and empire.

The square was thirty years in the making, and what one sees today [173] reflects the plan of architect Sir Charles Barry, best known for designing London's Houses of Parliament. He embarked on what he hoped would be a grand architectural achievement after the demolition of the Royal Mews and other buildings had made this new spacious square and the National Gallery building possible. Since the site had a distinct slope down toward the River Thames, Barry proposed leveling and paving it, thus creating a terrace in front of the National Gallery, which was being designed by William Wilkins. Because he thought it would be too dominant a presence in the square, Barry opposed the erection of Nelson's Column (1843), but he was overruled. William Railton designed the massive Corinthian column to support the statue (by Edward Hodges Baily) of the naval hero Lord Horatio Nelson (1758–1805), and this became the central landmark of the square. Long afterward, in 1867, four bronze lions by Sir Edwin Landseer were placed at each corner of the base of the column.

In the early 1840s, heeding the recommendations of several commissions—some fearing that vast public spaces encouraged congregations of riotous crowds as had happened in Paris—Barry decided to incorporate two large fountains as an attractive way to break up the expanse of pavement [172]. Completed by 1845, the fountains provided a striking complement to Nelson's Column. Water was obtained with some difficulty via artesian wells bored through layers of clay and chalk. At the time, a writer for The Builder described the fountains as:

... exceedingly chaste in design, plain, simple and unadorned as all works in granite ever should be... and in keeping with the prevailing design of the square.... They are the work of Messrs. Macdonald, the hydraulic part of the matter is entrusted to Messrs. Easton and Amos who are well known for their practical acquaintance with such matters. The water to supply the fountain is obtained from two wells, one in front of the National Gallery, and the other behind it, which are connected together by means of a tunnel, that passes directly under the National Gallery, behind which is also placed the engine house for raising the required water into the tanks, etc. before it is forced through the fountains.

In a May 1845 issue of The Civil Engineer and Architects Journal, a writer felt that the Trafalgar Square fountains, although they were made of beautiful red, polished granite, compared unfavorably to Paris fountains such as those in the Place de la Concorde and the Fontaine des Quatre Saisons. The writer repeated a complaint that they resembled "dumb-waiters with their tops knocked off." While praising the feat of supplying the fountains with ample water, there was further criticism that each fountain's jet spray scattered showers beyond the basin with every gust of wind. In spite of these initial reactions, the fountains prevailed until, towards the end of the nineteenth century, the original water supply dried up, necessitating a connection to the city's main water supply.

In 1938, Sir Edwin Lutyens began to redesign the two fountains as memorials to two admirals of the fleet, Lord John Rushworth Jellicoe and Lord David Beatty, both naval heroes of World War I. Although the work was interrupted by World War II, and by Lutyens death in 1944, the remodeling finally resumed under the direction of the Ministry of Works in 1947. Each fountain incorporates a central feature of two superimposed circular basins in Portland stone. The principal jets spout from the top basin, with the primary, central jet capable of reaching a height of eighty feet. The interior surfaces of the main pools are faced with light-blue tiles to enhance the water's aquamarine color and reflecting qualities. Bronze figures of tritons, mermaids and dolphins sculpted by Sir Charles Wheeler and William Macmillan further enliven the pools and water play [171]. The memorial fountains were unveiled with much fanfare on Trafalgar Day, 21 October 1948. Recently, new electric pumps and nozzles have been installed to increase the power of the jets which shoot dramatic splashes skyward and over the sculpture. The fountains are turned off at night. When the water is turned on again at ten o'clock each morning, the jets spring suddenly into the air startling flocks of pigeons and tourists.

The fountains of Trafalgar Square today play a role in the annual traditions of Londoners. As part of New Year celebrations, revelers gather in the square and dance in the fountains before and after hearing Big Ben chime midnight. The fountains, though, are now boarded over for the holiday period due to repeated incidents of damage to the fountain structures and a few cases of hypothermia. In the summer months, however, photographs of the fountains are even featured in the tabloid press. Over the years, to herald the arrival of summer or of a heatwave, the newspapers have sometimes published pictures of young people paddling in the fountains, the only sign of the passage of time being the increasingly revealing costume worn. When the water jets of the fountains are switched off, it is a public sign of an official drought. Most of the time, however, the prominently situated twin fountains, probably the most vigorously splashing waterworks in London, provide a refreshing public amenity while recalling the glory of Britain's once-reigning naval fleet.

Stephen Astley

∧ 171 One of the Trafalgar Square
fountains, London. Redesigned by
Sir Edwin Lutyens with sculptures
by Sir Charles Wheeler and
William Macmillan, 1938–47.

∨ 172 Trafalgar Square fountain
and the facade of the National
Gallery, London. Fountain designed
by Sir Charles Barry, 1845.
Photograph, 1905.

∧ 173 Aerial view of Trafalgar
Square with Nelson's Column and
one of the fountains redesigned by
Sir Edwin Lutyens.

fountains as
Spectacle
at international
expositions

"… as probably never was made before anywhere."

Frank Henry Norton, *Illustrated Historical Register of the United States Centennial Exposition, Philadelphia, 1876, and of the Exposition Universelle, Paris, 1878, 1879*

1851–1915

The great world's fairs of the latter half of the nineteenth and early twentieth centuries were a natural outgrowth of industrial and colonial expansion. A combination of nationalistic propaganda and spectacle, these displays fed an ever-increasing middle-class demand for entertainment and the most up-to-date consumer goods. Along with architecture, and eventually electricity, fountains, in combination with increasingly complex sculptural programs, played a central role in the rise and evolution of these events.

The first international exposition, which opened in London in 1851, was primarily conceived as a showcase for British manufacturers and merchants. Housed in Joseph Paxton's Crystal Palace, an innovative iron and glass exhibition hall some seven times the size of London's St. Paul's Cathedral, it displayed a vast accumulation of industrial products, ranging from household furnishings and military weapons to steam engines and the most advanced machinery for producing these commodities. Scattered among the exhibits were a variety of fountains, made of iron, zinc, cut glass, ceramic and terracotta. They included cast-iron basins "with all kinds of ornamental jets" for gardens; smaller fountains for inside the home; devices such as Jabez James's model bronzed fountain, complete with a steam engine to supply it with water; and the revolving "fountain for drawing and dining rooms, or boudoirs," manufactured by Sanders Thomas of Notting Hill which came with its own "musical arrangement."[1]

More prominent were a handful of monumental fountains, "suitable for the market place of a provincial town," which ornamented the main aisle and transepts of the exhibition hall. These included the Seeley Fountain, designed by John Woody Papworth and manufactured of "artificial stone"; John Bell's bronzed, cast-iron fountain, with its group of Cupid and the Swan forming a water jet cast by the Coalbrookdale Company; and Osler's Crystal Fountain [175, 176]. "Occupying the central place in the Crystal Palace," noted *The Art Journal Illustrated Catalogue of the Great Exhibition*, this "GLASS FOUNTAIN, by the Messers. Osler of Birmingham, is, perhaps, the most striking object in the exhibition; the lightness and beauty, as well as the perfect novelty of the design, have rendered it the theme of admiration with all visitors. The ingenuity with which this has been effected is very perfect; it is supported by bars of iron, which are so completely embedded in the glass shafts, as to be invisible, and in no degree interfering with the purity and crystalline effect of the whole object."[2]

In addition to their more conspicuous aesthetic function, the larger fountains also served as a source of drinking water for visitors to the fair which forbade the consumption of alcohol on the grounds. The "abundant supply of filtered water" that they offered, noted the official catalog, "was of great advantage to all connected with the Exhibition, but especially to the poorer class of visitors from the country, who came up bringing their dinner with them; a glass of water from the nearest

< 174 International Fountain and the Space Needle, Seattle Center, Washington. Fountain designed by Hideki Shimizu and Kazuyuki Matsushita, 1962; renovated by WET Design, 1995.

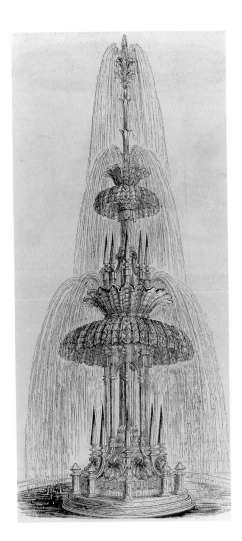

∨ 175 Osler's Crystal Fountain. Wood engraving from *The Art Journal Illustrated Catalogue of the Great Exhibition* (London, 1851).

> 176 View of the interior of the Crystal Palace with Osler's Crystal Fountain, Great Exhibition, London, 1851. Color lithograph by Chavanne. Of the 100,000 objects in the Great Exhibition, the most popular, and possibly the most beautiful, was Follett Osler's Crystal Fountain, made from four tons of pure crystal glass. In 1853, when the Crystal Palace was moved to Sydenham, the fountain moved with it, remaining as a glittering centerpiece for the next eighty-five years, until the Crystal Palace was destroyed by fire.

fountain or water-tap (sometimes mixed with that which was forbidden in the Refreshment Courts), forming an indispensable auxiliary to their comfort during their long summer day's pleasure."[3]

The overwhelming success of the London Great Exhibition inspired similar endeavors elsewhere: in Paris in 1855 and 1867, again in London in 1862, Vienna in 1873, and three years later in Philadelphia to celebrate the United States's centennial. Visitors to all of these expositions discovered decorative fountains inside and outdoors, as well as on display in the industrial and manufacturing exhibits. Characteristic of the larger examples were the cast-iron fountains manufactured by the Durenne foundry in France, which received awards in 1862, 1867 and 1873.[4] A Durenne fountain designed by Frédéric Auguste Bartholdi, the French sculptor best known for his Statue of Liberty in New York harbor, was placed at the center of the esplanade near the main entrance to the 1876 exposition in Philadelphia [178]. In common with earlier Durenne exhibits, as well as with many other freestanding pedestal fountains of the period, the Bartholdi Fountain featured a series of diminishing water basins supported by antique figures and a variety of classical architectural elements. With a bronzed surface, and weighing some fifteen thousand pounds, this ensemble stood thirty feet high. Set in the center of a broad stone pool, three female figures, balancing on a triangular pedestal ornamented with classical pilasters, shells and three water-spouting reptiles, held aloft a large cast-iron basin encircled with twelve gas lamps. Overhead, three titans supported a smaller bowl, above which water gushed forth from a crown to begin its cascade downward to the pool below. At night Bartholdi's novel gas-lamp illumination created a shimmering spectacle of water and light.[5]

Expecting to sell the piece, as well as to receive orders for others based on the same design, Bartholdi offered his fountain to the exposition free of charge. While further transactions failed to materialize, the exposition piece was purchased by Congress in 1877. The sculptor, however, was paid only six thousand dollars for his work, about half the sum that he originally had hoped to receive. In 1878 the Bartholdi Fountain was reconstructed in the Botanic Gardens at the center of the Mall in Washington, D.C., near Third Street, where it stood until 1927. It was subsequently moved to the corner of Independence Avenue and First Street, where it is today [177].[6]

In addition to the Bartholdi Fountain, others, such as the Sons of Temperance Fountain and the Catholic Total Abstinence Fountain, also served to ornament the 1876 exposition grounds and quench the thirst of fair-goers in a morally uplifting manner. Sculpted of marble and granite by Philadelphia artist Herman Kirn and funded by the Catholic Total Abstinence Union of America, the Catholic fountain depicted Moses poised atop a mound of rock, from which he produced a gush of cool water by striking his rod. About his feet, colossal statues of eight prominent Catholics alternated with drinking fountains.[7] Numerous smaller fonts entertained and cooled visitors inside the main exhibition buildings, among them Margaret Foley's marble fountain in the Horticultural Hall [179], an object that caught the attention of "Josiah Allen's Wife," the homespun feminist Samantha of Marietta Holley's popular novels of the era. Here, she enthused, was "a noble big vase bound with acanthus leaves,… shootin' up water, clear as a crystal, and at the foot of it on some rock work, sot three handsome children jest ready to plunge down into the cool, wet water; one of 'em was blowin' a shell, he felt so awful neat. There was lots of fountains in the Hall but none so uncommon handsome as this; and that noble fountain was the work of a woman."[8] Another work that appears to have gained acclaim was an elaborate, Renaissance-revival fountain exhibited by the J. L. Mott Iron Works in the Main Building, a model similar to those advertised in their trade catalogs.[9]

In contrast to the ornamental nature of most of the fountains at the fair, a very different "exhibition of water-power, waterfalls, and scientific and powerful pumping, such, as probably never was made before anywhere" could be found in the Hydraulic Annex of the Machinery Hall.[10] This curious display of industrial technology featured a thirty-six-foot cascade which poured thirty thousand gallons of water per minute into a large central basin. Exhibited around this tank was a variety of "hydraulic rams, presses, steam and hand pumps, pumps for mines, sugar refineries, and other special uses, turbine water-wheels and blowing machines and ventilating apparatus," all of whose "rushing streams" flowed in "parabolic curves into the waters below."[11] In order to accomplish this feat, as well as to operate the dozens of steam engines which were also displayed at the fair, a large pump house, capable of supplying seven million gallons of water per day to the exposition, was erected on the banks of the Schuylkill River.[12] At subsequent international exhibitions, these early hydraulic achievements were transformed into more explicit celebrations of industrial and technological wizardry. As a result, water rapidly became a central element in the design and iconography of the fairs.

At the Paris Universal Exposition of 1878, for example, the Trocadéro Palace and Cascade, which were designed as an ensemble by Gabriel Davioud and Jules Bourdais, formed the northern terminus of a symmetrical axis that ran south across the River Seine to the Palace of Industry, the main exhibition hall for the event [180]. Water for the Cascade emerged from a grotto set into the base of the palace at a rate of over a thousand gallons per minute. From here it spilled down a series of six cataracts to a reflecting basin and an array of fountains at the bottom of the embankment. All of this served, not only as a great public and ideological spectacle, but, as with a similar cascade at the Palais Longchamp at Marseilles (completed in 1869 [72]), as a key element in the regulation of the exposition's water system. Surrounded by personifications of the major continents and flanked with representations of Water and Air, the iconography of the Trocadéro's *château d'eau*, or upper grotto, symbolically positioned Paris at the center of her vast colonial empire, the various cultures and political dominions of which were prominently featured elsewhere at the fair.[13]

Eleven years later, at the Paris Universal Exposition of 1889 held to celebrate the centennial of the French Revolution, the axis of this iconography and the centrality of water were further extended when the Palace of Industry was razed to make way for the Eiffel Tower and a grand esplanade. This court, laid out by Jean-Camille Formigé, stretched southward across

"Occupying the central place in the Crystal Palace, this Glass Fountain, by the Messers. Osler of Birmingham, is, perhaps, the most striking object in the exhibition; the lightness and beauty, as well as the perfect novelty of the design, have rendered it the theme of admiration with all visitors. The ingenuity with which this has

been effected is very perfect; it is supported by bars of iron, which are so completely embedded in the glass shafts, as to be invisible, and in no degree interfering with the purity and crystalline effect of the whole object."

The Art Journal Illustrated Catalogue of the Great Exhibition, London, 1851

< 177 Bartholdi Fountain,
Washington, D.C. Designed by
Frédéric Auguste Bartholdi, 1876.

∨ 178 The Bartholdi Fountain,
United States Centennial Exhibition,
Philadelphia, 1876. Albumen print
stereograph.

∨ 179 Stereoscopic view of Miss
Foley's marble fountain, Horticultural
Hall, United States Centennial
Exhibition, Philadelphia. Sculpted
by Margaret Foley, 1876. Albumen
print stereograph.

> 180 Trocadéro Palace and
fountains, Universal Exposition,
Paris. Designed by Gabriel Davioud
with Jules Bourdais, 1878. Albumen
print.

> 181 The Fountain of Progress,
Universal Exposition, Paris.
Sculpted by Jules-Félix Coutan,
1889. Wood engraving from *Livre
d'or de l'exposition* (Paris, 1889).

the Champ de Mars to the dome of a new
exhibition hall, a structure that faced back
toward the Trocadéro Palace and Cascade,
both of which remained from the previous
fair. On the esplanade, between Eiffel's
monument and the new hall, stood Jules-
Félix Coutan's great celebration of French
political and industrial triumph, the
Fountain of Progress [181]. This allegorical
group of figures, also known as the Vessel
of the City of Paris, was placed in a circular
cascade and surrounded by shooting jets
of water and cavorting sea creatures.
Crowning the composition sat a winged
figure depicting the Genius of France,
illuminating the world with her
uplifted torch. Heralded by trumpeting
personifications of Fame, France was
accompanied by representations of
Science, Industry, Agriculture and Art.[14]

The opposite end of the esplanade was dominated by the Five Parts of the World, a fountain sculpted by Francis de Saint-Vidal. Here, six mythological figures swirled above reclining personifications of Europe, Asia, Africa, America and Australia. At the apex of this elaborate group, the figure of a woman held up an electric beam to enlighten the peoples of the earth.[15] The reflecting pond which united the two sculptural groups was itself decorated with water jets that were illuminated at night by electric beams that were controlled by mirrors and valves from subterranean chambers constructed beneath the esplanade [182]. The fountains and lights were constantly changing in height, intensity and color creating a great *pyrotechnie aquatique*, which was further animated by powerful searchlights and the incandescent illumination of the exhibition buildings that encircled this classic Beaux-Arts composition. Marking the first significant introduction of this technology to an international exposition, the populist reinterpretation of a tradition which stretched back more than two centuries to the royal celebrations at Vaux-le-Vicomte and Versailles caused considerable excitement among visitors and the press.[16]

When Chicago planned to commemorate the four-hundredth anniversary of the arrival of Columbus in the Americas with an international exposition of its own, it was decided that Paris would serve as the model for its fair. As determined by landscape designer Frederick Law Olmsted in collaboration with the architect Daniel Burnham, the focal point of this ambitious undertaking, held in 1893, was a formal Court of Honor surrounded by a Beaux-Arts ensemble of buildings in the French neoclassical style. At opposite ends of this central court stood Daniel Chester French's colossal Statue of the Republic and Frederick William MacMonnies's Columbian Fountain [183], an elaborate sculptural ensemble which was considerably indebted to Coutan's Fountain of Progress of four years earlier. In Chicago, MacMonnies depicted Columbia seated on a throne, resting her feet on a globe and holding a torch in her left hand. With Victory at the prow, and steered by Time, her barge was escorted by "the Sea-Horses of Commerce bearing riders representing modern Intelligence" and propelled by eight allegorical maidens personifying the arts (Music, Architecture, Sculpture and Painting) and the industries (Agriculture, Science, Industry and Commerce).[17] This ship of state, symbolic of the expanding aspirations of the nation, was set in the middle of a wide circular cascade and surrounded by cavorting mermaids, sprites and jets of water. To its left and right stood two electric fountains, which at night spouted choreographed and colored spumes of water to heights of 150 feet from over three hundred geyserlike orifices. As in Paris, this technological éclat was accompanied by the theatrical sweep of powerful searchlights and fireworks. Four massive pumps, with an aggregate ability to funnel forty million gallons of water per day through an underground tunnel five feet in diameter, and a battery of Westinghouse dynamos were required to sustain this extravagant and thrilling display of art and industry.[18]

While the Eiffel Tower survived, a new pageant of architecture, sculpture, water, and electricity was erected in Paris on the esplanade of the Champ de Mars for the Universal Exposition of 1900. Designed by Edmond Paulin, the Château d'Eau, or Water Castle, formed the culmination of its southern axis [184]. This structure complemented Eugène Hénard's Palais d'Électricité, which stood directly behind it and housed the impressive steam-driven dynamos that provided power for the entire exposition.[19] Surmounted by the Spirit of Electricity standing in a chariot drawn by hippogryphs, Paulin's Château d'Eau made palpable in a dazzling spectacle of illuminated water the otherwise invisible authority of this new technology [185]. Lit by thousands of multicolored incandescent lamps, the sinuous art-nouveau curves of the facade melted and merged with dozens of fountains, cascades, whirlpools and waterfalls in a radiant celebration of color

182 Night view of the Champ de Mars with the Fountain of Progress and illuminated water jet display, Universal Exposition, Paris, 1889. Wood engraving from *Livre d'or de l'exposition* (Paris, 1889).

183 The Columbian Fountain and Grand Basin, World's Columbian Exposition, Chicago. Sculpted by Frederick William MacMonnies, 1893. Photograph by William Henry Jackson.

and electricity that was likened to a great luminescent diadem or the unfolding of an enormous peacock's tail.[20]

The United States's claim to international status and hegemony over nature was reiterated in its third world's fair, held in Buffalo, New York, in 1901 shortly after the end of the Spanish-American War. Christened the Pan-American Exposition, this event represented an unabashed celebration of America's newly attained industrial and imperial power. Chosen in part because of its proximity to Niagara Falls, Buffalo milked its association with this famous natural wonder. Power for the exhibition was supplied by Westinghouse generators that had been installed at the falls in the 1890s, and the harnessing of this awesome cataract became a central metaphor for the fair's iconographic program.[21]

In the tradition of Chicago, the plan at Buffalo, as devised by John M. Carrère, centered on a Court of Fountains that marked the primary axis of a Beaux-Arts scheme, which the architect characterized

as "formality picturesquely developed."[22] All of the buildings were in a Spanish Renaissance style and ornamented with a complex sculptural program by Karl Bitter, who had worked at the World's Columbian Exposition. The iconography of this sculpture progressed from representations of the earth's natural resources and man in his primitive state to allegorical presentations of the nation's achievements. This evolutionary saga, which paralleled the message of the products on display in the fair's exhibition halls, culminated in the Electric Tower [186], "the crowning achievement of man," which stood at the head of the Court of Fountains and was "dedicated to the great waterways and the power of the Niagara."[23] Almost four hundred feet high, this monument, with the Goddess of Light by Herbert Adams at its apex, was illuminated by forty thousand incandescent bulbs. From its base flowed eleven thousand gallons of water per minute, which dropped some seventy feet over a series of ponds and ledges, down to the reflecting pool below. Flanking this cascade were two groups of statuary by George Grey Barnard "symbolizing its significance" as a metaphor for the subjugation of the Niagara Falls: The Great Waters in the Time of the Indian and The Great Waters in the Time of the White Man.[24]

At the opposite end of the Court of Fountains from the Electric Tower stood the Fountain of Abundance by Philip Martiny [187]. This elaborate composition depicted the Goddess of Abundance atop a pedestal supported by a group of dancing children, beneath which cupids tossed flowers into chutes down which playful boys and girls rode snails and swans. Reflecting a central motif of the exposition, the "plentifulness of nature" as controlled and exploited by modern industry and technology, the Fountain of Abundance was illuminated with rows of lamps set around its base.[25]

Both the Louisiana Purchase Centennial International Exposition held in St. Louis in 1904 and San Francisco's Panama-Pacific International Exposition of 1915 continued to build on the well-rehearsed themes of earlier fairs, adding to the growing corpus of literature generated by the City Beautiful movement, a new American approach to urban planning that was in part inspired by the phenomenal success of the World's Columbian Exposition in 1893. Taking

△ 184, 185 Château d'Eau and the Palais d'Électricité, Universal Exposition, Paris. Designed by Edmond Paulin and Eugène Hénard respectively, 1900. Illustrations from *Paris Exposition Reproduced from the Official Photographs* (New York, 1900). At night, thousands of multi-colored lamps transformed the fountains into a monumental iridescent diadem.

> 186 Electric Tower, Court of Fountains, Pan-American Exposition, Buffalo. Designed by John Galen Howard, 1901. Photograph by C. D. Arnold from *The Pan-American Exposition Illustrated* (Buffalo, 1901).

advantage of the natural topography of the site, a fanlike arrangement was chosen for the St. Louis fair by E. L. Masqueray in conjunction with the landscape architect George E. Kessler; the Festival Hall and Cascade formed the focus of a radiating system of avenues. As "the most important feature of the exposition," the Cascade was chosen by Karl Bitter—who again served as chief of the Department of Sculpture—as the heart of the fair's iconographic program.[26] At its head was Hermon Atkins MacNeil's Fountain of Liberty, flanked by allegorical representations of the Atlantic and Pacific Oceans by Isadore Konti, "symbolizing the fact that with the acquisition of the Louisiana region, the sway of liberty, truth and justice, illustrated in the center cascade, was extended from the Atlantic to the Pacific Ocean."[27] The flow of the Cascade itself was seen as an appropriate metaphor for this expansionist theme, one which was taken up again in San Francisco in 1915 to celebrate the opening of the Panama Canal and the city's recovery from the earthquake and fire of 1906.

The buildings of the 1915 San Francisco exposition were ornamented in a Moorish-Spanish style and grouped around courtyards that were intended to "reflect in plan, the walled cities of the Orient of the Mediterranean, where fountains play in the courts of palaces, in public squares and niches in the walls; and pools lie by the mosques, and in the gardens."[28] More than a dozen major fountains, all extravagantly illuminated at night like the architecture itself, ornamented this exotic setting. At its center stood the Court of the Universe, with the Fountains of the Rising and the Setting Suns by Adolphe Alexander Weinmann marking the east-west axis, and the Column of Progress and the Tower of Jewels standing to the north and south [188]. Through the gateway of the tower lay the South Garden with Alexander Stirling Calder's Fountain of Energy at its center [189]. Here, a "circle of figures, representing the dance of the oceans" supported the earth, on top of which was mounted the figure of Energy, on whose

∨ 188 Fountains of the Rising (right) and Setting (left) Suns with the Column of Progress in the background, Court of the Universe, Panama-Pacific International Exposition, San Francisco. Fountains designed by Adolphe Alexander Weinmann, 1915. Hand-colored photogravure from *The Splendors of the Panama-Pacific International Exposition* (San Francisco, 1915).

> 189 Fountain of Energy, Panama-Pacific International Exposition, San Francisco. Designed by Alexander Stirling Calder, 1915. Hand-colored photogravure from *The Splendors of the Panama-Pacific International Exposition* (San Francisco, 1915). Atop the Fountain of Energy was the equestrian statue of the Lord of the Isthmian Way. In the pool, figures symbolized the North and South Seas, and the Atlantic and Pacific Oceans.

< 187 Fountain of Abundance with the Temple of Music and Horticulture Building behind, Pan-American Exposition, Buffalo. Designed by Philip Martiny, 1901. Photograph by C. D. Arnold from *The Pan-American Exposition Illustrated* (Buffalo, 1901).

shoulders perched allegories of Fame and Victory. The exposition's official chronicler, Frank Morton Todd, observed that Calder's crowning figure of Energy, depicted on horseback, conveyed "the qualities of force and dominance that had ripped a way across the continental divide for the commerce of the world."[29] The grounds also housed the Fountains of Eldorado and of Youth by Gertrude Vanderbilt Whitney and Edith Woodman Burroughs; four fountains in the Court of Seasons by Furio Piccirilli; Edgar Walters's Fountain of Beauty and the Beast; and Robert Aitkin's Fountain of the Earth, which at night emitted a reddish-orange electric glow and was shrouded in steam to suggest the origins of the cosmos.[30]

As theatrical and ephemeral as these propagandistic displays may have been, their size and complexity served to fix them in the mind of the American populace as ideals of what cities might become. The 1893 World's Columbian Exposition, for example, was often cited as a primary influence on the City Beautiful movement in the United States, and many of its key participants, including Daniel Burnham, served as members of a congressional commission (the McMillan Commission),

which in 1901 and 1902 produced a model plan for Washington, D.C. The scheme looked back to the original 1791 plan for the American capital that had been conceived by the French military engineer, Major Pierre Charles L'Enfant, but it also recommended many of the design strategies that had been pioneered in Chicago.[31] These included using reflecting ponds and fountains to redefine the earlier plan, a suggestion which ultimately led to the placement of monuments such as Henry Bacon and Daniel Chester French's Dupont Memorial Fountain in Dupont Circle in 1921 [217].

A few years earlier, Karl Bitter, chief of sculpture for two international expositions, offered his own contribution to the City Beautiful movement in New York City in the form of the Pulitzer Fountain [160], placed in the Grand Army Plaza on Fifth Avenue and completed a year after Bitter's death in 1915. In a similar manner but on a grander scale, the Clarence Buckingham Memorial Fountain [218] by Edward H. Bennett and Marcel François Loyau was completed in 1927 to mark what would have been the central axis of Bennett and Daniel Burnham's important 1909 City

Beautiful Plan of Chicago.[32] Like those of the great exhibitions, this impressive fountain incorporates artificial illumination and choreographed hydraulic displays to delight visitors to Grant Park on hot summer evenings.

While the style of the architecture and sculpture may have changed, flamboyant polytechnic water displays, like the electric water jets of world's fairs in 1889 and in 1893 or the Château d'Eau at the Paris Universal Exposition of 1900, continued to play a central role in the layout and organization of subsequent expositions. The innovative wedding of technologies pioneered by the architects of these ephemeral spectacles still influences modern fountain designers such as the Los Angeles firm WET Design, and can be found at Disney's Epcot Center and in Las Vegas [246, 251]. As notable legacies of the great international expositions, fountains have become essential components in contemporary urban design, oases of entertainment, refreshment and distraction in the arid sprawl of the world's industrial and post-industrial cities and suburbs.

Kenneth Breisch

Celebrating the
Energy of the
Future

1925–1970

The enterprising optimism that had prompted Victorian England to undertake the first international exposition in 1851 as a way to show off the latest design and industrial innovations was similar to the spirit that launched modern international expositions. Like their predecessors, twentieth-century fairs continued as forums for new ideas, along with patriotic displays of recently developed products, artistic creativity and other expressions of traditional folk culture. Instead of a unifying architectural program and aesthetic style for the main exhibition halls or palaces, however, expositions after World War I featured smaller pavilions, reflecting more diverse cultural expressions and nationalistic interpretations of modern architecture. Corporations, too, played an increasingly visible role in developing exhibitions to promote their own commodities and latest advances. While both nineteenth- and twentieth-century international expositions sought to promote progress, modern fairs demonstrated a complete veneration for the beauty and power of the machine. Each successive exposition devised increasingly sensational displays of electricity and technological processes to convince an already predisposed public that these sources of energy were essential for creating better ways of life. There was an increased interest in the world of science and the process of discovery, and the fairs stimulated a growing public curiosity about the mysteries of natural phenomena. Displays of new communication technologies—bringing what was distant near—became popular. More than any of the earlier fairs, modern expositions after 1925 projected an eagerness to reach beyond the horizon to experience the promises of the future.

Fountains continued to be a persistent presence in modern expositions, some serving as ephemeral, yet memorable, landmarks, and others providing entertainment as awe-inspiring theatrical spectacles of water and light. Monumental fountains were often striking focal points along central walkways or lagoons, or marked building entrances. They also served as unifying design elements in otherwise heterogeneous architectural complexes. Breakthroughs in the evolution of fountain design and hydraulic technology involving more sophisticated pumps and equipment made it possible to move immense volumes of water to create an even greater variety of effects. Since the advent of electricity at the 1889 Paris exposition, where lavish water displays were for the first time combined with artificial lighting effects, architects and engineers developed equipment and technology so that each successive fair's illuminated fountain extravaganza surpassed its predecessor. Armed with the latest advances in hydraulics and light technology, designers became more adventurous in waterworks acrobatics and festive night-time presentations. The possibilities of harmonizing the nuances of light and water seemed vast. Astonishing fountain scenarios captivated a public who enthusiastically hungered for ever more surprising and dazzling effects. Expositions fountains from 1925 to 1970 ranged from conveying decorative elegance, such as those designed by René Lalique, to those by Isamu Noguchi, suggesting universal cosmic forces. The waterworks displays at international expositions became the primary means of demonstrating to the broadest possible audience the latest triumphs of hydraulic technology and fountain design, as well as major showcases for the ambitious ideas of their designers. Ultimately, these temporary fountains became models for more permanent monumental ones throughout the urban landscape of Europe and America.

< 190 The Springs and Rivers of France Fountain, Exposition Internationale des Arts Décoratifs et Industriels Modernes, Paris. Designed by René Lalique, 1925. Photogravure from *Exposition Internationale des Arts Décoratifs et Industriels Modernes Paris 1925: Rapport Général Rue et Jardin, vol. XI* (Paris, 1927).

The organizers of the Paris 1925 Exposition Internationale des Arts Décoratifs et Industriels Modernes sought to set aside traditional styles by encouraging the originality of modern design featuring new materials, such as plastic and chrome-plated steel, and new methods. Fountains were integrated throughout the fair as focal points in front of pavilions and as part of garden design displays, which were a novel feature introduced at this fair.[33] While some traditional fountains with figurative sculpture persisted, others used water to enhance abstract sculptures inspired by the ground-breaking art movements of cubism, fauvism, and futurism. Others were unprecedented in introducing stunning jewel-like qualities into the medium. Among the most dazzling monumental fountains at this fair was the glass fountain, entitled The Springs and Rivers of France [190], created by René Lalique, who was more renowned for designing elegant glass tableware and jewelry. Using plaques of frosted glass to clad a central pyramid set on an octagonal base, Lalique exploited the translucent material as a luminous complement to the shimmering water. Like a river casting off tributaries and rivulets, threads of water spilled from the fountain column. Colored lighting effects at night transformed Lalique's fountain into an ethereal apparition. While Osler's Crystal Fountain of 1851 [176] had impressed visitors to the Great Exhibition in London with its decorative use of fragile glass to create an enormous fountain chandelier, commingling the crystalline qualities and tinkling sounds of water, Lalique's fountain raised the integration of glass, water and light to a new level of fountain fantasy.

Marking the fiftieth anniversary of the first international exposition in London, the 1931 Exposition Coloniale in Paris was devised to broadcast the influence of French culture and commerce worldwide. The goal of the fair was to project the cultural vitality and richness that extended across the vast French empire where the "sun never sets." International admiration of France's prowess in fountain design was deemed further evidence of the superiority of French taste. Grandiose waterworks [191–93], spectacularly lit at night, far surpassed any of the fountains of the 1925 fair. Exotic motifs—pagodas, cacti, totems, lotuses—from French colonies inspired various fountain forms and the use of the fluidity of water in architectural ways. One fountain called Le Grand Signal, perhaps inspired by Lalique's 1925 fountain, resembled a diaphanous lighthouse. There were also immense water theaters and a graceful bridge, the Voûte d'Eau (Vault of Water), that were transformed through the magic of colored illumination into fantastic spectacles that astounded the public who beheld them.

V 191–93 (Clockwise from top) Le Grand Signal, Le Théâtre d'Eau and La Voûte d'Eau, Exposition Coloniale, Paris. Designed by André Granet and Roger-Henri Expert, 1931.

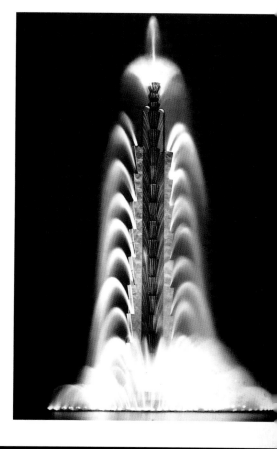

Architects viewed the planning of the 1937 Exposition Internationale des Arts et des Techniques Appliqués à la Vie Moderne in Paris as an opportunity to modernize urbanistically a prominent area as a grand counterpoint to the city's predominant landmark, the Eiffel Tower, which had been built for the 1889 exposition and had since endured as a feat of French engineering ingenuity. By the 1930s, the old Trocadéro Palace, the neo-Byzantine concoction with its wondrous Cascade designed for the 1878 Paris Universal Exposition, was appearing somewhat shabby. Once the decision to demolish the palace was made, a competition was held to determine what should permanently replace it. The winners Jacques Carlu, Louis H. Boileau and Léon Azema proposed to build the neoclassically modernist Palais de Chaillot to crown the brow of the hill of the same name and to serve as the majestic entrance to the fair. Its twin low-lying pavilions with curving wings frame the spacious esplanade that slopes down to the River Seine. The site offers a breathtaking vista of the Eiffel Tower and the Champs de Mars. The design of the esplanade gardens fell to Roger-Henri Expert with architects Paul Maître and Adolphe Thiers, the fountains and the rectangular fountain pool accentuating the axis toward the Eiffel Tower [195].

As the main fountain ensemble, strategically placed on the fair's dramatic entry esplanade, the forceful hydraulic display was calibrated to astonish visitors [194]. A battery of twenty hydraulic cannons, placed on the upper terrace and flanked by twin, sculpture-accented square basins, periodically shoot vigorous jets into the elongated, lozenge-shaped pool, lined with columns of vertical jets. When the cannons are silent, the fountain recalls the stately pools and jets found in France's formal gardens. When the cannons explode, people focus on the powerful machines propelling water toward an invisible enemy. The nearby River Seine readily supplies the fountain's abundant water needs. As one of the most spectacular fountains created for any exposition, the grand achievement of monumental landscaping remains today as one of the city's chief sights and most thrilling water displays.

Although the 1939 New York World's Fair commemorated the 150th anniversary of George Washington's inauguration as the first president of the United States, the exposition's main theme, the World of Tomorrow, generated exhibitions, pavilions, and inventions that looked forward to a "century in the making." In its official publication, *The Fair of the Future*, the

exposition's planners outlined their purpose: "The Fair should dedicate itself to the future, with the underlying social objective of demonstrating, not mere mechanical progress as in the past, but the ways in which new machines and merchandise could be used to improve economic conditions." The Trylon and Perisphere, the symbols and central landmarks of the fair, housed Democracity, an exhibition which envisioned the transportation systems, zoning, and recreational areas of an ideal American city in the future.

Water was incorporated throughout the parklike setting of the fair [196, 197]. Long, elegant pools and sculptural fountains, situated along major corridors and around pavilions gave a sense of formality and order. In contrast, other fountains emphasized water as a powerful, rapidly moving element associated with hydroelectric energy, while still others provided elegant, colorful entertainment.

Sponsored by 175 American utility companies, the Water Falls exhibit [198] promoted the industry's role in the progress of the nation. It recalled the form of major dams being constructed in various sections of the country in the 1930s. The fountain's noisy, plunging torrents, somewhat like a miniature Niagara Falls, accentuated the mastery of water power in hydroelectric waterworks which supplied America's rural areas with electricity. Mesmerizing patterns, similar to those in actual waterfalls, were created by the water flowing over the textured wall; the fountain was a forerunner of later waterwall and waterfall fountains.

References to hydroelectric energy were also found in the rapid activity of water in an imposing high-tech, multistory electric tower in the midst of the horseshoe-shaped Westinghouse and Manufacturing Building [200]. Created by sprays of water shot inward from the rim of the fountain's pool, the tower emerged from what appeared to be a cauldron of bubbling liquid.

By contrast, graceful, synchronized, rhythmic movement associated with dance inspired the Water Ballet Fountain which dramatically curtained the Consolidated Edison Building's facade [199]. The jets constantly pulsated, reaching a maximum height of forty-two feet. The use of colored lights on the spouting water and the reflections in the surrounding pools contributed to the theatrical air of the fountains. Inside the building, there was a spectacular diorama, The City of Light.

< 199 Water Ballet Fountain, Consolidated Edison Building, New York World's Fair. Designed by Alexander Calder, 1939.

The 1962 Seattle World's Fair launched the space age with a vision of the World of Century 21. The towering Space Needle was its beacon [174]. The first United States international exposition since 1939, the fair showcased an American city in a region better known for its tall timber, fishing and history of gold rushes. Seattle city leaders held an international competition for a monumental fountain that would dramatize the Pacific Northwest's abundant water resources being a major contributer to the country's hydraulic power industry. The fountain was to be a permanent centerpiece, first gracing the main plaza of the fair, and afterwards, as a civic landmark. The competition attracted 261 entries. The winners were two young Japanese architects who designed the enormous International Fountain [201] with parabolalike plumes of water in a sloped basin filled with irregular white rocks to suggest the galaxy's unexplored terrain. Changing water displays, shooting to heights of forty feet, created delightful star and flower shapes, including the popular fleur-de-lis pattern, which is still retained in the renovated fountain. The fountain symbolized man's effort to ascend to the heavens and to explore the farthest regions of outer space.

∧ 200 Symbol of Electric Power (detail), Westinghouse and Manufacturing Building, New York World's Fair. Designed by Skidmore & Owings and John Moss, 1939.

∧ 201 International Fountain, Seattle World's Fair, Washington. Designed by Hideki Shimizu and Kazuyuki Matsushita, 1962. Souvenir postcard, 1962.

> 202 Fountains in the Pond of Dreams, Japan World Exposition, Osaka. Designed by Isamu Noguchi, 1970.

In 1991, the site was adapted to become Seattle Center, a complex of theaters, museums, exhibition halls, restaurants, and sports arenas attracting almost eight million visitors annually, and the fountain plaza is now a popular location for cultural festivals and concerts. $6.5 million were allotted for the renovation of the International Fountain to improve its safety, to broaden accessibility, and to upgrade its status as a distinctive landmark. Nakano-Dennis redesigned the abruptly sloping basin, removed the hazardous rocks, and created an elegant, spiraling ramp from plaza level to the base of the fountain. WET Design adapted the fountain dome, replacing its tiles with stainless steel, and increasing its height and breadth. New jet nozzles were recessed beneath the surface, and computerized controls replaced the former hand-operated system. Completed in 1995, the fountain now presents an exciting sixty-minute water program every hour. The sequence of constantly changing water jet choreography is at times synchronized with music and light, but the climactic feature is a sudden burst of water exploding like a rocket 150 feet into the air. Throngs of people flock each week to the majestic fountain to watch children and young adults frolicking in the fountain sprays as if it were a giant sprinkler. To a generation well accustomed to space-age rocket launches, satellites and televised glimpses of planetary or lunar surfaces, the fountain that once aspired to suggest the extra-terrestrial, something beyond this world, is today a familiar and lovable, if oversized, water toy as well as a popular landmark.

The space theme was reiterated two years later at the 1964–65 New York World's Fair. The Unisphere, which rose to a height of 140 feet and hovered over a double ring of fountains, symbolized Man's Achievements on a Shrinking Globe in an Expanding Universe [206]. When visitors stood at the edge of the Unisphere's pool, the scale of the earth was shown as it appears from six thousand miles in space. Instead of peering at stars in the sky, people gazed at the Unisphere's world with the position of every national capital marked by a point of light.

The fair also featured the Fountain of the Planets, which, claiming to be the largest in the world, was 335 feet in diameter covering an area of 25,000 square feet. It comprised two thousand nozzles and 464 firework launchers, in addition to a lighting and sound system. Every evening there was a dramatic twenty-minute fountain program combining light, water, fireworks and sound, a spectacular type of feature pioneered in Paris in 1937. There was a variety of shows, each offering a different musical accompaniment. Great Masters included selections by classical composers, such as Tchaikovsky, Chopin, and Debussy, while Broadway presented a medley of tunes complementing George Gershwin's "Rhapsody in Blue," such as "Someone to Watch Over Me," "Begin the Beguine," and "Some Enchanted Evening." While most of the programs evoked celestial enchantment, there was also a forty-song program devoted to American patriotic favorites such as "Yankee Doodle Dandy," "Wild Blue Yonder," and "God Bless America."

For the first international fair in Asia, the 1970 Japan World Exposition held in Osaka, Japanese-American artist Isamu Noguchi was invited to design twelve fountains in three artificial lakes as a waterscape in the center of the site. The fair's theme of Harmony and Progress for Mankind balanced the domain of nature with that of technology. As with earlier fairs, Osaka's promoted technology as offering a wonderful future for mankind—an agenda emphasized by rapturous spectacles of light, color, sound, and water.

The Pond of Dreams with nine of Noguchi's fountains presented an exciting sight. The fountains expressed the vastness of the cosmos with water serving as the transitional element from the familiar world of nature on earth to the natural forces in outer space. Noguchi stated this intent: "The *objet* nature of the fountains must not be strong enough to overshadow the water—nature itself—which must be emphasized." Futuristic, gleaming, stainless-steel sculptural forms emitted masses of water or mist downward, outward, or in a rotary action to suggest rockets, orbits, comets, or nebulae [202]. Breezes created infinite variations on the fountain outpourings and sprays. The strength of water suggested the cosmic forces that ultimately dictate all natural phenomena. Noguchi's innovative Osaka fountains, fusing technological form and energy with water, launched a new style of monumental fountain which inspired the work he would later create in Detroit [270].

Non-stop, open-air entertainment has also played its part at Expo '98 in Lisbon, Portugal, in the form of huge water machines, fountains, and scintillating multimedia events combining water, fire, light, and sound. Fountains are still an essential component of the time-honored formula for international expositions. The latest wizardry in mastering water will continue to splash and glitter its way to the future.

Marilyn Symmes with Stephen Van Dyk

Remembering the Fountain of the Planets
at the New York World's Fair 1964–65

I began shooting pictures at age five, with a Kodak Brownie. By the time I was a teenager I had graduated to an Olympus-Pen, the now-legendary 35mm half-frame camera. With it, I documented the New York World's Fair during the course of many visits in 1964 and 1965, paying special attention to the fountains [205–07].

The Pool of Industry at the fair was an exhilarating place, especially at nightfall, when the crowds would gather for synchronized water, music, light and fireworks shows [203, 204]. There were several different programs. My absolute favorite was "Rhapsody in Blue."

It was an electric moment when, out in the middle of the pool, the Fountain of the Planets came alive with light and color, and the sounds of Gershwin began to fill the sweet summer evening air. It felt like Broadway under open skies.

The fountains became the music, matching and amplifying every mood. The surging waters changed in shape and intensity as they danced to Gershwin's classic. Underwater floodlights played the spectrum along with the orchestra, sending forth beams of liquid light in hues too intense to believe.

And then, launched from within the powerful geysers, fireworks. Fireworks! Dazzling brilliance that painted the sky whenever the score rose to a crescendo.

Within moments of the show's beginning the audience was hooked—hushed and mesmerized. It seemed like you were soaring on a magic carpet ride, but it was, after all, the 1960s.

The fair was all about THE FUTURE, and at that historical moment, mid-decade, the future still looked pretty good. Anything and everything seemed possible.

The space program was busy turning science fiction into science fact. So it was not much of a leap to believe that one day soon you could check into an underwater hotel, like the one in the General Motors Futurama exhibit. Commercial flights to the Moon? Just a matter of years, it seemed. By the turn of the century, at the latest. I yearned to go.

A generation of young people inspired by the idealism of the Kennedy years, myself among them, was set for change. It was an exuberant era filled with hope, promise and high expectations. America was pulsing with energy, and the big fountain in the Pool of Industry (the largest in the world, claimed the fair's guidebook) was that energy made manifest.

In hindsight it was, of course, a wildly innocent era. The theme song for one of the fair's exhibits promised "a great big beautiful tomorrow," and few were about to argue with that notion, least of all a sixteen-year-old boy.

So today, when I look at my photos of fountains that flowed long ago, I see more than images of artful water effects. I see a place and a time and an event that spoke a language beyond words. I see fountains that sang to me, sirenlike, of distant bright horizons.

The waters of the Fountain of the Planets had a particular, not unpleasant, brackish aroma. Somehow that added to the charged atmosphere of the night-time shows. There was the sense of watching a glorious act of nature—towering breaking ocean waves, glowing with phosphorescence.

It was a spectacle that transported me, leaving a lasting impression. The Fountain of the Planets occupies a portion of my memory reserved for vivid dreams. Even without looking at my pictures I can conjure up a vision of those waters in my mind. Years later, I can still see that fountain. And I hear Gershwin playing in the fresh night air.

Bart Barlow

203, 204 Fountain of the Planets, New York World's Fair, 1964–65. Views by night.

205 Fountain of the Planets, by day.

206 Aerial view of the fair and the Unisphere.

207 Taking a family snapshot with the Unisphere in the background.

203–07 are all photographs by Bart Barlow.

chapter 6
fountains as Commemoration

"A mortal's soul seems
Like the water,
From heaven coming
To heaven rising
Again renewed then
To earth descending
Ever changing."

from *Song of the Spirits over the Water*
by Johann Wolfgang Goethe (1779)

< 208 Shaftesbury Memorial
Fountain (also called the Eros
Fountain), Piccadilly Circus, London.
Designed by Alfred Gilbert, 1893.

Commemorative fountains and monuments can offer a sense of peace, hope or inspiration while honoring the memory of past lives or deeds. Tangibly acknowledging notable achievements, memorials exist in public arenas to prompt private, individual responses. The enduring benefits of water and its aesthetic visual and aural qualities, along with its spiritual associations, make it the supreme enhancer of memorials, triggering "vast reservoirs of sentiment and idealism" in the beholder.[1] Architects, designers, and artists choreograph the possibility for memory by using either grandiose or modest materials, form, scale, space and even information or symbolism, to fix the monument in time. They add the fluid continuity of water as the magical elixir to transform what has passed into eternity. Yet who or what ultimately provides the lasting element to a commemorative fountain's significance? The designer? Those memorialized? Or the beholder? Is it not perhaps water that commingles all reminders of vitality?

Like buildings and streets, fountains bearing the names of various individuals—some well known, others less so—dot countless cities and towns around the globe. Sometimes it is the donors who are commemorated, having given their own funds as gestures of conspicuous philanthropy to benefit fellow citizens with public fountains either for drinking or for beautifying an urban place (or for both). The Wallace Fountains in Paris [85] and the James Scott Memorial Fountain [214] are notable examples. Other commemorative fountains are designated by relatives, friends, communities or governing leaders as a way to perpetuate the memory of an admirable person or group [208, 212, 221]. Today, many such fountains are enjoyed in their own right as refreshing public adornments [218, 285], and the reincarnation almost eclipses the shadowy presence of those commemorated. As a gesture by the living in the name of the dead, those who commission or dedicate a fountain in someone's memory believe that water is so precious, that the ultimate life-affirming gift is to make it freely available for all to enjoy.

The tradition of uniting artistic expression with commemorative sentiment is centuries old. Funerary monuments as grand as the seventeenth-century Taj Mahal in India or as unassuming as the twentieth-century Memorial to the Deportees (on the tip of the Île de la Cité in Paris) endure to this day. Lamentations prevail in religious art and in musical requiems. Since the 1830s, however, the establishment of commemorative fountains as public amenities has become more prevalent. The impetus for these fountains may be traced partly to the exemplary grand-scale urban redesigning of Paris. Other influences include the more public display of mourning that arose following the deaths of such widely beloved men as Queen

Victoria's Prince Albert, Abraham Lincoln and Victor Hugo, as well as the inspirational and progressive splendor of international expositions after 1851.

Paris had an intermittent tradition of erecting monumental fountains after the creation of the Fontaine des Innocents (Fountain of the Innocents [63]). In the nineteenth century, with improved methods of providing and distributing water citywide, there was increased activity in designing major propagandistic fountains (for example, those in the Place de la Concorde [159]) and commemorative ones, which also fulfilled the city's ambitious urban embellishment program. Several notable fountains were designed by architect Ludovico (or Louis) Visconti, who is perhaps best remembered for designing Napoleon's tomb in Les Invalides. Dedicated in 1844 amid much pomp was a renovation of an earlier fountain as an elegant memorial to Molière [209], the great seventeenth-century dramatist whose plays still constitute part of the staple repertoire of the nearby Comédie Française theater. Visconti devised a Renaissance-style corner building with a niche for the bronze seated statue of Molière (a work

by Bernard-Gabriel Seurre), flanked by allegorical figures of both light and serious comedy (by James Pradier).[2] At the street-level base, almost as a functional afterthought, are lion-headed spigots discreetly spouting water into a trough. While the fountain served practical refreshment needs for those in the vicinity, the project was really an excuse to pay homage to one of France's most beloved cultural heros. Today, one can make a pilgrimage to the corner of Rue Molière and Rue Richelieu, where the Fontaine Molière still gurgles respectfully.

Another commemorative fountain in Paris, built with plaza-enhancing intent, pays tribute to four great French religious orators. Located in Place Saint-Sulpice, the Fontaine des Orateurs-Sacrés [211], also called both the Fontaine des Quatre-Évêques and the Fontaine de Saint-Sulpice (completed 1848), immortalizes four bishops: Bossuet (1627–1704) of Meaux, Fénelon (1651–1715) of Cambrai, Fléchier (1632–1710) of Nîmes and Massillon (1663–1742) of Clermont-Ferrand. At the top of the fountain is a French Renaissance-style temple structure sheltering statues of the bishops. Each is seated in a niche,

surmounted with his respective coat of arms, on the cardinal points of the compass.[3] The monument rests on a two-level octagonal cascade, with mascaron-sided urns emitting water from the upper tier. Four lions in repose (sculpted by François Derre), each supporting the coat of arms of Paris, are placed as diagonal accents on the lower cascade.

While Visconti took care to harmonize his design with the commanding solemnity of the church facade of Saint-Sulpice, critics of his day were less reverential about his efforts. Some complained that, from certain vantage spots, the fountain blocked views of the church portals. Others said that the water sounded like the fountain's lions were rumbling, since they were probably irritated by the water splashing their rumps.[4] Yet commemorative fountains such as these helped to aggrandize French patrimony, albeit with restrained classicism.[5] In modern Paris brimming with fountains from all eras, the fountain in Place Saint-Sulpice provides a welcoming refuge under the benevolent gaze of past religious leaders. Since the splashing masks intrusive traffic noise, the water has become a healer to modern-day annoyances.

209 Fontaine Molière, Paris. Designed by Ludovico Visconti, 1841–44. Engraving by Rudolf Pfnor from *Fontaines monumentales construites à Paris et projetées pour Bordeaux par Ludovic Visconti* (Paris, 1860).

210 Shaftesbury Memorial Fountain, Piccadilly Circus, London. Designed by Alfred Gilbert, 1893. Photograph *c.* 1900.

211 Fontaine des Orateurs-Sacrés, also called Fontaine de Saint-Sulpice, Paris. Designed by Ludovico Visconti, 1843–48.

While nineteenth-century England overflowed with monuments to royalty and great heroes, it had few memorials to distinguished individuals from its recent history. So the commission for a memorial to Anthony Ashley-Cooper, earl of Shaftesbury (1801–85) was, for its day, a remarkable tribute to a politician who had tirelessly devoted half a century to social and educational reform. Today, the Shaftesbury Memorial Fountain, commonly known as the Eros Fountain in Piccadilly Circus, is one of London's most beloved monuments [208]. Its decorative beauty anchors a setting where traffic and pedestrians hustle by; it is a jewel-like accent against a backdrop of blatant contemporary advertising. However, when it was first unveiled in June 1893, it caused tremendous public consternation because it memorialized a nationally-respected gentleman in the guise of a nude statue of Eros [210].[6]

The fountain was designed by Alfred Gilbert, one of England's foremost sculptors and goldsmiths, to convey Lord Shaftesbury's great humanity and philanthropy. Deliberately breaking with the Victorian tradition of coat-and-trousers portrait statues, Gilbert chose the god Eros as the symbol of selfless love, and the overflowing fountain was to represent Lord Shaftesbury's abundant generosity.[7] What Gilbert failed to anticipate was the high degree of Victorian prudishness, aggravated by the contextual associations of the site. The monument was derided as highly "indecent" and "hideous," and since the public misinterpreted Eros as Cupid, its association with a neighborhood notorious for prostitution was deemed exceedingly poor taste.[8] In the 1890s, people were somewhat aghast to see putti cavorting with writhing fish as the main decoration around the base emitting the water jets, and then there was the shock of looking up at a lissome Eros who was scantily covered by a bit of fluttering cloth. Furthermore, the design of the water jets and basin was such that those attempting to drink, instead got drenched, and the resulting spray made mud on the street.

FONTANA NEL GRAN CORTILE DEL PALAZZO VATICANO
detto Beluedere, Architettura di Carlo Maderno.

Gilbert never fully recovered from the vicious criticism for what he thought would be a triumphant masterpiece of original fountain design. He had spent years working on it, and he even adjusted it to accommodate the requests of the Memorial Committee (although possibly Gilbert's earlier ideas for the action of the water might have been more successful). Gilbert's earliest preparatory drawings for the memorial show a fontlike base, graduating upward into a spirited statue.[9] The pose of the maquette (originally modelled in plaster in 1891) for Eros, in flight and poised to shoot an arrow, revealed inspiration from Giambologna's *Flying Mercury* of 1564, a sculpture now in the Bargello, Florence, and from the figure of Bacchus in Titian's painting *Bacchus and Ariadne* (1522–23) in London's National Gallery.[10] Gilbert's skill for ornament is evident in the profusion of fish and putti around the lavish base. The architectural elements forming the foundation for the memorial were designed by Howard Ince.

The casting in bronze and aluminum of Gilbert's elaborate design proved to be exorbitantly expensive, costing the sculptor far more than he received as his fee. Gilbert went into debt and, in 1901, declared bankruptcy. This, and the lasting effects of his humiliation surrounding the Eros Fountain, prompted him to leave England to reside in Bruges, Belgium. Gilbert would

later return to see the fountain's initial frosty reception transformed to public fondness. With time people came to appreciate the memorial's exuberance, even if few associated it with one of the great benefactors of the previous century. The fountain has been dismantled and marginally resited several times over the years—during London Underground construction; to off-site storage during the war; and to accommodate changing traffic patterns. Following its most recent restoration, the Eros Fountain is again back in full glory, spritzing water and fulfilling its various roles as a charming attraction for Londoners and tourists; as a place for rebellious youths to hang out; as a focal point in one of the busiest intersections of central London; and above all as a spirited commemorative monument.

The same year that the Shaftesbury Memorial Fountain was completed, America celebrated the four-hundredth anniversary of Columbus's voyage of discovery. Inspired by the 1893 World's Columbian Exposition in Chicago, American architects and civic leaders championed beautification of cities across the United States, looking to great European cities, parks and gardens as models. Architects and artists, molded by the academic tradition of the École des

Beaux-Arts in Paris, composed unified, ornamental designs derived from classical elements and from various historical sources. Strategically placed fountains became part of city plans to serve as elegant focal points on grand, axial boulevards or vistas. Chicago architect Daniel H. Burnham, whose vision masterminded the Columbian exposition and the 1909 Plan of Chicago (which influenced city designs nationwide), advised: "Make no little plans, they have no magic to stir men's blood and probably themselves will not be realized. Make big plans: aim high in hope and work, remembering that a noble logical diagram once recorded will never die, but long after we are gone will be a living thing, asserting with growing intensity."[11] Between 1910 and 1930, in the wake of America's City Beautiful movement, several commemorative fountains in New York, Detroit, Chicago and Washington, D.C., were part of the gleaming magic that made their respective cities sparkle when they were first dedicated, and they remain landmark jewels in each city's crown today.

The Josephine Shaw Lowell Memorial Fountain [212] erected in 1912 in Bryant Park behind the New York Public Library was the city's first prominent monument honoring a woman. The fountain plaque proclaims: "This fountain commemorates/ the strong and beautiful character/ of Josephine Shaw Lowell 1843–1905/ wife for one year of a patriot soldier/ widow at

< 212 Josephine Shaw Lowell Memorial Fountain, Bryant Park, New York. Designed by Charles Adams Platt, 1912.

< 213 *Fountain in the Great Court of the Vatican Palace called the Belvedere, Architecture of Carlo Maderno*. Etching by Giovanni Battista Falda from *Le Fontane di Roma* (Rome, 1691).

∨ 214 James Scott Memorial Fountain, Belle Isle, Detroit. Designed by Cass Gilbert, with sculpture by Herbert Adams and Robert Aitken, 1914–25.

twenty-one/ servant of New York State and City/ in their public charities/ sincere candid courageous and tender/ bringing help and hope to the fainting/ and inspiring others to consecrated labors."[12] The pink granite fountain features a shallow, gently-contoured basin resting on a classically ornamented central pedestal. A dignified jet of water shoots up from the center of the basin and its falling water ripples and spills over the basin's rim to a large circular pool below.

Architect, garden designer, and artist Charles A. Platt based the design of the memorial on fountains he had admired during his travels through Italy. Loyal to the traditions of the Renaissance style, Platt may have modeled his gracefully classical bowl and basin design on Carlo Maderno's sixteenth-century fountain in the Vatican's Belvedere courtyard in Rome, which he might have seen or known from such prints as the one in Giovanni Battista Falda's *Le Fontane di Roma* [213].[13] Platt, who subsequently designed the Freer Gallery in Washington, D.C., knew Mrs. Lowell and the civic leaders in charge of awarding

the commission. A time-honored, stately fountain form without excessive ornament was an appropriate memorial to a pioneering social worker and reformer who eschewed personal extravagance in favor of working to benefit others less fortunate.[14]

While the Lowell Memorial Fountain is the epitome of classicizing restraint, architect Cass Gilbert designed a memorial in Detroit that derives its eclectic decoration from the great European fountains of Perugia, Florence, Rome, Versailles and Caserta.[15] An exuberant apotheosis of fountaindom, the James Scott Memorial Fountain [214] on the city's Belle Isle is also blessed with a superb setting. It can be seen, unobstructed by buildings, from American and Canadian shores and by thousands of boats sailing on the strait connecting Lake Erie and Lake Huron. Standing at the memorial, one enjoys a beautiful vista encompassing downtown Detroit and the Canadian city Windsor opposite.

One of the most glorious fountains in the United States, the Scott memorial commemorates a man few wished to honor so conspicuously. How did one of the country's leading architects come to design such an ennobling fountain for an ignoble man? During his lifetime, James Scott (1831–1910) was a ruthless citizen, seemingly without any philanthropic inclination, yet he left the city of Detroit his entire estate of $350,000 in order to erect a fountain on Belle Isle in his name.[16] Because of Scott's undesirable reputation, city officials were hesitant to fulfill the bequest. However the city rarely had such lavish funds to spend on public art and architectural beautification, and the potential benefits to Detroit citizens outweighed any reluctance. As one councilman urged: "If it is rightly done it will make Detroit famous the world over and be an attraction in just the same sense as St. Paul's Cathedral is an attraction in London."[17] Individual vanity joined city ambition, and the project proceeded, controlled by Scott's executors. The first idea was for an opulent fountain and public concert hall, much like the Trocadéro at the 1900 Paris Universal Exposition, but critics claimed this idea would taint Belle Isle's natural beauty. In 1914 a competition was held to select a design for the monumental fountain. Cass Gilbert, one of several prominent architects invited to submit, was the winner.[18]

The realization of his design [215, 216] took a period of years, however. Construction did not begin in earnest until 1921, partly due to World War I. Gilbert had also extravagantly elaborated his original scheme beyond the available financial resources, so adjustments had to be made. Then, the site preparation, which necessitated extending the island to accommodate the fountain's cascades and lagoon, took almost two years. The fountain was finally completed by 1925.

Gilbert's fountain features a large jet, soaring to a height of over seventy-five feet, within a ring of lower jets shooting from a raised basin from which water overflows into a larger circular basin below. Decorations around the pedestal supporting the smaller basin include putti riding spitting dolphins and spouting mascarons. The sides of the lower basin are carved with a frieze of trappers, traders, and Indians representing Detroit's early history, modeled on the European tradition of representing occupations, as on Perugia's Fontana Maggiore [99]. The climactic centerpiece is set within another larger fountain pool. Four lions spouting water, inspired by those in Rome, are placed symmetrically at four points near the pool's periphery. Other decorations include drinking horns, turtles and fish. Between the upper basins and the tip of the island are dramatic stepped cascades and tiers of scalloped masks emitting small jets, all of which descend to a lower basin and then a reflecting lagoon.

Gilbert fussed over every aspect of the commission, including the landscaping. He even suggested rewording the initial factual statement, "James Scott gave this fountain to the people of Detroit," to a more inspirational inscription, "A citizen of Detroit, he left his entire fortune to the City for the construction of a Fountain. From such good deeds great merit flows."[19]

Today, Detroit valiantly struggles to reverse the crippling effects of urban decay which have ravished major parts of the city. Driving to Belle Isle, one passes pockets of littered streets, vacant lots and abandoned buildings, as well as a growing panorama of spruced up, active neighborhoods and

commercial areas. Although Belle Isle suffered periods of neglect during the 1960s, the fountain has since been restored. When one arrives at the Scott Memorial Fountain, its dazzling imperial white Danby Vermont marble, its display of ornamentation and its profusion of water ceaselessly spraying, spouting and tumbling over statues, masks, basins and tiers constitute a wondrous vision made material by imagination and philanthropy.

In Washington, D.C., instead of abundant ornamentation and water, the theme is the mastery of water in the guise of three allegorical figures of ocean navigation. The Rear Admiral Samuel Francis Dupont Memorial Fountain at Dupont Circle [217] features the Sea, the Wind, and the Stars, who support a large circular basin from which two streams of water pour at opposite ends. With a dolphin at her feet and a gull on her shoulder, a classically draped Sea cradles a boat with her right arm. Wind holds a conch shell while he presses against the billowing sail of a ship, and on the third side of the pedestal, the goddess of the Stars holds a globe. Carved in brilliant white marble, the sculptural ensemble is the focal point of an island oasis beautifying the intersection of several busy avenues. Water is quietly present, not insistent, in complementing the more predominant sculpture. The descendants of Admiral Dupont (1803–65) wished to commemorate him as a Civil War naval hero, so they commissioned Daniel Chester French as sculptor and Henry Bacon as architect, both of whom designed the impressively commanding memorial in honor of President Abraham Lincoln.[20] The Lincoln Memorial was still under construction when the Dupont Memorial Fountain was completed in 1921. Today the fountain presides over a well-landscaped mini-park, providing a haven—for the fashionable and the homeless—in the midst of a commercial area, in contrast to the 1960s and 1970s when Dupont Circle was a popular spot for protest demonstrations and hippie singalongs.[21]

Chicago's Clarence Buckingham Memorial Fountain surpassed every American fountain, and it even rivaled those in Europe, when it was completed in 1927. It is a magnificent ornamental monument to water, inspired by the fountains of Versailles, but enlarged to the scale of the city's skyscrapers. Architect Edward H. Bennett, who worked with Daniel Burnham on his exemplary Plan of Chicago several decades earlier, viewed his design for the Buckingham fountain as the crowning triumph of the city's beautification goals. A regal focal point aligning with a major street axis, the memorial is prominently sited within the geometrically patterned gardens of Grant

< 215, 216 *General Plan* and *Elevation, Competition for the Scott Memorial Fountain, Detroit*, 1914. Pen, ink and wash drawings by Cass Gilbert.

∧ 217 Rear Admiral Samuel Francis Dupont Memorial Fountain, Dupont Circle, Washington, D.C. Designed by Henry Bacon and Daniel Chester French, 1921.

Park, near the shores of Lake Michigan [218]. Shortly after it was completed, the fountain was hailed as the world's greatest engineering feat dedicated to pure aesthetic beauty, and its spectacular rising and falling waters, dramatically illuminated at night, enthrall throngs of Chicagoans and out-of-town visitors during the summer months.[22]

Kate S. Buckingham had magnanimously provided $750,000 in order to establish this fountain in honor of the memory of her unmarried brother Clarence (1854–1913), who had unassumingly contributed to the social and cultural well-being of the city.[23] What was even more enlightened and farsighted is that her gift generously provided for a trust to cover future care and maintenance costs, so that Chicago citizens would never be burdened with perpetuating the memorial's glory. Made of pink Georgia marble, the fountain's basic wedding-cake design of three concentric basins was inspired by the Fontaine de Latone in Versailles [139], which Bennett probably saw during his student days at the École des Beaux-Arts in Paris, but the Chicago fountain is four times larger. Fed by the water of nearby Lake Michigan, which it then recycles, the Buckingham Memorial Fountain symbolizes that great water source that nurtures Chicago, and all life around its shores. In the ground-level pool, which is 280 feet in diameter, there are four pairs of bronze sea horses, sculpted by Marcel Loyau, representing the four states surrounding the lake (Illinois, Wisconsin, Michigan, and Indiana). The rest of the decorative dazzle is architectural ornament and an impressive array of constantly changing jets and cascades, lit at night in scintillating colors of blue, green, red and amber [219].

The challenge to Bennett and his engineering team was to achieve the most spectacular water display, with the least consumption of power, and thus cost. Using the most sophisticated hydraulic technology of the day, the fountain's elaborate electricity and pumping equipment can move almost sixteen thousand gallons of water per minute, though this expenditure of power is reserved for the major display presented only six times per week (the usual level ranges between 5,500 and

△ 218 Aerial view of the Clarence Buckingham Memorial Fountain, Grant Park, Chicago. Designed by Edward H. Bennett, 1927.

△ 219 Clarence Buckingham Memorial Fountain and the Chicago skyline by night.

> 220 J. C. Nichols Memorial Fountain, Kansas City, Missouri, 1960. Originally designed in 1910 with sculpture by Henri Greber and moved to Kansas City in the 1950s.

7,000 gallons per minute). Visible from some distance is the central vertical column of water shooting into the air, surrounded by twelve jets of lesser volume and height, and a series of jets rising from the lower tiers. The water gathered in the top basin descends in sheets to the lower basins, and finally to the outer pool to meet trajectories of water emitted from the sea horses. The fountain's standard program runs daily, from ten o'clock in the morning until eleven o'clock in the evening from 1 May to 1 October.

At the fountain's dedication ceremony on 26 August 1927, attended by fifty thousand people, John Philip Sousa conducted "Stars and Stripes Forever," and then waved his baton, and, as if on cue, the water began to perform its full repertoire of effects moving in a magical harmony of colored radiance and music. Newspaper accounts at the time focused on the fountain's technical wizardry. Readers learned that the fountain needed skillful "fountain players" to operate the daunting keyboard controlling the 134 jets and seven hundred lights (capable of thirty million candlepower) to create the wondrous symphonic effects. Another article following the dedication commented: "In a week the Buckingham fountain has captured the imagination of the town, enlarged its esthetic sense and done it spiritual good. The gift is more than a memorial to Clarence Buckingham. It is an expression of the lake by which it is fed and which it extols…. It is the lyric of the lake. It will never grow old or commonplace…. It will go on forever."[24]

And the majestic fountain today continues to be one of the spectacular landmarks of Chicago, perhaps far more flamboyant than a reserved Clarence Buckingham would have wanted, but it fulfills Miss Buckingham's wish to benefit people with free open-air waterworks entertainment guaranteed to divert them from their daily cares.[25]

Using monumental fountains as city beautifiers was an idea that rippled outward from Europe, then from Chicago, to heartland America. Dubbing itself the City of Fountains, Kansas City in Missouri boasts that its proliferation of fountains rivals Rome. The J. C. Nichols Memorial

Fountain, dedicated in 1960 [220], is Kansas City's equivalent of Bernini's Fountain of the Four Rivers in Piazza Navona, Rome [122]. Real estate developer Jesse Clyde Nichols (1880–1950) had been responsible for developing significant sections of Kansas City's residential and commercial areas, particularly the fashionable, European-inspired Country Club Plaza, known simply as The Plaza. He zealously adorned his sites with fountains throughout, as he had seen in the plazas, parks and gardens of Europe. After a 1922 trip abroad, he returned to his own city brimming with fresh ideas for using ornamental fountains and statues as community assets. After his death, his family and the city felt an appropriate memorial would be a fountain. However, rather than commission one anew, they opted to restore to its former glory a neglected one, originally designed in 1910 for the Long Island (New York) estate of industrialist Clarence H. Mackay. Mackay's home, designed by the noted architectural firm McKim, Mead & White, was complemented by the formal landscaping of Guy Lowell, and the garden's crowning feature was its monumental fountain, with sculpture by the French artist Henri Greber.[26]

Following Mackay's death in 1938, his estate fell to neglect and vandalism, and the bronze fountain sculpture ended up with a New York art dealer who sold the group to the Nichols family in 1952. There were four figures, each mounted on a rearing horse, and they had been placed at the cardinal points around a central two-tiered basin emitting a towering jet. The most dramatic figures symbolize the Mississippi and Volga Rivers: the former shows an Indian about to spear a menacing alligator, the latter combats a huge bear. The remaining two equestrian figures, each holding a reed cat's-tail and accompanied by tritons who restrain the horses, represent the Rivers Rhine and Seine. By the late 1950s, the city had approved the site and the necessary funding. The local firm of Tanner and Associates oversaw the conservation and resurrection of the fountain. During the spring and summer months, the water effects can be dramatic. The central jet propels water some forty feet into the air, while additional streams are aimed toward the center by putti astride dolphins which are placed in between the primary equestrian sculptures. The fountain exuberantly splashes in a park signaling the gateway to Kansas City's Plaza district, and local citizens regard it with pride as their greatest fountain.

...UNTIL JUSTICE ROLLS DOWN LIKE WATERS
AND RIGHTEOUSNESS LIKE A MIGHTY STREAM

MARTIN LUTHER KING JR

△ 221, 222 Civil Rights Memorial,
Southern Poverty Law Center,
Montgomery, Alabama. Designed
by Maya Lin, 1989.

▽ 223 A man drinking from a
segregated water fountain in North
Carolina, 1950. Photograph by
Elliott Erwitt.

belies the turbulence of the history that preceded it. Until 1960, public access to drinking water was an issue there. Black people were forbidden to drink from certain fountains [223], and they could not eat in certain restaurants, or sit in certain public places. Intimidation and violence were used against those who threatened the established order of white supremacy. Martin Luther King, Jr. and Mississippi NAACP (National Association for the Advancement of Colored People) official Medgar Evers were heroic leaders who opposed racial injustice, and became martyrs to the cause. No one had previously devised a memorial to honor them and the other ordinary citizens who acted courageously and suffered personal tragedies to influence the civil rights movement.

Maya Lin, the designer of the initially controversial, but now much admired, Vietnam Veterans Memorial in Washington, D.C. (completed 1981), was an appropriate choice for another monument that was meant to serve as an American shrine. The Vietnam Veterans Memorial, by using the eloquence of a unifying minimalist form in the landscape, acknowledges each individual who died, and has helped millions of Americans reconcile feelings of loss, anger and confusion generated by the Vietnam War. Similarly, the memorial to civil rights was to be about people's lives, and after receiving the commission, Lin read Martin Luther King's speeches, and found a passage that made it clear to her that the piece would also be all about water.[28] She then visited the site, later making sketches and a small-scale model to hone and place the forms in their final arrangement.

The Civil Rights Memorial stands in the entry plaza to the Southern Poverty Law Center. There Lin devised two minimal yet majestic forms of black granite that would subtly announce the contemplative place. On the curved granite wall, nine feet high and forty feet long, the words of Martin Luther King, Jr. greet all visitors: "...until justice rolls down like water and righteousness like a mighty stream." This famous variant on the biblical passage (Amos 5:24) rallied people to civil rights action.[29] The quiet, constant presence of water on the granite surfaces gives potency to King's words.

While the way European fountains link decorative sculpture and ornament with water remains a model for many American fountains, several contemporary designers, notably Maya Lin and Lawrence Halprin, have studied how water moves in nature, and they emphasize its flowing and falling qualities as metaphoric currents in commemoration.

The Southern Poverty Law Center in Montgomery, Alabama, commissioned Maya Lin to design the first monument dedicated to civil rights achievements and to those who died during the struggle for racial equality. The Civil Rights Memorial, which was completed in 1989, features a smooth veil of water flowing like a soothing spring [221].[27] The serene, continuous motion of the water in this memorial, located in the heart of America's South, an area which encouraged segregation, almost

A low, elliptical, black granite table—11½ feet in diameter at its top, and tapering to a twenty-inch base—rests in front of the wall. Inscribed on the table's surface as rays radiating from the center is a chronology of fifty-three landmark events in the civil rights movement incorporating the death dates of forty people who died for freedom. The first entry reads: "17 May 1954 Supreme Court outlaws school segregation in Brown vs. Board of Education." The last is: "4 Apr 1968 Dr. Martin Luther King, Jr. assassinated, Memphis, TN." Some of the events and people mentioned are well known, others not: "7 May 1955 Rev. George Lee killed for leading voter registration Drive, Belzoni, MS.... 1 Dec 1955 Rosa Parks arrested for refusing to give up her seat on bus to a white man Montgomery, AL.... 1 Feb 1960 Black students stage sit-in at whites only lunch counter Greensboro, NC.[30]... 28 Aug 1963 250,000 Americans march on Washington for Civil Rights." In order to read all the entries and to engage emotionally with the memorial, one must walk around the periphery of the table on an intimate journey to commune with reminders of a now-public history. Water discreetly bubbles from a source off-center to wash uniformly over the entire surface. At the edge, water wraps around clinging to the tapered underside until it drops down from near the base. Encouraging introspection and connection, the fountain invites visitors to touch the names through the water [222], thus gently disturbing the flow—non-violently, just as civil rights activists influenced the course of history.

Lin states: "The water [is] as slow as I could get it. It remains very still until you touch it. Your hand carves ripples, which transform and alter the piece, just as reading the words completes the piece."[31] At the memorial's dedication ceremony, Lin recalls: "Emmett Till's mother was touching his name beneath the water and crying, and I realized her tears were becoming part of the memorial."[32] Simultaneously fixed and yet fluid, the controlled power of the water moving over the inscribed granite conveys a calm invincibility.

> 224 Model of the Franklin Delano Roosevelt Memorial (detail), Washington, D.C. Designed by Lawrence Halprin, memorial completed in 1997.

Themes of freedom and the vigorous presence of water also characterize the design of the Franklin Delano Roosevelt Memorial in Washington, D.C. However, in contrast to the Civil Rights Memorial's use of barely moving water as a quiet, but righteous, healer, the F. D. R. Memorial features rushing waters that roar and splash. As a great twentieth-century American president touching the lives of many, Roosevelt (1882–1945) brought the nation out of its worst economic depression, set up public works projects and social programs, and led the country through world war. Years in the making, but finally dedicated on 2 May 1997, the memorial showcases a harmonious sequence of cascading waterfalls, granite walls, paving, plants, trees, figurative sculpture and quotations from Roosevelt's famous speeches [224]. Instead of classically inspired architecture and statues, the memorial is a scenic 7½-acre park, bounded by the Potomac River and the Tidal Basin, on the Cherry Tree Walk (between the Thomas Jefferson and Abraham Lincoln Memorials) with majestic vistas of the Washington Monument.[33]

Designed by landscape architect Lawrence Halprin of San Francisco, the $48 million memorial is the biggest project of his fifty-year career. It culminates a lifetime of studying the movement and sounds of water amid rock formations in natural settings of the American West [281].

Halprin and his design associates pioneered monumental waterfall fountains that offer the "experiential equivalent" of awe-inspiring nature to revitalize city park settings and plazas. While dramatically descending cascade fountains were popular features in Italian villas, they were unusual in American cities before Halprin. Halprin has designed major public places featuring water that successfully thrive today in Portland, Oregon [283–86], Seattle, San Francisco and Los Angeles.

Halprin was awarded this prestigious commission only after other architectural proposals had tried and failed to win approval. Creation of monuments to greatness in the capital city have a history of being hotly debated and subjected to lengthy delays.[34] In 1960, a national competition attracted 574 proposals, including one by Halprin with Minoru Yamasaki and Associates. The prize-winning design by architects William F. Pedersen and Bradford S. Tilney, with sculptor Norman Hoberman, offered a modernist grouping of colossal concrete stelae inscribed with Roosevelt's words. Dubbed in the press as "a set of bookends just out of the deep freeze," "instant Stonehenge," and an "eccentric graveyard," the Pedersen–Tilney design endured a tug-of-war between praise and criticism before its ultimate rejection in 1965.[35] A year later, after the F. D. R. Memorial Commission

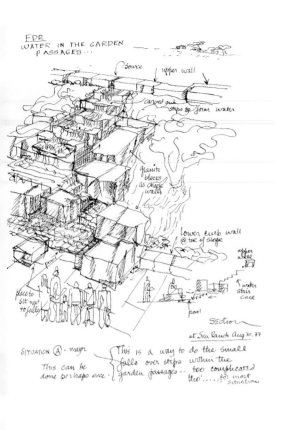

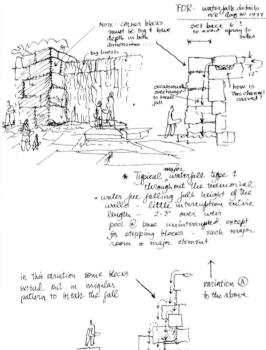

△ 225, 226 An early proposal for the flow of water in the garden passages and waterfall details for the Franklin Delano Roosevelt Memorial, Washington, D.C. Sketchbook drawings by Lawrence Halprin, 30 August 1977.

invited over fifty architects to submit new proposals, internationally acclaimed architect Marcel Breuer was selected to shape the memorial. In 1967 his design— a grand pinwheel-like arrangement of triangular-shaped granite—was also rejected. By 1970 the commission had abandoned all ideas of heroic modernism or of traditional ennobling architecture. Instead, they favored a rose garden surrounding a statue. This decision opened the way for a landscape architect to lead the design process that would result in the first presidential memorial as a park to be enjoyed, rather than as an iconic monument to be revered. In 1974 the commission chose Halprin, and by 1978, his proposal had received all the necessary governmental approvals. Following further design development and fund raising, ground breaking occurred in 1991.

From the mid-1970s until the memorial's dedication over twenty years later, Halprin filled his diaristic sketchbooks with hundreds of drawings, notes and jottings pertaining to the commission, amid ideas for other concurrent projects and design workshops, and many studies of water. However, Halprin's original concept of a narrative path through four outdoor rooms with major waterfall fountains remained basically the same. His entry dated 7 December 1976 articulated his goal: "The intent is to develop an *integrated* memorial environment which will be a place for people to be involved in many different qualities of experiences related to F. D. R.—solemn, quiet, contemplative, biographical, inspirational, the politics of the new deal, etc. *PLUS* the pure & simple enjoyment of being within an intricate and beautiful garden environment. It should be a place to visit for its own sake for personal enjoyment—as well as for its national significance."[36]

Sketches dating to 1976 and 1977 detail the scale and texture of the stone blocks, and how the water should emerge and run over wall surfaces [225, 226]. He noted sound decibels of different amounts of falling water. He even scored a visitor's passage through the park with places for experiencing the water, sitting and reading inscriptions. Drawings from 1991 show Halprin still fussing over the precise

placement of various elements, seeking to fine tune the integrated whole. These later sketchbooks are filled with visible musings on how the water should fall in each cascade.

From the beginning, water in various states of activity was planned as a primary feature, serving both practical and symbolic purposes. Roosevelt's associations with water included his love for the sea and sailing; his service as assistant secretary of the Navy (under President Woodrow Wilson); the source of his polio; and his swimming treatments at Warm Springs, Georgia, where he died. On a practical level, the memorial's rushing water masks the noise of jets flying to and from the nearby airport. As Halprin noted in preparation for one of the national committee meetings: "The site carries the burden of an incredibly difficult environmental pollutant. Aircraft jet noise… generates enough decibels to prevent conversation, much less the poetic and reverent contemplation appropriate for a memorial. The use of falling water as a 'white noise' can… ameliorate the problem."[37] Water also enlivens the stark roughness of the pavement and massive walls constructed from over six thousand tons of pinkish granite.

To experience the memorial, the visitor strolls through four landscaped rooms—each with a slightly different, dramatic water feature—symbolizing both Roosevelt's election to an unprecedented four terms and the Four Freedoms that he immortalized in his 1941 State of the Union address as the right of all citizens: Freedom of Speech, Freedom of Worship, Freedom from Want, and Freedom from Fear. At the entrance to the park are the words: "This generation has a rendezvous with destiny," followed by the first open area devoted to The Early Years 1932–36. Dominating the space is a broad sheet of water falling from the top of a wall about twelve feet high. In the second room associated with Roosevelt's second term, Social Policy 1936–40, visitors encounter George Segal's popular *Bread Line* and *Fireside Chat* sculptures, as well as an installation by Robert Graham, in front of a stepped cascade waterfall, reminiscent of dams built by the Tennessee Valley Authority under Roosevelt [227].

After passing through a restful garden with a small water shoot, one discovers jagged boulders and the most turbulent and cacophonous waterfall symbolizing the disruptive force of The War Years 1940–44 [228]. Neil Estern's statue of Roosevelt, seated besides his dog Fala, presides.[38] Leonard Baskin's funeral cortège bas-relief installed over a reflecting pool and Estern's portrayal of Eleanor Roosevelt as the first United States delegate to the United Nations signal one's arrival at the last, most spacious room devoted to The Seeds of Peace 1944–45 and the Four Freedoms. Here the visitor confronts the grand waterfall finale, where water exuberantly creates its finest splashing spectacle. Few resist the chance to step on to large stones dotted in the fountain pool to experience the water more closely.[39] While a visitor is put in touch with the history of Roosevelt's twelve-year presidency through his words and the somewhat literal sculptural narrative, it is the orchestration of the enduring qualities of water that makes the F. D. R. Memorial so rewarding. It was in this vein that Halprin described his vision of a visit to the memorial: "F. D. R. was multi-faceted and so must the memorial be… the whole environment of the memorial becomes sculpture: to touch, feel, hear and contact—with all the senses."[40]

After those modeled on Europe's grandest or on nature, what can memorial fountains of the future hope to achieve? Perhaps their goal is the ethereal quality of cloudlike vapor beckoning upward, like each day's changing tableau in the skies. For the new national United States Air Force Memorial (to be on an axis with the Washington Memorial), architect Emilio Ambasz, one of eight selected in 1994 to compete in designing the memorial, has proposed swirling clouds of mist hovering over a circular plaza, on to which are projected changing images of the earth, as seen from outer space. Thus, he envisions that visitors would feel that they are flying above the veil of clouds while glimpsing our world beyond. The fluidity of water is bound by the laws of gravity, but mist, and flight technology, briefly defy gravity. Ambasz's vaporous fountain addresses the tip of a sleek triangular memorial building, dynamically tilted to convey skyward thrust. On its runwaylike roof are statues

representing all levels of air force personnel, who, as they approach the highest point, sprout wings to take off into the heavens, above the puffy clouds of mist in the plaza fountain.[41]

It is a memorial dedicated to uniting the elements of earth, water and air, while it acknowledges the soaring achievements of human technology and universe-conquering ambition. Reaching from sources deep to lofty heights, commemorative fountains will long reverberate as amplifiers of memory and aspiration.

Marilyn Symmes

∧ 227 Memorial visitors beside the waterfall cascade in the second room of the Franklin Delano Roosevelt Memorial, Washington, D.C.

∧ 228 Water tumbles over the rusticated red granite blocks in the third room of the Franklin Delano Roosevelt Memorial.

fountains as
Entertainment
and
Pleasure

"…Happy in all that
ragged, loose
Collapse of water, its
effortless descent

And flatteries of spray…"

Richard Wilbur, "A Baroque Wall-Fountain
in the Villa Sciarra," 1956

< 229 Avenue of the Hundred
Fountains, Villa d'Este, Tivoli.
Garden design by Pirro Ligorio,
1550–72. This long terrace with
rows of successive water sprays
and spouts alludes to the Aniene
River, which was partially diverted
to supply the villa.

Over the centuries, the collaboration of artists, architects and hydraulic engineers has resulted in inventive fountains whose waters can sing and dance, drench and delight. From kings and popes to ordinary citizens, fountains have exhilarated the viewer with their imaginative play of water, ingenious sculptures, alluring sound and refreshing spray. A notable example is Gian Lorenzo Bernini's Fountain of the Four Rivers in Piazza Navona [122]. As the work neared completion in 1651, Pope Innocent X asked Bernini if he could preview the fountain before its unveiling. Bernini agreed, but apologized that the conduits were not ready. Satisfied with the work, the pope gave his blessing and turned to leave. Just then, with a great roar, water gushed from the fountain. To Innocent's great pleasure, he declared that the surprise rejuvenated him by ten years.[1]

Fountains can take almost any form and are found in a variety of locations, including private and public parks, royal estates and city centers. Their sculptural subjects can range from classical mythology, like the Bassin d'Apollon at Versailles [142], to the slightly indiscreet (but immensely popular) Manneken-Pis fountain in Brussels [106]. Some of the most intriguing fountains were originally private pleasures, the centerpieces of Italian villas.

In sixteenth-century Italy, as urban centers swelled, those who could afford to abandoned the sweltering heat of the city and retreated to the country and its promise of clean, cool air and refreshing waters. Endless delights and surprises waited to be discovered in the gardens of these magnificent villas. Fountains, ranging from small, gurgling spigots to roaring cascades, from water-propelled automata to drenching water jokes, entertained and revitalized the visitor.

One of the most spectacular of these country retreats was the Villa d'Este at Tivoli. Begun by Cardinal Ippolito d'Este when he was appointed governor by Pope Julius III in 1550, the villa took twenty-two years to create.[2] Although the usurpation of land and the partial diverting of the River Aniene to feed his fountains did not endear the cardinal to the people of Tivoli, he continued to focus his money and attention on the creation of his villa as a retreat from the court at the Vatican, after his failed attempts to gain the papal tiara, and as a place beneficial to his health. A former monastery overlooking a steep hill was transformed into the *casino* while Pirro Ligorio, architect, archeologist and renowned antiquarian, was responsible for the garden's concept and design, comprising nine longitudinal axes intersected by thirteen others. Entering at the base of the hill through the Porta delle Colle, one was continually diverted from the garden's main axis throughout the ascent and urged to explore its paths by following the varying sounds of water.

∧ 230, 231 Water Organ Fountain (overall view and close-up of the upper level), Villa d'Este, Tivoli. Designed by Pirro Ligorio, 1568; water jets and falls added later.

> 232 The Fountain of Rome, Villa d'Este. Fountain work by Curzio Maccarone, c. 1568.

∨ 233 Diana of Ephesus, Villa d'Este, completed c. 1568. Water from Diana's breasts symbolizes fertility from springs and rivers nourishing the earth.

∨ 234 View of the Fountain of Tivoli and the Tiburtine sibyl, Villa d'Este. Designed by Pirro Ligorio; fountain work by Curzio Maccarone, completed 1566. A seventeenth-century visitor described the water as moving "so transparently and smoothly as to resemble the sheerest veils floating in the air, and spraying into minute drops that form a dewy cloud."

The fame of the Villa d'Este's fountains spread quickly. Never before had water been manipulated to create the sensual effects achieved here. "Water," as landscape historian David R. Coffin writes, "was molded like clay in the hands of a sculptor, assuming a variety of shapes, including vertical jets, fan sprays [13], and even the Este lily.… Not only did water express a variety of visual forms, but it also was controlled to convey a variety of sounds. Contemporary accounts speak of the water jets of the Fountain of the Dragons not only changing in form from single tall jets to wide-spreading umbrella-like sprays, but uttering different sounds like the gentle patter of rain or the sharp explosion of a musket."[3] Visitors included ambassadors from Moscow and Poland, Japanese princes, European nobility, intellectuals and artists. Later recounting what they had seen, the beauty of the garden with its many marvels became legendary.

The Fountain of Tivoli, the most prominent of the works and key to the garden's iconographic program, has a large oval basin surrounded by a wall punctuated by arches and niches containing nymphs [234]. The water flowing from their urns is overwhelmed by the cascade that forms the centerpiece of this fountain. Its semicircular form stretches the water, creating a veil, behind which one can walk along a narrow and wet passageway. Moving through the cavelike darkness behind this curtain of water, wet with its spray and deafened by its roar, the visitor has the unique experience of becoming part of the fountain. Above this cascade sits the figure of the Tiburtine sibyl with her son, flanked by river gods, and at the apex stands the winged Pegasus from whose hoof the water flows through this new Parnassus.

In front of the Tivoli fountain is the Avenue of the Hundred Fountains, each small fountain adorned by carved reliefs and capped by an Este eagle [229]. Its small, controlled jets of water, operating in continuous succession, set a quick rhythm for those walking from the Fountain of Tivoli to the scenographic Fountain of Rome located at the other end of the alley.

The Fountain of Rome, commonly known as the Rometta, has seven stucco-covered brick buildings, raised on a terrace, symbolizing the seven hills of Rome, while below jets of water collected by a small stream recall the River Tiber [232]. The use of water is minimal, a striking contrast to its pendant, the Fountain of Tivoli, but its purpose was to serve as a backdrop for theatrical performances. Its small choreographed jets provided a muted background for the principal action in front.

Theater was one of Cardinal d'Este's preferred entertainments at the villa. A man of cultivated tastes and literary pursuits, the cardinal populated his estate with a select group. Marc-Antoine Muret, the cardinal's resident humanist, wrote: "[the] house [was] crammed by learned men from whose society and conversation one was always learning something… so that [it] might seem to have been an academy."[4] Indeed, one needed to be well read to unravel the complex and multileveled iconographic program of the garden's fountains and statuary that equated the villa at Tivoli with the mythical gardens of the Hesperides and likened the cardinal to the hero Hercules.

For the casual visitor, the garden offered other entertainments. Among the Villa d'Este's great delights were the water-driven automata, exemplified by the Fountain of Nature or the Water Organ [230, 231]. Located at the top of a cross-axis, the fountain's architectural frame supports an abundance of sculpture, including hermes, genii and the Este eagle. Its central niche once housed a figure of the many-breasted Diana of Ephesus who concealed the unusual hydraulic works created by the French engineer, Luc Le Clerc [233]. The water necessary to activate the organ was stored in reservoirs and hidden from sight. As the water was regulated, the organ pipes were played automatically,[5] delighting the unsuspecting visitor.

The Fountain of the Owl, like the Water Organ, was a water-driven automaton. A bronze group of birds sang in a thicket—their song in fact small flutes—until an owl appeared and frightened them into silence.[6] The French chronicler Michel de Montaigne noted that this action would be repeated as often as it pleased the viewer.[7] Although these hydraulic devices had their roots in antiquity, known in the Renaissance through ancient authors like Vitruvius, their resurgence was probably inspired by the Islamic gardens of Spain. Detailed descriptions of the Generalife at Granada [297] were written in the sixteenth century and watery features of that garden surfaced at Tivoli, lending an exotic flavor.[8] However, it took the talents of the *fontanieri*, hydraulic specialists, to implement the mechanical water devices. Curzio Maccarone was responsible for the large fountains, such as the Fountain of Tivoli and the Rometta, while the special ability of Luc Le Clerc, assisted and then succeeded by his nephew Claude Venard, was employed to create such masterworks as the Water Organ and the smaller automata.

> 235 *Water Jokes (Giochi d'Acqua or Trick Fountains) at Villa d'Este, Tivoli*. Etching by Giovanni Francesco Venturini from *Le Fontane del giardino Estense in Tivoli* (Rome, 1691).

The amusements provided by the automata were equaled by the engineering feats of the *giochi d'acqua*, or hidden waterworks, common features in sixteenth-century gardens. Meant to startle, water would suddenly shoot up from the floors of grottoes, or flood benches that visitors rested upon. The mechanics of these water surprises fascinated the recipient and provided refreshing respite from the heat.

At the Villa d'Este, water jokes ranged from the subtle to the outrageous. The Fountain of the Dragons, situated in the center of the garden, shows a sculpted dragon surrounded by a variety of water jets [236].[9] Encircling the fountain were curved stairways. As one placed a hand on the rail to ascend the steps, water flowed over it, a cooling surprise. In contrast, the later seventeenth-century etching by Giovanni Francesco Venturini [235] shows visitors fleeing as gardeners, hidden from sight, open the faucets, allowing jets of water to rain down upon the unsuspecting company.

Although the sheer spectacle of the fountains at the Villa d'Este—their music, their mechanical magic, and their jokes that surprised yet delighted—offered an unparalleled experience for the visitor, other villas challenged Tivoli's fame with their splendors. The Medici Villa at Pratolino, near Florence, begun in 1569 and completed in 1589 by the mannerist architect Bernardo Buontalenti, for Duke Francesco I de' Medici, was designed to surpass the Villa d'Este.[10] Its plan is T-shaped with the palace in the middle of the long north-south axis. Fountains are situated at the ends of this axis with the Fountain of Jove at the north and at the south, the Basin of the Laundress where a young woman wrings out her white marble cloth. Pratolino's numerous grottoes, located in front of and inside the palace itself, were famous for their *giochi d'acqua* and automata. Michel de Montaigne was amazed by the waterworks and wrote: "By a single movement the whole grotto is filled with water, and all the seats squirt up water to your backside; and if you fly from the grotto… it may let loose a thousand jets of water from every two steps of that staircase."[11] The well-known Grotto of Fame and Pan at Pratolino combined hydraulic automata with illusionistic landscape paintings to create its theatrical setting. Within this grotto, music played and mechanical figures enlivened the scenes

∧ 236 Fountain of the Dragons, Villa d'Este. During his visit in 1646–47, the Englishman John Raymond remarked that the fountain's dragons "vomit forth the water with a most horrid Noyse."

∧ 237 Fountain of the Giants, Villa Lante, Bagnaia, near Viterbo. Designed by Giacomo Barozzi da Vignola, 1564–86.

< 238 Cardinal's Table, Villa Lante. Designed by Giacomo Barozzi da Vignola.

populated by automated animals who bent their heads to drink while spectators were subjected to the water jokes described by Montaigne. It was this combination of grottoes, *giochi d'acqua* and automata that made Pratolino such a curiosity, and its fame spread throughout Europe via published travel journals, diaries and engravings.

Unlike the villas at Tivoli and Pratolino, distinguished by their mechanical and hydraulic works, Cardinal Gianfrancesco Gambara's Villa Lante at Bagnaia, near Viterbo, was renowned simply for being the most beautiful villa in Italy. Situated within a parklike setting, an abundance of pure spring water allows for a variety of fountains with a myriad of shapes as water flows down three terraces along a central axis. At the top, the waters of the Fountain of the Deluge course through that of the Dolphins to spew from the mouth of a stone crayfish—*gambero* in Italian, a pun on the cardinal's name—through a series of interlocking basins that mimic the claws of the crayfish until they reach the Fountain of the Giants, personifications of the Rivers Arno and Tiber [237]. The gray-colored stone used throughout and the flowing water tie together these otherwise diverse fountains. The harmony of parts complements the natural setting, and man's presence is acknowledged without appearing to dominate.

This bucolic impression could hardly prepare the visitor for the lavish banquets and celebrations for which the Villa Lante was famous. On the middle terrace stands the fountain known as the Cardinal's Table [238] where, in imitation of ancient Roman villas, food and drink would have been laid in the summer. This large stone table has a water channel carved into it where bottles of wine could be cooled as guests dined. Gambara's entertainments were so extravagant that he was reprimanded for his foolish expenditures by Cardinal, and later Saint, Carlo Borromeo, while Pope Gregory XIII canceled his annual pension of one thousand *scudi*, reserving it for needier cardinals.[12] Gambara, however,

was only following the tradition that had been revived by Agostino Chigi in the early sixteenth century at his suburban retreat in Rome, now known as the Villa Farnesina. Chigi's legendary banquets included such delicacies as eels imported from Constantinople and relish made from parrots' tongues.[13]

The extravagant playfulness of these Italian gardens was emulated throughout Europe, including at Prince Archbishop Marcus Sitticus von Hohenems's country retreat of Hellbrunn Palace in Salzburg, Austria.[14] Santino Solari was commissioned in 1613 to build a small castle to be used as a summer residence, whose garden was completed six years later. To the north of the castle is the pleasure garden, furnished with an unusual variety of grottoes and fountains, and famous for its *Wasserspiele*, or water games, which recall those at Pratolino, but with a more ominous edge. In the celebrated Grotto of Neptune, encrusted with multicolored shells and spouting sea horses, is the white marble sea god. Triggered by the flow of water, his eyes roll and his tongue sticks out, mocking the visitor. As one stands absorbed before this spectacle, jets of water soak the person standing before Neptune, adding injury to insult.

Hellbrunn's Grotto of the Song of Birds revisits the Villa d'Este's Fountain of the Owl. At Hellbrunn, one hears the birds' singing, mechanically produced by water pressure, but upon investigation the birds do not exist and one's curiosity is rewarded by criss-crossing squirts of water. This grotto denies the viewer the pleasure of seeing the mechanical birds, offering instead a mischievous soaking.

Hellbrunn also includes a Prince's Table in its garden [239]. A long stone slab with a central trough used to cool wine recalls the Villa Lante's, but the crafty archbishop included another feature. When the host wished to enliven the party, a signal released jets of cold water in every direction. The startled guests were forced to remain seated since etiquette demanded that no one rise before the archbishop, whose place remained unaffected by the waterworks. The archbishop, as these few examples demonstrate, seemed to have preferred water games to the simple pleasures and respites offered by garden fountains.

> 239 Garden theater with the Prince's Table, Hellbrunn Palace, Salzburg, Austria. Designed by Santino Solari, 1612–19.

By the end of the sixteenth century, garden fountains were associated with a variety of functions, including dining and theater. In the seventeenth century, the role of fountains was further expanded, reaching its pinnacle at Versailles.

Versailles was celebrated for the fêtes, performances and fireworks—the royal court's principal entertainments—that took place in its gardens, which were large enough to accommodate the crowds who arrived for these events. The inventive and elaborate ephemeral settings for these fêtes often inspired permanent works such as the fountain/theater known as the Salle de Bal or Ballroom [240]. This outdoor oval theater set within a bosquet, or grove, was designed by the landscape architect André Le Nôtre in 1680 and finished five years later. In the center was a small stage, enclosed on one side by five adjacent waterfalls arranged in eight tiers that were decorated with loosely attached shells brought by the Royal Navy from the Red Sea and the Indian Ocean. As the water flowed over them, their sound blended with the music, provided by the musicians on stage, to which the guests of Louis XIV danced.[15] Gilt-lead torchères illuminated the marble dance floor, creating the illusion that one was inside rather than outside in the garden. Within palaces, it was not unusual to find fountains adorning the walls of dining rooms, where water could be used to wash fruit and rinse glasses. With the Salle de Bal, the palace's ballroom was recreated outdoors and walls became fountains, as torchlight mingled with starlight.

With the ascension of Louis XV to the throne, the extensive formal gardens, elaborate bosquets and spectacular fountains gave way to endless flowers, meandering paths and simpler waterworks, as Versailles became a center for the cultivation of rare plants and for botanical study. It was Le Nôtre's seventeenth-century park and not, however, this eighteenth-century garden, that provided the inspiration for the gardens and fountains at Herrenhausen[16] in Germany and for the king of Spain's country residence at Aranjuez. Although both these gardens were developed after the 1680s and well into the eighteenth century, the spectacular play of water that

∨ 240 *The Salle de Bal, Versailles*. Designed by André Le Nôtre. Etching by Adam Perelle from *Vues des belles maisons de France* (Paris, 1693). Inspired by Roman amphitheaters, a fan-shaped bank of stepped cascades, decorated with rock and shellwork, urns and torchères, provided an enchanting backdrop for this outdoor ballroom.

∨ 241 *Great Fountain Waterworks (Ta Shui Fa)*, engraving from the suite *Yuan-Ming-Yuan Summer Palaces and Gardens of the Chinese Emperor Qianlong*, 1786. Fountains designed by Giuseppe Castiglione and Michel Benoist.

> 242 *Stage Design: Garden Scene with a Fountain*, c. 1740–44. Etching with engraving by Johann Andreas Pfeffel after Giuseppe Galli Bibiena, from *Architecture e prospettive dedicate all Maestà di Carlo Sesto*.

> 243 *Garden with Classical Buildings and a Fountain*, 1743. Watercolor with pen and brown ink, by Isaac de Moucheron.

characterized their fountains and their lavish entertainments recalled earlier times and other places.

The Italian and French taste for splendid palaces, gardens and fountains that provided entertainment and pleasure also reached beyond Europe to places as far away as China. As exotic chinoiserie ornament inspired the West in the eighteenth century, Western styles reached the imperial court of Qianlong in Peking (now Beijing). Giuseppe Castiglione, a Milanese Jesuit sent to China as a missionary, was attached to the Imperial Academy of Painting which served the glory and pleasure of the Ching dynasty emperor. In 1747, Qianlong, after seeing a picture of a European fountain, asked Castiglione if he knew of a European missionary who could design one like it. Michel Benoist, a French Jesuit priest who was a mathematician and astronomer with some knowledge of hydraulics, was summoned to make a model. Delighted with the results, the emperor immediately commissioned Castiglione, with Benoist as the waterworks expert, to design his summer retreat, Yuan-Ming-Yuan (Garden of Perfect Clarity) as European-style palaces and gardens recreating Paradise.[17] While both Castiglione and Benoist oversaw the project, they recruited other missionaries who were knowledgable about aspects of architecture, interior furnishings and botany.

Skilled Chinese architects and engineers, as well as hundreds of workmen and craftsmen, also worked to realize the elaborate estate, which developed in stages over the next two decades. By 1768 most of Yuan-Ming-Yuan was complete, although additions were built into the 1780s. The extensive grounds featured Xieqiqu (the Palace of Delights of Harmony), with a water tower to supply its fountains, an aviary, a labyrinth, Changchunyuan (a Garden of the Long Spring), a Bamboo Pavilion, an elaborate water clock, and even Yuanyingguan (an Observatory of the Distant Waters). Although Yuan-Ming-Yuan was never the emperor's long-term residence, it was ideal as his occasional leisure retreat and as a place for imperial festivities. Letters written by the missionaries noted that whenever the emperor planned a visit to his summer palace, workmen would scurry in advance to carry up supplies of water to the

immense basin so that all the fountains could play as the emperor strolled through the gardens.[18] The palace buildings were constructed of the costliest materials, including marble, polychromed terracotta and Venetian glass, and the fountains were powered by intricate machinery, all of which required constant maintenance to look and perform at their best.

In order to immortalize Yuan-Ming-Yuan, Qianlong asked Castiglione to create a series of engravings, subsequently executed under the artist's direction by Chinese students. This exceedingly rare suite of twenty prints, published after Castiglione's death in 1786, is the only contemporary visual record of the magnificent summer palace and its gardens. The images show fantastic pagodalike fountains [241], and an elaborate Horological Fountain with twelve

sculpted figures representing the signs of the zodiac in front of the Palace of the Calm Sea.[19] Though the exotic fountains were Western in conception and design, their style commingled Chinese and European cultural traditions in an extraordinary way. Following the end of Qianlong's reign in 1795, the palace complex and gardens gradually deteriorated. In 1860 French and British troops plundered or destroyed much of what remained, leaving only ruins, some of which still stand.

European gardens with fountains had served as settings for theatrical productions since the Renaissance, but artificial gardens were also recreated on indoor stages. A print after Giuseppe Galli da Bibiena's design for an opera, possibly *Sirita* by Antonio Caldara which was performed in Vienna to celebrate the 18 August 1719 marriage of Maria Josefa of Austria to Frederick Augustus, elector of Saxony,[20] shows an ornate, imaginary scene with a fountain surmounted by a figure of Neptune as its centerpiece [242]. Bibiena, the chief theater architect for the imperial Hapsburg court, was well known throughout Europe as a gifted master of illusionistic perspective and of startling spatial effects. Prints such as this, documenting royal European decorations, festivals, theater and garden designs, and fountains, found their way into the libraries of royalty and nobility throughout the world. It is conceivable that such prints made their way to the royal courts in China, too. The proliferation of prints, drawings and paintings of garden views in the seventeenth and eighteenth centuries meant that the cultivated pleasure and serenity afforded by outdoor fountains could be savored indoors. The jewel-like watercolors by Isaac de Moucheron, a Dutch artist who had spent time in Italy in the 1690s, later transmitted visions of idealized landscapes and garden scenes in a classically inspired Italianate style to northern Europe. One of his prized garden views shows a stately fountain of spouting dolphins in front of a flamboyant rocaille, gazebolike folly [243].

Two centuries later, the grandeur and spectacle of Europe's great garden fountains and the astonishing aquatic feats displayed at nineteenth-century world's fairs inspired the American industrial tycoon and financier Pierre S. du Pont, great-grandson of the founder of the du Pont chemical company, to have elaborate fountains built at Longwood Gardens, his private country estate. In 1906 du Pont acquired the property, thirty miles west of Philadelphia, to save one of America's finest private arboretums from lumber interests, and he proceeded to transform its fields and thickets into one of the country's horticultural treasures.

Trained as an engineer, but self-taught as a garden and fountain designer, du Pont had been deeply impressed by the innovative fountains he had seen in his youth at the United States Centennial Exposition in Philadelphia in 1876, the Paris Universal Exposition in 1889 and the 1893 World's Columbian Exposition in Chicago. His extensive library of gardening books served as a resource for classical designs. His most important catalyst for ideas, however, were his travels in Europe. Captivated by Italian and French gardens, particularly the Villa d'Este and Versailles, du Pont would return home eager to devise traditional-style fountains using modern

technology to create fantastic jetting displays. Rather than use sculpture or architectural ornament as focal points, he enlivened his garden through the decorative activity of water.

In 1907 du Pont laid out the first of Longwood's flower gardens, and his first fountain was a single circular pool sporting a simple jet. Following his 1913 trip to Italy to visit the Villa d'Este and twenty-three other villas and gardens, he designed an open-air water theater, which debuted in 1915. Ten years later du Pont made a tour of fifty French châteaux and gardens. This trip, and the memory of Italian villa gardens, prompted the creation of three elaborate water gardens at Longwood, each employing the latest wizardry in fountain effects. Complex calculations for the hydraulic requirements fill du Pont's personal notebooks.[21]

From 1925 to 1927, du Pont developed his Italian Water Garden with more than six hundred jets shooting nine spectacular variant displays from six blue-tiled pools and twelve pedestal basins [245]. From 1926 to 1927, du Pont and his master electrician Russell Brewer extensively

< 244 Main Fountain Garden, Longwood Gardens, Brandywine Valley, Pennsylvania. Designed by Pierre S. du Pont, 1928–31.

∧ 245 Italian Water Garden, Longwood Gardens. Designed by Pierre S. du Pont, 1925–27.

> 246 Fountain of Nations, Epcot Center, Walt Disney World, Orlando, Florida. Designed by Mark Fuller, 1982.

redesigned the 1915 water theater to provide greater hydraulic power and to accommodate hundreds of lights that spectacularly illuminated the versatile display of jets. A newspaper account of a 1928 public presentation of the water theater declared that the new fountains were "like fireworks, rockets upside down, or weird deep-sea mysteries of coral and fan-shaped fungus, colored in turn ghostly violet or flaming gold, fiery scarlet, yellow, blue and green."[22] The great success of this water feature propelled du Pont to create the Main Fountain Garden from 1928 to 1931, in an area bordered by maple trees and boxwood hedges [244]. Its water effects are reminiscent of the dazzling jets and cascades du Pont had seen at the Villa d'Este [230]. The setting also recalls Le Nôtre's unerringly symmetrical garden designs at Vaux-le-Vicomte and Versailles, combined with du Pont's memories of the thrilling hydraulic spectacle at the 1893 Chicago fair [183]. Du Pont wanted his newest fountain garden to surpass everything he had ever seen. In two long canals, two circular pools and a huge rectangular basin, there are almost four hundred fountain heads and jets, some capable of shooting jets as high as 130 feet. Eighteen pumps circulate ten thousand gallons of water per minute, supplying a fifty-foot waterfall as well as the animated symphony of constantly changing jets. After du Pont's death in 1954, Longwood Gardens were opened to the public. While in their founder's day all the waterworks were controlled by hand-operated systems, they have since been computerized to synchronize light and music with dramatic water action. Longwood's Festival of Fountains is a popular summer attraction to this day, thrilling spectators with a profusion of water acrobatics against a backdrop of luxuriant gardens.

Without any political agenda or special celebration to proclaim, the theatrical waterworks of Longwood Gardens were designed solely to entertain and delight. Their wildly kinetic and colorful water displays anticipated the lavish, attention-seeking fountains created more recently for American performing arts centers, theme parks and resorts. These grandiose water features, like the glittering appearance of star celebrities, help to lure visitors to these recreational attractions.

The fountains at Epcot Center, the Experimental Prototype Community of Tomorrow, the educational theme park at Walt Disney World in Orlando, Florida, make just such an enlivening and entertaining splash. Before his death in 1966, Walt Disney, the master impresario of popular cartoon films and imaginatively plotted theme parks, was more excited about announcing his plans for the utopian Epcot, than he was about building another Magic Kingdom, which was also underway. Disney envisioned Epcot as a showcase for the marvels of new ideas and technologies emerging from American industry and research centers. The park was patterned after the world's fairs, but was created as a permanent place where visitors could always experience a blueprint for the future. Offering amazing entertainment along with opportunities for edifying discovery, Epcot opened in 1982. The park was created by Walt Disney Imagineering, the Disney design company of "imagineers" (architects, designers, and engineers) responsible for all Disney resorts, theme parks and attractions. On the team was Mark Fuller, the "illusioneer" who devised the special-effects fountains. It was at Epcot that he first tried out his vast repertoire of fountain tricks that would

later become the staple of WET (Water Entertainment Technologies) Design, the innovative fountain-design firm Fuller established in Universal City, outside Los Angeles, when he left Disney in 1983.[23]

At the Epcot Center entrance, just beyond the Spaceship Earth geosphere, is the Innoventions Plaza, with its large, oval, computer-animated Fountain of Nations [246]. The most elaborate waterworks feature at Epcot, this fountain sends almost thirty thousand gallons of water (the equivalent of two large swimming pools) cascading down tiered walls, while twelve individual SuperShooter jets propel fifty gallons of water 150 feet into the air. These aquatic feats are accompanied by a display of forty MiniShooters (capable of shooting five gallons a hundred feet into the air) and 212 MicroShooters. To make all this exciting water wizardry happen, there are about four miles of pipes and thirty-five miles of electrical wire installed out of sight. Every fifteen minutes, water ballets have been specially choreographed by computer to synchronize each jet with tunes from movie soundtracks. The Fountain of Nations exemplifies the modern high-tech fountain that utilizes sophisticated engineering and physics expertise to stretch the limits of moving water in order to generate the most exciting visual and aural effects for the viewer.

More playful, human-scaled fountains
are located in the garden outside the
Journey into Imagination Pavilion. For
this space, Fuller invented the LeapFrog
Fountain, the Jellyfish Fountain and Pop
Jets. Similar to the joke fountains that
surprised visitors to European villas or
palaces centuries before, the LeapFrog
Fountain depends upon nozzles in planters
hidden within shrubbery. At unpredictable
intervals, these nozzles project smooth,
arching streams of water over visitors'
heads. Each arch jumps in succession from
planter to planter, looking like a perfectly
formed solid, glass rod, but it readily
shatters into drops, sprays and splashes
whenever people touch it. Once the finger
or other obstacle is removed, the water
immediately resumes its smooth, glassy
appearance. Children delight in trying to
perform the magic trick of transforming the
apparent solid into liquid, but the pre-
programmed leaping water moves quickly
and often eludes its pursuers.[24] The
Jellyfish Fountain ejects three-foot-wide
jellyfishlike blobs of water some twelve
feet into the air, while the Pop Jets send up
jiggling balls of water which collapse like
confetti on the ground or on visitors
standing in the water's path.

While the wonders of Epcot's fountains
have amused tourists from all over the
world, they have also attracted the attention
of businessmen wishing to revitalize city
centers. One Texan developer recruited a
team of top architects, landscape designers
and Mark Fuller's WET Design to create
Fountain Place in Dallas, a refreshing urban
oasis which opened in 1986 [42–44, 295].
For what may have been the first time in
a public city plaza, people could directly
experience the myriad surprises of water
emerging from holes in the pavement, and,
if they chose to, they could walk into the
midst of the water action since there is no
basin or pool wall to hinder them. With the
success of Fountain Place, other designers
have introduced similar playful fountains as
a prominent feature in urban public spaces
[299]. In 1987, the plaza of the Los Angeles
Music Center, a cluster of buildings
devoted to symphonic music, opera, dance
and theater designed by Welton Becket

Associates (1964–69), was enhanced by the addition of a WET Design fountain comprised of a cruciform grid of water jetting from holes around a 1969 sculpture by Jacques Lipchitz [247]. The challenge to WET's project designer Claire Kahn was to create a fountain that would be a scintillating feature for the cultural center without overwhelming the sculpture that was already in place.[25] By day, the banks of jets dramatically dance in unison like a precisely choreographed corps de ballet. Sunlight reflects and refracts through the prismlike jets. The heights of the jets vary, tempting people to run through them when low; however, the jets can suddenly rise to almost fifteen feet. While the computer-programmed fountain sequence looks simple to figure out, the water movement is not as predictable as people think; those who saunter leisurely through parts of the fountain may find they suddenly get very wet. At night, the fountain is skillfully lit from below, the light beams uniting with banks of water jets which rise and collapse around the sculpture, to create a shimmering, kinetic light sculpture.

Another WET Design water spectacle in downtown Los Angeles is the California Plaza Watercourt located at the foot of two office towers, designed by Arthur Erickson Architects. The plaza is oriented around a large pool in front of an open-air stage used for occasional live entertainment events. Most of the time, however, the daily performance consists of a complex panoply of magnificent fountain effects. Designed in 1992, this theatrical waterworks display pulsates with a chorus of jets of varying heights sweeping quickly back and forth across the platform [248]. After the jets, there are rushing cascades, and, then, for the grand finale, there is a large wave that undulates from the back of the stage across the pool to end up lapping over the toes of visitors venturing too close to the pool's edge. Nearby is another fountain that constantly creates tall spiral patterns of water. California Plaza is one of the few major urban settings where one can experience water as a highly versatile, multitalented entertainment—and the show is free!

In 1992 the Jerde Partnership, masters of shopping mall design, completed Universal CityWalk, a recreational attraction for Hollywood's Universal Studios. Conflating popular clichés of stage-set architecture and moviedom, Universal CityWalk is a concourse that is part shopping center and part carnival. In the midst of a variety of stores and restaurants, complete with flashy neon signs, large cut-outs of King Kong and a gigantic electric guitar, is a plaza which also sometimes serves as a stage. When no one is performing, a WET-designed fountain grid of shooting jets provides surprise entertainment and diversion for children [249]. The fountain's display includes a fog feature, which produces a cloud of mist that suddenly obscures the scene.

Fountains have also become prime attractions at major sports arenas. In Kansas City, Missouri, the Royals Stadium Fountain celebrates athletic agility at the Harry S. Truman Sports Complex for professional baseball games. The enormous two-part water display flanks an electronic scoreboard to give spectators a unique visual treat [250]. Starting in 1970, Ewing Kauffman, owner of the American League Kansas City Royals Baseball Club, assembled a design team to develop the new stadium, including architect Kenneth von Aachen and Anthony C. Mifsud, head of New York City's Canal Electric Motors, Inc., who had designed water displays for the 1964–65 New York World's Fair.[26] The stadium opened in 1973. The fountain, comprising six hundred nozzles and colored

< 248 California Plaza Watercourt, Los Angeles. Designed by WET Design, 1992.

∨ 249 Universal CityWalk Fountain, Universal City, California. Designed by WET Design, 1993.

∨ 250 Royals Stadium Fountain, Kansas City, Missouri. Designed by Kenneth von Aachen and Anthony C. Mifsud with Peter Micha, 1973. This view shows the fountain performing to a sellout Independence Day holiday crowd on 4 July 1993.

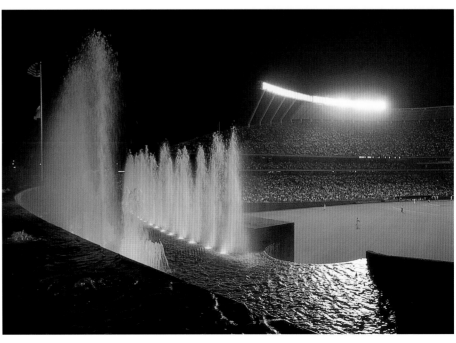

lights arranged in two tiers and placed high in the bleachers, presents an eye-catching program of multicolored water castles, cone shapes, colossal patterns of water sprays, and cascades at every game. Whenever the home team hits a home run, the fountain engineer activates the controls creating a spectacular spiraling column that grows taller as the fans' cheers and applause grow louder.

The focal point at Centennial Olympic Park in Atlanta, Georgia, site of the 1996 Olympics, was the Fountain of Rings. EDAW, Inc. with William Hobbs Ltd Architectural Fountains designed the fountain with 251 water jets and four hundred fog jets forming the five interconnecting circles, twenty-five feet in diameter, of the Olympic logo. At night during the Olympics, the fountain jets were illuminated in shades of amber and red. Like Epcot's Fountain of Nations, which synchronizes water action to music, the Fountain of Rings also features a changing program of sequential light and water play performed to music such as Tchaikovsky's 1812 Overture Finale or Vangelis's "Chariots of Fire." This fountain remains today as a highly popular recreational destination for Atlanta residents and tourists.

In Las Vegas, America's gambling mecca in the Nevada desert, water and glitzy neon have transformed The Strip, the casino-lined Las Vegas Boulevard, into a scene of dazzling opulence unlike any other in the world. Without the nearby

Colorado River and Hoover Dam abundantly catering for all of Las Vegas's excessive water and power needs, the arid area would never have developed into a city capable of supporting over a million residents plus thirty million tourists annually. While popular 1950s casinos capitalized on the desert theme with such names as the Desert Inn, the Sands, the Dunes and the Sahara, recent mega-resorts, such as the Luxor, a casino-hotel shaped as an immense, glass Egyptian-style pyramid, have become grandiose fantasy theme parks, offering the ultimate in synthetic settings. Caesar's Palace, the casino inspired by the extravagant luxury of the Roman Empire just before its fall, was among the first resorts to appropriate sparkling European-style fountains into its lavish décor.

Since 1989, when entrepreneur Steve Wynn, chairman and chief executive of Mirage Resorts Inc. opened the Mirage Casino as a paradise oasis of the South Seas, the entertainment value of water has been developed to new heights—literally, as well as in terms of extreme showmanship. In the Mirage Casino's entrance lagoon, visible from the street and sidewalk, is a fifty-nine-foot-high mountain covered by a cascade during the day. At night, the waterfall is transformed into a live volcano erupting every few minutes, by spewing a hundred feet into the air water jets and steam illuminated in reds and oranges to mimic fiery lava [251]. The volcano extravaganza

concludes each performance with real flames descending to the lagoon surface. Anyone who might be concerned about water conservation is assured that the vast amounts of water used in this amazing spectacle are recycled after each eruption. Details about the design development and process behind such casino fountains are usually cloaked in secrecy since competition in the mega-resort business is so intense. All aspects of designing Mirage Resorts casinos—the hotel buildings, interiors, landscaping and special attractions—are overseen by Wynn's own design division called Atlandia, but Wynn himself is credited with providing the vision behind the casino theme concepts, including the Mirage volcano.

While the Mirage presents an illusion of one of nature's most awesome phenomena, at another casino, the sidewalk water attraction is based on a manmade use of water. The New York-New York Casino, designed by Jon Jerde (Jerde Partnership), opened in 1996. New York City with its skyscrapers and other famous sights has been transplanted to The Strip. The Brooklyn Bridge and a Coney Island roller coaster, with yellow taxis as the cars, are arranged around New York Harbor complete with the Statue of Liberty and tugboat fountains with large nozzles spouting graceful arcs of water.

Another billion-dollar Mirage mega-resort is scheduled to open in the summer of 1998. Bellagio, named after the scenic northern Italian lake town, will aim to recreate an atmosphere of deluxe European sophistication. Bellagio's three-thousand-room casino-hotel will look out on to a landscaped garden with a nine-acre lake featuring a $30 million mile-long water ballet of jets, devised by Atlandia with WET Design. Such awesome fountains and colossal water features are certainly far bigger and more expensive than any ever created before. Yet the ambition driving such fountain designs is not unlike that of Louis XIV's monumental efforts to bring water to Versailles for the elaborate fountains there. Louis XIV also spent vast sums on impressive fêtes with water spectacles and fireworks. Today the commercial profit motive has replaced royal pomp and vanity, and fountains have become part of a shrewd business strategy that utilizes the novel, the dramatic and the ostentatious to create irresistible attractions for hordes of holiday seekers.

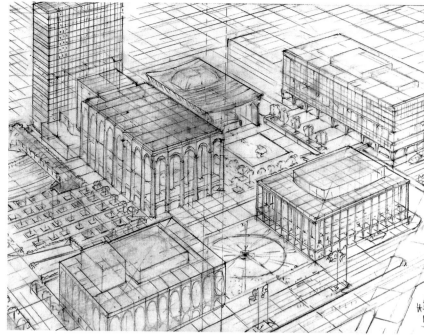

While elaborate water displays provide a palpable air of reality for the creation of artificial paradises, fountains can also be used as glittering chandeliers to adorn grand outdoor drawing rooms or salons. One important example of this kind of fountain is the centerpiece at New York's Lincoln Center for the Performing Arts, promoted in the 1950s by Robert Moses, a powerful city official, and by John D. Rockefeller III, along with other important cultural leaders. Three buildings, the New York State Theater, the Metropolitan Opera House and Avery Fisher Hall, define three sides of the elegant Lincoln Center Plaza that fronts on to busy streets. Having a fountain as a central feature was an idea that first appeared in an early master plan devised by a team of architects headed by Wallace K. Harrison, who had also been instrumental in the designs for Rockefeller Center and the United Nations Complex.[27] Marcel Breuer, the Hungarian-born international-style architect based in New York, and Sven Markelius, a Swedish architect and urban planner who had participated in the designs for the U. N. buildings, were among the advisory architects who suggested that the Lincoln Center Plaza should be modeled on such elegant European squares as that of San Marco in Venice (an enclosed plan) or Michelangelo's Piazza del Campidoglio in Rome (a plaza open on one side). The latter ultimately became the formal inspiration for the finished space. Drawings from 1955 by Harrison's office show a fountain as the pivotal accent in a

circular space radiating to the main buildings and the street [252]. The buildings facing on to the plaza were designed by different architects over the course of several years. A perspective drawing of 1960 shows the final site plan with a more rectangular plaza [253], anticipating the Lincoln Center that was realized several years later. Philip Johnson, with Richard Foster, was the architect of the New York State Theater (1964), now home to the New York City Ballet and New York City Opera, located on the plaza's south side. Johnson and Foster also designed the fountain [254].

< 251 Volcano, Mirage Casino, Las Vegas. Designed by Steve Wynn and Atlandia, 1989.

< ∧ 252, 253 *Preliminary schemes for Lincoln Center for the Performing Arts, New York: Aerial View at Night, c.* 1955 and *Perspective View*, 1960. Designed by architect Wallace K. Harrison. Architectural renderings by Hugh Ferriss.

∧ 254 Lincoln Center for the Performing Arts Plaza, New York. Fountain designed by Philip Johnson with Richard Foster, completed 1964. Ezra Stoller © Esto.

< 255 Mosaic Fountain,
Grosser Garten, Dresden, Germany.
Designed by Hans Poelzig, 1926;
restored 1995.

∨ 256 Fountain of Wisdom,
Seattle Public Library, Seattle,
Washington. Designed by
George Tsutakawa, 1959.

∨ 257 Naramore Fountain,
Naramore Park, Seattle. Designed
by George Tsutakawa, 1967.

> 258 Revolving Torsion Fountain,
St. Thomas's Hospital, London.
Designed by Naum Gabo, 1972–75.

By the mid-1950s, Philip Johnson, who had been director of the Department of Architecture and Design at New York's Museum of Modern Art, was already well known as the designer of the oasislike Rockefeller sculpture garden at the Museum of Modern Art, which includes understated fountains. He was also working with architect Ludwig Mies van de Rohe on the Seagram Building (1958), one of the icons of modern architecture. It was Johnson's experience on the Seagram project that partly molded his ideas about using a fountain to benefit the Lincoln Center Plaza. As he once said: "I am into water and light. Anything that moves, anything that makes a focal point, anything that is exciting in time. I always wanted fountains at Seagram's and not sculpture. Mies and I never agreed on that.... I was the one who always pushed for fountains.... I think the noise, the accidental sprays, the lights, the fact that it's living is what interests me. I feel about it the way I do about processionals. It's an emotional feeling that is in space—the way to decorate that space to enhance it, that is unique."[28] Johnson believed fountains fill spaces, touching

one's senses with their changing noise, energy and coolness, similar to the way glowing fires in fireplaces fill rooms. He realized that flickering fountains can add their own movement to architecture, and, like magnets, they also attract people.[29]

The Lincoln Center's circular fountain, which contains a dense network of 577 nozzles and eighty-eight spotlights and is over forty-two feet in diameter, was completed by the mid-1960s. It was programmed (in pre-computer days, by tape) to provide a constantly jumping water dance,[30] variations of which would later be echoed in fountains by WET Design and others. Besides visually and spatially complementing the modern facades of the three surrounding theaters, the sparkling fountain, over thirty years later, has become the lively heartbeat of the plaza, where people enjoy lingering before and after performances.[31]

While providing diversion or an urban accent, some fountains are intended to be viewed as works of art offering aesthetic pleasure. Many modern artists and

designers have exploited water's malleability as a sculptural element interacting with hard, static metal or stone shapes in order to explore new avenues for artistic expression. In 1926, Hans Poelzig, the German architect of Berlin's Grosses Schauspielhaus (or Great Theater, completed in 1919 and later demolished), designed a Mosaic Fountain for Dresden's International Exposition of Garden Design. The fountain has been restored to its original location in one of the city's main parks, the Grosser Garten [255]. Inspired by ancient Egyptian lotus columns, the fountain recalls the tall, light sculptures Poelzig had earlier devised for the Grosses Schauspielhaus foyer. As the fountain's multicolored tile pattern radiates upward like a growing plant, delicate veils of water fall over the tiers resulting in an overall shimmering effect of flowing light.[32]

The fountains by the Seattle-based sculptor George Tsutakawa draw upon his heritage of Asian art and philosophy, where every part of nature lives in harmony with the whole. As he explains: "My fountain sculptures are an attempt to unify water—

the life force of the universe that flows in an elusive cyclical course throughout eternity —with an immutable metal sculpture."[33] In his first fountain, the Fountain of Wisdom at the Seattle Public Library (1959), Tsutakawa stacked hollow, abstract forms partly inspired by *obos* (Tibetan rock mounds), with water spilling over the edges [256]. The flowing water is alternately separated and united by each of the sculptural shapes, evoking the harmonious balance of the world's liquid and solid elements, and the integration of one life cycle with another.[34] In Tsutakawa's view, all sculptural fountains of the West remain fundamentally unchanged since Roman times: "They do two things: they either squirt water at the sculpture or the sculpture squirts water at you."[35] Tsutakawa wanted his fountains to flow quietly, rather than jet, spout or gush dramatically, thereby presenting viewers with an aesthetic experience that transports immediate temporal spectacle into a more spiritual realm. Other Tsutakawa fountains, such as the Naramore Fountain, located in a small park beside a major Seattle freeway,

∧ 259 Archimedes Screw, 's-Hertogenbosch, The Netherlands. Designed by Tony Cragg, 1993.

∧ 260 Carnival Fountain, Basel, Switzerland. Designed by Jean Tinguely, 1977. In the foreground is the fountain sculpture called Rocker. In the background, from left to right, are Wagger, Fountain, Spider, and Whistler.

> 261 Blair Fountain, Riverfront Park, Tulsa, Oklahoma. Designed by Athena Tacha, 1982–83.

suggest hardy plant growth that survives even the harshest urban environment [257]. The sculpture recalls leaves and petals symmetrically arranged on a strong central stalk; the water suggests the source of regenerative strength.

While most sculptors devise static forms with water as the animator, others have created emphatic fountain structures that also move. Naum Gabo's Revolving Torsion Fountain of the 1970s, installed in London just across the River Thames from Big Ben, harks back to his early constructivist experiments with non-objective form and structure [258]. In his *Realistic Manifesto* of 1920, Gabo declared that space is "a structural part of the object… conveying volume" and that by incorporating an "experience of time," a form reveals an "experience of life." Adapting the shape of an open spherical tetrahedron, the fountain evolved from clear plastic models of 1929 (now at the Tate Gallery, which also owns the fountain). These models emphasize the diaphanous quality of defining open spaces with taut filaments of nylon or steel. Decades later, Gabo ingeniously recreated the effects of a tracery of lines on his stainless-steel fountain by placing 140 water jets along the structure's curved edges. Futher kinetic energy is created by the ten-minute revolution of the fountain during which the light changes as the angles shift. Integrating abstract geometric form, water as torquing lines of light, and a slow, turning movement, Gabo defines the fountain space with a strong sculptural anchor cloaked within the constantly dissolving materiality of water.

The Swiss sculptor Jean Tinguely, impresario of quirky kinetic contraptions that playfully squirt water in various directions, created a captivating fountain installation in Basel [260]. His Igor Stravinsky Fountain (1983), a collaboration with Niki de Saint-Phalle in Place Igor Stravinsky by the Centre Georges Pompidou in Paris, is one of the most colorful and exuberant fountains in the world [268, 269].

Tony Cragg's Archimedes Screw (1993), a large mechanical fountain in 's-Hertogenbosch, The Netherlands, utilizes water neither for its dematerializing effects, nor for its amusing, carnivalesque qualities [259], but returns instead to the fundamentals of water hydraulics. When Cragg, a British artist who resides in Germany, first received the commission for this sculptural fountain, he was hesitant to accept. He believed: "Fountains are decorative, that's a fact of cultural history. They rely on the decorative 'translation' of nature: demonstrating the power of water in an attractive manner. That causes problems for the sculptor, because he isn't interested in making ornaments but autonomous artworks."[36] The prospect of inventing a new type of fountain, however, became more tantalizing to Cragg when he conceived the idea of using a monumental Archimedes Screw, the water-moving machine shaped as a cylindrical helix, said to have been invented by the third-century B.C. Greek scientist and mathematician Archimedes. As an artist known for his sculptures inspired by utilitarian tools and objects, Cragg devised his Archimedes Screw as an inclined, industrially pristine, spiral-grooved metal cylinder moving large quantities of water upward as it turns, causing water to shower from its tip. Since this mechanical fountain reveals how it works, it removes the threat that it could be deemed merely "decorative." Instead, the fountain celebrates human ingenuity in devising a means to move the earth's most plentiful element more easily. However, Cragg's fountain, sited in a pond, also alludes more specifically to the spiral pumps that helped to reclaim the Netherlands from water, thereby transforming the landscape.

Two fountain installations in the United States—one by artist Athena Tacha and the other by artist-architect Maya Lin—both evoke the earth's topographic terrain, although Tacha's work is about the domain of water, and Lin's piece relies on the immutability of granite. Tacha's Blair Fountain (1982–83) in Tulsa, Oklahoma, is set within a small recreational lake formed by damming the Arkansas River. Maximizing the advantage of the river's continual flow, terraced waterfalls ring the basin containing the Blair Fountain, which exalts the phenomena of moving water as it courses downstream [261]. Tacha designed an island of concentric pools of varying

heights, ranging from four to sixteen feet above the basin. Jets shoot up from the center of the upper pools as well as from a ring around the central pools. Tacha's design was inspired by natural flow or wave patterns, such as concentric ripples generated by drops on a water surface, bubbling mud pools, or curved terraces of mineral deposits formed by water dripping over millennia, as at Minerva Springs in Yellowstone National Park. In Lin's Sounding Stones (1996), four sequentially placed granite blocks mark a path in the pedestrian plaza of the Federal Courthouse in Lower Manhattan, bordering on Chinatown. In Chinese culture, rocks shaped naturally by water forces over the millennia are prized as "scholars' rocks" or "philosophers' stones," and represent a naturally derived microcosm of the universe, and thus constitute an ideal vehicle to prompt contemplation.

Lin's deliberately human-scaled fountains invite one-on-one interaction that results in an intimate aesthetic experience based on her subtle modulations of materials with light, sound, texture, scale and placement. Each block exhibits rough-cut sides—suggesting the subtle undulations of topography—as well as highly polished

surfaces. On top of the lowest block, one can see a small basin filled with water bubbling over the rim. Otherwise, the water is not readily visible from the exterior, flowing instead inside the cavern within each block. When one stands close by, one hears the gentle sound of falling water, but to see the water, one has to look through a viewing hole. These were bored to enable one to glimpse at the water spilling inside the stone, and to allow one to reach inside and touch the water. Thus, while the fountain exists in a public setting, the experience of the water is intensely private.[37]

Part of the enduring appeal of fountains is the way designers orchestrate water's effects for our pleasure, so that we anticipate the next wondrous display as we are enjoying the present one. The spectrum of fountain design ranges from recreations of pleasurable paradises and waterworks extravaganzas to distinctive, contemplative experiences. In every case, water is the animator, the design element continually affected by changing light, physical forces, and weather conditions so that the viewer's aesthetic appreciation alters with every passing moment. As the artist Jean Tinguely once remarked: "Everything moves continuously. Immobility does not exist."[38] The fountain experience, like the beauty of water, is inevitably transitory, not fixed.

Maria Ann Conelli and Marilyn Symmes

153

The
Fountains at Chatsworth

∧ 262 *The Willow Tree Fountain at Chatsworth*, fountain originally completed by 1693. Wood engraving from *The Stately Homes of England* by Llewellynn Jewett and S. C. Hall (London, n.d.).

From 1687 to 1706, William Cavendish, the first duke of Devonshire, created the grand Palladian manor house and extensive formal gardens which today, with additions and changes by successive heirs, rank as one of the most splendid estates in England. Waterworks and fountains, while not as lavish as those at Versailles or at other villas and palaces on the Continent, were an important feature at Chatsworth from the time of the first duke.

The Willow Tree Fountain, made in 1693, reflected the European taste for ingenious joke fountains that suddenly drenched unsuspecting visitors who had paused to admire its lifelike qualities [262]. According to the Chatsworth accounts, a Mr. Ibeck was paid sixty pounds for an "artificiall tree of brass for a Fountaine at Chatsworth." During a visit to the estate in 1696, Celia Fiennes wrote in her diary: "There… in the middle of ye grove stands a fine willow tree, the leaves, barke and all looks very naturall, ye roote is full of rubbish or great stones to appearance and all on a sudden by turning a sluice it raines from each leafe and from the branches like a shower, it being made of brass and pipes to each leafe, but in appearance is exactly like any willow."[1]

By the time Joseph Paxton was made head gardener of Chatsworth by the sixth duke of Devonshire in 1826, the Willow Tree Fountain had long fallen into disrepair, so Paxton arranged for a new one. It was composed of eight thousand pieces of copper and brass and had eight hundred jets of water hidden in the branches and leaves.

Paxton erected the fountain, not in the original location in the center of the Ring Pond, but in a partially concealed glade fashioned from Paxton's new naturalistic rock works. It was to be an artificial element in the middle of the artfully arranged natural landscape. A new reservoir was dug on top of the hill to supply water to the fountain, which was later dubbed a "squirting tree" by the delighted thirteen-year-old Princess Victoria, who was to become queen of England in 1837.

The joke element did not fade with time. In his book *On Foot Through the Peaks* (1862), James Croston wrote: "We were in a party of which one member was a 'know all'. When we reached the willow, the gardener, with a malicious smile, appealed to our 'expert' for the name. Certainly he would just examine the formation of the leaf [to identify it]. No sooner said than done; he… stepped on the grass, and in an instant a thousand jets were pouring their… streams upon his head. He [made] his escape all dripping and drenched, and, disappearing among the [bushes] we saw him no more."[2] Since then, the Willow Tree Fountain has been replaced twice, most recently in 1983.

The Cascade is a dramatically splashing and rushing water feature, originally designed in the 1690s by Grillet, a pupil of André Le Nôtre. Several years later, this Cascade was dug up and extended, and a Temple Pavilion designed by Thomas Archer was placed at the top of the Cascade in 1703 to provide a dramatic vista from the east side of the house. Around 1830, Paxton supervised the relaying of more than half the Cascade to align it better with the house. A new aqueduct, filling new ponds and reservoirs, and pipework were built to supply it. Later in the nineteenth century, some criticized the Cascade, which was rather unique for an English garden. Joshua Major, in his book *The Theory and Practice of Landscape Gardening* (1852) remarked on how the Cascade's combination of "art and nature… thus bringing together gaiety and sombreness, order and wildness… opposes the dictates of good taste." However, pushing the limits of water power and its effects had interested Paxton, and his innovative work on the Cascade and other fountains, as well as his designs for the gardens, still delight visitors today. At the Cascade [264], a sheet of water flows over the series of elegant steps, down from the baroque pavilion to disappear abruptly into a culvert at the bottom (and thus into pipes feeding another fountain, the Sea-Horse Fountain on the South Lawn close to the house).

Paxton's most spectacular fountain achievement was the Emperor Fountain, which rises dramatically from the Canal Pond [263]. The sixth duke had visited Russia where he met Tsar Nicholas and greatly admired the fountains of Peterhof. In late 1843, upon learning that the tsar intended to visit Chatsworth the following year, the duke immediately made plans to create a bigger and better fountain than those he had seen in Russia. Despite there being only six months before the planned visit, Paxton made surveys to check what water levels were necessary to create a colossal jet of water, and began to supervise the extensive hydraulic work. 2½ miles of pipe were laid across the moor to drain water into a newly excavated eight-acre reservoir, 350 feet above the house. The duke wrote in his diary: "I walked up with Paxton to see the new reservoir, half frightened by the immense work." Work continued at night, lit by flares, to ensure completion on time. The duke wrote to Paxton from Brighton on 3 July 1844: "I want to know how the reservoir has borne the rain… you must tell me as soon as 'the Emperor' has begun to play. I do not want him to wait for me or anybody."

The Emperor Fountain was powered by a system of hydraulic technology that was remarkable for its day. The lake could release almost four thousand gallons per minute at peak capacity to activate the gigantic jet. In 1844, *The Magazine of Botany* described the engineering work:

Much consideration was given to the nature of the pipes which were to convey the water from the reservoir, down the sloping hill to the fountain, in order that, while security and strength may be obtained on the one hand, no unnecessary waste of metal may be occasioned on the other. Various hydraulic and pneumatic

experiments were made, so as to arrive at a proper conclusion of the important part of the business. The results appeared so perfectly satisfactory to Mr. Paxton that he at once fixed upon the various forms and dimensions and the work commenced…. Near the fountain was a double-acting valve, which took five minutes to open or close fully, so that shock damage to the pipes could be avoided. The nozzles of the jet were made of brass, and the normal jet would play 267 feet and is on record as having reached 296 feet.

Never before had water jets in England achieved such heights. While Paxton succeeded in completing the fountain by the appointed date to the duke's immense satisfaction, the tsar's visit never took place. The duke was jubilant when he first beheld the Emperor Fountain, as he noted in his diary entry for 16 July 1844: "It is a glorious success, the most majestic object of a new glory at Chatsworth. O Paxton!" Not all reactions were so rapturous, however. In his book *The Theory and Practice of Landscape Gardening* (1852), Joshua Major remarked:

With regard to the grand jet, it is more calculated to surprise than to excite permanent interest. To many it may appear a wonderful example of the height to which water may be thrown; but even in producing this effect, the column is forced too high for its substance. It consequently becomes incapable of retaining its solidity, and it is dispersed by the wind, deluging to a considerable distance the dress ground about it, thereby destroying much of its interest, and becoming in reality a nuisance… no jet ought ever to rise higher than it has power to remain solid, otherwise, instead of falling in drops or bubbles, it is spread into mist or spray, and it is liable to be forced out of perpendicular with the least wind, thereby destroying the effectiveness of the fountain, the form and regularity of which constitute its main beauty.

Almost a century later, on 26 September 1939, the girls of Penrhos College in Wales, evacuated because of the war, arrived at Chatsworth, their home for the next six years. To welcome them upon their arrival, "every fountain, on the Duke's instructions was playing…. The Great Emperor in the Long Lake shot, sparkling into the sky, and as the girls poured out of the coaches… it was a breath-taking fairy-tale landscape that met their eyes."[3]

Stephen Astley

< 263 Emperor Fountain, Chatsworth. Designed by Joseph Paxton, completed 1844.

> 264 Cascade with Temple Pavilion, Chatsworth. Original Cascade designed by Grillet in the 1690s; later renovated under the direction of Joseph Paxton, *c.* 1830.

Swaying, Sprinkling and Splashing

The Fountains of Jean Tinguely

In the early 1960s, the Swiss sculptor Jean Tinguely was already deeply immersed in the construction of complex kinetic sculptures from mechanical parts when he found new inspiration in simple utilitarian lawn sprinklers that spewed out arcs of water from double twirling heads. By combining convoluted rubber hoses with wheels and various sundry decorative metal parts set in motion by an electric motor, he fabricated a special kind of sprinkler that could be wheeled around the garden. In a sense, the emission of water from forceful jets and fanning sprays was a visual expression of the energy generated by the motion below. These effects were multiplied when, in another imaginative stroke, Tinguely placed these fragile, rotating waterworks into fountain pools where they ruffled the surface of the water into infinite patterns.

The City of Basel in Switzerland commissioned Tinguely to create a municipal fountain to enliven a rather desolate plaza below its new State Theater and to serve as a central meeting place. He devised ten mechanical forms for it using rubber tubes, nozzles, wheels, electric motors and the scrap-iron remains of the old theater. These elements possess tremendous personality and verve as they rotate gracefully like a corps de ballet of soloists [260]. Seemingly oblivious of one another, their multiple sprays and jets of water interweave like wisps of chiffon drifting in the wind which wraps them into a whole. During the inauguration on 14 June 1977 of Fasnachtsbrunnen (Carnival Fountain, after the famous Basel Carnival that Tinguely knew well), dancers from the Basel Ballet waded into the shallow pool to interact with their mechanical counterparts. The fountain became an instant symbol for the city, and schoolchildren even sing about the memorable idiosyncrasies of its individual components.

At one end of the 52-by-62-foot basin, the Theater Head, based on the mask for comedy from the old theater's facade, appears to lead the other fountain elements as it rocks back and forth like the conductor of an orchestra. Streams of water pouring from its eye sockets transform its facial features into those of a tragic muse. Unforgettable are the Sisyphean tasks performed by the Sieve, which strains water repeatedly into gentle rain, and the Shoveler, with its metal elbows and cupped hands that busily toss water into the air. As if they are spinning out history, the reel-like wheels of the Rocker and the Wagger recall speeding film projectors, with the latter's long spout swinging with the regularity of a metronome. Plumes of water above the spoked wheels of the Fountain and the Whistler [266] are ejected in an array of strong jets and fanlike sprays that Tinguely referred to as male and female respectively. From opposite diagonal corners, the Squirter and the Turtle (installed later in 1983) send out simple hoselike squirts, the latter from under a hard shell, and the Spider [267], with legs curved in several directions, churns the water with a hoelike protrusion.

In addition to the fountain's vigorous and pulsating aquatic sounds, the impression of a musical ensemble is enhanced by the scrolls of decorative ironwork that transform several of the hydrokinetic contraptions into hybrid stringed instruments. Their linear black forms are like drawings in air that gain complexity as one is superimposed visually on another, their sprays intermingling with rainbows in the sun. In winter, as the fine mists and dripping water of the Carnival Fountain freeze over the machines, they are encased in marblelike ice and then resemble the classical carved figures of their cousin fountains in Rome.

In his drawings for the fountains, Tinguely claimed he sought a solution between "dream and reality" while establishing a liaison between form and movement. He achieved remarkable dimension and layering in these works on paper simply by varying the thickness of lines executed primarily with either pencil, felt-tipped or ballpoint pens [265]. With detailed mechanical directions, and a scattering of nuts and bolts, the sketches convey the immediacy of creation, even when drawn in retrospect, often as letters to friends. Sometimes the water sprays he drew explode into brilliant displays of fireworks against a night sky.

Not long after the completion of the Carnival Fountain, the French composer Pierre Boulez visited Basel with colleagues and discovered in Tinguely's humorous and radical constructions, and in their special

< 265 *Study for a Figure in the Basel Carnival Fountain*, 1977. Pencil, ink, ballpoint pen, paintstick drawing by Jean Tinguely.

music, the appropriate creative concept for the Place Igor Stravinsky in Paris. This bland plaza, honoring one of the twentieth century's most innovative composers, covers the underground studios of the Institut de Recherche et de Coordination Acoustique/ Musique founded by Boulez. Situated symbolically between past and future— the sixteenth-century Gothic facade of the Église Saint-Merri to the south; the 1977 constructivist building of the Centre National d'Art et de Culture Georges Pompidou to the north; a row of typical old Parisian houses and the institute itself on the east and west— a fountain in this location would add to the theatricality of the Beaubourg area and also coincide with a program initiated by Jacques Chirac, then mayor of Paris, to build more fountains in the city.

Tinguely accepted the commission provided he could work with his long-time collaborator, the French-American artist Niki de Saint-Phalle, known for her balloon-shaped polyester women painted in bright primary colors. Unlike its quirkier antecedent made from scrap materials in Basel, the Igor Stravinsky Fountain more consciously addresses its subject and its location. For the sake of lightening the load over the studios, Tinguely's constructions are fabricated in aluminum painted black, and de Saint-Phalle's brightly painted figures are made of polyester and fiberglass. The shallow water basin, almost twice as long as Basel's, retains an illusion of depth, and its stainless-steel rim serves as a bench for the public. On 16 March 1983, with all sixteen fountain elements in place (divided evenly between the two artists), the Igor Stravinsky Fountain was officially turned on [268].

∧ 266 Whistler, Carnival Fountain, Basel. Fountain sculpture by Jean Tinguely, 1977.

< 267 Spider, with Fountain in the background, Carnival Fountain.

∨ 268 View looking toward Centre Georges Pompidou, Igor Stravinsky Fountain, Paris. Designed by Jean Tinguely and Niki de Saint-Phalle, 1983.

> 269 The Firebird, Igor Stravinsky Fountain. Sculpture by Niki de Saint-Phalle.

"Sas isch e Giigeli Gaageli, Wiigeli Waageli, Ringgeli Ränggeli, Springgeli Spränggeli, Spritzli Bräuseli Gstell, e Spritzli Bräuseli Gstell."

Chorus of "Bim Tinguelybrunne"

"This is a tinkling, creaking, swaying, swinging, curving, climbing, jumping, sputtering, splashing, springing rack, a splashing, springing rack."

Chorus of "By the Tinguely Fountain"

While the Basel sculptures may hint at chamber music, the Paris fountain is like a fully staged theatrical performance paying tribute to Stravinsky's ballets, operas and other vocal and instrumental works and to his collaboration in the colorful folktale productions mounted by Serge Diaghilev's Ballets Russes. Circus sideshows come to mind in the twistings and turnings and splashings and spurtings of the individual performers, whose movements hark back to the animated fountains of the baroque period. Crowned with golden spikes spouting water, the Firebird [269] gazes across the pool to the Nightingale, which spins slowly and makes waves by dipping one wing. The glossy primary colors of these Stravinsky ballet characters, fabricated in the picturesque rotund style of Niki de Saint-Phalle, echo the brightly painted, exposed conduits of the Centre Georges Pompidou as well as the café umbrellas that flank the fountain on the adjacent Rue Brise-Miche.

Tinguely's enormous G Clef overtly sets the musical tone of the composition along with Life, a bountiful cornucopia with four spouts evoking the earthy pagan rituals of Stravinsky's *Rite of Spring*. At the far end, Tinguely's Ragtime (after the composer's jazz composition for eleven instruments) has become a signature motif of the fountain's exuberance, rendered by the artist time and again in drawings that capture its three massive wheels turning in on each other with no less than five nozzles that, in the paper versions, appear to eject sprays of confetti.

Accompanied by the rhythmical gushing and sprinkling of water, the remaining sculptures gyrating in the fountain begin with a Spiral that rotates and flips surface water; next is Love in the shape of spitting red lips; an Elephant spouts through his trunk (Stravinsky once composed an elephant ballet for the Ringling Brothers and Barnum & Bailey Circus); the Diagonal, shaped like a scroll with two jet sprays; a little golden Siren on a blue rock (a later replacement); a Clown's Hat skimming out of reach; a spinning red Heart; Renard, the fox from a Russian burlesque Stravinsky turned into a chamber opera, rendered as an armadillolike spiky barrel that whips the water; a coiling Serpent; Death coupling a Niki de Saint-Phalle skull-cum-nozzle with a skeletal body by Tinguely; and finally the Frog, spouting and adding an occasional croak in the guise of a periodic clanking sound.

In his 1939–40 lectures on the "Poetics of Music" at Harvard College in Massachusetts, Stravinsky spoke of the creative imagination as being "the faculty that helps us to pass from the level of conception to the level of realization." This is compatible with Tinguely's own search to transform dream into reality and to define daily life in terms of change, in the constant movement and flow of mechanical fountains that imitate nineteenth-century machinery. Stravinsky also wrote of drawing inspiration from accidents that he defined as observations of the unforeseen. This phenomenon magically occurs at the Igor Stravinsky Fountain when the viewer steps back to visualize the elements moving in concert as a harmonious whole. For a moment, the multiple sprays criss-cross on high into ethereal Gothic arches against the Gothic windows of the Église Saint-Merri.

Spectators respond with joy to Tinguely's fountains, which have been commissioned by other European cities on a smaller scale. But no one expresses public sentiment better than Basel schoolchildren in a performance of the rousing chorus from "Bim Tinguelybrunne" ("By the Tinguely Fountain").

Paula Deitz

fountains as urban Oases

With its surging waters and spectacular modeling, the Trevi Fountain in Rome epitomises the appeal of urban dwelling. Historically, the functional aspect of drawing water from a source within the city demanded human attendance each day. But for the Trevi, as for so many fountains, the metaphorical dimension has rivaled, if not surpassed, physical measure and artistic standards. In these aspects—functional, social and symbolic—the Trevi has stood as an urban oasis [128, 271], and has served as a prototype for fountain design in the United States to this day.

The word "oasis" derives from the Greek via Latin and applies equally to a verdant area in a desert and to a relief from boredom.[1] The term "urban oasis" implies a sense of respite from the exigencies of the environment, a balm to the tribulations of life in the twentieth-century United States. It also questions the efficacy of any fountain design to mitigate social ills, and the broader notion of vital public space. If the contemporary fountain constitutes an urban oasis, just what does it offer and how does it succeed? And, furthermore, are there any lessons to be learned from fountain design that are more broadly applicable to current urban design practice and the policies behind it?

The ancient oasis provided escape from the aridity of the climate, the sand storms, the inhospitability of the terrain and transport by animal. To the early dwellers of the desert, the oasis was a life necessity, a place where water was sure, if not always plentiful. Its springs supported plants and, on a larger scale, agriculture, and were therefore the source of continuing life. In the wake of water and greenery came trade and more permanent settlements. These were the "cities" in the desert, communities at the intersections of trade routes, that attracted life. The oasis was, in short, an intimation of an earthly paradise cast in opposition to the hardships of reality, and an escape from their burden.[2] Paradise was a garden; water vitalized that garden; the fountain nourished Paradise.

Within the city, the water source addressed different purposes and acquired appropriate forms. Functional requirements could demand a mechanism as simple as a spout and a pool from which the folk could draw for their needs. Where spring, lake or river were far away, channels or aqueducts bore the liquid to its urban outlets.[3] The symbolic dimensions of these fountains increased over time; their makers understood the communicative potential of an urban element to which people came on a daily basis. The popes and the aristocracy capitalized on fountain design in seventeenth- and eighteenth-century Italy, creating works that have both served necessity and narrated stories through the centuries. In some instances, for example in the square of St. Peter's in Rome, the fountains stand as objects in a space which one must traverse to reach the waters.

< 270 Horace E. Dodge & Son Memorial Fountain, Detroit, Michigan. Designed by Isamu Noguchi, completed 1979.

Their purpose, however, is less one of dispensing water than of providing architectural and ceremonial forms which lend life and scale to the vast piazza.

Gian Lorenzo Bernini's Fountain of the Four Rivers in Rome's Piazza Navona conflates in its waters the world's continents, proclaiming the unification of their peoples under the doctrine of Catholicism. Bernini's counterpoised figural composition embodies the exuberance of the baroque period, and in its modeled rockwork [122], it prefigures the naturalistic slopes of the Trevi Fountain executed some eighty years later.[4]

In its architectural and modeled forms, the Trevi Fountain's design conjoins the organic and constructed worlds of stone: pilasters rise from sculptured trees or retreat into natural forms. The base of the fountain's facade, and the transition zone between building and basin, is a mass of scogli, or stone seemingly left in its original

form. Yet each rock is as carefully crafted as the architecture that rises above it. John Pinto, the Trevi's biographer, recounts how architect Nicola Salvi, the fountain's designer, devoted almost maniacal attention toward the forming of these natural rocks: "Salvi took infinite care in the design of the scogli, studying each detail by means of small models in wax and clay and repeatedly rearranging the travertine masses themselves. Moreover, he often climbed out onto the scogli with charcoal stick in hand to sketch particular details onto the surface of the travertine for the stonecutters to follow."[5] The water falls in sheets, animated by gravity and a host of small nozzles, spilling from basin to basin, spreading and gaining in volume with each inferior tier. The arrangement of three basins of diminishing widths—added by Giuseppe Pannini, in opposition to the more naturalistic treatment of Salvi's original design— forces the perspective and exaggerates the apparent depth of the cascade.

∧ 271 Trevi Fountain, Rome.
Designed by Nicola Salvi,
completed 1762.

> 272 Marcello Mastroianni and
Anita Ekberg in the Trevi Fountain,
Rome. From the film *La Dolce Vita*
(directed by Federico Fellini, 1960).

The Trevi's basin penetrates deep into its urban space; roughly half the piazza is aqueous, pushing visitors back to the perimeter of the plaza. Caught in the brilliance of sunlight, the sparkle and spectacle of the fountain's waters contrast markedly with the shaded periphery, augmenting their visual effect. The fountain's primary basin sits approximately six feet below street level; the steps descending to its edge define a shallow amphitheater reinforced by the rings of bollards and railings that protect it. Here urban life is transformed into urban spectacle, in a non-stop performance from dawn to the evening hours. The Trevi design, with its allegorical sculptures and animated flow, provides a focal point for the piazza and magnetic appeal. One can view; one can be viewed. One can be a part of the crowd or alone in the crowd, sheltered in a niche provided by the *scogli*, that appear smoothed as if by the passage of water over the centuries rather than by the artisan's hand.

One can also read the fountain and its piazza—which must be regarded as a amalgamated unit—as an oasis within urban Rome. Visually and haptically they offer relief from the city's estival heat and humidity. The melting *scogli* and flora counter the substantiality of the palace above and beyond the fountain, creating "an exquisite choreography uniting sculpture and architecture, which climaxes in the foamy crescendo of the central cascade."[6] One may even read the juxtaposition of water, rockwork, mythological figures and architectural facade as a gradient of reference from the factual to the dreamed. The architecture and its allegorical personages inhabit a "natural" terrain with water at their feet, suggesting that the human world must have nature as its base, and that oases continue to enrich life, even within cities.

The Trevi figures strongly in our contemporary image of Rome, given its inspiration for a symphonic work by Ottorino Respighi; his 1916 suite *Fontane di Roma* (*Fountains of Rome*) includes "La fontana di Trevi al meriggio" ("The Trevi Fountain at Noon") as one of its four parts. Lush harmonies and swimming themes, like the fountain's own waters, flow into one another in this symbiosis of ancient and contemporary manners. While the work was ill received at the time of its premiere in 1917, it has become a staple of the twentieth-century orchestral repertoire, and one of the best-known Italian compositions of our era.[7]

Since its completion in the eighteenth century, the fountain has been celebrated in countless images and stories, and more recently, in film as well. *Three Coins in the Fountain*, for example, glorifies the waters of Rome and Tivoli, opening with a portfolio of jets, falls and sprays set in a picturesque montage.[8] Miss Maria Williams, newly arrived in Rome and somewhat star-struck, is taken by her new roommates to the Trevi Fountain for the requisite tourist call. You toss a coin in the fountain and make a wish, she is told; the wish must always be the same, however, to return to Rome.[9] "Keep me in Rome at least a year, Mr. Fountain," says Maria tossing in her penny. Surrounded by the hubbub of quotidian Rome, the women begin their life in the Eternal City.

A memorable scene in Federico Fellini's 1960 film *La Dolce Vita* shows the journalist played by Marcello Mastroianni accepting Anita Ekberg's bid to join her in the Trevi's great basin, as she splashes abstractedly under the cascade [272]. At the end of the scene, there is silence, and, as the camera moves backward, we witness not only a Trevi stilled, but a poignant rendering of the "tabloid reporter adrift in meaningless cafe society."[10] By that silence and in that absence, we are forced to comprehend the tremendous effect—both sonic and visual—of water gushing over the stone. When Mastroianni died in December 1996, the Trevi was again hushed temporarily in tribute to his memory and his silenced voice.[11]

Waves pulsing outward from the Trevi reached the banks of the Mississippi River two and a half centuries later. As part of urban renewal plans for New Orleans there would be a magnificent public set piece, like the Trevi, wedding fountain and plaza. It would be called St. Joseph's Fountain, or the Piazza d'Italia, in case the reference to the Italian-American community it acknowledged might be missed [273].[12] Located at the base of a high-rise office

tower, and intended to be an extravagant center for hotel and commercial development, the fountain would be designed by architect Charles Moore (of the Urban Innovations Group based at the University of California in Los Angeles) with August Perez Associates of New Orleans.[13] It was to be one of the most extreme, and most controversial, fountains of our era.

In 1975 the project began; the work was more or less complete three years later. Unlike the Trevi, which abutted a real palace, Charles Moore and company had to construct the scenic backdrop for their waterworks from scratch. By the late 1970s the historicism that accompanied postmodernism already held sway, and Charles Moore was himself one of its most baroque proponents. In many prior works, Moore's elaboration tended to be spatial rather than iconographic, using insubstantial planes of gypsum board to articulate complex configurations of form and space. In New Orleans, he again used thin stucco walls—painted the reds and ochres common to Italy—to create an intricate *scaena* of several layers, in the best baroque theatrical tradition. From cutouts in these walls, water was extruded in pencil-like jets, testing the limits of nozzles and filtration [274]. Moore's involvement with water and architecture was already several decades old at the time the Piazza d'Italia was designed, and some years earlier he had served as project designer for Portland's Lovejoy Fountain discussed later. In New Orleans, however, Moore left the abstract naturalism of his earlier fountain and looked instead to the architectural history of Europe. With great wit, Moore used water streams to define the flutes of columns with stainless-steel capitals and bases. "Nothing quite like it has even been seen in America before," wrote architecture critic Martin Filler enthusiastically shortly after the fountain's inauguration in 1978. He continued: "Moore and his collaborators have manipulated water in ways that one would scarcely have thought possible. But here it is, washing sensuously over the stainless-steel arch of the Doric wall, sliding down stucco surfaces with surprising richness of texture, dancing in the sunlight in thousands of permutations in the course of a sultry Southern summer afternoon."[14] Here was water used as *disegno*, a medium with which to render, a medium with which to connect the dots. The fountain's overspray cooled those who explored the backstage of this water theater on a sultry summer afternoon, completing visual delight with physical pleasure.

At the center of the composition, a black-and-white relief map of the Italian peninsula, executed in slate, marble and cobblestones, assumed the guise of sculpture and inverted basin, turning upside down the void of the Trevi's three tiers [275]. Sicily, birthplace of the progenitors of much of New Orleans's Italian population, occupied center stage of the map fed by three rivulets representing the Rivers Arno, Po and Tiber. When everything was working properly the Piazza d'Italia was indeed a magnificent place, with the prominence of the almost-kitsch architecture melting under an aqueous blanket.[15] Unfortunately, those instances were rare, and over time the fountain operated less and less.

In part, the problem was the lack of the maintenance necessary to keep such finely tuned waterworks in operation. In addition, the proposed development around the piazza never materialized, and this was compounded by alleged jurisdictional disputes between city agencies over responsibility for the fountain's care. The fountain stayed dry; the stucco cracked; architectural elements fell victim to the environment and to vandalism. Today, St. Joseph's Fountain is a relic from a past, postmodern age, a wonderful if experimental voice now muffled, except, that is, on St. Joseph's Day, when the Piazza d'Italia still offers a dynamic stage for community celebration.

A fountain of far different color and material is the Horace E. Dodge & Son Memorial Fountain in Detroit, designed by sculptor Isamu Noguchi [270, 276]. As happened in so many American cities in the 1960s, Detroit's downtown suffered from population decline and neglected infrastructure. The call for a vibrant civic space in the center city traces back to the 1920s, but no design had ever progressed much beyond the proposal stage. In the

1970s, however, with the infusion of sizable amounts of capital into such mixed-use developments as the Renaissance Center, the impetus for a fresh urban heart grew in momentum. Shortly after his success at the 1970 Japan World Exposition in Osaka [202]—where he created a series of exuberant fountains—Noguchi received the invitation to design a monumental waterworks at the head of Woodward Avenue, to be funded by a two-million-dollar donation from Anna Thomson Dodge.[16] In his Detroit design, the sculptor would invert the quiet animation of his 1964 sunken water garden for the Chase Manhattan Bank Plaza in New York [163]. There, incised as a circle within the bank's upper plaza, the garden's shallow pool and water jets overlay movement and change

< 273 Piazza d'Italia, New Orleans, Louisiana. Designed by Charles Moore, 1978.

< 274 Detail showing the play of water, Piazza d'Italia.

< 275 Piazza d'Italia, model showing the map of Italy.

∧ 276 Horace E. Dodge & Son Memorial Fountain, Detroit, Michigan. Designed by Isamu Noguchi, completed 1979.

∧ 277 Aerial view of the Dodge Fountain, showing the riverfront plaza designed by Isamu Noguchi. Crowds flock to the plaza for the city's summer ethnic festivals, outdoor concerts and Independence Day fireworks.

> 278 Entrance to Paley Park, New York. Designed by Robert Zion and Harold Breen, 1967.

upon the static superstructure of rocks and paving. Although the references to classic Japanese rock gardens such as Ryoan-ji in Kyoto are evident, Noguchi used water flow and a modeled base plane to bring the work conclusively into the twentieth century.

Noguchi's first scheme for Detroit proposed a monumental hollow beam of metal spanning two granite piers, supporting a ring from which dense masses of water shot downward, to be answered by an opposing field of jets thrusting upward. It was essentially a grand entry arch under which only the eye might pass. Noguchi's metaphor was compelling. To the fountain committee, he cast the design as an engine for water, "plainly associating the spectacle to its source of energy—the automobile motor—so closely a part of Detroit." He claimed that "it recalled

and commemorated the dream that has produced the automobile, the airplane, and now the rocket. The machine now a poem."[17] Because the area surrounding the proposed fountain had been assigned to parking—an unsuitable setting for such an artwork—Noguchi suggested that he expand his purview to include the entire project area [277].[18] The Dodge Fountain therefore became but a single element— albeit the central one—in a landscape that embraced an amphitheater, a 120-foot-high twisting aluminum-clad pylon, a stepped pyramid assigned to seating, a restaurant, a riverfront promenade and shopping. Noguchi explained the revised 1973 scheme: "The plaza, viewed as a whole, will present a series of pyramidal shapes: that of the fountain, that of the stepped pyramid of the theater, the blue exhaust stack of the road and the greater pyramid of the festival amphitheater as it rises to the plaza plane." He then played his trump card, no doubt devised to win the heart of the Middle American: "I like to think that the effect will be American, unlike anything elsewhere."[19] He assured the populace that it would not be a monument, but a "people's park."[20] Because the unstable clay soil and existing seawall could not support the volumes of earth required to raise the grade to the desired height, the plaza would be constructed on a deck supported by a field of some five hundred columns. The lower story was assigned to stalls to be used during various fairs, including the city's annual Ethnic Festival.

The fountain's infancy was not an easy one. Skeptics saw the project as an ungainly white elephant. Noguchi's metallic doughnut met few citizen expectations for a monumental fountain, lacking as it did all traditional iconography. The essentially post-and-lintel scheme apparently bothered Noguchi as well. In its revised form the central torus, clad in stainless-steel panels, is supported by two inclined metal cylinders, and a far greater unity is achieved. Despite its comeliness the metallic structure alone is not the sculptor's whole work. Instead, it is the water that makes the fountain [270]. Gone are the river gods, the sea horses and the allegorical deities that dominate classical fountain design. "Today electronically programmed fountains have done a complete about face," asserts a hyperbolic press release for the Renaissance Center. "Today water is the star; decoration is minimal or non-existent."[21]

All well and good if the water performs correctly, but from its opening day on 24 July 1979, the fountain never worked properly, confirming the dire predictions of pessimists. Like the St. Joseph's Fountain in New Orleans, the designer's vision seemed to have superseded technological capabilities. Even before its official inauguration, the fountain had been slated for a renovation, a victim of apathy and vandalism. Costs grew, as did the criticism. Irritation plagued the designers, the builders and the public alike. "What a mess," exclaimed a 1979 *Detroit Free Press* editorial. "If the Dodge Fountain were Detroit's only place to get a drink, the population would have perished of thirst years ago."[22] Maintenance had not been factored into the costs of the fountain, despite being mandatory to keep such a finely tuned engine running. To achieve the symphony of water effects—downward, upward and outward sprays—faultless execution and upkeep were required, neither of which were in great supply.

Fortunately, Noguchi and the fountain had a strong ally, city engineer Louis Klei, who took on the fountain's proper operation as a personal crusade and did not rest until it was all working smoothly. The process took years, and Klei spent many of his free hours trying time and again to make everything work; he was described as obsessed. "I call him Bela Lugosi," said Carl Miles, a construction inspector who worked with Klei. "You see him in the control room at night turning knobs and punching buttons on the computer panel, and he looks just like the Phantom of the Opera. He wants to see it dance."[23]

It had to work, Klei argued, or there was no sculpture. He had adopted Noguchi's own litany: "I look at it not so much as a piece of sculpture like a traditional fountain, but as a water and light show. The water and lights are the sculpture. The actual structure is secondary, it is simply a means to carry the water and lights. The sculpture itself is constantly changing."[24] This was true only if the water design performed correctly, however, which it often did not.

As one would-be wit phrased it: "How do you squeeze some pizzazz out of a lemon that looks like a doughnut?"[25] Only after another renovation in 1988, when fountain technology had sufficiently advanced, did the hydraulics become reliable. To quell anxiety about the spartan quality of the plaza, Noguchi stressed in writing that he had "reserved at least a third of the area for grass or trees."[26]

The Dodge Fountain story has a happy ending, despite the less-than-perfect results of downtown renewal efforts. A sculptural object set on the plane of the plaza, it is indeed a mighty fountain; if it is an engine for water, it is definitely a V-8. Supported by its inclined legs, the ring spews downward a cylinder of water countered by upward-surging jets manipulated in numerous configurations. "The fountain rises eighteen feet in the air," Noguchi wrote, "hovering in a cloud of water, incandescent at night."[27] Computer-controlled, the thirty-one variants offer a visual play of liquid in constant movement.[28]

Photographs record the public's fascination with the dancing waters that draw everyone to them, especially children. As a social design, it has unquestionably

triumphed. Noguchi wrote in a letter to the committee: "Emerging out of classical symmetry toward a controlled asymmetry and the river beyond, the mood is that of the primeval land we inhabit within America. The vista is defined by primary forms which themselves invite participation as places of relaxation: to sit, listen to the sounds of the river, the sounds of voices, or even music and theater at times. There are in effect four such communally enjoyable configurations."[29] As a form, it is a stunning water sculpture supported by a metal armature: "This work is a synthesis of unity and plurality, of balance and imbalance, of fusion and fission, of stability and change of all imaginable pairs of opposites."[30] As a technological accomplishment, however, flaws have marred its performance, and again like the Piazza d'Italia, it may have pushed the limits of hydraulic equipment a bit too far, too fast, too soon. As a sculpture, however, the Horace E. Dodge & Son Memorial Fountain is arguably the most handsome of late twentieth-century fountains, a credit to its design and construction teams and the city to which it was given.[31]

By most standards Paley Park in New York City is really quite small for an urban public park, measuring barely forty-four by one hundred feet. But the impact of the park, designed by landscape architects Robert Zion and Harold Breen, has far

exceeded its meager dimensions [279]. Within the dense fabric of midtown Manhattan, this bounded space of masonry, vegetation and water has been, since its opening, a most welcome palliative to the bustle and crush of urban life. It is at once both an urban oasis and a tranquil void within the city's solid blocks, a place of both retreat and destination. During the week, it is a haven in which to have a drink or grab a sandwich, to read a newspaper or chat with a colleague. On the weekends, the tenor becomes less formal, with more shopping bags and fewer neckties, business suits and high heels in evidence.

The idea for Paley Park traces back to the exhibition "New Parks for New York" sponsored by the Architectural League of New York in May 1963. Zion and Breen Associates proposed a series of "vest pocket parks" to relieve the relentless congestion of the central city. "Where," they asked, "does the midtown office worker in New York spend his lunch hour? Where can he find outdoor relaxation, chatting in the shade of a tree? Where, in our commercial districts, can the tired shopper pause for a moment's rest?"[32] While their immediate influence would be local, with a system of parks that could be built on hundreds of vacant spaces throughout the city, their presence would be pervasive. The parks would offer greenery and shade where formerly there was only concrete and brick. They would offer a brief moment for the individual to be alone within a public setting, seen and physically present, perhaps, but psychologically detached. Chairs rather than benches would be a necessity, allowing visitors the choice to join others or to remain alone. Water would provide animation and "white noise" to counteract staccato human shouts and car horns.

The timing was right. Broadcasting executive William S. Paley underwrote the cost of the park on a piece of land on Fifty-third Street between Fifth and Madison Avenues in memory of his father Samuel.[33] Zion and Breen's design as implemented is a perfecting of the exhibition scheme,

adjusting the plantings for the slightly reduced dimensions.[34] To set the space off from the street, three steps invite the visitor to ascend, quite literally, to another level [278].

The honey locusts, arranged on a quincunx rather than a rigid grid, appear as the perfect choice of species. The trees offer a delicate texture when in full leaf, a handsome yellow color in fall, and are appropriately deciduous in colder seasons when the warmth of sunlight is more welcome. The landscape architects intended this canopy to "create a solid roof of shade and a uniform, bold and restful silhouette."[35] Boston ivy planted on the side walls—termed by Zion and Breen as "vertical lawns"—mitigated the pressure of the bounding walls, "requiring none of the care which the traditional lawn demands." To reinforce public life within the space, kiosks at the entrance to the park serve beverages and light food, pairing with iron gates to form a gateway to the park. Wire chairs designed by Harry Bertoia provide seating that can be reconfigured by the visitors, a flexible element in the fixed, virtually symmetrical, composition.

The vertical cascade on the north wall of the site is a thunderous torrent that operates during the clement months [280]. The water sparkles as it catches the sunlight during the day and glows warmly with artificial illumination at night. The Paley Park waterwall is a simple gesture, a mere sheet of falling water that addresses the open street end of the park to the south. There is no figurative statement as at the Trevi, there are no references to natural systems as we will see at the Lovejoy and Ira C. Keller Fountains in Portland. Instead, this simple design answers the restricted conditions of the site and the need for a kinetic element to animate the space even when only a visitor or two are present. Paley Park is an uncompromisingly modernist park that employs the elements of its vocabulary functionally, and with great sensitivity.

The critical and popular success of Paley Park spawned offspring around the midtown area, which have been fertilized by modified zoning regulations that have traded increased floor area for public amenity. Some of these "parks" are interior or arcaded spaces, such as the glassed court of the IBM Building and the AT&T (now Sony) Building nearby; most of them use water in only a limited way, or not at all.[36]

279 Aerial view of Paley Park.

280 Waterwall, Paley Park. The streaming water, looking somewhat like a large, monochromatic abstract painting with constantly changing forms and hues, provides both sparkling animation and "white noise" to screen out traffic sounds. The park is a welcome outdoor retreat for relaxing, eating lunch, reading or visiting with friends.

Some retain their identities as exterior spaces, their number of seats carefully calculated to meet the stipulations of the law. None of these spaces, however, approach the succinct elegance of Paley Park, its overall cohesion, or its popularity. None of them uses a simple sheet of tumbling water so effectively or so elegantly.

Water enjoyed its greatest postwar moments, perhaps, after the construction of two major fountains in Portland, Oregon [283, 285]. Created principally by landscape architect Lawrence Halprin as part of a major urban renewal program during the years 1961–68, the Lovejoy Fountain and the Ira C. Keller Fountain mark a departure from tradition in two important ways.[37] Firstly, both works merge fountain and

V 281, 282 *Study of a California Mountain Stream*, 1960s, and *Sketch for Lovejoy Fountain, Portland, Oregon,* 1965. Drawings by Lawrence Halprin from his notebooks.

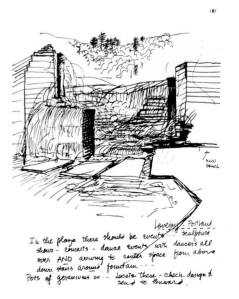

plaza under a barrage of water; secondly, they draw not upon the imagery of mythology and allegory, but upon the abstraction of natural systems. Halprin found inspiration in the High Sierra mountains of California, referring back to observations recorded in his personal sketchbooks as early as 1959.[38] In annotated drawings he described the geologic structure of the granite outcroppings and boulders, and the hydraulic movement in and around them [281]. Recalling personal experience and the pleasure he gained by fully engaging with water in the mountains, Halprin proposed a language for bringing his experience to the city. "What I want is to design *events*," he told an interviewer in 1961, "which occur—which have no necessary or recognizable *form* but which generate qualities of experience."[39] Urban dwellers should not only look at the flow of the liquid, but should truly experience it: wade in it, pass under it, walk over it, and delight in its volume and forms.

The basis of the Lovejoy and Ira C. Keller designs lies not in any ideas borrowed, for example, from art and architecture, but in an understanding, and most importantly an abstracting, of natural conditions. Recording a walk taken in 1961, Halprin outlined his theory of landscape architecture. The "elements of a natural landscape," he explained, are characterized by nine qualities: unpredictable rhythms, relatedness of things, small counter rhythms, quiet but persistent sounds, edges softened by natural process, evolution by

addition or subtraction, non-completion of spaces, variability of light, and a context conducive to participation.[40] While it may never be appropriate to include all of these categories in a single urban project, as a whole they circumscribe the design of any landscape. To these should probably be added the constraints applied by personal and civic considerations, ranging from budget and zoning to a desire for interpretative structures—and taste.

As the Portland renewal scheme developed, Halprin determined that there should be two parks linked by a green corridor. The first would be soft and green, the other paved and featuring water (a second fountain would be added as the project progressed). The landscape architect's inspiration in the High Sierras complemented that of architect Charles Moore, Halprin's collaborator on the Lovejoy Fountain design. Halprin's ideas "resonated with images I carried of a cascade on slanted ledges just above Fallen Leaf Lake, near Lake Tahoe, California," wrote Moore some years later. "I take it as corroboration of the effectiveness of Larry's skills in inviting participation, that to this day when each of us lectures about Lovejoy, he shows his source and I show mine." In 1986, Moore was no longer able to recall who had done what on the design: "It was my notion, probably, that water would well up at the top higher than where one was sitting in order to give a sense of imminent inundation and the cascade down to a lower level."[41]

The fountain and plaza were completed in 1966, constructed for economic reasons entirely of exposed concrete with a hammered texture. The swirling cascade of cast planes recalls the Sierras, perhaps as viewed through the baroque path of the Spanish Steps in Rome. "The layers grow just gradually enough to suggest the erosive patterns of a natural landscape," one critic wrote, "yet their willful shapes pull just back from representation [282]."[42] Like his wife, dancer Anna Halprin, the landscape architect has been gripped with the importance of movement in space, and the revelation of form and space solely through movement, that is to say, over time.[43] His designs more often than not involve what he terms "scores," treating the landscape not as a static composition but as a setting for human activity and kinetic exploration

[284]. This movement is also central to the Portland projects, both in the path from a small source through a pedestrian corridor to the Lovejoy Fountain and in the mounded and tree-canopied Pettigrove Park to the Ira C. Keller Fountain. One sees each space in relation to the other, and each element of the fountains as a part of the greater whole.

The geometry of the designs is foreign to the streets and buildings that surround the site; this was not a contextual design whose geometry derived from a simple extension of the urban or architectural grid. The form of the fountains purposely confronts the grid, instigating associations with natural and not constructed landscapes. The concrete planes of wandering angular shapes recall the pieces of cardboard used to depict the contours of landform on architectural models. Here, however, they are writ full-size. The upper pool—shallow but broad and inviting—welcomes the

visitor and portends the fall. Within a bounded bowl, the water tumbles briskly, gathering in volume and velocity as it plummets. The cascade finds its tranquil resolution in a second shallow basin at the lower level, whose supporting edge is sufficiently high to serve as an angular bench. A path of stepping slabs lures the visitor across the pool, the first stage, perhaps, in a more active involvement with the water.

The fountain that is the Auditorium Forecourt, now known as the Ira C. Keller (or simply Ira's) Fountain, was completed several years later [285]. Its configuration furthers the drama of the Lovejoy Fountain by increasing the height of the fall to eighteen feet, its width to over eighty feet, with concrete planes articulated to recall the sheared stone facets of mountains. Taking advantage of the site's slope, project designer Angela Danadjieva recessed the forecourt below street level and used the

< 283 Aerial view of Lovejoy Plaza
and Fountain, Portland, Oregon.
Designed by Lawrence Halprin
and Charles Moore, 1966.

> 284 Walking down the water
steps of Lovejoy Fountain. The
spiraling cascade with water
exuberantly splashing over its
concrete steps has an irresistible
climb-in, walk-through, look-at,
and listen-to-me allure.

fountain's face as a dam, creating a pool at the upper level to play the role of the serene mountain waterhole. The tranquil effect of this shallow basin is heightened by the violent fall of the water as it comes tumbling over the precipice. Danadjieva refined the form and fall of the fountain using a clay model, essentially shaping the fountain's contour by a process of subtraction until it felt right. Despite the radical differences in formal vocabularies, the quest for an experience analogous to that of nature recalls Nicola Salvi's project for the Trevi.

Like the Lovejoy Fountain, a pathway of slabs sponsors engagement with the water at the auditorium end of the site. The issue of safety has been an insistent concern, both during design and in the public's perception of the fountain: "The fountain was designed to *appear* very dangerous but to *be* relatively safe."[44] Halprin's team ingeniously addressed the building code's requirement for a forty-two-inch railing height by creating pools of that depth just behind the edge of the weir. The result is an edge unfettered by external railings although each weir serves as a protective parapet at the required height. The design team, which included engineer Richard Chaix as hydraulic consultant, also conjured the impression of massive amounts of falling water when in fact the average depth of the fountain is only three inches.

The fountain's inauguration in June 1970 was cause for grand celebration. During the suitably staid formal ceremonies, a group of

hippies jumped into the fountain, followed by Halprin himself, much to the chagrin— or delight—of the crowd [286]. One irate taxpayer, not at all pleased by the expenditure of municipal funds on such frivolity wrote in the *Oregonian*, a local newspaper: "What kind of city is this that is too broke to install proper traffic lights for school crossings, but can afford to pay $500,000 for a pile of cement designed by some San Francisco hippie for his people?"[45] In fact, the fountain was privately underwritten. The presence of those with alternative lifestyles, however, seems to dominate the public's perception of the fountain, as a number of newspaper stories from the early 1970s testify.

One of the city's art commissioners hoped that "as the novelty of its presence wore off… the enthusiasm of youth would be more 'constrained,' so that a broader cross-section of the public would be availed its pleasures."[46] And this came to pass within a few years of the fountain's opening: "On the relatively quiet street-level plaza at the upstream end, elderly people sit and talk and babies dabble in the shallow water. The brink of the falls is obviously for the more adventurous; there is real danger, but anyone who has waded into knee-deep pools to reach the edge is bound to be aware

of that." There is also a record of at least one baptism in the fountain, perhaps one of the few uses not foretold by the designers.[47]

In some ways the areas of the Ira C. Keller Fountain are less integrated than the elements of the Lovejoy Fountain. There are distinct upper and lower portions of the former's site, for example, and the whole is less tied to its surroundings. But we reach this conclusion only if viewing the concrete superstructure in isolation. We must keep in mind that a fountain has two elements: the physical support and hardware of the jets (which give the fountain structure), and the water itself (which gives it life). Cast in relatively crudely-made concrete, these fountains may lack sophistication of form but the sheer volume of water, and the way in which it moves, literally drowns any compositional shortcomings. In these two water spaces, the Halprin team have developed a new idiom that joins support with liquid, fountain with urban space, and visual subject with experiential object. They have become landmarks in the city, drawing people to and into them,

△ 285 Ira C. Keller Fountain, Portland, Oregon. Designed by Lawrence Halprin & Associates, 1970. About thirteen thousand gallons of water per minute surge over the twenty-foot high waterfall, providing what Lawrence Halprin calls an "experiential equivalent of nature" in the middle of the city.

< 286 At the June 1970 inauguration of the Ira C. Keller Fountain (then called Auditorium Forecourt Fountain), people enthusiastically jumped into the water to celebrate.

functioning truly as antidotes to the urban condition.[48] To the credit of the municipal authorities, there has been no major crackdown on wading, save posted notices that one does so at one's own risk. Attempting to be unobtrusive, a security guard monitors the area "to protect toddlers and disoriented drug users" from possible harm.[49] Although there seem to have been no major accidents or instances of litigation, we can never fully proscribe all bodily risk in public places. The success of the Lovejoy and Ira C. Keller Fountains suggests something quite contradictory, that marginally dangerous spaces might attract more people than those considered completely safe.[50] If, as Halprin notes, the landscape designer is to "interpret nature's mode of operations *not* her results," the landscapes must, of necessity, include some element of risk.[51] That is to say, if we are to understand the processes and not merely mimic the forms, we must include the uncertainty that lies at the base of the human experience of nature.

The Halprin office continued the development of the fountain-as-mountain idea in several works. Principal among them is Freeway Park in Seattle, Washington. Completed in 1976, it is a brilliant example of urban design strategy, expanding a 1968 plan to construct a park along the highway, Interstate 5. Rather than lining the side of the road, Halprin proposed bridging the central freeway with a green platform linking the downtown and First Hill districts. This would inject a dose of much-needed green space into the city while repairing the tear to its fabric. Some trees, intended as a windbreak, were planted in large boxes; openings in the platform allow views of the cars whizzing by below.[52] Well within the park, staggered vertical planes enclose a "canyon" of concrete which intensifies the sound and visual effect of the torrential waterfall. The vocabulary—the Sierra metaphor—is familiar, but here earlier essays are made more precise and architectural. With the completion of Freeway Park, the notion of the fountain as event space, and the formal idiom first proposed in Portland, achieved

maturation.[53] The overall plan of the Portland redevelopment embodies the key aspects of Halprin's ideal built environment, using tree-lined passages to link urban spaces. The city thus becomes an interwoven progression of fountains, events, pedestrian movement, and places just to sit. The Portland projects sought a fusion of fountain and public space; in Seattle, the park and the fountains become one.

If the fountains of Lawrence Halprin inserted a range of constructed mountains into the city, New York architects Philip Johnson and John Burgee's Water Gardens in Fort Worth, Texas, excavated a series of valleys from the urban floor, left as if in the wake of a primordial glacier [287]. Instead of a green and wooded park on the more pervasive model of New York City's Central Park, there is a brilliant water display inspired by those of the Villa d'Este in Tivoli. The craters are vivified with plants and an array of water-casting devices, conceived by the architects as the project's essential element.

Perhaps influenced by the stepping terraces of Dan Kiley's Oakland Museum landscape (1968) in California, or perhaps by Halprin's successes in Oregon, Johnson

and Burgee configured the park's five water zones in a similar "bio-cubic" idiom of planar layers.[54] Again, exposed concrete is the material throughout, lending an almost manic unity to the elements of the site. Walls define the limits of pools of varying volumes and sprays and bound the site together; at the same time, however, they somewhat unfortunately isolate the garden from the city around it. This is a park adrift, a water world in and of itself, "at once useless and absolutely splendid," as architecture critic Paul Goldberger wrote.[55] The landscape design by Vernon Swanson and Bill Cornett claims five hundred plant species, including coastal live oaks, sweet gums, white wisteria, and a bosk of ginkgoes. Although the project fact sheet tells of 32,000 items being planted (including grasses and ground cover), there is little sense of greenery within the block except around the edges.

One enters the park, and departs Fort Worth, for a calm or wild ride. Modulated like a television aerobics class offering a range of involvement from light to heavy, each of the pool areas exploits a different type of water system, from simple pencil-like jets and conical sprays [289] to falling torrents.[56] In the hot summer months, the overspray cools the air, making even a simple promenade more pleasant. The intensity of the sound changes with one's proximity to the water features,

> 287 Overall view of the Active Water Pool, Fort Worth Water Gardens, Fort Worth, Texas. Designed by Philip Johnson, 1974.

varying from a gentle whoosh to a mighty roar. The Water Gardens' climax is the deep Active Water Pool, into which one gingerly descends over a series of slabs without the support of any handrail. The bowl continuously narrows and steepens, causing the water to increase in velocity and volume as one ventures lower [288]. Standing at the bottom of the pool and looking up, one is struck by a vertiginous sensation, and by a strong premonition of imminent inundation as masses of water tumble from all sides. It is an exhilarating experience, not without a mild dose of terror, a distant cousin of that described by Edgar Allan Poe in his story "A Descent into the Maelström": "The edge of the whirl was represented by a broad belt of gleaming spray; but no particle of this slipped into the mouth of the terrific funnel… speeding dizzily round and round with a swaying and sweltering motion."[57] The magnitude of the sound increases with the constriction of the basin's space and with the tumult of the assembled waters, again recalling Poe's whirlpool which sent "forth to the winds an appalling voice, half shriek, half roar, such as not even the mighty cataract of Niagara ever lifts up in its agony to Heaven."[58]

As one ascends, the play of phenomena reverses. Moving higher, one feels the water calm and the clamor subside. Arriving at street level, with a furtive sigh of relief,

the visitor re-enters the urban environment which in contrast appears tranquil and sane. In the 1970s, the Water Gardens offered a unique experience and constituted, perhaps, the greatest water park since Renaissance Italy. Since that time, however, we have witnessed the advent of water theme parks with names such as Wet 'n' Wild, which may partially explain why the Fort Worth experience today appears somewhat diminished. One also wishes for a stronger connection to the streets and buildings that surround the site, and for water features that address the city rather than the interior of the park alone. The concrete terraces that once excited visitors now appear almost as a monotonous period piece, and one longs for greater masses of

∨ 288 At the bottom of the Active Water Pool at Fort Worth Water Gardens, people are surrounded by water crashing and roaring down the stepped walls.

∨ 289 The Aerated Water Pool with forty jet sprays, Fort Worth Water Gardens.

> 290 The Transco Waterwall, composed of a curved waterwall and a Roman-inspired arched screen, Houston, Texas. Designed by Philip Johnson, 1985.

> 291 Philip Johnson in front of the Transco Waterwall. As a modern-day nymphaeum celebrating water, Johnson wanted to provide people with the exhilarating experience of being surrounded by the sixty-foot semicircular wall covered every minute by eleven thousand gallons of surging water.

greenery to soften the concrete lines. Only in the great basin does the power remain in full force—a fountain that is a space, a fountain that offers an urban white water ride for those who would remain (relatively) dry.

The water mountain grew to extreme proportions in Houston, when the Transco Waterwall, designed by John Burgee Architects with Philip Johnson, arrived in 1985 [290, 292]. Given the moment—a high point in postmodern eclecticism—architecturally the structures could be termed "temple-pastiche."[59] But the project will not be remembered for its style. Instead it will be remembered, like the Portland fountains, for the height of the wall and the height of the fall. The idea for the waterwall is somewhat bizarre—a freestanding structure whose sole purpose, which it accomplishes quite well, is to elevate a sheet of water. "Neither part of the fountain design bears any relationship to the building [the Transco Tower]," noted critic Carleton Knight.[60] The original scheme linked the fountain to the tower with a three-hundred-foot-long reflection pool, a feature which proved to be impractical and was left unrealized.

Historical precedents for the fountain's semicircular enclosure (unfortunately dull when seen from its outer, convex side) include the sixteenth-century Villa Giulia in Rome, whose celebrated nymphaeum's

rear wall bounds a subterranean rather than an elevated space. Beyond the villa, one sees glimpses of the primitive grotto, so popular in Renaissance gardens. Cool, removed, laden with mythological associations, the grotto mixes sensuality with poetry, and stone with water.

The Transco Waterwall became a tourist destination almost immediately upon completion. Situated at the base of a high-rise tower, also designed by John Burgee Architects with Philip Johnson, the waterwall was intended to create a destination on the fringes of the ring road, the Houston Loop. And people come. With an annual attendance of almost 140,000, mostly on spring and summer weekends, they come for family excursions, for picnics, for the requisite wedding portraits—or even the nuptials themselves. "A favorite game," one writer tells us, "is to get close, face away from the wall and bend backward. Seen like this, the wall really does look as though an impossible cloudburst is dropping from the sky."[61] Challenge was built into its sixty-foot height: "It is, after all, our very own man-made Niagara, just off Loop 610, challenging hordes of amateur and professional photographers and those brave enough to stand close to the strobing, pulsing water, risking getting wet when the wind picks up [291]."[62] Like its

∧ 292 Night view of the Transco Tower and the Transco Waterwall.

175

architecture, however, even the nature of the structure has been questioned. Another writer was less sanguine, noting that "although the Transco Fountain appears to invite participation, the invitation is an illusion, for the steps up the sides of the fountain lead not into a pool but nowhere…. Looking around, one suddenly feels cold, like an intruder in an eerie Swiftian world."[63]

The Transco Waterwall stands out in a remarkably homogeneous cultural landscape, as do the over-lifesize mustangs in Williams Square in Las Colinas, outside Dallas. While the giant bronze statues of horses offer little relief from the sun, and the effect of their splashes can be greater in photographs than in reality [166], the Transco Waterwall is a distinct event in a built environment that reads almost as an extrusion. Johnson spoke of the office building as the steeple of a suburban village, "Transco is its own skyline."[64] The boldness of the scale and enclosure, the volume of liquid, and the basic fascination that only moving water can instigate together make the waterwall a predominant feature of Houston's suburban fabric. If the tower is the village steeple, the waterwall is its well.

The most extreme melding of fountain and plaza is also found in Texas, in Dallas. Here, in 1986, landscape architect Dan Kiley, with Peter Ker Walker and WET Design, brought the shade of the forest to the sweltering city and water to its pavement [293]. On more than one instance Kiley has stated: "We are one with the universe. Man *is* nature. Is that not exciting to realize? It's not man *and* nature. It's not man *with* nature. Man *is* nature, just like the trees."[65]

The trees at Fountain Place are carefully positioned on a regular grid. To Kiley, there is no conflict in reading a geometrically-based field as natural. He does not mimic irregular planting in order to appear natural, thereby confronting the long-held tradition of naturalistic design championed so effectively by nineteenth-century landscape designer Frederick Law Olmsted.[66] For Kiley, there are no natural, no artificial systems. Geometry and ecological patterns both reflect natural process. Seen in this way, there is no conflict between geometry in a more natural landscape and a forest—or a swamp species—within a city.

Dallas can be extremely hot in the summer months, and it also tends to be humid. To mitigate the reflected heat from paving, Kiley proposed to eliminate the typical plaza-as-plaza among the slick glass prisms of the First Interstate Bank Tower (formerly Allied Bank), designed by I. M. Pei and Harry Cobb. The design came quickly: "The very first second I saw the Dallas Fountain Place I knew all six acres should be water," said Kiley, "and there would be some bald cypress trees and people would walk flush with the water, and there would be geometric waterfalls." And yet on the other hand, "it took two years to work out the details but the design was there, right like that."[67] He planted a forest of 440 native bald cypresses on fifteen-foot centers, and their foliage joins together in a dense mass of greenery. At their feet, terraces of water, each spilling into the lower level, provide the excitement of falling water, enhanced by 263 bubbler fountains in the granite-bounded squares of water. The cypresses, being deciduous, offer a thick shield of needles against the summer sun, but allow more light during the cooler winter months. In thermal and lighting effect, Fountain Place becomes a swamplike forest in downtown Dallas, a curious, even bizarre, transposition of a "natural" setting into the city. What could better illustrate Kiley's belief that man is nature?

An open pocket of space that employed fountain technology still in its infancy complements Kiley's architectural landscape of cypress, cascading water and granite [294]. Hydraulics consultants WET Design developed the idea for the plaza area, using a computer-controlled grid of 160 water jets to create aqueous sweeps and figures that literally dance before the eyes of the delighted spectators [295]. For events requiring a greater flat area, the fountain, whose nozzles are recessed beneath the pavement, can be silenced, leaving a sheet of granite in its place. While aspects of the design had several precedents—Noguchi's work among them—the advent of computer technology offered a host of new possibilities for intricate sculptural water patterns and fountain designs.

Fountain Place has been an unqualified success. It may have generated from a far-fetched idea of submerging the bank's plaza in water, but it has become a sophisticated balance of solids and liquids, static and moving, creating ultimately its own ecology.[68] The space beneath the bank's heroic glass walls welcomes people as a pleasant place to take a light meal or drink, and is the site of numerous fashion and wedding shoots. Its field of trees softens the building's base and as an urban ensemble neatly joins Kiley's sculpture garden for the Dallas Museum of Fine Arts nearby. Perhaps the greatest acknowledgment of its acceptance has been the inclusion of Fountain Place on tourist bus excursions, when visitors dutifully exit their minibus, and spread out under the canopy of cypresses to stand and watch the titillating sequence of the dancing waters. But Fountain Place serves the native more than the tourist as a highly popular urban retreat.

Since the completion of Fountain Place, the programmed rise and fall of water jets has recurred in landscape design in several parts of the world. A grid of water needles creates less precise forms than those of architecture and suggests the periodicity of nature, itself familiar but incalculable. Think of the play of waves or flames and their ability to attract human interest. There seems to be an inherent fascination with this use of water to draw lines, planes and masses, particularly when the exact moment of release eludes prediction. For the reinvigoration of Plaza Park in San Jose, California, in 1989, Hargreaves Associates utilized a network of water jets to create a field that can be touched and entered. Unlike the densely packed mass of the Fountain Place jets, Plaza Park displays water on a laser field; it is illuminated from below for night-time viewing. Like the Halprin fountains in Portland, Plaza Park also offers direct contact with water, although normally only children, adolescents, and the occasional dog risk getting wet.

The field of jets idea, pioneered by WET Design at Fountain Place, finds its most dramatic and architecturally-satisfying applications in an urban park completed in 1992. Parc André-Citroën, designed by a conglomerate team that included Gilles Clément, Patrick Berger, Alain Provost and Jean-Paul Viguier, is the most recent major green space to open in metropolitan Paris.[69]

< 293 Aerial view of the cypress grove water terrace, Fountain Place, Dallas, Texas. Designed by Dan Kiley and Peter Ker Walker, 1986.

∧ 294 Cascade and cypress tree reflected in the mirrored windows of the First Interstate Bank Tower, Fountain Place, Dallas.

Built on the reclaimed site of a former automobile factory, it is a vast project of highly intricate design [300]. Naturalistic areas—the *jardin en mouvement*—play against more intimate spaces of thematic designs.[70] Seven water stairs conjoining the fountain and the pool link the glass houses with the broad central lawn. Between the two monumental glass houses that mark the park's eastern entrances, a field of water jets plays in staccato, yet subtle, repetition. The spurts fascinate all visitors, particularly children. They take as great sport the challenge to run through the field at water's ebb. Can they make it through the jets before the program starts anew? A second sport is to balance a soccer ball on a jet when the water is low and keep it balanced there as the pressure increases.

Although accidents have occurred, children are undeterred, fascinated instead by the dance of the waters.[71] The city, however, sees the situation in a quite different light, and in recent years signs prohibiting running and playing have appeared around the fountain's periphery. The city faces an uphill battle as neither signs nor guards have effectively negated the inexorable draw of the waters and their sirenlike allure, which captivate people with dimensions beyond the visual.

Most recent urban fountains hold two properties in common: they employ large volumes of water, and they are configured in complex patterns. Despite the impact provided by these masses of water and their intricate displays, we should not overlook the power of the fountain to exert its influence in just the opposite way, by stilling intrusive noise through simple animation. The effect of such muffling was one of the important lessons of the Moorish gardens of Spain. Mountains of water are not always required, nor are fabulous plays of spouts and sprays. In their place, a diminutive bubbler, effectively positioned, can set a stream in flow that commands attention through the most meager means.

In 1988, Dan Kiley designed planted spaces to complement architect Harry Wolf's round tower for the North Carolina National Bank in Tampa, Florida. At once plaza, garden, and terrace—elevated to roof the bank's garage below—this tartan plaid of fountains, water courses, zoysia grass and pre-cast concrete paving joins the city streets with the Hillsborough River.[72] To weave a spatially intricate carpet of landscape Kiley uses trunks and arboreal canopies, playing a rigid grid of lanky sabal palmettos against irregular swaths of six hundred crape myrtles, brilliantly pink when in bloom. A glass-roofed entry to the

parking garage feeds nine water rills that penetrate deep into the terrace's carpet of concrete and grass. Each one is enlivened at its terminus by a small bubbler fountain, which suffices to enliven the narrow rills, which in turn energize the planted or paved surfaces of the terrace [296].

Although uncompromisingly modern in its configuration and plantings, the NCNB project exudes a diffidently Islamic air, recalling the magnificent gardens of the Alhambra and the Generalife in Granada, Spain [297]. These, too, are oases cast against both the neighboring city and the arid countryside. The Koran describes Paradise as the confluence of four rivers, where water is plentiful and living good. "Paradises have a certain family likeness," cultural geographer Yi-Fu Tuan explains, "because the excesses of geography (too hot or too cold, too wet or too dry) are removed. In all of them, plants and animals useful and friendly to man abound. Paradises also differ in their respective excellences: some are rich pastures, others are magical forests, perfumed islands, or mountain valleys."[73]

The gardens of the Moorish tradition rely on the use and display of water as a source of life, as blood for a living entity. The sparkle and tinkle of the long rows of jets in the Patio de la Acequia or the arching geometries of the Garden of the Sultana at the Generalife suggest the same effects as those of the Tampa terrace. But in its distillation of complexity into an ultimate unity, the Kiley design refers to no other project as much as to the Court of the Myrtles at the Alhambra,[74] although the dimensions are vastly different, the number of components greatly expanded, and the

architectonic enclosure of the Granada palace is missing. In Tampa, as in Spain, the power of still sheets of water and a diminutive bubbler effectively tranquilize the pressures and noises of life, providing instead, a mysterious paradoxical element, water that excites while it calms.

It is the designers of fountains who imagine their potential and determine their form and their magic. Ultimately, however, it is their management that determines their success, although at times, the people prevail despite municipal policy. The Lovejoy and Ira C. Keller Fountains have been enjoyed for three decades without major restrictions, mishaps or litigation. This is also true of the Water Gardens in Fort Worth, whose descent into the maelström—without any handrails—could be considered dangerous to those lacking the sure step of the mountain goat. Of course, signs caution potential waders that they are not encouraged to intrude, and warn them that they do so at their own risk. Considering the plethora of building codes that dictate the forms of our urban environment, however, these slight transgressions are nothing short of miraculous and suggest some degree of enlightenment on the part of governmental authorities.

In closing, let us examine the nature of two urban fountains and their relations to governmental policy. The Los Angeles Community Redevelopment Agency and Broadway Spring Center agreed to dedicate a small space in the center of a downtown block to the memory and contributions of the ex-slave and midwife Biddy Mason.[75] This link between Broadway and Spring Streets would be an almost exclusively paved area—termed "hardscape" in the profession—linking a new parking garage with a proposed office and commercial development. Neither lavish vegetation nor water was planned; maintenance would need to be minimal considering the rough character of the location. The owners wished no basin that could be considered a potential source of litigation or used by the homeless for washing. The landscape architects Pamela Burton and Katherine Spitz saw a need for the kinetic relief that a fountain would provide. Bending slightly to their argument, the client then modified the program to include a fountain, as long as all potential liability could be removed, and it could remain virtually free of maintenance.

< 295 Fountain jets in the plaza, Fountain Place. Designed by WET Design.

< 296 Low bubbler fountain, North Carolina National Bank Plaza, Tampa, Florida. Designed by Dan Kiley, 1988.

∧ 297 Patio de la Acequia, Generalife, Granada, Spain, 13th century; with fountains added later.

179

Burton and Spitz, building on a concept by the local sculptor Eino, fashioned a laudable solution to the programmatic compromise, taking a liability and turning it into an asset. The result was a grove of copper and stainless-steel pipes of various diameters, with water gushing from their tops far above arm's reach. Water spirals down the length of one pipe, while in others, water emerges and clings to the sides of the metallic cylinders. All waters disappear into the paving below [298]; there is no pool. Compared to a true fountain the net effect is minimal, the inclusion of this water feature in the "park" is itself a major contribution, the one "living" element of the design besides the visitors themselves. The project also reveals the state of municipal interest in fountains in less glamorous areas and reflects the problems of design in relation to civic policy. Even with this political caution, however, both the fountain and the park have been treated well "despite the area's high vandalism rate."[76]

An even happier ending is the story of urban renewal in West Palm Beach, Florida. Here a flagging area of the city was raised to public prominence through considerate urban design—and by a fountain. An energetic mayor, Nancy Graham, bent on reversing the fortunes of the downtown as a pilot project, commissioned urban designers Andres Duany and Elizabeth Plater-Zyberk to redesign the district so that "West Palm Beach could become the downtown for the whole county."[77]

< 298 Fountain in Biddy Mason Park, Los Angeles. Designed by Pamela Burton and Katherine Spitz, 1991.

< 299 Centennial Fountain, West Palm Beach, Florida. Designed by the Office of Dan Kiley and Team Plan, Inc., 1994.

> 300 Parc André-Citroën at sunset, Paris. Designed by Jean-Paul Viguier (plaza) and Patrick Berger (greenhouse), 1992.

Centennial Fountain, designed by Dan Kiley with the landscape architecture firm Team Plan, Inc. and consultant Peter Hoyle, would be the showpiece of the renovated Clematis Street [299]. The project has been successful beyond all anticipations, described positively by one supporter as "a mob scene" after dark when the area was previously deserted with everyone back in their houses. "It's like Madrid after the sun goes down. You can hardly move," says another.[78] Can a fountain do all of this?

Certainly not, or certainly not in isolation. The reinvigoration of central West Palm Beach cannot be tied to a fountain alone, but the project is indicative of an energetic and effective leader who pushed to get things done. Centennial Fountain is an urban element that was proposed by the designers and backed by the mayor. The fountain, completed in 1994, "quickly fill[ed] up with splashing children, but the mix of visitors also often reflects the city's diverse racial makeup. The scene there looks more like a multicultural Coca-Cola video than reality."[79] Like all fountains of this genre its identity disappears when the water is turned off, leaving a bold triangular paving pattern that visually animates the plaza.

The crowds continued to grow, understandably considering Florida's climate and the lure of a social place that seems like a reverie from a distant, mythical past. It has become a target destination, which has forced a redefinition of the site: "When day camps started busing children downtown to use the fountain as a public pool, the city simply changed the designation from 'fountain' to 'pool' and furnished it accordingly."[80] The mayor had more ideas: "'I hired a lifeguard and put in that lifeguard chair,' Ms. Graham said proudly, pointing to a stately white throne overlooking the geysers. 'And we also added more chlorine to handle more people. And public bathrooms.'"[81] Children play in it, seniors watch them play in it, and "the middle-aged wonder if they're still young enough to play in it."[82]

This is the point at which a city's legal counsel usually begins to recoil, suggesting that the increased risk outweighs potential economic and social advantages. Ms. Graham disagrees: "Oh, if we worried about [liability], we'd never do anything."[83] And she's right. The West Palm Beach story quite clearly demonstrates the effect of political policy on the success of public urban spaces. In this case a fountain serves as the protagonist, its splash, spectacle and coolness all draw people inexorably to it. However, good designs are not made without good designers, despite powerful tools such as computer-controlled systems for water display. Tools are little without talent. The polity and its policies must offer the designers the means for invention, and allow the people sufficient interaction with the end product. Only then will the site become a truly vital urban oasis, experienced with all the physical amenity and spiritual relief that the metaphor implies.

Marc Treib

Chronology

Unless stated otherwise, the date given is the date the fountain was completed.

13th century
Generalife, Granada, Spain
Fountains added later.

1277–78
Fontana Maggiore, Perugia, Italy
Sculptors: Nicola Pisano (1220/25–before 1284)
with Giovanni Pisano (1245/50–before 1319)
Hydraulics: Fra Bevignate and Boninsegna

14th century
Fountain of the Lions, The Alhambra,
Granada, Spain
Basin added to 11th-century group of
twelve stone lions.

Begun 1386
Schöner Brunnen (Beautiful Fountain),
Nuremberg, Germany

1419
Fonte Gaia, Piazza del Campo, Siena
Sculptor: Jacopo della Quercia (c. 1374–1438)
Replaced in 1868 with a copy by Tito Sarrocchi
(1824–1900).

c. 1540
Gänsemännchenbrunnen
(Geesebearer Fountain), Nuremberg, Germany
Designer: Pankraz Labenwolf (1492–1563)

1542–46
Kindlifresserbrunnen (Ogre Fountain),
Kornhausplatz, Bern, Switzerland
Sculptor: Hans Gieng (died 1562)

1543
Fountain of Justice, Bern, Switzerland

1549
Fontaine des Innocents
(Fountain of the Innocents), Paris
Architect: Pierre Lescot (c. 1500/10–78)
Sculptor: Jean Goujon (c. 1510–c. 1565)
Renovated and resited late 18th century,
and again in the 1860s by architect
Gabriel Davioud (1824–81).

< 301 Frontispiece to Bernard
Forest de Bélidor, *Architecture
hydraulique, ou l'art de conduire,
d'élever et de ménager les eaux
pour les différens besoins de la vie*
(Paris, 1737–53). The fountains'
waterwheel and pipes are hidden
by a pumphouse in the style of a
classical temple, which harmonizes
with the balustrades and château
beyond.

1550–72
Villa d'Este, Tivoli, Italy
Garden design: Pirro Ligorio (c. 1520–85)

> Avenue of the Hundred Fountains
>
> Fountain of the Dragons
>
> Fountain of Tivoli
> Fountain work: Curzio Maccarone, 1566
>
> Fountain of Nature, or the Water Organ
> Hydraulics: Luc Le Clerc with
> Claude Venard, 1568
>
> Fountain of Rome, called the Rometta
> Fountain work: Curzio Maccarone, c. 1568

c. 1554–57
Fountain of Neptune, Messina, Italy
Sculptor: Giovanni Angelo Montorsoli
(1507?–63)

1559–60
Fountain of Hercules and Antaeus,
Villa Medici, Castello, Italy
Designer (of base): Niccolò Tribolo (1500–50)
Sculptor: Bartolomeo Ammannati (1511–92)

c. 1560–75
Fountain of Neptune,
Piazza della Signoria, Florence
Sculptor: Bartolomeo Ammannati (1511–92)

1561–68
Il Bacco (Fountain of Bacchus),
Boboli Gardens, Florence
Sculptor: Valerio Cioli (1529–99)

1563–66
Fountain of Neptune, Piazza Nettuno,
Bologna, Italy
Sculptor: Giambologna (1529–1608)

1564–86
Villa Lante at Bagnaia, Viterbo, Italy
Designer: Giacomo Barozzi da Vignola
(1507–73)

> Water chain cascade (*catena d'acqua*)
> Fountain of the Giants (Arno and Tiber
> river gods)
> Fountain of the Deluge
> Fountain of the Dolphins

1565–68
Fountain of Neptune,
Boboli Gardens, Florence
Sculptor: Stoldo Lorenzi (1534–83)

1567
Fountain of Oceanus,
Boboli Gardens, Florence
Sculptor: Giambologna (1529–1608)
Oceanus replaced with a copy; original marble
statue is now in Bargello, Florence.

1569–89
Medici Villa (later Villa Demidoff) and gardens,
Pratolino, near Florence
Architect and hydraulics: Bernardo Buontalenti
(1531–1608)
Most grottoes and water automata destroyed by
the late 19th century.

1585–88
The Acqua Felice
(Fountain of Moses), Rome
Designer: Domenico Fontana (1543–1607)

Late 16th century
Fontana del Facchino
(Water Porter Fountain), Rome
Resited 1872 from the Corso to Via Lata.

Begun 1602
Water theater and water stairs,
Villa Aldobrandini, Frascati, Italy
Designers: Carlo Maderno (1556–1629),
with later additions by Giacomo della Porta
(1537–1602) and Giovanni Fontana
(1540–1614)

1609–11
Mount Parnassus grotto fountain,
Somerset House, London
Designer: Salomon de Caus (1576–1626)
Destroyed 18th century.

1610–12
Il Fontanone
(Fountain of the Acqua Paola), Rome
Designers: Giovanni Fontana (1540–1614)
and Flaminio Ponzio (c. 1559–1613),
with pool added in 1690 by Carlo Fontana
(1638–1714)

1612–19
Garden theater with the Prince's Table,
Hellbrunn Palace, Salzburg, Austria
Designer: Santino Solari (1576–1646)

1615
Book: Salomon de Caus, *Les Raisons des forces
mouvantes* (Frankfurt)

1618
Manneken-Pis, Brussels, Belgium
Designer: Jérôme Duquesnoy (c. 1570–1641/42)
The original statuette has been replaced.

c. 1626
Fontana del Mascherone (Big Mask Fountain),
Via Giulia, Rome

1642–43
Triton Fountain, Piazza Barberini, Rome
Designer: Gian Lorenzo Bernini (1598–1680)

1648–51
Fountain of the Four Rivers,
Piazza Navona, Rome
Designer: Gian Lorenzo Bernini (1598–1680)
Sculptors: Jacopo Antonio Fancelli (1619–71,
the Nile), Claude Poussin (died 1661,
the Ganges), Antonio Raggi (1624–86,
the Danube), and Francesco Baratta
(died 1666, the Plata)

1660–68
Neptune Fountain,
Nuremberg, Germany
Sculptor: Georg Schweigger (1613–80)

c. 1661
Cascades, Saint-Cloud, France
Designer: Antoine Le Pautre (probably
[1621–91]); enlarged in 1697 by
Jules Hardouin-Mansart (1646–1708)

1664
Book: Georg Andreas Böckler, *Architectura
Curiosa Nova, Die Lustreiche Bau- und
Wasserkunst* (Nuremberg)

1667
Fountains, St. Peter's Square, Rome
Architects: Carlo Maderno (1556–1629) for the
design of the original fountains in 1614; rebuilt
by Gian Lorenzo Bernini (1598–1680)

Fontaine d'Eau Chaude
(Hot Springs Fountain), later called
Font Moussu (Mossy Fountain),
Aix-en-Provence, France
Sculptor: Jacques Fossé
Original sculpture does not survive.

1668–late 1680s
Versailles
　　Fontaine de la Piramide (Pyramid
　　Fountain) and the North Parterre, 1668–70
　　Sculptor: François Girardon (1628–1715),
　　after design of Robert de Cotte
　　(1656–1735) or Charles Le Brun (1619–90)

　　Fontaine de Latone
　　(Latona Fountain), 1668–70
　　Sculptors: Gaspard (1624–81) and
　　Balthazar Marsy (1629–74); sculpture
　　arranged on tiers, 1687–89

　　Bassin d'Apollon (Fountain of Apollo), 1671
　　Sculptor: Jean-Baptiste Tuby (1635–1700)
　　Hydraulics: François de Francine

　　Labyrinth, 1672–74
　　Thirty-nine fountains with animal
　　sculptures depicting the fables of
　　Jean de La Fontaine
　　Sculptors: Étienne Blanchard (1633–93),
　　Jacques Blanchard (1634–89),
　　Jacques Houzeau (1624–91),
　　Étienne Le Hongre (1628–90),
　　Balthazar (1629–74) and Gaspard Marsy
　　(1624–81), Pierre Mazeline (1632–1708),
　　Jean-Baptiste Tuby (1635–1700)
　　Labyrinth destroyed 1775, but some
　　sculptures remain in the Musée du
　　Château de Versailles.

　　Salle de Bal (Ballroom), 1680–85
　　Designer: André Le Nôtre (1613–1700)

　　Bassin de Neptune, begun 1679 with
　　sculpture added 1741
　　Sculptor: Lambert Sigisbert Adam
　　(1710–59)

1682–1720s
Grosser Garten and fountains,
Herrenhausen, near Hanover, Germany
Designers: Martin Charbonnier (died 1720)
and Electress Sophie (1630–1714, wife
of Ernest-August, elector of Hanover).
Great Fountain erected 1720s, based on 1690
hydraulic plans by Gottfried Wilhelm Leibniz
(1646–1716).

1685–99
Celestial and Terrestial Sphere Fountains
and others, Het Loo, The Netherlands
Designer: Daniel Marot (1663–1752)
Renovated 1979–84.

1690s–1830s
Chatsworth, England
　　The Willow Tree Fountain,
　　completed by 1693
　　Replaced 1826, and in the 20th century.

　　Cascade, begun 1690s following
　　designs of Grillet
　　Renovation by Joseph Paxton, *c.* 1830.

　　Emperor Fountain (see 1844)

1696
Book: Carlo Fontana, *Utilissimo trattato
dell'acque correnti* (Rome)

1709
Book: Antoine-Joseph Dézallier d'Argenville,
La Théorie et la pratique du jardinage (Paris)

1714–34
The Grand Cascade and other fountains,
Peterhof, Russia
Designers: Jean-Baptiste-Alexandre Le Blond
(1679–1719), Niccolò Michetti (died 1759),
and others

Begun 1717
Formal garden parterre and fountains,
Augustusburg Palace (now called
Brühl Castle), Brühl, Germany
Designer: Dominique Girard (died 1738)

1721–28
Fountains at La Granja,
San Ildefonso, Spain
Sculptors: René Frémin (1672–1744),
Jean Thierry (1669–1739), and others

1732–62
The Trevi Fountain, Rome
Designer: Nicola Salvi (1697–1751), completed
by Pietro Bracci (1700–73), and others

1737–53
Book: Bernard Forest de Bélidor, *Architecture
hydraulique, ou l'art de conduire, d'élever et de
ménager les eaux pour les différens besoins de
la vie* (Paris)

1745
Fontaine des Quatre Saisons
(Fountain of the Four Seasons),
Rue de Grenelle, Paris
Designer: Edme Bouchardon (1698–1762)

1751–55
Fountain of Neptune, Place Stanislas,
Nancy, France
Architect: Emmanuel Héré (1705–63)
Sculptor: Barthélémy Guibal (1699–1757)

1752–72
Cascade with sculptural tableaux,
Palazzo Reale, Caserta, Italy

Architects: Luigi Vanvitelli (1700–73) and
Martin Biancour
Sculptors: Paolo Persico (1729–80),
Angelo Brunelli (1740–1806), and
Pietro Solari (died 1790)

1768–80s
Yuan-Ming-Yuan (Garden of Perfect Clarity),
Peking (now Beijing)
Designers: Giuseppe Castiglione (1688–1766),
Michel Benoist (1715–74), and others
Much destroyed in mid-19th century;
ruins remain.

1773
Book: Claude Mathieu Delagardette
(attrib. to), *L'Art du plombier et fontainier* (Paris)

1775
Fontaine de la Croix-du-Trahoir
(Fountain of the Cross of Trahoir), Paris
Architect: Jacques-Germain Soufflot (1713–80)
Sculptor: Simon-Louis de Boizot (1743–1809)
Originally erected in the 16th century, rebuilt
1606, dismantled 1636, and then rebuilt again.

1780–86
Fuenta de Cibeles
(Fountain of Cybele), Madrid
Architect: Ventura Rodríguez (1717–85)
Sculptors: Francisco Gutierrez (1727–82) and
Robert Michel (1720–86)

1806–08
Fontaine du Fellah (Egyptian Fountain or
Water Carrier Fountain), Rue de Sèvres, Paris
Architect: Louis-Simon Bralle
Sculptor: Pierre-Nicolas Beauvallet (1750–1818)
Statue replaced in 1844 by sculptor
Jean-François-Théodore Gechter (1796–1844).

1836–39
Fontaine de la Place Louvois, Paris
Architect: Ludovico (or Louis) Visconti
(1791–1853)
Sculptor: Jean-Baptiste-Jules Klagmann
(1810–67)

1836–40
Fountains, Place de la Concorde, Paris
Restored 1861–62
Architect: Jacques Ignace Hittorff (1792–1867)
Sculptors: Isidore-Hippolyte Brion
(1799–1863), Auguste-Hyacinthe Debay
(1804–65), Antoine Desboeufs (1793–1862),
Achille-Joseph Valois (1785–1862),
Jean-Jacques Elshoecht (1791–1856),
Jean-François-Théodore Gechter (1796–1844),
Franz Hoegler (1802–55), Honoré-Jean Husson
(1803–64), Jean-Jacques Feuchère (1807–52),
François-Gaspard Lanno (1800–71),
Louis-Parfait Merlieux (1796–1855),
Antonin-Marie Moine (1796–1849)

1841–44
Fontaine Molière, Paris
On site of a fountain originally built in 1671
Designer: Ludovico (Louis) Visconti
(1791–1853)
Sculptors: Bernard-Gabriel Seurre (1795–1867)
and James Pradier (1792–1852)

1842
Fountain, City Hall Park, New York
The fountain no longer exists.

1843–48
Fontaine des Orateurs-Sacrés, also called
Fontaine de Saint-Sulpice or Fontaine des
Quatre-Évêques (Fountain of the Sacred
Orators or Saint-Sulpice Fountain), Paris
Designer: Ludovico (Louis) Visconti
(1791–1853)
Sculptors: François-Gaspard Lanno (1800–71),
Jean-Jacques Feuchère (1807–52),
Louis Desprez (1799–1870),
Jacques-Auguste Fauginet (1809–47),
and François Derre (died 1888)

1844
Emperor Fountain, Chatsworth, England
Designer: Joseph Paxton (1803–65)

1845
Fountains, Trafalgar Square
Designer: Sir Charles Barry (1795–1860)
Redesigned with sculpture 1938–47.
Architect: Sir Edwin Lutyens (1869–1944)
Sculptors: Sir Charles Wheeler (1892–1974)
and William Macmillan (1887–1977)

1850–53
Atlas Fountain, Castle Howard,
Yorkshire, England
Designer: William Andrews Nesfield
(1793–1881)
Sculptor: John Thomas (1813–62)

1851
Osler's Crystal Fountain, The Crystal Palace,
Great Exhibition, London
Designer: Follett Osler
Moved to Sydenham 1853–54; destroyed
by fire 1936.

1858–60
Fontaine Saint-Michel, Paris
Architect: Gabriel Davioud (1824–81)
Sculptors: Saint-Michel group by
Francisque-Joseph Duret (1804–65)
on a rock by Félix Saupin;
dragons by Henri-Alfred Jacquemart (1824–96)
Restored 1872 and 1893.

1862
Gothic Revival fountain,
Streatham Green, London
Designer: William Dyce (1806–64)

Victoria Fountain, Victoria Park,
Hackney, London
Architect: Henry Darbishire

1867–74
Fontaine de l'Observatoire
(Observatory Fountain), Paris
Architect: Gabriel Davioud (1824–81)
Sculptors: Jean-Baptiste Carpeaux (1827–75),
Eugène Legrain (1837–1915),
Emmanuel Frémiet (1824–1910),
and Louis Villeminot (1826–1914)

1869
Château d'Eau, Palais Longchamp,
Marseilles, France
Architect: Henry Espérandieu (1829–74)

1871
Tyler Davidson Fountain
(The Genius of the Waters or
The Blessings of Water),
Fountain Square, Cincinnati, Ohio
Sculptor: August von Kreyling (1819–76);
original setting designed by architect
William Tinsley

1872
Wallace Fountains, Paris
Sculptor: Charles-Auguste Lebourg
(1829–1906)

1873
Bethesda Fountain (Angel of the Waters),
Central Park, New York
Sculptor: Emma Stebbins (1815–82);
substructure by Calvert Vaux (1824–95)
and Jacob Wrey Mould (1825–84)

1876
United States Centennial Exhibition,
Philadelphia
    Bartholdi Fountain
    Sculptor: Frédéric Auguste Bartholdi
    (1834–1904)
    Fountain purchased in 1877
    by U.S. government and installed in
    Botanic Gardens, Washington, D.C.;
    moved in 1932 to First Street, S.W., and
    Independence Avenue, Washington, D.C.

    Miss Foley's marble fountain,
    Horticultural Hall
    Sculptor: Margaret Foley (died 1877)

1878
Trocadéro Palace and Cascade
Universal Exposition, Paris
Architect: Gabriel Davioud (1824–81)
Engineer: Jules Bourdais

c. **1884–90**
Cogswell Fountains, installed in Boston,
New York, San Francisco, Washington, D.C.,
and over twenty other cities in the
United States.

1886
Jet d'Eau, Geneva, Switzerland
Moved in 1891 to present site;
upgraded in 1951.

1888
Skidmore Fountain,
Portland, Oregon
Designer: Olin L. Warner (1844–96)

1889
Fountain of Progress (Vessel of the
City of Paris) and Five Parts of the World,
Universal Exposition, Paris
Sculptor: Jules-Félix Coutan (1848–1939)

1893
Columbian Fountain,
World's Columbian Exposition, Chicago
Sculptor: Frederick William MacMonnies
(1863–1937)

Shaftesbury Memorial Fountain
(Eros Fountain), Piccadilly Circus, London
Designer: Alfred Gilbert (1854–1934)

1897–98
Court of Neptune Fountain, Library of
Congress Main Building, Washington, D.C.
Architects: J. L. Smithmeyer, Paul J. Pelz, and
Edward Pearce Casey
Sculptor: Roland Hinton Perry (1870–1941)

1900
Château d'Eau and the Palais d'Électricité,
Universal Exposition, Paris
Architects: Edmond Paulin (1848–1915) and
Eugène Hénard (1849–1923) respectively

1901
Pan-American Exposition, Buffalo
    Court of Fountains
    Architect: John M. Carrère (1858–91)

    The Fountain of Abundance
    Sculptor: Philip Martiny (1858–1927)

1912
"Benson Bubblers," Portland, Oregon
Architect: A. E. Doyle

Josephine Shaw Lowell Memorial Fountain,
Bryant Park, New York
Designer: Charles Adams Platt (1861–1933)

1913–16
Pulitzer Fountain (Pomona),
Grand Army Plaza, New York
Architect: Thomas Hastings (1860–1929)
Sculptor: Karl Bitter (1867–1915)

1914–25
James Scott Memorial Fountain,
Belle Isle, Detroit
Architect: Cass Gilbert (1859–1934)
Sculptors: Herbert Adams (1858–1945) and
Robert Aitken (1878–1949)

1915
Panama-Pacific International Exposition,
San Francisco
    Fountain of the Rising Sun and
    Fountain of the Setting Sun
    Designer: Adolphe Alexander Weinmann
    (1870–1952)

    Fountain of Energy
    Sculptor: Alexander Stirling Calder
    (1870–1945)

1915–31
Longwood Gardens, Brandywine Valley,
Pennsylvania
Designer: Pierre S. du Pont (1870–1954)
    Italian Water Garden, 1925–27
    Main Fountain Garden, 1928–31

1917
The Fountain, readymade (signed R. Mutt)
submitted to Society of Independent Artists
Exhibition, New York
Artist: Marcel Duchamp (1867–1968)

1921
Rear Admiral Samuel Francis Dupont
Memorial Fountain, Dupont Circle,
Washington, D.C.
Architect: Henry Bacon (1866–1924)
Sculptor: Daniel Chester French (1850–1931)

1925
The Springs and Rivers of France Fountain,
Exposition Internationale des Arts Décoratifs
et Industriels Modernes (International
Exposition of Modern Decorative and
Industrial Arts), Paris
Designers: René Lalique (1860–1945),
with Marc Ducluzeaud and L. Amaury

1926
Mosaic Fountain, Grosser Garten,
Dresden, Germany
Architect: Hans Poelzig (1869–1936);
restored 1995

Shemanski Fountain, with a statue of Rebecca,
Portland, Oregon
Architect: Carl L. Linde
Sculptor: Oliver L. Barrett

1927
Clarence Buckingham Memorial Fountain,
Grant Park, Chicago
Designer: Edward H. Bennett (1874–1954)
Sculptor: Marcel François Loyau (1895–1936)
Renovated 1994 by architects Harry Weese
Associates.

1931
Grand Signal, Voûte d'Eau and Théâtre d'Eau,
Exposition Coloniale, Paris
Designers: André Granet and
Roger-Henri Expert (1882–1955)

1934
Prometheus Fountain,
Rockefeller Center, New York
Sculptor: Paul Manship (1885–1966)
Renovated 1988; hydraulics by WET Design.

1937
Fountains of the Trocadéro (Fountains of the
Palais de Chaillot), Exposition Internationale
des Arts et des Techniques Appliqués à la Vie
Moderne (International Exposition of the
Applied Arts and Crafts in Modern Life), Paris
Architects: Roger-Henri Expert (1882–1955),
Paul Maître, and Adolphe Thiers
Sculptors: Daniel Bacque, Léon-Ernest Drivier,
Georges-Lucien Guyot, Paul Jouve,
Pierre Poisson, and Pierre Traverse

1939
New York World's Fair
Lagoon
Fountain consultants: Basset Jones
and A.K. Morgan

Water Falls, Electric Utilities Exhibit
Architects: Wallace K. Harrison
(1895–1981) and J. André Fouilhoux
(1879–1945)

The Water Ballet Fountain,
Consolidated Edison Building
Designer: Alexander Calder (1898–1976)

Symbol of Electric Power Fountain,
Westinghouse and Manufacturing Building
Designers: Skidmore & Owings and
John Moss

1940
Meeting of the Waters
(Wedding of the Rivers), St. Louis, Missouri
Sculptor: Carl Milles (1875–1955)

1949–56
General Motors Technical Center,
Warren, Michigan
Architect: Eero Saarinen (1910–61)
Sculptor: Alexander Calder (1898–1976)

1959
Fountain of Wisdom, Seattle Public Library,
Seattle, Washington
Designer: George Tsutakawa (1910–97)

1959–61
El Alamein Memorial Fountain
(first dandelion fountain), Sydney, Australia
Designer: Robert Woodward (born 1923)

1960
J. C. Nichols Memorial Fountain,
Kansas City, Missouri
Sculptor: Henri Greber (1854–?)
Sculpture and structure originally
designed in 1910.

1961–64
Chase Manhattan Bank Plaza sculpture
garden and fountains, New York
Sculptor: Isamu Noguchi (1904–88)
Architects: Skidmore, Owings & Merrill

1962
International Fountain, Seattle World's Fair,
Washington
Designers: Hideki Shimizu and Kazuyuki
Matsushita; John O. Phillips and Associates,
Harry B. Rich (resident architects)
Renovated 1995 by WET Design
(JoAnn Matyas and Mark Fuller, project
designers; Dave Duplanty, project architect;
Long Pham and Alan Robinson, project
engineers); Nakano-Dennis, landscape
architect; TRA, architect-structural engineer.

1964
Fountain, Lincoln Center for the
Performing Arts Plaza, New York
Designers: Philip Johnson (born 1906) with
Richard Foster

1964–65
World's Fair, New York
Unisphere (Fountain of the Continents)
Architects: Gilmore D. Clarke with
consultants Hamel and Langer

Fountain of the Planets (Pool of Industry)
Fountain consultants: Hamel and Langer,
Clarke and Rapuano, Inc.; "spectacle"
program: Leon Leonidoff, producer, and
Jacques Belasco, music director/composer

1966
Lovejoy Plaza and Fountain, Portland, Oregon
Designer: Lawrence Halprin (born 1916),
Lawrence Halprin & Associates, San Francisco
(Satoru Nishita, partner in charge)
Architects: Charles Moore (1925–93),
Charles Moore & William Turnbull;
David Thompson, resident landscape architect;
Gilbert, Forsberg, Deikman & Schmidt,
structural engineers; Yanow & Bauer,
mechanical engineers

1967
Naramore Fountain, Naramore Park, Seattle
Designer: George Tsutakawa (1910–97)

Paley Park, New York
Landscape architects: Robert Zion (born 1921)
and Harold Breen (1923–95), Zion & Breen
Associates; A. Preston Moore, architectural
consultant

1970
Fountains in the Pond of Dreams,
Japan World Exposition (Expo '70), Osaka
Designers: Isamu Noguchi (1904–88), with
Makoto Suzuki and Takasi Sasa

Ira C. Keller Fountain, or Ira's Fountain
(formerly Auditorium Forecourt Fountain),
Portland, Oregon
Designer: Lawrence Halprin (born 1916),
Lawrence Halprin & Associates, San Francisco
(Angela Danadjieva, project designer;
Satoru Nishita, partner in charge;
Byron McCully, project director)
Fountain consultants: Beamer/Wilkinson
and Associates (Richard Chaix)

1971
Greenacre Park, New York
Designer: Sasaki, Dawson, De May Associates

1972–75
Revolving Torsion Fountain,
St. Thomas's Hospital, London
Sculptor: Naum Gabo (1890–1977)
Fountain consultants: Sir Robert McAlpine &
Sons, Matthew Hall Engineering Ltd

1973
Royals Stadium Fountain, Kansas City, Missouri
Architect: Kenneth von Aachen
Engineers: Anthony C. Mifsud of Canal
Electric Motors, Inc., with Peter Micha,
Pem Fountain Company

1974
Fort Worth Water Gardens, Fort Worth, Texas
Architect: Philip Johnson (born 1906), Philip
Johnson and John Burgee, New York; Vernon
Swanson and Bill Cornett, landscape architects;
Thomas S. Byrne, Inc., Fort Worth, engineer
and general contractor

1977
Fasnachtsbrunnen (Carnival Fountain),
Basel, Switzerland
Designer: Jean Tinguely (1925–91)

1978
St. Joseph's Fountain, Piazza d'Italia,
New Orleans, Louisiana
Architects: Charles Moore (1925–93), Urban
Innovations Group, Los Angeles (Ron Filson,
project coordinator) with August Perez
Associates, New Orleans (R. Allen Askew
and Malcolm Heard, Jr., project directors)

1979
Horace E. Dodge & Son Memorial Fountain,
Detroit, Michigan
Designers: Isamu Noguchi (1904–88)
with Shoji Sadao
Architects: Smith, Hinchman & Grylls
Associates, Inc.
Fountain consultant: Richard Chaix

1980
Williams Square, Las Colinas, Texas
Commissioned by Ben Carpenter
Architects: SWA Group, Houston
(James Reeves, project director);
Robert Glen, sculptor
Fountain consultant: Richard Chaix

1982
Levi's Plaza, San Francisco
Designer: Lawrence Halprin (born 1916)
Fountain consultant: CMS Collaborative
(Richard Chaix, Tom Mallonee, and
Richard Schuder)

Fountain of Nations, Epcot Center,
Walt Disney World, Orlando, Florida
Designer: Mark Fuller (born 1951)

1982–83
Blair Fountain, Riverfront Park,
Tulsa, Oklahoma
Designer: Athena Tacha (born 1936)
Architect: James Manzelmann,
Benham-Holway-Spragins
Fountain consultant: Jack Tumilty,
W.R. Holway and Associates, Division of the
Benham Group

1983
Igor Stravinsky Fountain, Paris
Designers: Jean Tinguely (1925–91) and
Niki de Saint-Phalle (born 1930)

Butler Ice Fountain, Buffalo State College,
Buffalo, New York
Sculptor: Carl Nesjar (born 1920)

1984
Tanner Fountain, Harvard University,
Cambridge, Massachusetts
Designers: Peter Walker (born 1932) and the
SWA Group, with steam artist Joan Brigham
Fountain consultant: CMS Collaborative
(Richard Chaix, Tom Mallonee, and
Richard Schuder)

1985
Transco Waterwall, Houston, Texas
Architects: Philip Johnson (born 1906),
Philip Johnson and John Burgee Architects,
New York; associated architects, Richard
Fitzgerald and Partners, Houston
Landscape architects: SWA Group, Houston
Fountain consultant: CMS Collaborative
(Richard Chaix, Tom Mallonee, and
Richard Schuder)

1986
Fountain Place at First Interstate Bank Tower
(formerly Allied Bank), Dallas, Texas
Architects: I.M. Pei and Partners; Harry
Weese Associates
Landscape architects: Dan Kiley (born 1912),
Kiley-Walker, Vermont (Peter Ker Walker,
partner in charge)
Fountain consultant: WET Design
(Mark Fuller and Nina Vaughn, project
designers, and Alan Robinson, project engineer)

1987
Los Angeles Music Center Fountain
Designers: WET Design (Claire Kahn and
Mark Fuller, project designers with
Alan Robinson, project engineer)

1988
Fountains and Water Garden, North Carolina
National Bank Plaza, Tampa, Florida
Landscape architect: Dan Kiley (born 1912),
Office of Dan Kiley, Vermont
Architect: Harry C. Wolf Associates
Fountain consultant: William Hobbs, Ltd.

1989
Nicholas J. Melas Centennial Fountain and
Water Arc, Chicago River, Chicago
Designer: Lohan Associates
Fountain consultant: CMS Collaborative
(Richard Chaix, Tom Mallonee, and
Richard Schuder)

Civil Rights Memorial, Southern Poverty
Law Center, Montgomery, Alabama
Designer: Maya Lin (born 1959)

Lagoon, water mountain/volcano,
Mirage Casino, Las Vegas, Nevada
Designers: Steve Wynn and Atlandia

1991
Fountain, Biddy Mason Park, Los Angeles
Designers: Pamela Burton (born 1948) and
Katherine Spitz (born 1952), Burton and Spitz
(now Pamela Burton & Company),
Santa Monica

1992
Parc André-Citroën, Paris
Designers: Patrick Berger (born 1947),
architect, with Gilles Clément (born 1943),
landscape architect; and Jean-Paul Viguier
(born 1946), architect, with Alain Provost (born
1938), landscape architect
Fountain consultants: M. Labbyt and M. Llorca
First phase completed in 1992 but designs in
progress to extend park to the River Seine.

California Plaza Watercourt, Los Angeles
Architect: Arthur Erickson
Designers: WET Design (Mark Fuller,
JoAnn Matyas, Linda Wall, Traer Price and
Claire Kahn, project designers, with
Alan Robinson, project engineer)

1993
Universal CityWalk Fountain,
Universal City, California
Architect: The Jerde Partnership
Designers: WET Design (JoAnn Matyas,
Traer Price and Mark Fuller, project designers,
with Long Pham and Alan Robinson, project
engineer)

Archimedes Screw, 's-Hertogenbosch,
The Netherlands
Sculptor: Tony Cragg (born 1949)

1994
Centennial Fountain,
West Palm Beach, Florida
Designers: Office of Dan Kiley, Vermont
Landscape Architects: Team Plan, Inc.,
North Palm Beach, Florida
Fountain consultant: Peter Hoyle, London

1996
Fountain of Rings, Centennial Olympic Park,
Atlanta, Georgia
Designers: EDAW, Inc., Atlanta, with
William Hobbs Ltd

Sounding Stones, New York
Designer: Maya Lin (born 1959)

1997
Franklin Delano Roosevelt Memorial,
Washington, D.C.
Designer: Lawrence Halprin (born 1916)
Sculptors: Leonard Baskin (born 1922),
Neil Estern (born 1926), Robert Graham
(born 1938), Tom Hardy (born 1921) and
George Segal (born 1924)
Fountain consultant: CMS Collaborative
(Richard Chaix, Tom Mallonee, and
Richard Schuder)

Notes

Abbreviated author/date references are given in full in the Bibliography.

Chapter 1

1 Lao-Tze, *Tao Te Ching*, v. 78 (6th c. B.C.), as quoted in Moore 1994, p. 40.

2 Text accompanying the chromolithograph plate for the Great Fountain, Enville, Staffordshire in *The Gardens of England*, 1857.

3 The fountain also celebrates the purifying of Chicago's drinking supply while it commemorates the thousands who died in epidemics caused by the city's once-polluted river.

4 From Alberti, *L'Architettura*, vol. I, p. 15 as quoted in Coffin 1991, p. 103.

5 Lines 10 and 8 respectively from a letter dated 26 July 1543. See C. Tolomei, *Delle lettere di M. Claudio Tolomei*, Venice, 1550, as quoted in MacDougall 1978, pp. 5–6, 12–14. Also found in Coffin 1991, p. 36.

6 Duchamp submitted the urinal (manufactured by Mott Iron Works, a New York company that actually made fountains, in addition to plumbing fixtures) to a 1917 Independents exhibition as a work of art by "R. Mutt," but *Fountain* was rejected by the exhibition jury. An article published at the time came to Duchamp's defense: "Whether Mr. Mutt with his own hands made the fountain or not has no importance. He CHOSE it. He took an ordinary article of life, placed it so that its useful significance disappeared under the new title and point of view—created a new thought for that object." (Quoted in Anne d'Harnoncourt and Kynaston McShine, eds., *Marcel Duchamp*, Philadelphia, 1973, p. 283.)

7 Almost 1,800 drawings by Giuseppe Barberi, the largest group outside Italy, are in the collection of Cooper-Hewitt, National Design Museum.

8 See Campbell 1978, for a lucid overview of the qualities of water, hydraulics and the fountain design process.

9 The Medici Villa (now known as Villa Demidoff) was designed with astonishing water effects to rival those at the Villa d'Este. It also boasted a grotto fountain in the form of a rocky Mount Parnassus and an amphitheater with Giambologna's colossal statue of Appennino (symbolizing the Appenines, the mountains of Tuscany). Many of the spectacular water and garden features were destroyed in the nineteenth century.

10 Coffin 1991, pp. 50–53.

11 Ibid., pp. 53–54.

12 Ibid., p. 54.

13 Mount Parnassus and the Muses was a favorite theme in Renaissance gardens, and this Mount Parnassus fountain was undoubtedly inspired by the one at Pratolino. See Strong 1979, pp. 73–97 for an excellent account of de Caus's career; pp. 90–93 discuss Mount Parnassus. De Caus's print, or the original in Pratolino, probably inspired Charles Le Brun's elegant design for a similar fountain for Versailles [138]. Also, I am indebted to Leslie Overstreet, Smithsonian Institution Libraries Special Collections Department (Dibner), for providing information on de Caus and the other important figures in hydraulic engineering history cited here.

14 Ibid., p. 165: "the world of late Renaissance mechanical manuals and magical science lived on into the age of Enlightenment." Isaac's book was translated into English by John Leak, and when Stephen Switzer published *An Introduction to a General System of Hydrostatics and Hydraulics* (1729), he acknowledged his debt to Salomon de Caus.

15 Sextus Julius Frontinus compiled his *De aquis urbis Romae* (or *De aquaeductibus urbis Romae*) while he served as Rome's water commissioner and civil engineer from A.D. 97 until his death, thought to be A.D. 103 or 104. His hydraulics knowledge was based on his personal inspection of the city's many aqueduct systems, and on his own records of water volume and flow rates. This classical text was the most comprehensive source on the engineering of ancient Roman water systems. It was lost until 1429, when it was found in the monastery library of Monte Cassino. By Carlo Fontana's day the text was more widely known. Since he was working on upgrading Rome's water systems, he would have consulted it. It is not surprising that he would have wished to follow his esteemed predecessor's example, contributing his own observations to hydraulics literature.

16 See Bélidor 1739, vol. 2, Chapter 5, "De la manière de distribuer & de diriger les Eaux jaillissantes pour la décoration des jardins," pp. 389–98. Also summarized in Moore 1994, pp. 43–45.

17 Bélidor 1739, p. 389.

18 Quoted in Elizabeth K. Reilly, *Water in the Garden… Prints and Books of the XVI to XX Century*, New York, 1980, p. 21.

19 Chaix worked on the Portland fountain when he was with Beamer/Wilkinson and Associates. In 1977, he established his own firm, Richard Chaix Fountain Consultant; in 1981, he was cofounder of CMS Collaborative. His two articles for *Architectural Record* (Mar. 1969 and Dec. 1970) elucidate the role of the contemporary hydraulic engineer in fountain design.

20 The Butler family has played a significant philanthropic role in the Buffalo community. Edward H. Butler, founder of the *Buffalo Evening News*, supported the college in its early years. His son Edward H., Jr., was responsible for the Edward H. Butler Library, named for his father, and Kate Butler Wallis, the granddaughter, was the patron of the library's expansion and its fountain.

Chapter 2

1 See D'Onofrio 1991, pp. 78–100; Sanfilippo 1996, p. 173; and Morton 1966, pp. 108–10. Once thought by some to be by Michelangelo, scholars now reject this attribution. D'Onofrio suggests it might be by Stoldo Lorenzi, p. 80. The fountain still survives today. In 1872 it was moved from its original location on the Corso to a niche of a building on the Via Lata, just off the Corso. Unfortunately, the porter's face is damaged, partly due to being repeatedly bumped by water vessels.

2 Koeppel 1994, p. 20.

3 Krautheimer 1952, p. 271. Since the mid-thirteenth century, the city of Siena had placed itself under the special protection of the Virgin, so council members ruled in her name. Duccio's *Maestà* (1315), the splendid altarpiece created for Siena's cathedral, depicts the Virgin in Majesty as the city's protector. Ambrogio Lorenzetti's mural *The Virtues of Good Government* (1338–39) for the Palazzo Pubblico proudly projects the city's civic and artistic achievements. The fresco's iconography features Justice, who governs for

the common good, aided by Fortitude, Prudence, Temperance, Peace and Magnanimity. Thus, the public fountain combines already established aspects of Siena's religious and civic symbolism.

4 Ibid., p. 265; Seymour 1968, p. 97.

5 Krautheimer 1952, p. 265; Hanson 1965, pp. 22–25; Seymour 1968, pp. 93–94; Peter Ward-Jackson, *Italian Drawings, Fourteenth-Sixteenth Century*, Vol. 1, Victoria and Albert Museum Catalogues, London, 1979, pp. 21–24; Jacob Bean and Laurence Turčič, *15th- and 16th-Century Italian Drawings in the Metropolitan Museum of Art*, New York, 1982, pp. 210–11.

6 Morton 1966, p. 31.

7 Schama 1995, p. 286, note 74, cites Pliny, *Natural History*, trans. H. Rackham, Cambridge, Mass., 1986, 36.24; a variant of this quote is in Morton 1966, p. 31.

8 Sanfilippo 1996, p. 43.

9 For a history of the making of the fountain, see D'Onofrio 1962, pp. 85–95. The project started with the 1 June 1585 purchase from Marzio Colonna of land rights for the source of the water, followed immediately by the aqueduct work to connect the water to Rome. Sanfilippo 1996, p. 88. Also, see Torgil Magnuson, *Rome in the Age of Bernini*, 2 vols., Stockholm, 1982, vol. I, p. 14. He observes that before any undertaking to bring water to Rome could proceed, the pope waged a successful campaign to eliminate crime perpetrated by roaming bandits who had long terrorized everyone who ventured into the countryside surrounding Rome.

10 Sanfilippo 1996, p. 43. Also, Schama 1995, p. 284, states Domenico Fontana was in the pope's good graces as he had successfully masterminded the reerection of the Egyptian obelisk in the square in front of St. Peter's—one of Sixtus's most notable projects. According to D'Onofrio 1962, pp. 89–92, Giovanni Fontana, architect to the pope and Domenico's brother, also worked on the Acqua Felice.

11 See D'Onofrio 1962, pp. 141–48, for a history of the creation of this fountain.

12 "Si sentira un gran strillare a far pagar il vino per condurre l'acqua," as quoted in ibid., p.145.

13 Ibid., p. 148. The edict was addressed to greengrocers, gardeners and vineyard workers prohibiting the washing of themselves, their clothes and their vegetables by day or night in the fountain. Later edicts banned bathing and swimming. Also see Sanfilippo 1996, p. 44.

14 Miller 1968, pp. 270–77, and Chapter V of Miller 1977a remain important definitive studies on this fountain. These are key references for the text here. Please also see her discussion in Chapter 3 of this book on pp. 69–70. Also important are Marion Boudon's "La Fontaine des Innocents" and Daniel Rabreau's "Sculpture et iconographie" in Massounie et al. 1995, pp. 52–55 and 150–57.

15 Miller 1968, p. 272.

16 Ibid., pp. 273 and 276.

17 Ibid., p. 272.

18 Massounie et al. 1995, pp. 54–55.

19 Miller 1977a, p. 124; Massounie et al. 1995, p. 55; "The Fountains of Paris," *Architectural Review* 37, Feb. 1915, p. 35.

20 Richard A. Etlin, *The Architecture of Death: The Transformation of the Cemetery in Eighteenth-Century Paris*, Cambridge, Mass., 1984, p. 17.

21 Also, the monument was in need of some restoration since centuries of exposure to the elements had damaged delicate details of Goujon's sculpture. Some of the original reliefs are now preserved in the Musée du Louvre. Montorgueil 1928, p. 34.

22 Ibid., p. 35.

23 Jeffrey Chipps Smith, *German Sculpture of the Later Renaissance, c. 1520–1580: Art in the Age of Uncertainty*, Princeton, 1994, p. 221.

24 Schenk 1949, p. 13. Gieng is thought to have also done the statues for two other Bernese fountains: the 1507 Bagpiper (inspired by an engraving by Albrecht Dürer) and Samson. Also see Chapter 3, p. 63.

25 See Aynaud 1968, pp. 135–40.

26 André Bouyale D'Arnaud, *Évocation du vieil Aix-en-Provence*, Paris, 1964, p. 212.

27 The text here depends on Daniel Rabreau's chapters in Massounie et al. 1995, pp. 98–103 and 150–57. Also see Roserot 1902, pp. 353–72.

28 This drawing is now in the Musée Vivenel, Compiègne. See Pinto 1986, pp. 112–13, fig. 75.

29 Eighteen drawings relating to the Fontaine des Quatre Saisons are in the Musée du Louvre, see Jean Guiffrey and Pierre Marcel, *Inventaire général des dessins du Louvre et du Musée de Versailles*, Paris, 1908, vol. 2, nos. 867–84. Also see Gerold Weber, "Dessins et maquettes d'Edme Bouchardon," *Revue de l'art* 6, 1969, pp. 43–47, illustrating the maquettes, which are in the collection of the Musée des Beaux-Arts, Dijon.

30 This glorification is reinforced by the fountain's Latin inscription. See Roserot 1902, p. 360 and Rabreau in Massounie et al. 1995, p. 100.

31 Renzo Salvadori, *Architect's Guide to Paris*, London, 1990, p. 67.

32 Massounie et al. 1995, pp. 138–40.

33 "The Fountains of Paris," p. 38; Montorgueil 1928, p. 110; Massounie et al. 1995, p. 297. The fountain originally featured a statue by Pierre-Nicolas Beauvallet which was based on one in the Louvre, but his figure was replaced with one by J. -F. -T. Gechler in 1844.

34 M. Symmes is indebted to Caroline Mathieu and Bruno Girveau, Musée d'Orsay, for information about this drawing. Darcel and Alphand's hydraulics expertise were later tapped to create the magical waterworks for the Paris Universal Expositions of 1867, 1878, and 1889 (see Chapter 5, pp. 106–09). Also see Paul Smith, "Fontaines jaillissantes artésiennes," in Massounie et al. 1995, pp. 202–04.

35 See Vial 1991 for a history of the project.

36 The canal system goes through the countryside surrounding Aix-en-Provence, thus irrigating and enriching a region known for its bountiful harvests and markets.

37 Vial 1991, pp. 40–43, 55–56. Models of Bartholdi's Palais Longchamp proposals are now in the Musée Bartholdi, Colmar. In 1859, his designs were carefully reviewed by a commission comprised of the most august architects of the day: Léon Vaudoyer, Henri Labrouste and Victor Baltard. While they found some merit in Bartholdi's proposals, they also suggested improvements, hesitating to endorse him fully. Bartholdi, naturally, was deeply disappointed not to get the major commission. When the final Palais Longchamp design by Espérandieu was unveiled, Bartholdi claimed that it heavily relied on his initial design. The dispute lasted for years; he finally lost his claim for fees in 1901.

38 Ibid., pp. 60–61, 78–79, for detailed descriptions of the iconography and water effects.

39 The design of Palais Longchamp influenced Gabriel Davioud's Trocadéro Palace and Cascade at the 1878 Paris Universal Exposition [180], as well as the monumental fountain in Barcelona's Parque de la Ciudadela (1877–82), by Josep Fontseré assisted by the young Antoni Gaudí.

40 See Koeppel 1994, pp. 19–30, for a more detailed account of the history of New York's water systems. See esp. pp. 22–24 and 26, for the role of Aaron Burr (who was vice president during the 1801–05 term of President Thomas Jefferson) and the early years of the Manhattan Company. Tapping people's water needs to develop a healthy business was the prime purpose of the company. However, the Manhattan Company quickly capitalized on the revenues derived from supplying water to establish a more thriving bank business, in fact the forerunner of Chase Manhattan.

41 Ibid., pp. 26–27. John B. Jervis, who had worked on the Erie Canal, was chief engineer on the Croton project. There were many difficulties to be overcome, funds to be raised, feats of design and engineering to be achieved before the water could travel the forty miles from the Croton Dam to New York City. One of the distributing reservoirs within the city, located at Fifth Avenue and Forty-second Street, was later razed to make room for the New York Public Library. An updated Croton system still furnishes about one tenth of the daily water supply required by Manhattan inhabitants.

42 Ibid., p. 30. The words are by George Pope Morris.

43 *The Builder*, 11 June 1859, p. 392.

44 Gloria-Gilda Deák, *Picturing America, Prints, Maps, and Drawings Bearing on the New World Discoveries…*, 2 vols., Princeton, 1988, vol. l, pp. 384–85, no. 568.

45 M. Symmes is indebted to Sally Pierce, Boston Atheneum, for providing a copy of the official Boston Water Celebration program and published record.

46 *Celebration of the Introduction of the Water of Cochituate Lake into the City of Boston, October 25, 1848*, pp. 44–45.

47 Davies 1989, p. 8. See also Chapter 5, p. 105.

48 Ibid., p. 8. There were devastating cholera epidemics in 1848–49 and 1853–54. The link between cholera and filthy water was established in 1854 when Dr John Snow traced one outbreak to a specific London pump.

49 Ibid., pp. 13, 15. Interestingly, besides those advocating temperance, among the early fountain patrons were those whose wealth came from breweries.

50 *The Builder*, 26 Nov. 1859, pp. 776, 777. "Water Is Best" was inscribed on a 1861 fountain outside Bath Abbey, as noted in Davies 1989, p. 28.

51 Originally, the fountain was to be placed on a wall adjacent to the burial ground of St. Andrew's, Holborn, but *The Builder* voiced objections to London's first drinking fountain being placed unwholesomely next to the remains of many generations. The advice was heeded, and the fountain was relocated. A subsequent article in *The Builder* (14 May 1859, p. 325) found great fault in this fountain's ill-proportioned Norman design. Also see Davies 1989, pp. 13–14 and 41. Although the fountain was dismantled in 1867 due to construction of the Holborn viaduct, it was reinstalled in 1913. It is one of the few to retain its original bronze drinking cup and chain (giving meaning to the inscribed reminder "Replace the Cup"). Communal fountain cups were removed in response to modern public health policies.

52 *The Civil Engineer and Architect's Journal* 23, 1 Oct. 1860, pp. 315–16.

53 *The Builder*, 26 Nov. 1859, p. 776.

54 M. Symmes acknowledges the contribution of Stephen Astley, Sir John Soane's Museum, London, who kindly provided research and this text on Dyce. For further information on this artist, see Marcia R. Pointon, *William Dyce, 1806–1864: A Critical Biography*, New York, 1979, and *Centenary Exhibition of the Work of William Dyce R.A. 1806–1864*, Aberdeen Art Gallery, Aberdeen, Scotland, 1964.

55 Davies 1989, p. 18.

56 Many readers may be more familiar with another Wallace legacy in London, the Wallace Collection, which has one of the finest collections of French art outside France.

57 See François Ozanne's chapter "Les Fontaines Wallace," in Massounie et al. 1995, pp. 205–07 for further information.

58 There is a resemblance between these figures and the larger ones found on Bartholdi's 1876 fountain [177] at the United States Centennial Exhibition in Philadelphia.

59 The original passage, paraphrased here, is quoted in full in Ozanne, in Massounie et al. 1995, p. 206.

60 See Moffatt 1992, pp. 123–43, for a thorough account of Cogswell Fountains.

61 Ibid., p. 124.

62 Ruth Teiser, "Dr. Cogswell's Unloved Statues," *Westways* 3, no. 7, July 1949, p. 21, as quoted in Moffatt 1992, p. 137.

63 Teiser, ibid., p. 138.

64 New York's Cogswell Fountain was restored in 1992. At that time, the city Department of Parks removed the statue of Hebe (a figure manufactured by the J. L. Mott Iron Works Company of New York) to protect it from air pollution, and it was deposited with the New York Municipal Art Society.

65 Emil Corwin, "Cogwell's Great Fountain Crusade," *Yankee* 35, no. 3, Mar. 1971, p. 106.

66 Ibid., pp. 140–41.

67 Karl Klooster, "Skidmore: The Fountain Hits 100," *This Week*, 20 Sep. 1988.

68 As quoted in "Skidmore's Portland," *Portland Commerce Magazine*, 1 Mar. 1974, p. 29.

69 Ibid.

70 This sentiment was echoed by American sculptor Loredo Taft, who made a pilgrimage to visit the fountain in Nov. 1934, as noted in Paul F. Hauser, Jr., "Skidmore Left a Fountain… and a Controversy," *The Sunday Oregonian*, 9 Nov. 1941. Although in the years since there was some thought to relocate the fountain to a park setting, preservationists prevailed, and it still adorns the intersection in the historic section of the city, on the original site for which Warner designed it.

71 Information here about the Shemanski and Benson drinking fountains comes from several incompletely identified newspaper clippings from the Oregon Historical Society's "Fountain Subject File." M. Symmes is grateful to the society's reference staff for accommodating her research needs.

72 Sam Howe Verhovek, "A Few Cities See a Profit in Bottling L'Eau de Tap," *The New York Times*, 6 Aug. 1997, pp. A1, A14.

Chapter 3

Data gleaned from guidebooks or classical dictionaries is not cited. The author would like to thank Beye/Deppe for their help with the Latin inscriptions.

1 These themes, particularly the fountain as a source of wisdom and inspiration, are discussed in Miller, "Domain of Illusion. The Grotto in France," in MacDougall 1978, pp. 175–206, esp. pp. 201–05.

2 Paul Underwood, "The Fountain of Life in Manuscripts of the Gospels," *Dumbarton Oaks Papers* 5, 1950, pp. 41–138. For the Oberlin painting, see Lotte Brand Philip, *The Ghent Altarpiece and the Art of Jan van Eyck*, Princeton, 1971, pp. 11–13, 66–70.

3 F. A. Gruyer, *Chantilly: les quarante Fouquet*, Paris, 1897, pp. 97–98.

4 Oleg Grabar, *The Alhambra*, Cambridge, Mass., 1978, pp. 34, 124–29, 144, 151, 206. Also, Frederick Bargebuhr, *The Alhambra. A Cycle of Studies on the Eleventh Century in Moorish Spain*, Berlin, 1968.

5 See Miller 1977a, pp. 64–85.

6 Plotinus, *The Enneads*, trans. MacKenna, 2nd ed., London, 1957, III.8.10, p. 249.

7 Hesiod, *Works and Days*, trans. H. G. Evelyn-White, Cambridge, Mass., and London, 1914, lines 110–20.

8 Reinhild Janzen, *Albrecht Altdorfer. Four Centuries of Criticism*, Ann Arbor, Mich., 1980, pp. 88–89.

9 Jacqueline and Maurice Guillaud, eds., *Altdorfer and Fantastic Realism in German Art*, New York, 1985, p. 94, fig. 104.

10 Alison Stewart, "Sebald Beham's Fountain of Youth-Bathhouse Woodcut: Popular Entertainment and Large Prints by the Little Masters," *Register, Spencer Museum of Art*, 6, 1989, pp. 64–88. See too G. Hartlaub, *Der Jungbrunnen*, Stuttgart, 1958, which discusses Lucas Cranach's *Fountain of Youth* (1546), its large pool centered about a statue of Venus and Cupid; see pp. 26–28 for Hans Sachs's verses, "Der Traum vom Jungbrunnen," 1557, and Anna Rapp, *Der Jungbrunnen in Literatur und bildender Kunst des Mittelalters*, Zurich, 1976.

11 See Miller 1986, pp. 137–53, esp. pp. 145–52, and notes.

12 S. Samek Ludovici, *Il "De Sphaera" estense e l'iconografia astrologica*, Milan, 1958, p. 44, pl. 41. See also Paul Watson, *The Garden of Love in Tuscan Art of the Early Renaissance*, Philadelphia, 1979.

13 See Giusta Nicco Fasola, *La Fontana di Perugia*, Rome, 1951, pp. 14–17; and Kathrin Hoffmann-Curtius, *Das Programm der Fontana Maggiore in Perugia*, Düsseldorf, 1968.

14 Ludwig Zintl, *Der Schöne Brunnen in Nürnberg und seine Figuren*, Nuremberg, 1993, gives a history of the fountain from 1385 to the present and is copiously illustrated with polychrome figures and a plan of the octagonal fountain, indicating all its components.

15 For the most comprehensive work on Roman fountains, see D'Onofrio, *Le Fontane di Roma*, Rome, 1957, 3rd rev. ed., 1986. For the most pleasurable introduction to these fountains, see Morton 1966 (for the Fountain of Moses, see pp. 127–33; the Evelyn citation is on p. 133). Cf. "The Song of the Well" (Nos. 21:16–18), a poetic insertion in praise of the miraculous gift of water provided to the Israelites during their wanderings in the desert.

16 Dominique Jarasse, "Les Fontaines et le décor urbain," in *Gabriel Davioud Architecte (1824–1881)*, Paris, 1981–82, pp. 42–51, esp. pp. 42–47, where the author presents unexecuted projects as well as the final version.

17 Marie Donald Mackie Hottinger, *The Stories of Basel, Berne and Zurich*, Nendeln-Liechtenstein, 1933, reprint 1970, pp. 212–15.

18 *Pasquinata* was the nickname of an ancient statue in Rome on which lampoons were posted in the sixteenth century. See Morton 1966, pp. 108–10.

19 Stewart, "Sebald Beham's Fountain," p. 70, fig. 8.

20 See M. Bernos, N. Coulet, C. Dolan-Leclerc, P. A. Février et al, *Histoire d'Aix-en-Provence*, Aix-en-Provence, 1977, fig. 63, for a reproduction of this fountain.

21 Joseph Mordaunt Crook, *William Burges and the High Victorian Dream*, Chicago, 1981, pp. 68–69, fig. 6. Also Crook, ed., *The Strange Genius of William Burges 'Art-Architect' (1827–1881)*, London, 1981, p. 15. Stephen Astley, Sir John Soane's Museum, London, kindly provided additional information on this drawing.

22 Virgil, *The Aeneid*, trans. H. R. Fairclough, London and New York, 1929.

23 Sheila Ffolliott, *Civic Sculpture in the Renaissance: Montorsoli's Fountains of Messina*, Ann Arbor, Mich., 1984.

24 Miller 1977b, pp. 14–39.

25 Eve Borsook, *Companion Guide to Florence*, New York, 1966, pp. 47–49.

26 Weber 1985, pp. 284–86, fig. 147. Lablaude 1995, p. 79, reproduces Jean Cotelle's painting of the Bassins de Neptune and du Dragon, and the Allée d'Eau (1693). Also, A. and J. Marie, *Versailles au temps de Louis XIV*, Paris, 1976, pp. 371–72.

27 Pierre Marot, *La Place Royale de Nancy: image de la réunion de la Lorraine à la France*, Nancy, 1966, pp. 53–60, and pls. 23, 24 from Emmanuel Héré, *Recueil des fondations*, 2nd ed., 1762.

28 See Goode 1974, pp. 69–70. In the wake of the artistic success of the World's Columbian Exposition in Chicago, painters and sculptors were called to Washington, D.C., to decorate the new Library of Congress building with ornamental moldings, mosaics, statuary, and frescoes portraying allegories of the arts and sciences.

29 Giorgio Vasari, *Le vite de piu eccellenti pittori scultori ed architettori*, ed. Milanese, 9 vols., Florence, 1906, vol VI, pp. 72–86, in the life of Tribolo.

30 Coffin 1979, ed. 1988, pp. 328–29.

31 Paul Laumonier, *Pierre Ronsard. Oeuvres complètes*, 20 vols., Paris, 1937, vol. 8, p. 224.

32 See Miller 1977a, pp. 104–12, and notes.

33 Miller 1968, pp. 270–77.

34 Miller 1977a, pp. 301–07, discusses the fountains in the *Hypnerotomachia Poliphili*.

35 Howard Hibbard, *Bernini*, Baltimore, 1965, pp. 39–40 and 110–14. Also, Ovid, *Metamorphoses*, trans. F. J. Miller, 2 vols., London, 1984.

36 Hibbard, *Bernini*, pp. 118–24; Morton 1966, pp. 176–87.

37 Schneider 1977, vol. 1, pp. 397–424, and notes.

38 Boudon 1991, pp. 81–83, and notes.

39 Kowsky 1979, pp. 231–37.

40 There is ample documentation for this fountain. For a summary, see Marianne Doezema and June Hargrove, *The Public Monument and Its Audience*, Cleveland, 1977, cover and pp. 41–43. See also Mary S. March, "Henry Probasco and Ferdinand von Miller Create the Tyler Davidson Fountain," *Queen City Heritage: The Journal of the Cincinnati Historical Society* 45, Spring 1987, pp. 3–18; also, Gerhard Bott, "Der Tyler-Davidson-Brunnen in Cincinnati," in Katharina and Gerhard Bott, eds., *ViceVersa: Deutsche Maler in Amerika, Amerikanische Maler in Deutschland, 1813–1913*, Munich, 1996, pp. 150–64.

The Bethesda Fountain in New York City

1 For Stebbins, see Charlotte Streifer Rubinstein, *American Women Sculptors: A History of Women Working in Three Dimensions*, Chicago, 1990, pp. 63–66; Michael Elliman and Frederick Roll, *The Pink Plaque Guide to London*, London, n.d., pp. 56–57.

2 *The Holy Bible Containing the Old and New Testaments Translated Out of the Original Tongues.* New York, 1873, John 5:4; also quoted in Board of Commissioners of the Central Park, *Third Annual Report 1872–73*, New York, 1875, p. 8.

3 *Third Annual Report*, p. 8.

4 "The Bethesda Fountain," *New York Herald*, 1 June 1873, and "The Bethesda Fountain," *New York Times*, 1 June 1873.

5 Tony Kushner, *Angels in America Part Two: Perestroika*, New York, 1994, pp. 143–46.

Chapter 4

* The term "propaganda" may seem pejorative today when describing forms of political or economic manipulation, but it is used here in its broader sense— as a form of iconography that persuasively conveys to the observer ideas about power and patronage.

1 For an introduction to Cosimo's patronage, see Janet Cox-Rearick, *Dynasty and Destiny in Medici Art*, Princeton, 1984; Paul William Richelson, *Studies in the Personal Imagery of Cosimo I de' Medici, Duke of Florence*, New York, 1975.

2 Wiles [1933] 1975, pp. 22–31.

3 Quoted ibid., p. 51.

4 Giusto Utens's 1599 painting of the Pitti Palace, in the Museo di Firenze com'era, reveals the expanse of the gardens and documents the location and original appearance of the fountains. On the Pitti Palace and its gardens, see Mario Bucci and Raffaello Bencini, *Palazzi di Firenze*, Florence, 1973, pp. 11–27, and Francesco Gurrieri and Judith Chatfield, *Boboli Gardens*, Florence, 1972, pp. 17–36.

5 The fountain was transferred in 1636 to the Isolotto, designed by Alfonso Parigi in 1618, and located in the expanded portion of the gardens.

6 James Holderbaum, *The Sculptor Giovanni Bologna*, New York and London, 1983, pp. 149–50.

7 Montorsoli's 1557 Fountain of Neptune in Messina (Sicily) provided the inspiration for later sculptural fountain designs, although Ammannati's Florentine Fountain of Neptune remains the best known of this type. The Florentine commission had been given originally to the sculptor Baccio Bandinelli, but upon his death in 1560, Cosimo opened the competition and Benvenuto Cellini, Ammannati, Vincenzo Danti and Giambologna all submitted models (now lost). Ammannati, who had considerable experience with fountains, won. Giambologna may have utilized his design in his two later fountains: that of Oceanus in the Boboli Gardens and the Fountain of Neptune in Bologna. In 1563, Giambologna was offered the commission for the Bologna Neptune by Pope Pius IV. With the exception of the stone receiving basin and marble steps, the fountain is entirely of bronze and is dominated by a single standing figure of the sea god. Upon his return to Florence in 1567, Giambologna created the Boboli fountain featuring the powerful Oceanus. See Wiles [1933] 1975, pp. 50, 54–56.

In the same year as the Oceanus commission, Cosimo instructed Pietro Paolo Galeotti to strike twelve commemorative medals, one bearing a portrait of Cosimo on the obverse and the aqueduct with part of Ammannati's Neptune on the reverse. Cosimo attached such importance to his role in this construction that upon his death in 1574 it was featured in his funerary apparatus. See Eve Borsook, "Art and Politics at the Medici Court I: The Funeral of Cosimo I de' Medici," *Mitteilungen des Kunsthistorischen Institutes in Florenz* XII, 1965, pp. 31–54; Kurt W. Forster, "Metaphors of Rule: Political Ideology and History in the Portraits of Cosimo de' Medici," *Mitteilungen des Kunsthistorischen Institutes in Florenz* XV, 1971, pp. 80–81. See also Igino B. Supino, *Il Medagliere mediceo nel R. Museo Nazionale di Firenze (Secoli XV, XVI)*, Florence, 1899, p. 134, nos. 384–85.

8 The fountain was removed in the seventeenth century to a rectangular basin behind the amphitheater and was replaced by a Ganymede fountain. The Neptune fountain retained its cylix form for a short time which was then replaced by its present rocky base.

9 Malcolm Campbell, "Observations on Ammannati's Neptune Fountain: 1565 and 1575," *Renaissance Studies in Honor of Craig Hugh Smyth*, Florence, 1986, II, pp. 113–32; See also, Charles Avery, *Giambologna: The Complete Sculpture*, Mt. Kisco, N.Y., 1987.

10 Wiles [1933] 1975, pp. 22–31.

11 Virginia Bush, *The Colossal Sculpture of the Cinquecento*, New York, 1976, p. 180; see also, Lazzaro 1990, p. 194.

12 Edmund P. Pillsbury, "Drawings by Jacopo Zucchi," *Master Drawings* 12, 1974, p. 21.

13 The curved theater, with or without a fountain, is a common feature of the Renaissance villa from the Villa Belvedere to the Villa Giulia. A segmented water theater on axis behind the main block of the villa is found at Palladio's Villa Maser and its plan is illustrated in his *Quattro libri dell'architettura* of which Maderno owned a copy. See Howard Hibbard, *Carlo Maderno and Roman Architecture, 1580–1630*, University Park, Pa., 1971, pp. 47–50, 131–33.

14 The standard work on the Villa Aldobrandini remains Karl Schwager's "Kardinal Pietro Aldobrandinis Villa di Belvedere in Frascati," *Römisches Jahrbuch für Kunstgeschichte*, 1961–62, vols. IX–X, pp. 289–382. See also Carla Benocci, *Villa Aldobrandini a Roma*, Rome, 1992; Steinberg 1965, p. 453.

15 Earl Rosenthal, "Plus Ultra, Non Plus Ultra and the Columnar Device of Emperor Charles V," *Journal of the Warburg and Courtauld Institutes*, 1971, vol. XXXIV, pp. 204–28.

16 Coffin 1979, pp. 41, 59.

17 For comprehensive information about the creation of Versailles and its fountains, see Robert W. Berger, *The Château of Louis XIV*, University Park, Pa., 1985; Gerald van der Kemp, *Versailles*, New York, 1978; Walton 1986; Weber 1985.

18 Woodbridge 1986, pp. 181–95.

19 Walton 1986, p. 164.

20 Ibid., p. 165.

21 Ibid.

22 Ibid., p. 166.

23 Alfred Marie, *Versailles au temps de Louis XIV: troisième partie, Mansart et Robert de Cotte*, Paris, 1976.

24 Charles Le Brun, the *premier peintre du roi*, was the most influential artist at Versailles, masterminding its décor which included the painted decoration as well as the designs for tapestries, furniture, sculpture and fountains.

25 Nationalmuseum, Stockholm, *Versailles à Stockholm, dessins du Nationalmuseum: peintures, meubles, et arts décoratifs des collections suédoises et danoises*, Paris, 1985, p. 22 (exhibition organized on the occasion of the "Colloque Versailles," Institut Culturel Suédois, Hôtel de Marie, Paris, Sep.–Oct. 1985); Lablaude 1995, p.53.

26 Thomas Hedin, *The Sculpture of Gaspard and Balthazar Marsy: Art and Patronage in the Early Reign of Louis XIV*, Columbia, S.C., 1983, pp. 140–42.

27 Ibid., pp. 140–46.

28 Walton 1986, p. 164 notes that the growth of the palace with its fountains and waterworks outpaced the ability of engineers to provide water. Despite new reservoirs and many windmills to drive pumps, it was not possible to keep the existing fountains playing most of the day. Today's visitors to Versailles are apt to see Latona and the other fountains without full moving water jet action just as in Louis XIV's day, when there was careful orchestration of when each fountain was turned on; some were reserved to play in full force only for major festivities. Today, the fountains are turned on only in the summer months, and then, only on Sundays and special occasions. Since the fountains are powered by gravity-driven water pressure and hydraulic pumps, water slowly drains from reservoirs hidden in one wing of the palace and in other buildings in the city of Versailles. By afternoon's end, after the water has flowed from the higher fountains to the lower ones, the water level in the reservoirs is low, so the fountains are turned off. They can be turned on again when the reservoir is replenished. We acknowledge the assistance of Arnaud Ramière de Fortanier, directeur des Archives Départementales des Yvelines in Versailles, for indicating which buildings contain water to supply the grounds of the royal palace.

29 Berger, *Château of Louis XIV*, p. 23.

30 Jacques Wilhelm, "Le Labyrinthe de Versailles," *Revue de l'histoire de Versailles*, vol. 38, no. 1, Jan.– Mar. 1936, pp. 44–63.

31 The first edition of La Fontaine's fables, published in 1668, was dedicated to the dauphin. Ibid., p. 48.

32 The animal sculptures appear to be the work of a single hand, but were in fact the result of the group effort of more than twenty sculptors. Many versions were modeled before the final selections were made. A document dated to the 1670s, in the Tessin Collection, Stockholm, identifies each sculptor by name, notes the fees paid, and the sculpture's placement within the maze, but it does not clearly link each sculptor with his work. Ibid., pp. 51–52.

33 Its name changed in 1944 to Petrodvorets, reverting to Peterhof in 1993.

34 Anxious to see the newest and most ingenious creations in the fields of Western art and technology, the tsar visited Europe in 1697, 1712, and 1717. Politics prevented him from visiting France until 1717, so he relied upon books, such as Salomon de Caus's *Les Raisons des forces mouvantes* (1615), which impacted upon the hydraulics he employed and the importation of designers like Jean-Baptiste-Alexandre Le Blond who left the clearest mark on the layout of the garden. For further discussion, see Margrethe Floryan, *Gardens of the Tzars: A Study of the Aesthetic, Semantics and Uses of Late Eighteenth-Century Russian Gardens*, Aarhus, 1996.

35 Floryan, *Gardens of the Tzars*, p. 194.

36 The palace and gardens received their name from the recreational *granja*, or grange, of the Hieronymite order of El Parral that had previously existed on the site.

37 In 1726, Procaccini converted the royal residence of La Granja, built only six years earlier by Teodoro Ardemans, into a baroque palace whose curvilinear facade shows the influence of the seventeenth-century Italian architect Francesco Borromini. Ardemans, trained in the classical tradition, had designed a square plan with an interior courtyard and four corner towers, an unmistakable reference to the earlier alcazars of the Spanish Hapsburg kings.

38 George Kubler and Martin Soria, *Art and Architecture in Spain and Portugal and Their American Dominions 1500–1800*, Harmondsworth, 1959 (1969 ed.), pp. 43, 163.

39 This discussion depends upon the excellent study, Pinto 1986, pp. 5–27.

40 Ibid., p. 31.

41 Ibid., p. 43.

42 Ibid., p. 79. The obelisk was later erected in front of the Trinità ai Monti and the *tazza* was set below the obelisk of the Quirinal.

43 Ibid., pp. 91–93.

44 Ibid., p. 99.

45 Hibbard, *Bernini*, p. 120.

46 Ibid., p. 122.

47 Pinto 1986, pp. 220–26.

48 A copy of this pamphlet, dated "14 brumaire an VIII" in the French Revolutionary calendar adopted in 1793 (i.e. dated 5 Nov. 1799), is in the British Library, London. In 1992, James A. Leith, Queens University, Kingston, Canada, notified Cooper-Hewitt, National Design Museum, of the pamphlet's existence and very kindly provided his transcription of the text for the museum's research files on this drawing. The iconographical explanation for this fountain design relies on Mr. Leith's transcription of Hoüel's own words. A print based on this drawing was executed in 1802.

49 See Katia Frey, "L'Entreprise Napoléonienne," in Massounie et al. 1995, pp. 120–21, for an account of this fountain.

50 While zoomorphic architecture and sculpture had their origins in ancient civilizations, with elephants figuring significantly in India, Egypt, and North Africa (particularly in Carthage during the times of Hannibal), European monumental sculpture in the form of an elephant was not common. Live elephants were creatures of great curiosity in royal menageries. Europe's increasing familiarity with this exotic beast prompted its use as a popular decorative motif in the sixteenth and seventeenth

centuries. In 1758, M. Ribart had his idea for an elephant monument to be placed on the Champs Élysées published. In his *Architecture singulière: l'éléphant triomphal, grand kiosque, à la gloire du roi*, the elephant was to support a tower decorated with trophies and banners, capped by a statue of Louis XV. See Clay Lancaster, *Architectural Follies in America, or Hammer, Saw, Tooth and Nail*, Rutland, Vt., 1960, p. 190.

51 See Jean Guiffrey and Pierre Marcel, *Inventaire général des dessins du Musée du Louvre et du Musée de Versailles, École Française*, Paris, 1907, vol. 1, pp. 4–5, nos. 6–15. Three drawings show alternative ideas for the elaborate golden palanquin; the elephant's exotic attendants; and a view with a different water action. Of the remaining drawings, one depicts the huge hangar erected on the construction site, while the fifth drawing shows an idea for a camel and crocodile fountain. Prints after Alavoine's Elephant Fountain watercolors also exist.

52 Frey in Massounie et al. 1995, p. 121. Also see Schama, *Citizens: A Chronicle of the French Revolution*, New York, 1989, pp. 3–6. Schama begins his book with a passage describing how the massive plaster model of the "unforgettable" imperial elephant monument, left standing in Place de la Bastille, gradually crumbled into ruins, while the pendulum swing of French patriotic memory sought instead to commemorate the revolutionary events of 1789 and 1830.

53 For a history of the redesign and iconography of this major Paris square, see Schneider 1977, Chapter VI, pp. 365–430; and *Hittorff* 1986, pp. 75–109.

54 Two important Paris buildings designed by Hittorff are the church of Saint Vincent de Paul (1824–44) and the Gare du Nord (1858–66).

55 Schneider 1977, p. 382.

56 Several people may have influenced the king on Hittorff's behalf, including the esteemed German scientist and explorer Alexander von Humboldt, the German diplomat H. A. A. von Werther, the French Minister of the Interior Adolphe Thiers, and C. P. B. Rambuteau, appointed prefect of the Seine in 1833. Rambuteau's appointment came in the wake of a terrible cholera epidemic, so besides overseeing practical water systems matters, he welcomed involvement in a major civic fountain project celebrating water. Ibid., pp. 365, 384; and Dominique Massounie, "1830–1848: L'Essor des fontaines monumentales," in Massounie et al. 1995, pp. 171–73.

57 A version of this fountain was installed at the Rond-Point of the Champs Élysées, only to be replaced in the 1860s with one by Gabriel Davioud. See Massounie in Massounie et al. 1995, p. 173.

58 The first fountain in front of St. Peter's was originally designed by Carlo Maderno in 1614. In 1667, it was remodeled and relocated by Gian Lorenzo Bernini when he was redesigning the piazza. In 1668–78, another fountain was constructed as a twin to the first in order to create a symmetrical and ordered approach to the church. Both fountains received an abundant supply of water from the Acqua Paola. See Chapter 2, p. 54.

59 Schneider 1977, p. 392.

60 *Hittorff* 1986, p. 105; Schneider 1977, p. 399.

61 Tremendous care was taken to ensure the evenness of flow from the top basins to the lower ones, so that the overall effect would be maintained regardless of fluctuating water pressures or gusts of wind. An ingenious trough, hidden by the edges of the middle basin, controlled the flow of water over the rim. See Schneider 1977, p. 400, fig. 215.

62 See Massounie in Massounie et al. 1995, pp. 172, 298. For another description of the iconography, see Schneider 1977, pp. 400–01. The sculptors were Auguste-Hyacinthe Debay (the Atlantic and the Mediterranean); Antoine Desbouefs (Coral and Fish); Achille-Joseph Valois (Shells and Pearls); Isidore-Hippolyte Brion (Maritime Navigation, Astronomy and Commerce); Jean-François-Théodore Gechter (the Rhône and the Rhine); François-Gaspard Lanno (Flowers and Fruit); Honoré-Jean Husson (Wheat and Grapes); Jean-Jacques Feuchère (River Navigation, Industry and Agriculture). The tritons and nereids were by Jean-Jacques Elshoecht, Louis-Parfait Merlieux and Antonin-Marie Moine. The other decorative sculptures were by *ornemaniste* Hoegler.

63 Schneider 1977, p. 397.

64 Bitter's influential role derived, in part, from his contribution to the sculptural programs and pageantry of four American world's fairs: the World's Columbian Exposition (1893), the Pan-American Exposition in Buffalo (1901), the Louisiana Purchase Centennial International Exposition in Saint Louis (1904), and the Panama-Pacific International Exposition in San Francisco (1915). See Chapter 5, pp. 109–13.

65 Bogart 1986, p. 57. Pulitzer's will left $50,000 expressly for "the erection of a fountain at some suitable place in Central Park preferably at or near the Plaza entrance at 59th street, and to be, as far as practicable, like those of the Place de la Concorde, Paris." As Bogart's article recounts, this was Pulitzer's parting response to his arch rival, newspaper publisher William Randolph Hearst, who had previously commissioned the Maine Memorial (1901–13) for another major corner of Central Park (at what is now Columbus Circle). The memorial was for 260 sailors who died when the battleship Maine exploded in Havana Harbor, triggering the Spanish-American War. Pulitzer was highly critical of Hearst's exploitation of the controversial naval tragedy to sell more papers. Pulitzer wanted the grandeur of his fountain and plaza to surpass Hearst's monument.

66 A presentation drawing of the fountain design, inscribed "Approved May 12, 1913" is in the Art Commission records in the New York City municipal archives. With Bitter's death in an automobile accident in 1915, Pomona had to be completed by his studio assistants.

67 See Harry Rand, *Paul Manship*, Washington, 1989, p. 141. Also see Edith Hamilton, *Mythology: Timeless Tales of Gods and Heroes*, New York, 1962, pp. 68–73. Because of his aid to mortals, Prometheus subsequently had to suffer Zeus's cruel revenge. As punishment, Prometheus was bound to a mountain top, where, unable to escape, he was tortured daily by an eagle feasting on his liver. Eventually, Hercules came to his rescue, killing the eagle and releasing Prometheus.

68 Alan Balfour, *Rockefeller Center*, New York, 1978, p. 195.

69 Donald Martin Reynolds, *Masters of American Sculpture: The Figurative Tradition from the American Renaissance to the Millennium*, New York, 1993, pp. 46–47.

70 Carol Herselle Krinsky, *Rockefeller Center*, Oxford, London, and New York, 1978, p. 56.

71 Rand, *Paul Manship*, p. 139.

72 Ibid., p. 142. Two other sculptures, one of a male figure the other of a female figure, represented the human race. They were originally placed on either side of the wall behind Prometheus, but Manship was bothered by their relationship to the central figure. In 1935 they were resited to the Palazzo Italia roof

garden of the Rockefeller Center complex, where they remained until 1984. These sculptures are now back in the plaza near the Prometheus Fountain, but sited differently from 1934.

73 Named for the English Channel, the Channel Gardens are the narrow passageway linking the British Empire Building and La Maison Française. At the high end of each pool, then and now, is a small sculpture of a triton (alternating in the next pool with a nereid) riding a fish spouting water. These fountainheads, by sculptor René Chambellan, symbolize, according to Donald Reynolds (*Masters of American Sculpture*, p. 47), "Leadership, Will, Thought, Imagination, Energy, and Alertness, attributes that have enabled mankind to succeed in the course of civilization." At the bottom of each pool, the drain is covered by marine creature sculptures, such as a crab or starfish, also by Chambellan.

74 As quoted in Balfour, *Rockefeller Center*, p. 218.

75 Ibid. (and note 78) as from "Look at Rockefeller Center," *Harper's Magazine*, Oct. 1938, pp. 506–13.

Fountains as Globes, Symbols of the Universe and Democracy

1 Louis Villeminot designed the bronze garland of shell work and marine plants that decorates the pedestal supporting the Carpeaux figures. Emmanuel Frémiet was the sculptor of the wildly rearing sea horses and writhing, spouting dolphins who, in turn, are doused by sprays of water from the mouths of turtles near the pool's periphery.

2 For more information pertaining to the design of the Perisphere, see Victoria Newhouse, Chapter 9, "1939: The World of Tomorrow," *William K. Harrison, Architect*, New York, 1989, pp. 80–93. Also shown at the fair was a plaster Celestial Sphere by Paul Manship, artist of the Prometheus Fountain [161]. Later in 1939, to honor the League of Nations and President Woodrow Wilson, a bronze version of the Celestial Sphere—13½ feet in diameter—was installed as the Wilson Memorial in the midst of a reflecting pool at the Palais des Nations, Geneva, headquarters of the European offices of the United Nations. See Harry Rand, *Paul Manship*, Washington, D.C., and London, 1989, pp. 124–26.

3 For further discussion of New York world's fairs' fountains, see Chapter 5, pp. 109–19.

Chapter 5

1 *Official Descriptive and Illustrated Catalogue of the Great Exhibition 1851*, 3 vols. with supplementary vol., London, 1851, vol. 1, pp. 235, 326. For examples of other fountains exhibited at the 1851 fair, see also vol. 1, pp. 311, 473; vol. 2, pp. 598, 600, 658, 704, 728, 767, 853; and vol. 3, pp. 1066, 1205, 1229, 1283. Beaver 1986, pp. 11–67; and Allwood 1977, pp. 13–24.

2 *The Art Journal Illustrated Catalogue of the Great Exhibition*, London, 1851, pp. 255–56; and *Official Descriptive and Illustrated Catalogue*, vol. 2, pp. 658, 700, 852; and supplementary vol., p. xxviii. When the Crystal Palace was enlarged and moved to Sydenham in 1853, Osler's Crystal Fountain was moved with it, and the exhibition hall itself was surrounded with elaborate gardens and outdoor fountains. The fountain, along with the palace, was destroyed in 1936. Beaver 1986, pp. 69–104 and 141–46.

3 *Official Descriptive and Illustrated Catalogue*, supplementary vol., p. 131.

4 These were all designed in collaboration with the French sculptor Jean-Baptiste-Jules Klagmann. Virginie Granval, "Fontaines éphémères," in Massounie et al. 1995, p. 212; and Allwood 1977, pp. 25–41.

5 Kowsky 1979, pp. 231–37. See also Allwood 1977, pp. 42–57; and John Maass, *The Glorious Enterprise: The Centennial Exhibition of 1876 and H. J. Schwarzmann, Architect-in-Chief*, Watkins Glen, N.Y., 1973.

6 Kowsky 1979, pp. 233–34; and Goode 1974, pp. 250–51.

7 James D. McCabe, *The Illustrated History of the Centennial Exhibition*, Philadelphia, 1876, reprint 1975, p. 116 This was just two years after the founding of the National Women's Christian Temperance Movement in Cincinnati.

8 Marietta Holley, *Josiah Allen's Wife as a P. A. and P. I., or, Samantha at the Centennial*, Hartford, 1877, p. 464. Margaret Foley was an American artist working in Rome.

9 For this and other fountains, see McCabe, *Illustrated History*, pp. 29, 68 and 188; and Frank Henry Norton, *Illustrated Historical Register of the United States Centennial Exposition, Philadelphia, 1876, and of the Exposition Universelle, Paris, 1878*, New York, 1879, pp. 259, 286 and 301; Wayne Craven, *Sculpture in America*, New York, 1968, pp. 330–32; and *Illustrated Catalogue of Statuary: Fountains, Vases, Settees, etc. for Parks, Gardens and Conservatories, Manufactured by the J. L. Mott Iron Works*, New York, 1873.

10 Norton, *Illustrated Historical Register*, p. 212.

11 Ibid., p. 166; and McCabe, *Illustrated History*, p. 168.

12 McCabe, *Illustrated History*, p. 116.

13 Granval in Massounie et al. 1995, pp. 214–18; Norton, *Illustrated Historical Register*, pp. 325–26 and 336.

14 Granval in Massounie et al. 1995, pp. 219–25; and Frantz Jourdain, "La Fontaine monumentale," *L'Exposition de Paris de 1889* 1, no. 15, 8 June 1889, pp. 115 and 120.

15 "La Fontaine de M. Saint-Vidal," *L'Exposition de Paris de 1889* 1, no. 7, 15 Mar. 1889, p. 50.

16 See, for example, Good 1889, pp. 115–18; or Carl Henning, "Electricity," in *Reports of the United States Commissioners to the Universal Exposition at Paris*, Washington, D.C., 1891, vol. 4, pp. 98–99.

17 *Picturesque World's Fair: An Elaborate Collection of Colored Views*, Chicago, 1894, p. 63; Wim de Wit, "Building an Illusion: The Design of the World's Columbian Exposition," in Neil Harris et al., *Grand Illusions: Chicago's World's Fair of 1893*, Chicago, 1993, p. 85; Stanley Applebaum, *The Chicago World's Fair of 1893: A Photographic Record*, New York, 1980, p. 21; and Craven, *Sculpture in America*, p. 424.

18 *Report of the President to the Board of Directors of the World's Columbian Exposition: Chicago 1892–1893*, Chicago, 1898, pp. 43–45; and Hubert Howe Bancroft, *The Book of the Fair*, Chicago, 1893, vol. 1, pp. 402 and 424.

19 Allwood 1977, pp. 96–109; Wolfgang Friebe, *Buildings of the World's Exhibitions*, trans. J. Vowles and P. Roper, Leipzig, 1985, pp. 116–33. These are the dynamos that so enthralled the American visitor, Henry Adams. See *The Education of Henry Adams: An Autobiography*, Boston, 1918, pp. 379–90.

20 The volume of water being displayed was more than twenty thousand gallons per minute (Granval in Massounie et al. 1995, pp. 226–29).

21 Robert W. Rydell, *All the World's a Fair: Visions of Empire at American International Expositions, 1876–1916*, Chicago, 1984, pp. 127–28; and C. D. Arnold, *The Pan-American Exposition Illustrated*, Buffalo, 1901.

22 Rydell, *All the World's a Fair*, p. 132.

23 Ibid., p. 134; and Craven, *Sculpture in America*, pp. 469–70.

24 Arnold, *Pan-American Exposition*, pp. 17, 19 and 46; Craven, *Sculpture in America*, pp. 445–46; and James M. Dennis, *Karl Bitter: Architectural Sculptor 1867–1915*, Madison, Wis., 1967, pp. 104–10.

25 Other major fountains at the fair that reiterated its primary iconographic themes were The Birth of Venus and The Birth of Athena (by "Mr. and Mrs. Michel Tonette"), which flanked the main pool, and The Fountain of Man outside the Government Building by Charles Grafly. Arnold, *Pan-American Exposition*, pp. 32, 54, 62 and 66; and Craven, *Sculpture in America*, pp. 439–40.

26 Quoted in Susan E. Luftschein, "The Changing Face of an Expanding America: The City Beautiful Movement, the Myth of the Frontier, and the Louisiana Purchase Exposition, St. Louis, 1904," Ph.D. Diss., The City University of New York, 1996, p. 64; Dennis, *Karl Bitter*, pp. 110–15; and also David R. Francis, *The Universal Exposition of 1904*, 2 vols., St. Louis, 1913.

27 Luftschein, "The Changing Face of an Expanding America," pp. 63–67; and John Wesley Hanson, *The Official History of the Fair, St. Louis, 1904: The Sights and Scenes of the Louisiana Purchase Exposition*, St. Louis, 1904, p. 489.

28 Ben Macomber, *The Jewel City: Its Planning and Achievement; Its Architecture, Sculpture, Symbolism, and Music; Its Gardens, and Exhibits*, San Francisco, 1915, p. 83.

29 Frank Morton Todd, *The Story of the Exposition: Being the Official History of the International Celebration held at San Francisco in 1915 to Commemorate the Discovery of the Pacific Ocean and the Construction of the Panama Canal*, New York, 1921, vol. 2, p. 310; and Macomber, *The Jewel City*, pp. 83–95.

30 Elizabeth N. Armstrong, "Hercules and the Muses: Public Art at the Fair," in Benedict, Burton et al., *The Anthropology of World's Fairs: San Francisco's Panama Pacific International Exposition of 1915*, London and Berkeley, 1983, p. 119. A small fountain designed by the San Francisco architect William Faville for the Palace of Education was later donated by him to the city of Sausalito. It was completely recast in 1977 and presently stands in Depot Park, now called Plaza Viña del Mar. Jack Tracy, *Sausalito "Moments in Time": A Pictorial History of Sausalito First One Hundred Years, 1850–1950*, Sausalito, Calif., 1983, pp. 116–17.

31 William H. Wilson, *The City Beautiful Movement*, Baltimore, Md., 1989; and also Thomas S. Hines, "The Imperial Mall: The City Beautiful Movement and the Washington Plan of 1901–1902," and Jon A. Peterson, "The Mall, the McMillan Plan, and the Origins of American City Planning," in Richard Longstreth, ed., *The Mall in Washington, 1791–1991*, Washington, D.C., 1991, pp. 79–115.

32 Goode 1974, p. 291; Dennis, *Karl Bitter*, pp. 230–44.; and Draper 1982, pp. 14–24.

33 See Granval in Massounie et al. 1995, pp. 231–46, for a description of the variety of fountains at this exposition and the Paris fairs of 1931 and 1937 discussed later in this chapter.

Chapter 6

1 See Coles 1973, p. 20. Coles used this phrase in remarking on Cass Gilbert's belief that memorials rise above practical utility to the ideal.

2 Massounie et al. 1995, p. 176.

3 The statues are by Jean-Jacques Feuchère, François-Gaspard Lanno, Louis Desprez and Jacques-Auguste Fauginet, respectively. Sometimes the fountain was also called the Fontaine des Quatre Points Cardinaux, being a French play on words meaning either "Fountain of the Cardinal Points" or "Fountain of the Four Cardinals Who Never Were" because none were ever appointed cardinal.

4 Massounie et al. 1995, p. 177.

5 A memorial tribute to Visconti, subsequently appointed architect to Napoleon III, was the publication in 1860 by Léon Visconti of a set of engravings documenting for posterity (and future preservationists) the architect's monumental fountain designs (shown in perspective, plan and section). Other noteworthy Visconti-designed fountains in Paris are Fontaine Gaillon (1828) and Fontaine de la Place Louvois (1836–39 [123]).

6 For an excellent account of the history, design process and significance of the Shaftesbury Memorial Fountain, see Marc Girouard, "The Background to the Shaftesbury Memorial: Memorials and Public Open Spaces in Victorian London," pp. 33–38 and Richard Dorment, "The Shaftesbury Memorial 1886–1893," pp. 135–43, in Dorment, *Alfred Gilbert, Sculptor and Goldsmith*, London, 1986.

7 Dorment, ibid., pp. 135–36.

8 Ibid., p. 136. The Piccadilly Circus site was selected in Jan. 1890 (ibid., p. 135). At about this time, a newly devised street, leading down to Piccadilly Circus, was named Shaftesbury Avenue (see Girouard, ibid., p. 36).

9 Dorment, ibid., pp. 138–39, shows illustrations of sketchy drawings in the collection of the Jean van Caloen Foundation (Loppem, Belgium) and in the Greater London Record Office.

10 Ibid., pp. 141–42.

11 Wolfe 1996, p. 296.

12 See Keith N. Morgan, *Shaping an American Landscape: The Art and Architecture of Charles A. Platt*, Hanover, N.H., 1995, pp. 102–04 for a biography of Mrs. Lowell and an account of the creation of the memorial.

13 This shape exemplifies one that became standard for fountains during and after the Renaissance. In fact, since Maderno's fountain used the huge granite basin that had been excavated from the Thermae of Titus, the basin form derives from the Romans. (See Morton 1966, p. 215.) Two of Platt's drawings for the Lowell Memorial Fountain (one being a quarter plan of the basin, half-elevation, half-section, a section of the curb, and an elevation of the plaque; the other showing details of the fountain, plus quarter plans and elevations) are in the collection of the Avery Architectural and Fine Arts Library, Columbia University, New York.

14 Initially intended for a Lower East Side park where Lowell had worked, the fountain was instead placed on a more prestigious site near the William Cullen Bryant Memorial on the east side of Bryant Park. Today, the fountain, recently restored, graces the west side of the park.

15 Coles 1973, p. 9. This article furnishes much information about the story behind the James Scott Memorial Fountain, the design competition and Gilbert's prolonged involvement in the project.

16 Ibid., p. 5.

17 Ibid., p. 6.

18 By this time, Cass Gilbert was famous for the grand Beaux-Arts style U.S. Customs House (now the Smithsonian Institution's National Museum of the American Indian) and the Gothic-inspired Woolworth Building, the world's first skyscraper, both in New York City. He would later design the Detroit Public Library and the U.S. Supreme Court Building in Washington, D.C.

19 Coles 1973, pp. 19 and 20.

20 See Michael Richman, *Daniel Chester French: An American Sculptor*, New York, 1976, pp. 155–63. In 1882, Congress had named the intersection of Massachusetts and Connecticut Avenues (then an elegant residential area) Dupont Circle to honor the admiral for his military services. A statue of him had been erected there, but in 1917 Dupont family members wanted a more graceful memorial. Richman's text outlines in detail the collaborative process between architect, sculptor and patrons. The presentation model and working models are preserved at Chesterwood, French's former home in western Massachusetts.

21 Few associate the Dupont Memorial Fountain with a naval war hero of the last century. More accessible and popular is the modern United States Navy Memorial on Pennsylvania Avenue (halfway between the Capitol and the White House). Designed by the New York architectural firm Conklin Rossant in 1987 as a circular plaza for office workers to enjoy at lunchtime, it features four low, curved, stepped fountains, each topped by a row of small jets. These surround a huge pavement map of the world, on which stands the *Lone Sailer* (1987), a sculpture by Stanley Bleifield. At the base of the fountains are reliefs depicting major naval victories and events since the American Navy's founding. The four abstract fountains are perhaps meant to symbolize the sea, but the formulaic water steps lack inspirational power. Instead the fountain is dictated by practical design solutions devised so a minimum of water can provide the maximum glistening effect and rushing sound, while not splashing passers-by when gusts of wind prevail. The disadvantage of structural designs like this is that when the water is turned off, visitors see less attractive rows of concrete steps. This utilitarian mastery of water is becoming more prevalent in many urban plazas and malls worldwide. Yet fountains featuring the evocative sculptural qualities of water, with or without iconographic sculpture or classic forms, as in the Dupont Memorial Fountain, may more successfully fulfill commemorative purposes.

22 I am indebted to Mary Woolover, Ryerson & Burnham Archives, Art Institute of Chicago, for furnishing copies of newspaper clippings and Bennett, Parsons, and Frost archival architectural information pertaining to the fountain, as well as biographical information on Buckingham. The archive also includes a 18 May 1927 letter to Bennett from landscape architect Frederick Law Olmsted congratulating him on his great fountain and inquiring about the results of his experiments with different jet nozzles.

23 The Buckingham fortune derived from their father's lucrative grain business. Clarence's charity work included establishing children's playgrounds, contributing to local boys' schools and homes caring for elderly men, in addition to serving as a long-time trustee of the Art Institute of Chicago, helping to found its prints department. He was an avid collector of Japanese prints, which he first saw at the 1893 World's Columbian Exposition. Kate's 1937 bequest to the museum left funds to care for and augment the collections of oriental art, Old Master prints, and medieval art.

24 Information here comes from identified and unidentified newspaper clippings, including "50,000 Attend Dedication of New Fountain," *Chicago Tribune*, 27 Aug. 1927; "City Seeks 'Fountainist' to Play Symphonies with Water and Light," *Chicago Tribune*, 28 Nov. l927; "Great Fountain in Grant Park a Color Lyric," *Chicago Daily News*, 1 June 1929; and one undated, unidentified clipping.

25 In May 1995, Harry Weese Associates completed the restoration of the Clarence Buckingham Memorial Fountain which had operated without disruption since 1927. By the early 1990s, repairing freeze/thaw damage and upgrading the lighting and pump equipment with the latest computerized technology were necessary.

26 For complete information regarding this fountain and J. C. Nichols, please see Piland and Uguccioni 1985, esp. pp. 160–67.

27 The Southern Poverty Law Center was established in 1971 to protect the legal rights of minorities and the poor, while it advocates teaching tolerance. The idea for the Civil Rights Memorial originated with the center's cofounder Morris Dees. Edward Ashworth, then a board member, proposed Lin as the designer. Sara Bullard and Richard Cohen, also of the S. P. L. C. staff, researched the events and names for the memorial. I thank JoAnne Chancellor and Ashley Alred, S. P. L. C., for furnishing information about the Civil Rights Memorial and the Southern Poverty Law Center.

28 Zinnser 1991, p. 35.

29 Ibid. The phrase became famous in King's "I Have a Dream" speech that culminated the 1963 civil rights march in Washington, but he also used it earlier in a speech given at the start of the 1955 Montgomery bus boycott.

30 This Woolworth Store lunch counter is now part of the collection of the National Museum of American History, Smithsonian Institution, Washington, D.C.

31 Zinnser 1991, p. 38. Lin designed a similar water table fountain for Yale University in New Haven. The Women's Table marks a spiraling history of women students at the university, marking a few events from its founding in 1701 to 1969, when it became coeducational, followed by an increasing number of dates up to 1993, when the fountain was installed.

32 Ibid., p. 35.

33 In fact, there is also a modest F. D. R. Memorial more in keeping with the president's own wishes to have a stone memorial no larger than his desk. This was dedicated in 1965, and it is located in the grounds of the National Archives on Pennsylvania Avenue, Washington, D.C. In London, there is also an F. D. R. Memorial Fountain (1948; Sir William Reid Dick, designer) in Grosvenor Square.

34 This site for a presidential monument had been designated by the 1901 McMillan Commission extension of Pierre Charles L'Enfant's original 1791 city plan for Washington (which previously indicated three monumental focal points: the Capitol, the Washington Monument and the White House). The McMillan plan was a kite-shaped arrangement with the key points being the Washington Monument (completed 1884), the Lincoln Memorial (completed 1922), a future presidential memorial (now the new F. D. R. Memorial) and the Jefferson Memorial (completed 1943).

35 *Newsweek*, 5 July l965, p. 20. I thank Rolf Myller, one of the six preliminary finalists in the 1960 F. D .R. Memorial competition, for kindly sharing his clippings file documenting the publicity surrounding the 1960 competition and the subsequent controversy.

36 I am grateful to Lawrence Halprin for generously permitting me to study and cite excerpts from his unpublished notebooks. See Halprin Notebook 57.

37 Ibid., page dated 6-21-90.

38 Shortly before it opened, disabled Americans protested the memorial's minimal acknowledgment of Roosevelt's polio and his reliance on a wheelchair, cane or crutches for mobility. Since during his presidency Roosevelt himself veiled his own disability in the belief that acknowledging it would weaken his image as a strong leader, Roosevelt family members and the design team opted to focus on his presidential achievements and not his disability. However, bowing to public pressure, President Clinton promised to support legislation modifying the memorial with an additional sculpture showing Roosevelt in a wheelchair. Information from David Stout, "Clinton Calls for Sculpture of Roosevelt in Wheelchair," *New York Times*, 24 Apr. 1997, p. B8.

39 In fact, the water was so alluring that the National Park Service has since banned wading and swimming in the waterfall pools. A site manager declared that people thought the memorial was a recreational "Water World." Linda Wheeler, " No More Frolicking in FDR Pools," *The Washington Post*, 23 July l997.

40 Halprin Notebook 71, page from Dec. 1980, p. 41.

41 I am grateful to Emilio Ambasz, architect and industrial designer in New York and Bologna, for sharing information about this memorial project.

Chapter 7

1 Howard Hibbard, *Bernini*, Harmondsworth, 1965, pp. 121–22.

2 Coffin 1960 and Coffin 1979, pp. 311–40.

3 Coffin 1979, p. 327.

4 Ibid., p. 336.

5 Ibid., p. 319.

6 MacDougall 1978, p. 9.

7 Michel de Montaigne, *Travel Journey*, trans. Donald M. Frame, San Francisco, 1983, p. 98.

8 Coffin 1979, p. 327.

9 The Fountain of the Dragons was originally to have featured the many-headed dragon vanquished by Hercules, but was altered to display the *impresa* of Pope Gregory XIII in honor of his visit.

10 Webster Smith, "Pratolino," *Journal of the Society of Architectural Historians* XX, 1961, pp. 155–68; Coffin 1981, pp. 279–82. Coffin notes the importance and influence of Pratolino. The French hydraulics expert Salomon de Caus visited Italy between 1595 and 1598 and thoroughly investigated the waterworks at Pratolino. In 1611, de Caus was in England and designed a grotto for Queen Anne for her garden at Somerset House [25]. He later followed Elizabeth, the sister of Henry, prince of Wales, and the wife of the elector Palatine, to Heidelberg where for the remainder of his life he created the great *Hortus Palatinus*. His younger brother, Isaac de Caus, stayed in England and continued his brother's work.

11 Michel de Montaigne, *Journal d'un voyage en Italie… 1580–1581*, Paris, 1906, pp. 271–72, quoted in Miller 1982, p. 48.

12 Coffin 1979, p. 340.

13 Ingrid D. Rowland, "Render Unto Caesar the Things Which Are Caesar's: Humanism and the Arts in the Patronage of Agostino Chigi," *Renaissance Quarterly*, XXXVI, 1986, p. 688.

14 Patricia Schultz, "Hellbrunn: The Sacred and the Profane," *Garden Design*, V, 1986, p. 41.

15 Woodbridge 1986, p. 213.

16 Although landscape gardener Michael Grosse began to design the gardens of Herrenhausen in 1666 and his work was subsequently developed by Henry Perronet after 1674, they did not truly follow Le Nôtre's example until later. In 1682 Electress Sophie (wife of Ernest-August, later elector of Hanover) appointed Martin Charbonnier (d. 1720), a pupil of Le Nôtre, to undertake all the major design work in the garden, and their vision made it the finest example of the French style in Germany. While initial hydraulic planning for the Great Fountain took place in 1690, the actual construction of the fountain did not begin until 1720.

17 Many scholars have written about these palaces, including Michèle Pirazzoli-t'Serstevens, "The Emperor Qianlong's European Palaces," in *Orientations*, Nov. 1988, pp. 61–71. Also by the same author, "A Pluridisciplinary Research on Castiglione and the Emperor Chien-Long's [Qianlong's] European Palaces, Parts I and II" in the *National Palace Museum Bulletin*, Taipei, Taiwan, vol. xxiv, nos. 4 and 5, Sep.–Oct. 1989, pp. 1–11 and Nov.–Dec. 1989, pp. 1–16.

18 L. F. Delatour, *Essais sur l'architecture des Chinois*, Paris, 1803, as quoted in Pirazzoli-t'Serstevens, "Emperor Qianlong's European Palaces," p. 63.

19 Two bronze heads, one of a boar and one of a monkey from Yuan-Ming-Yuan's series of zodiac sculptures, were auctioned at Sotheby's, New York, 9 Oct. 1987, lots 134, 135.

20 However, some scholars believe this print records a scene from *Ipermestra* by Pietro Metastasio which was performed at the Hoftheater, Vienna, on 8 Jan. 1744.

21 Randall 1995, p. 5. This guidebook provides the best overview of the history of the gardens and fountains. Colvin Randall kindly furnished further information about Longwood Gardens.

22 Quoted ibid. The only American public fountain to rival these impressive effects was Chicago's Clarence Buckingham Memorial Fountain, dedicated in 1927, see Chapter 6, p. 129.

23 Mark Fuller's design and engineering of unusual water features was based on his own hydraulic research about how water behaves when turbulence is removed, as published in his 1976 Stanford University thesis on "axisymmetric laminar flow." The Guest Relations Division of Walt Disney World Co. provided detailed information about the Epcot fountains designed by Fuller. For other information about designing and building Disney theme parks, see Beth Dunlop, *Building a Dream: The Art of Disney Architecture*, New York, 1996, with pp. 54–61 discussing Epcot Center.

24 Although modern hydraulics technology have advanced so these leapfrog effects are possible, water arches existed earlier. Seventeenth-century French prints depict an arcade of arched water streams at Versailles, with promenaders passing underneath without being touched by a drop. See Lablaude 1995, p. 83.

25 Although the realized fountain relies on computerized sequencing to orchestrate its movements and lighting, Claire Kahn began to design the fountain

by first drawing on paper an array of possible water patterns. Her precise geometric drawings of dots and lines show the points of each jet's genesis and the lines of each jet's trajectory. Kahn's drawings are then subsequently developed by engineers, who use the computer as a tool to fine-tune, coordinating the hardware with the design requirements for the desired water effects.

26 See Piland and Uguccioni 1985, pp. 277–82. For the Kansas City Royals Fountain action, Mifsud devised eight programs capable of more than 150 combinations. Peter Micha, owner of Pem Fountain Company of Ontario, Canada, designed and fabricated the fountain components, as well as the hydraulic systems.

27 Harrison was the architect of the Metropolitan Opera House (1966). For a detailed history of the making of Lincoln Center, see Victoria Newhouse, *Wallace K. Harrison: Architect*, New York, 1989, pp. 186–235.

28 As quoted in John Peter, *The Oral History of Modern Architecture: Interviews with the Greatest Architects of the Twentieth Century*, New York, 1994, p. 77. Christian Bjone, formerly with Philip Johnson, Ritchie & Fiore and now with Pei Partnership Architect, brought this quote to our attention, and provided important information about this and other fountain projects designed by Johnson.

29 Ibid.

30 Johnson and Foster worked with mechanical engineers Syska and Hennessy, along with lighting designer Richard Kelly.

31 In fact, the increasing success of the Lincoln Center Plaza as a meeting place means the fountain is frequently turned off for plaza concerts and dance events. During the summer months, the Lincoln Center Fountain Café has tables and umbrellas next to the fountain to create a pleasant ambience for diners, although the café blocks the overall view of the plaza from passers-by. The fountain has been such a popular Lincoln Center symbol that its image is the logo on one version of Lincoln Center's office stationery.

32 Tanja Poppelreuter kindly shared specific information about this fountain received from Prof. Dr. L. M. Fiedler, Johann Wolfgang Goethe-Universität, Frankfurt-am-Main.

33 As quoted in Sumio Kuwabara, "The Fountain Sculpture of George Tsutakawa," in Kingsbury 1990, p. 13.

34 Tsutakawa's fountain designs typically evolve from small three-dimensional models, made of cardboard, sliced ping-pong balls, wire, foil and copper sheets. Water patterns emerge separately from the artist's drawings or by his "playing around" with how water passes over different shapes and through various openings. The artist's son Gerard Tsutakawa and Jack Uchida make the mechanical drawings necessary for the fountain hardware and hydraulic details. See ibid., p. 101.

35 Ibid., p. 112.

36 Poodt 1993, p. 7. Jos Poodt, Museum Het Kruithuis, 's-Hertogenbosch, graciously provided information about this Cragg fountain and about his city's exciting program of commissioning monumental fountains from internationally recognized sculptors to reinforce the city's association with the Dutch history of water.

37 This text is based on a 1996 brochure about Sounding Stones produced by the federal Art-in-Architecture Program, Washington, D.C.

38 Quoted from Tinguely's manifesto which he distributed at his gallery exhibition in Düsseldorf, (Jan. 1959). Violand-Hobi 1995, pp. 30, 33.

The Fountains at Chatsworth

1 As quoted in Chatsworth Garden guidebook, 1996, from C. Morris, ed., *C. Fiennes Journeys*, 1947, p. 98.

2 James Croston, *On Foot Through the Peaks*, London, 1862, pp. 162–63.

3 Monica Beardsworth, *Penrhos College 1880–1980: The Second Fifty Years*, 1981, p. 37, as quoted in Chatsworth Garden guidebook, 1996, p. 49.

Chapter 8

For help with providing research materials I am grateful to Marilyn Symmes and Jeannette Redensek, Cooper-Hewitt, National Design Museum, and Amy Hau and Bruce Altshuler, Isamu Noguchi Foundation, New York City; Dorothée Imbert critically, but kindly, reviewed an early draft.

1 *Webster's Ninth New Collegiate Dictionary*, Springfield, Mass., 1986, p. 813.

2 Paradise provided in abundance all that was missing in normal life, substituting shade for parching sunlight, water for aridity, milk and honey for personal want. See Tuan 1974, pp. 113–28.

3 The Roman aqueducts are celebrated historical constructions, many of them still active today. To traverse valleys, elaborate masonry structures spanned the slopes bearing their cargo downward, following gravity. The Pont du Gard in southern France is one of the more magnificent remaining examples. See Guilhem Fabre et al., *The Pont du Gard: Water and the Roman Town*, Paris, 1992. In ancient Persia, the rapid evaporation caused by the hot arid climate was thwarted by underground channels called *qanats*, which brought water from mountain sources to the fields and settlements. "A main shaft was sunk to the permanent subterranean water level, usually at the base of hills or mountains. Workers then dug a tunnel from where the water was needed to the source. At intervals of about fifty feet or less, shafts from the surface were dug to remove the excavated material and provide air for laborers.... The tunnel was slightly inclined toward the source; hence the water system was propelled by gravity." Elizabeth B. Moynihan, *Paradise as a Garden in Persia and Mughal India*, London, 1982, p. 26.

4 John Pinto notes that "the range of water effects employed by Bernini in the Four Rivers Fountain—from slender jets to broad sheets and conch-like sprays—was unsurpassed until the completion of Salvi's design for the Fontana di Trevi." Pinto 1986, p. 52.

5 Ibid., p. 150.

6 Ibid., p. 168.

7 "My *Fountains of Rome* is being given today at the Augusteo," Respighi wrote in a letter at the time of its premiere. "They'll open the taps and drench the Roman audience with water—fetid water. Let's hope they don't protest by hissing too much. But we must be resigned to even this! 'We will teach you the lust for hissing'—the futurists used to say—but that did not prevent them from becoming hyenas when they were hissed!" Elsa Respighi, *Ottorino Respighi*, trans. Gwyn Morris, London, 1962, p. 52.

8 *Three Coins in the Fountain*, with Dorothy McGuire, Jean Peters and Maggie McNamara as the female leads, was directed by Jean Negulesco and released in 1954. Its title song won an Academy award and popularized both Rome and the Trevi Fountain internationally.

9 "Workmen in rubber boots retrieve approximately 70,000 lire each week from the basin as a result of the coin-throwing custom, which seems to have begun or to have been revived in the latter part of the 19th century." Campbell 1978, p. 41.

10 Celestine Bohlen, "Marcello Mastroianni, Self-Deprecating Charmer of Italian Film, Is Dead at 72," *New York Times*, 20 Dec. 1996.

11 Ibid.

12 Actually, the fountain was only one part of the Piazza d'Italia, but over time the two names have become conjoined. More often than not, the fountain project is referred to as the Piazza d'Italia.

13 Moore had long been interested in the role of water and architecture. It had been his dissertation subject at Princeton University (1957) later updated in his book Moore 1994. For the long and winding tale of the Piazza d'Italia's rise and fall see (for its rise) Filler 1978, pp. 81–87, and (for a post mortem) Jennifer C. Toher, "Piazza d'Italia," in Tod A. Marder, *The Critical Edge: Controversy in Recent American Architecture*, New Brunswick, N.J. and Cambridge, Mass., 1985, pp. 149–62. The design credits for the project are extensive. Piazza design: August Perez Associates, New Orleans; R. Allen Eskew and Malcolm Heard, Jr., project directors; Robert Kleinpeter, project coordinator; Robert Landry, field representative. Fountain design: Charles Moore, Urban Innovations Group, Los Angeles; Ron Filson, project coordinator.

14 Filler 1978, p. 86.

15 Charles Moore noted that among the architectural orders, the design team had used the Doric, Ionic, Tuscan, Composite and one additional, of Moore's design, the "Delicatessen Order." Ibid.

16 Anna Thomson Dodge's 1970 bequest left funds to create a memorial fountain honoring her husband, the automobile magnate, and her son, to be called the Horace E. Dodge & Son Memorial Fountain, now usually referred to as the Dodge Fountain. Noguchi's contribution to the Osaka fair comprised a series of nine fountains that animated water as downward sprays, vertical and spiraling jets, and clouds of mists. Perhaps it was these works which suggested the potential for the Dodge Fountain in Detroit. In awarding the commission to Noguchi, the selection committee rejected a proposal by "David Elgin Dodge, grandson of the lady who left the money." Like every other civic project, the fountain would suffer from communication and coordination problems. Ladd Neuman, "Dodge Fountain: Artistic or Awful?," *Detroit Free Press*, 7 Sep. 1971.

17 Noguchi, letter to The Horace E. Dodge Fountain Selection Committee, 25 Aug. 1971, Noguchi Foundation.

18 "There was a large parking lot by the river for which a plan had been made by the architects. But, realizing this to be inappropriate to the fountain concept, I was asked by the chairman of that firm, Robert Hastings, to do the entire plaza as well." Noguchi, letter to Ada Louise Huxtable, 25 Apr. 1979, Noguchi Foundation. Noguchi nominated Smith, Hinchman & Grylls of Detroit as the plaza architects.

19 "Design for Detroit Civic Center Plaza Focuses on Fountain of Jetting Water," *AIA Journal*, Aug. 1973. Noguchi characterized the scheme's revisions as achieving a better "functional relationship between the fountain, the plaza, and what goes on below. The Dodge Fountain remains the focal point of the plaza, and its new location permitted me to re-orient the axis of the plaza on a diagonal from the intersection with Woodward and Jefferson. Now the fountain itself takes the form of a bird rising... though it still retains an evocation of the airplane and jet propulsion." James Gallagher, press release, Smith, Hinchman & Grylls, 30 Mar. 1973, Noguchi Foundation.

20 Peter Benjamin, "River Plaza to be Park—Not a Monument," *Detroit Free Press*, 31 Mar. 1973.

21 Gladys Sanders, "Aqua Pura: What Would Bernini Say?," press release for Renaissance Center, n.d., Noguchi Foundation.

22 "Noguchi: The Fountain and the Artist Deserve Better of the City," "In Our Opinion," *Detroit Free Press*, 23 Apr. 1979.

23 Nolan Finley, "City Pulls Plug on Bugs in Dodge Fountain Flow," *The Detroit News*, May 1980. Noguchi himself acknowledged the role played by the engineer during a visit to the troubled fountain in 1979: "The sole reason the fountain does as well as it does... is because Louis Klei, the city engineer, has been so passionately committed to it." Polk Laffoon IV, "Fountain Flaws Anger Artist," *Detroit Free Press*, 20 Apr. 1979.

24 Finley, "City Pulls Plug on Bugs."

25 N. Scott Vance, "A Fresh 'Doughnut', At Last," *The Detroit News*, 3 July 1987. In an article published the previous month Vance had noted that an additional $800,000 would be spent "to put the spray and sparkle back into the Hart Plaza's troubled Dodge Fountain." N. Scott Vance, "Hart Fountain May Be Fixed," *The Detroit News*, 16 June 1987.

26 Noguchi to Detroit Civic Center Plaza Development Committee, 16 Feb. 1973, Noguchi Foundation. Noguchi would continue to lament the city's reluctance to install the vegetation as specified.

27 Noguchi to The Horace E. Dodge Fountain Selection Committee, 25 Aug. 1971, Noguchi Foundation.

28 Richard Chaix Fountain Consultant (successor to Beamer/Wilkinson and Associates, Oakland, California) provided the hydraulic expertise for the project. "Splashy Fountain Bejewels Motor City Plaza," *Engineering New Record*, 6 Oct. 1977.

29 Noguchi to The Horace E. Dodge Fountain Selection Committee, 25 Aug. 1971, Noguchi Foundation. In a memo to the committee, William H. Kessler summarized the suggestions for plaza activities solicited from civic leaders. John D. Ryan of the J. Walter Thomson Co. emphasized that the plaza should be destined to "ongoing activities as opposed to single events." General Motors's Charles Hagler suggested that "activity should not encourage [a] 'hippy haven' or 'protestor center.'" It should be "truly a place where people can sit and enjoy a view of the river." He added parenthetically that the "Information Center [should be] accessible by auto." Noguchi Foundation.

30 Tanaka 1981, p. 147.

31 Noguchi tended to keep a close watch on his projects even after completion. In 1979, he wrote to the mayor's office, troubled by lighting standards and kiosks which had been added without his consultation. He offered alternatives. Noguchi to Mayor Coleman Young, 22 Aug. 1979, Noguchi Foundation. Again, in 1988 on the eve of a major renovation, Noguchi wrote to the Central Business District Association President, establishing his credibility by reminding him that: "As you must know I am the one who worked on what is there starting in 1971, over a period of about seven years. The design is

mine in the smallest detail. The Pylon was my free gift to get things going." Now, the integrity of the design was being undermined by additions: "It would be nice and appropriate if the designer's work could be respected when changes and 'improvements' are made by others. I was not informed." Noguchi to Diane J. Edgecomb, 8 July 1988. Noguchi Foundation.

32 Zion and Breen 1963, unpaginated.

33 Paley was chairman of The Columbia Broadcasting System (CBS) in New York at the time. Ralph Blumenthal, "Paley is Donating a Vest-Pocket Park to the City on Stork Club Site," *New York Times*, 2 Feb. 1966. See also the adjacent article by Ada Louise Huxtable, "Experiment in Parks."

34 The exhibition scheme was fifty by one hundred feet, the actual lot, forty-four by one hundred feet.

35 Zion and Breen 1963.

36 For the development of these spaces see Marc Treib, "Arte pubblica e spazi pubblici," *Casabella*, Jan.–Feb. 1992, pp. 94–99.

37 The Lovejoy Fountain has retained its name from the time of its construction. Ira's Fountain, also known as The Ira C. Keller Fountain (renamed in 1978 to honor a major civic leader who championed the urban redevelopment of downtown Portland), was first called the Auditorium Forecourt Fountain after the piece of land it occupies in front of the performing arts center.

38 See Halprin 1972, pp. 16–27 ff.

39 Ibid., p. 43.

40 Ibid., pp. 64–65.

41 Charles Moore, "Still Pools and Crashing Waves", Fried et al. 1986, pp. 19–20.

42 Donlyn Lyndon, "Concrete Cascade in Portland," *Architectural Forum*, July–Aug. 1966, p. 76.

43 In the 1960s, Halprin developed a system of graphic notation to record and/or direct movement's paths: motation. See Halprin, "Motation," *Progressive Architecture*, July 1965, reprinted in Halprin 1978, pp. 51–62.

44 Felice Frankel and Jory Johnson, *Modern Landscape Architecture: Redefining the American Garden*, New York, 1991, p. 144.

45 Mrs. K. D. Beaver, letter to the editor, *Oregonian*, 2 July 1970.

46 "Fountain Design Praised," *Portland Journal*, 3 July 1970.

47 "Portland's Walk-in Waterfall," *Architectural Forum*, Oct. 1970, p. 58. "Unusual Sites Selected for Weekend Baptism," *Oregonian*, 19 July 1971.

48 That role has changed somewhat over the years, as the Ira C. Keller Fountain and its public have matured. Forms have softened, trees have grown, and moss has appeared on shaded surfaces. "The fountain has also changed. Visitors once shared a common experience of a single sculptural form. What they now find is more fragmented, private, reflective. The growth of the original plantings has isolated the fountain from the surrounding streets and separated the upper and lower sections." Carl Abbott, "Two Portland Fountains Come of Age," *Landscape Architecture*, Mar. 1993, p. 48.

49 "Portland's Walk-in Waterfall," p. 58.

50 This interest in risk is corroborated by the longevity of the San Francisco cable car—now a national landmark—whose manner of boarding and riding would never pass current codes. Franco Zagari observed: "In this [the Lovejoy Fountain], as in other of

Halprin's spaces, each person's safety is his or her own responsibility, as it would be in a natural setting." *L'Architettura del giardino contemporaneo*, Milan, 1988, p. 122.

51 Halprin 1972, p. 312. He notes: "The Portland fountains are 'natural' not because they mutate nature but because the processes by which natural effects of this kind *operate* have been understood and recycled into an art form, i.e., *form followed process*." Even this degree of abstraction is insufficient, according to landscape architect Dan Kiley. "Larry's always great for waterfalls. I disagree with his thinking about nature, though, about the way he wants to take nature and recreate a man's scene out of it. I think that's wrong. As I told you, we *are* nature." Byrd and Rainey 1983, p. 33.

52 Halprin 1978, p. 231.

53 The vocabulary of the Portland fountains seems to have informed several Halprin projects, among them Skyline Park in Denver (1970), Manhattan Square Park in Rochester, New York (1975), and Levi's Park in San Francisco (1978). Most recently, aspects of these projects appear in the F. D. R. Memorial in Washington, D.C., which opened in May 1997 (see Chapter 6, pp. 133–35). Despite their unqualified social success, at some point one must question the aesthetic and geographic appropriateness of an abstracted mountain terrain set on a coastal site, a flat one in the Tidewater, for example.

54 The Portland/Fort Worth connection seemed obvious to a writer for *Progressive Architecture*: "Ever abashed to use a good idea, Johnson might be said to be 'Learning from Larry' (Halprin that is), yet the result bears Johnson's touch." Jan. 1975, p. 23. The Fort Worth Water Gardens were a gift of The Amon G. Carter Foundation to the citizens of Fort Worth. Johnson had previously been the architect of The Amon Carter Museum of Western Art.

55 Paul Goldberger, "In Fort Worth, a Water Garden Is an Urban Space," *New York Times*, 1 Feb. 1975.

56 The fact sheet lists the garden's water effects in the following way: Active Water Pool, the great basin, with 10,500 gallons of water per minute; an Aerated Pool, with forty special nozzles; a Cascade Pool, located on the northwest entrance; a Wet Wall, 650 feet long and built into the retaining wall; and a Quiet Water Pool, surrounded by concrete walks and sweet gums. Thomas S. Byrne, Inc., engineers and general contractors, "Memo: Interesting Facts on Fort Worth Water Garden," 9 Oct. 1974.

57 Edgar Allan Poe, "A Descent into the Maelström," in *Arthur Gordon Pym and Related Tales*, Oxford, 1994, p. 226.

58 Ibid.

59 Architect Philip Johnson himself used a classical term, *scenae frons*, to describe the pavilion set before the great wall; seen a decade later, one wishes the references to historic forms had been far less overt and cloying.

60 Knight 1985, pp. 182–87.

61 Louis B. Parks, "Fountains: Drop by Houston's Water Wonders," *Houston Chronicle*, 26 Feb. 1986.

62 Mimi Crossley, "Wondrous Water Wall," *Houston Style*, Jan. 1986, p. 52.

63 Elizabeth McBride, "The Transco Fountain," *Cite, a Publication of the Rice Design Alliance*, Summer 1985, pp. 19–20.

64 Philip Johnson, "Transco Tower & Park," fact sheet, n.d.

65 Dan Kiley, "Dan Kiley Lecture," in Byrd and Rainey 1983, p. 8.

66 It should be noted, however, that Frederick Law Olmsted (1822–1903) himself often relied on architectural spaces in and around buildings, even those in highly naturalistic settings. His work at Biltmore, the Vanderbilt estate near Asheville, North Carolina, or even the areas around the Bethesda Fountain in New York's Central Park, both utilize more architectonic planning.

67 Dan Kiley in Robin Karson, "Conversation with Kiley," *Landscape Architecture*, Mar./Apr. 1986, p. 54.

68 The cylindrical planted boxes for the swamp cypresses to some degree circumscribe the trees' root system and prevent the trees from growing beyond a certain size. Evaporating water helps cool the plaza and its visitors.

69 The competition for the park's design was held in 1985, with top prizes given to two teams. In the French manner, the four laureates were commissioned to execute the park's design as a joint venture, although elements of the master plan became the responsibility of the various team members. See Jean-Claude Garcias, "Un lustre après, le concours Citroën revisité," in "Espaces publics," *Paris Projet*, Paris, no. 30–31, 1993, pp. 110–15.

70 See Gilles Clément, *Le Jardin en mouvement: de la vallée au Parc André-Citroën*, Paris, 1994.

71 During a visit to the park in 1993, I witnessed one boy falling on the slick granite surface and receiving a cut to his forehead in the process. He used the water jet to rinse the cut—a use for which it was, no doubt, never intended—and resumed the same risky play. It may be the sense of impending danger, in fact, that lures children through the sprays.

72 The terrace is essentially a centrifugal space moving outward from the tower and adjacent banking hall that uses the Fibonacci series of numbers to generate the proportions of paving to green areas. Each number in this series is generated by adding the two previous numbers: for example, 1, 2, 3, 5, 8, 13, etc.

73 Tuan 1974, p. 247.

74 See Jonas Lehrman, *Earthly Paradise: Garden and Courtyard in Islam*, Berkeley, 1980, pp. 95–99.

75 Born in Georgia, Biddy Mason (1818–91) settled in Los Angeles in 1866, working as a midwife and nurse. The current park "sits atop Mason's 19th-century homesite, which was also a clinic for the sick and refuge for poor black families." The project includes commemorative murals by Sheila de Bretteville and Bettye Saar. Ann Wilson Lloyd, "A Park Called Hope," *Landscape Architecture*, Apr. 1993, p. 70.

76 Ibid.

77 Mayor Nancy Graham, quoted in Barbara Flanagan, "Good Design Creates Another Palm Beach Story," *New York Times*, Thursday, 12 June 1997, pp. c1, 6. The details of the design are discussed in Michael Redd and Frank Baynham, "Back from the Brink: People Make the Difference in Downtown Design," *Landscape Architect & Specifier News*, July 1996, pp. 46–47.

78 Flanagan, "Good Design Creates Another Palm Beach Story," p. c1.

79 Ibid., p. c6.

80 Ibid.

81 Mayor Nancy Graham, quoted ibid.

82 Ron Hayes, "Fountain of Youth," *The Palm Beach Post*, 23 July 1995.

83 Ibid.

Bibliography

Abercombie, Stanley. "Evaluation: A Prototype Left Unreplicated [Paley Park, New York, Zion and Breen]." *Architecture* 74, no. 12 (Dec. 1985), pp. 54–55.

Adams, William Howard. *The French Garden: 1500–1800.* New York, 1979.

Allwood 1977: Allwood, John. *The Great Exhibitions.* London, 1977.

Amaury, Duval. *Les Fontaines de Paris, anciennes et nouvelles.* Paris, 1816.

"Architecture & Water." *Architectural Design No. 113.* London, 1994.

Aronvici, Carol. *The Public Fountain in Civic Art.* Greenwich, Conn., 1946.

Augur, Helen. *The Book of Fairs.* Detroit, 1992.

Aynaud 1968: Aynaud, Albert. *Aix-en-Provence, ses fontaines et leurs secrets.* Aix-en-Provence, 1968.

Bargagli-Petrucci, Fabio. *Le Fonti di Siena e i loro aquedotti.* Siena, 1906.

Beardsley, John. "Like a Mighty Stream: Maya Lin's Memorial to Civil Rights Workers." *Landscape Architecture* 80, no. 1 (Jan. 1990), pp. 78–79.

Beaver 1986: Beaver, Patrick. *The Crystal Palace: A Portrait of Victorian Enterprise.* Chichester, England, 1986.

Bélidor 1739: Bélidor, Bernard Forest de. *Architecture hydraulique, ou l'art de conduire, d'élever et de ménager les eaux pour les différens besoins de la vie.* Paris, 1737–53.

Belloncle, Michel. *La Ville et son eau: Paris et ses fontaines.* Paris, 1978.

Berger, Patrick. "André Citroën Park, Paris, France: 1988–1992." *A+U* 6, no. 309 (June 1996), pp. 28–54.

Berger, Robert W. *In the Garden of the Sun King.* Washington, D.C., 1985.

Bischofberger, Christina. *Jean Tinguely.* Zurich, 1990.

Bishop, Minor L. *Fountains in Contemporary Architecture.* Exh. cat., American Federation of Arts, New York, 1965.

Bizzarri, Giulio, Marco Guidi, and Aurora Lucarelli. *Il Nettuno del Giambologna: storia e restauro.* Milan, 1989.

Böckler, Georg Andreas. *Architectura Curiosa Nova, Die Lustreiche Bau- und Wasserkunst.* Nuremberg, 1664.

Bogart 1986: Bogart, Michele H. "Maine Memorial and Pulitzer Fountain: A Study in Patronage and Process." *Winterthur Portfolio* 21, no. 1 (Spring 1986), pp. 41–63.

Bogart, Michele H. *Public Sculpture and the Civic Ideal in New York City, 1890–1930.* Chicago, 1989.

Bogart, Michele H., and Deborah Nevins. *Fauns and Fountains: American Garden Statuary, 1890–1939.* Exh. cat., Parrish Art Museum, Southampton, N.Y., 1985.

Boudon 1991: Boudon, Françoise. "Visconti et le décor urbain: les fontaines parisiennes." *Visconti 1791–1853.* Paris, 1991.

Brigham, Joan. "Steam Heat: Winter Fountains in the City." *Places* 6, no. 4 (Summer 1990), pp. 42–49.

Brown, Mark, and Graham Stansfield. *The Fountains of Witley Court.* Great Witley, England, 1992.

Byrd and Rainey 1983: Byrd, Warren T., and Reuben Rainey, eds. *The Work of Dan Kiley, A Dialogue on Design Theory.* Symposium proceedings, University of Virginia. Charlottesville, Va., 1983.

Campbell 1978: Campbell, Craig S. *Water in Landscape Architecture.* New York, 1978.

Chaix, Richard. "Fountain Scale Model Serves as an Engineering Design Tool." *Architectural Record* 145 (Mar. 1969), pp. 165–67.

Chaix, Richard. "Achieving Effective Collaboration in the Design of Fountains." *Architectural Record* 148 (Dec. 1970), pp. 105–08.

Coffin 1960: Coffin, David R. *The Villa D'Este at Tivoli.* Princeton, 1960.

Coffin 1979: Coffin, David R. *The Villa in the Life of Renaissance Rome.* Princeton, 1979.

Coffin 1981: Coffin, David R. "The Wonders of Pratolino." *The Journal of Garden History* 1, no. 3 (July–Sep. 1981), pp. 279–82.

Coffin 1991: Coffin, David R. *Gardens and Gardening in Papal Rome.* Princeton, 1991.

Coffin, David R., ed. *The Italian Garden.* Washington, D.C., 1971.

Cohn, Anna. "Robert Woodward, Fountain Maker." *Art in Australia* 22, no. 3 (Autumn 1985), pp. 382–86.

Coleman, Jonathan. "First She Looks Inward, Profile, Architect, Maya Lin." *Time* 134 (6 Nov. 1989), pp. 90–94.

Coles 1973: Coles, William A. "The History of America's Greatest Fountain: The Scott Memorial Fountain on Belle Isle, Detroit." *Classical America,* no. 3 (1973), pp. 5–26.

Collins, Tim, Reiko Goto et al. *Aqua Pura.* San Francisco, 1992.

Cooke, Jr., Hereward Lester. "The Documents Relating to the Fountain of Trevi." *Art Bulletin* 38 (Sep. 1956), pp. 149–73.

Cooper, Guy, Gordon Taylor, and Clive Boursnell; foreword by Sir Geoffrey Jellicoe. *English Water Garden.* Boston, 1987.

Cresti, Carlo. *Le Fontane di Firenze.* Florence, 1982.

Croutier, Alev Lytle. *Taking the Waters: Spirit, Art, Sensuality.* New York, 1992.

Davies 1989: Davies, Philip. *Troughs & Drinking Fountains: Fountains of Life.* London, 1989.

De Buyer, Xavier; photographs by François Bibal. *Fontaines de Paris.* Paris, 1987.

De Caus, Salomon. *Les Raisons des forces mouvantes.* Frankfurt, 1615.

Dézallier d'Argenville, Antoine-Joseph. *The Theory and Practice of Gardening: wherein is fully handled all that relates to fine gardens, commonly called pleasure-gardens, as parterres, groves, bowling-greens & c.* Trans. John James, London, 1712.

D'Onofrio 1962: D'Onofrio, Cesare. *Le Fontane di Roma, con documenti e disegni inediti.* 2nd ed., Rome, 1962.

D'Onofrio 1991: D'Onofrio, Cesare. *Il Facchino di Via Lata et altre fontane minori, con acqua di Trevi.* Rome, 1991.

Draper 1982: Draper, Joan E. *Edward H. Bennett, Architect and City Planner, 1874–1954.* Chicago, 1982.

Dybwad, G. L., and Joy V. Bliss. *Annotated Bibliography: World's Columbian Exposition, Chicago 1893 with Illustrations and Price Guide.* Albuquerque, N. Mex., 1992.

Fachard, Sabine, Claude Martinand et al. *Eaux et fontaines dans la ville: conception, techniques, financement.* Paris, 1982.

Filler 1978: Filler, Martin. "The Magic Fountain, Piazza d'Italia, New Orleans." *Progressive Architecture* 59, no. 11 (Nov. 1978), pp. 81–87.

Fontana, Carlo. *Utilissimo trattato dell'acque correnti.* Rome, 1696.

Fontinalia: The Art of the Fountain and the Fountain in Art. Exh. cat., University of Kansas Museum, Lawrence, 1957.

Forgey, Benjamin. "Lawrence Halprin: Maker of Places and Living Spaces." *Smithsonian* 19, no. 9 (Dec. 1988), pp. 160–71.

Forgey, Benjamin. "F. D. R., Like the Man, the Memorial Breaks with Tradition." *The Washington Post,* 27 Apr. 1997.

Fried et al. 1986: Fried, Helene et al. *Lawrence Halprin: Changing Places.* Exh. cat., San Francisco Museum of Modern Art, San Francisco, 1986.

Futagawa, Yukio, ed. "Transco Tower, Works & Projects/John Burgee Architects with Philip Johnson." *GA Document 12* (Jan. 1985), pp. 109–13.

Gasparini, Leone. *Antiche fontane di Napoli.* Naples, 1979.

Gayle, Margot, and Michele Cohen. *The Art Commission and the Municipal Art Society Guide to Manhattan's Outdoor Sculpture.* New York, 1988.

Girard, Jacques. *Versailles Gardens: Sculpture and Mythology.* London, 1985.

"GM's Industrial Versailles." *Architectural Forum* 104 (May 1956), pp. 122–28.

Good 1889: Good, Arthur. "La Fontaine lumineuse de l'exposition universelle." *L'Exposition de Paris de 1889* 1, no. 15 (8 June 1889), pp. 115–18.

Goode 1974: Goode, James M. *The Outdoor Sculpture of Washington, D.C.* Washington, D.C., 1974.

Grabar, Oleg. *The Alhambra.* Cambridge, Mass., 1978.

Greenhalgh, Paul. *Ephemeral Vistas: The Expositions Universelles, Great Exhibitions, and World's Fairs, 1851–1939.* Manchester, England, 1988.

Gutheim, Frederick. "Landscape Design: Works of Dan Kiley." *Process: Architecture,* no. 33 (Oct. 1982).

Halprin, Lawrence. *RSVP Cycles: Creative Processes in the Human Environment.* New York, 1970.

Halprin, Lawrence. *Cities.* Rev. ed., Cambridge, Mass., 1972.

Halprin 1972: Halprin, Lawrence. *Notebooks 1959–1971.* Cambridge, Mass., 1972.

Halprin 1978: Halprin, Lawrence. *Process: Architecture 4, Lawrence Halprin.* Tokyo, Feb. 1978.

Hanson 1965: Hanson, Anne Coffin. *Jacopo della Quercia's Fonte Gaia.* Oxford, 1965.

Hibbard, Howard, and Irma Jaffe. "Bernini's Barcaccia." *Burlington Magazine* 106 (Apr. 1964), pp. 159–70.

Higuchi, Shoichiro. *Water as Environmental Art.* Trans. Shig Fujita, Tokyo 1991.

Hittorff 1986: Hittorff, un architecte du XIXe. Exh. cat., Musée Carnavalet, Paris, 1986.

Hoffmann, Gretl. *Modern Fountains.* London, 1980.

Holmes, Ann. *Presence: The Transco Tower.* Houston, 1985.

Hulten, Pontus. *Tinguely.* Exh. cat., Centre Georges Pompidou, Paris, 1988.

Hulten, Pontus. *Niki de Saint-Phalle.* Exh. cat., Kunst und Ausstellungshalle der Bundesrepublik Deutschland, Bonn, 1992.

Hunt, John Dixon. *Garden and Grove: The Italian Renaissance Garden in the English Imagination 1600–1750.* Princeton, 1986.

Hunt, John Dixon. *Gardens and the Picturesque.* Cambridge, Mass., 1992.

Hunt, John Dixon, ed. *Garden History: Issues, Approaches, Methods.* Washington, D.C., 1992.

Hunt, Peter, ed. *The Book of Garden Ornament.* London, 1974.

Hunter, Sam. "Isamu Noguchi: 'I Know Nothing About Anything, and That's Why I'm So Free.'" *Art News* 77, pt. 5 (May 1978), pp. 124–30.

Jellicoe, Susan, and Geoffrey Jellicoe. *Water: The Use of Water in Landscape Architecture.* London, 1971.

Jellicoe, Susan, and Geoffrey Jellicoe. *The Landscape of Man: Shaping the Environment from Prehistory to the Present Day.* 3rd ed., London, 1995.

Johnson, Eugene J., ed. *Charles Moore: Buildings and Projects 1949–1986.* New York, 1986.

Johnson, Jory. "Presence of Stone [Tanner Fountain, Harvard University]." *Landscape Architecture* 76, no. 4 (July–Aug. 1986), pp. 64–69.

Juaristi, Victoriano. *Las Fuentes de España.* Madrid, 1944.

Kahler, Sonja. *Franklin Delano Roosevelt, The Memorial.* Washington, D.C., 1997.

Katz, Bernard. *Fountains of San Francisco.* San Francisco, 1989.

Keim, Kevin P., ed. *An Architectural Life: Memoirs & Memories of Charles W. Moore.* New York, 1996.

Kiley, Dan. "A Way With Water." *Landscape Design,* no. 208 (Mar. 1992), pp. 33–36.

Kiley, Dan. *Process: Architecture, Dan Kiley: Landscape Design II: In Step with Nature.* Tokyo, Jan. 1993.

Kingsbury 1990: Kingsbury, Martha. *George Tsutakawa.* Seattle, 1990.

Knight 1985: Knight III, Carleton. "High-Tech Skin on a Form from an Earlier Era" [Transco Tower, Houston]. *Architecture* 74, no. 5 (Jan. 1985) pp. 182–87.

Koeppel 1994: Koeppel, Gerard. "A Struggle for Water." *American Heritage, Invention & Technology* 9, no. 3 (Winter 1994), pp. 19–30.

Kowsky 1979: Kowsky, Francis R. "The Bartholdi Fountain: A Model for All Our Cities." *Gazette des Beaux-Arts,* sec. 6, vol. 94 (Dec. 1979), pp. 231–37.

Krautheimer 1952: Krautheimer, Richard. "A Drawing for the Fonte Gaia in Siena." *The Metropolitan Museum of Art Bulletin* 10, no. 10 (1952), pp. 265–71.

Lablaude 1995: Lablaude, Pierre-André. *The Gardens of Versailles.* London, 1995.

Lazzaro 1990: Lazzaro, Claudia. *The Italian Renaissance Garden: From the Conventions of Planting, Design, and Ornament to the Grand Gardens of Sixteenth-Century Central Italy.* New Haven, 1990.

Lewis, Hilary, and John O'Connor. *Philip Johnson: The Architect in His Own Words.* New York, 1994.

Lindner, Werner. *Schöne Brunnen in Deutschland.* Berlin, 1920.

Littlejohn, David. *Architect: The Life and Works of Charles W. Moore.* New York, 1984.

MacDougall, Elisabeth B. "The Sleeping Nymph: Origins of a Humanist Fountain Type." *Art Bulletin* 56, no. 3 (Sep. 1975), pp. 357–65.

MacDougall and Miller 1977: MacDougall, Elisabeth B., and Naomi Miller. *Fons Sapientiae: Garden Fountains in Illustrated Books, Sixteenth–Eighteenth Centuries.* Washington, D.C., 1977.

MacDougall 1978: MacDougall, Elisabeth B., ed. *Fons Sapientiae: Renaissance Garden Fountains.* Washington, D.C., 1978.

MacDougall, Elisabeth B., and Richard Ettinghausen, eds. *The Islamic Garden.* Washington, D.C., 1976.

Masello, David. "Liquid Symbol: Centennial Fountain is Lohan Associates' Symbolic Salute to the 1889 Reversal of the Chicago River." *Architectural Record* 178 (Mar. 1990), pp. 92–95.

Massounie et al. 1995: Massounie, Dominique, Pauline Prévost-Marcilhacy, and Daniel Rabreau. *Paris et ses fontaines de la Renaissance à nos jours.* Paris, 1995.

Mays, Vernon. "Fountain of Youth [International Fountain, Seattle Center]." *Landscape Architecture* 86, no. 6 (June 1996), pp. 30–35.

Metz, Erhard, and Gerd Spies. *Der Braunschweiger Brunnen auf dem Altstadtmarkt.* Brunswick, Germany, 1988.

Meyer, Peter. "Brunnen." *Das Werk* 23 (Feb. 1936), pp. 37–58.

Miller 1968: Miller, Naomi. "The Form and Meaning of the Fontaine des Innocents." *Art Bulletin* 50 (Sep. 1968), pp. 270–77.

Miller 1977a: Miller, Naomi. *French Renaissance Fountains.* New York, 1977.

Miller 1977b: Miller, Naomi. "Piazza Nettuno, Bologna: A Paean to Pius IV." *Architectura* 7 (Sep. 1977), pp. 14–40.

Miller 1982: Miller, Naomi. *Heavenly Caves: Reflections on the Garden Grotto.* New York, 1982.

Miller 1986: Miller, Naomi. "Paradise Regained: Medieval Garden Fountains." In *Medieval Gardens,* edited by Elisabeth B. MacDougall. Washington, D.C., 1986, pp. 135–54.

Miller, Naomi. "Fountains." *The Dictionary of Art,* edited by Jane Turner, New York, 1996, vol. 11, pp. 338–47.

Mique, Richard. *Les Jardins de Versailles et de Trianon d'André Le Nôtre.* Exh. cat., Musée National des Châteaux de Versailles et de Trianon, Versailles, 1992.

Moffatt 1992: Moffatt, Frederick C. "The Intemperate Patronage of Henry D. Cogswell." *Winterthur Portfolio* 27, no. 2–3 (Summer/Autumn 1992), pp. 123–43.

Montorgueil 1928: Montorgueil, Georges. *Les Eaux et les fontaines de Paris.* Paris, 1928.

Moore, Charles W. "Water and Architecture." Ph.D. diss., Princeton University, 1957.

Moore 1994: Moore, Charles W.; photographs by Jane Lidz. *Water and Architecture.* New York and London, 1994.

Morton 1966: Morton, H. V. *The Waters of Rome.* London, 1966.

Möseneder, Karle. *Montorsoli Die Brunnen.* Mittenwald, Germany, 1979.

Mosser, Monique, and Georges Teyssot, eds. *The History of Garden Design.* London, 1991.

Mousset, Albert. *Les Francine: Créateurs des eaux de Versailles intendants des eaux et fontaines de France de 1623 à 1784.* Paris, 1930.

National Geographic Special Edition. *Water, The Power, Promise, and Turmoil of North America's Fresh Water* 84, no. 5A. Washington, D.C., 1993.

Nefzger, Ulrich. *Salzburg und seine Brunnen: Spiegelbilder einer Stadt.* Salzburg, 1980.

Paczowski, Bohdan. "The Trevi Fountain on the Ambiguity of the Concept of Nature." *Architectural Review* 164, no. 978 (Aug. 1978), pp. 72–78.

Pardoe, Bill. *Witley Court: Witley Court and Church, Life and Luxury in a Great Country House*. Great Witley, England, 1986.

Paris 1937. Exh. cat., Musée d'Art Moderne de la Ville de Paris, 1987.

[Petrodvorets] Peterhof: Palaces and Pavilions, Gardens and Parks, Fountains and Cascades, Sculptures. Leningrad, c. 1978.

Pfanneschmidt, E. E. *Fountains and Springs*. New York, 1969.

Phillips, Roger, and Nicky Foy. *A Photographic Garden History*. New York, 1995.

Pica, Agnoldomenico. "Ad Osaka: acqua in movimento." *Domus*, no. 490 (Sep. 1970), pp. 8–9.

Picon, Antoine. *Architectes et ingénieurs au siècle des lumières*, Marseilles, 1988.

Piland and Uguccioni 1985: Piland, Sherry, and Ellen J. Uguccioni. *Fountains of Kansas City: A History and Love Affair*. Kansas City, Mo., 1985.

Pinto 1986: Pinto, John A. *The Trevi Fountain*, New Haven, 1986.

Pinto, John A. "The Trevi Fountain and its Place in the Urban Development of Rome." *AA Files*, no. 8 (Spring 1995), pp. 8–20.

Piranesi: Rome Recorded. Exh. cat., American Academy in Rome, New York and Rome, and the Arthur Ross Foundation, New York, 1990.

Plantier, Louis. *Les Fontaines de Haute Provence*. Aix-en-Provence, 1989.

Plumptre, George; photographs by Hugh Palmer. *The Water Garden: Styles, Designs and Visions*. London, 1993.

Poodt 1993: Poodt, Jos, ed. *Tony Cragg, Archimedes Screw/ De Schroef von Archimedes: A Fountain Sculpture for the City of 's-Hertogenbosch*. Museum Her Kruithuis, 's-Hertogenbosch, The Netherlands, 1993.

Randall 1995: Randall, Colvin; photographs by Larry Albee. *Longwood Gardens*. Kennett Square, Pa., 1995.

Reed, Gervais. "The Fountains of George Tsutakawa." *AIA Journal* 52 (July 1969), pp. 49–51.

Robertson, Jaquelin. "Renowned Landscape Architect Dan Kiley Reviews His Life and Times in a University of Virginia Symposium." *Inland Architect* 27, no. 2 (Mar.–Apr. 1983), pp. 10–25.

Rosasco, Betsy. "Review of Gerold Weber, *Brunnen und Wasserkünste in Frankreich*." *Art Bulletin* 69 (Mar. 1987), pp. 143–49.

Rosasco, Betsy. "Bains d'Apollon, Bain de Diane: Masculine and Feminine in the Gardens of Versailles." *Gazette des Beaux-Arts* 112 (Jan. 1991), pp. 1–26.

Roserot 1902: Roserot, Alphonse. "La Fontaine de la rue de Grenelle à Paris par Edme Bouchardon." *Gazette des Beaux-Arts* 28 (1902), pp. 353–72.

Rydell, Robert W. Introduction to *The Books of the Fairs: Materials about World's Fairs, 1834–1916, in the Smithsonian Institution Libraries*. Chicago, 1992.

Rydell, Robert W., and Nancy E. Gwinn, eds. *Fair Representations: World's Fairs and the Modern World*. Amsterdam, 1994.

Sanfilippo 1996: Sanfilippo, Mario; photographs by Francesco Venturi. *Fountains of Rome*. Milan, 1996.

Scardino, Barrie. "Fifty Fountains" and "Waterworld." *Cite*, no. 37 (Spring 1997), pp. 12–15, 16–19.

Schama 1995: Schama, Simon. *Landscape and Memory*. New York, 1995.

Schenk 1949: Schenk, Paul. *A Chronicle of the Fountains of Berne*. Bern, 1949.

Schneider 1977: Schneider, Donald. *The Works and Doctrine of Jacques Ignace Hittorff (1792–1867)*. 2 vols., New York, 1977.

Schomann, Heinz. *Die Alten Frankfurter Brunnen*. Frankfurt, 1980.

Seymour 1968: Seymour, Jr., Charles. "'Fatto di sua mano': Another Look at the Fonte Gaia Drawing Fragments in London and New York." In *Festschrift Ulrich Middendorf*, edited by Antje Rosegarten, Berlin, 1968, pp. 93–105.

Snyder, Eugene E. *Portland Potpourri: Art, Fountains and Old Friends*. Portland, Oreg., 1991.

Sorvig, Kim. "Water Design: Special Effects." *Architecture* 81, no. 12 (Dec. 1991), pp. 72–75.

State University College at Buffalo. *The Butler Ice Fountain*. Buffalo, N.Y., 1984.

Steinberg, Ronald Martin. "The Iconography of the Teatro dell'Acqua at the Villa Aldobrandini." *Art Bulletin* 47 (Dec. 1965), pp. 453–63.

Strong 1979: Strong, Roy. *The Renaissance Garden in England*. London, 1979.

Suzaki, M. "Osaka World's Fair: Fountains and Sculpture." *Japan Architect* 45 (May–June 1970), pp. 162–63.

SWA Group. *Process: Architecture 103, Landscape Design and Planning at the SWA Group*. Tokyo, May 1992.

Switzer, Stephen. *An Introduction to a General System of Hydrostaticks and Hydrauliks, Philosophical and Practical*. London, 1729.

Tacha, Athena. "*Blair Fountain*, River Sculpture." *Landscape Architecture* 74, no. 2 (Mar.–Apr. 1984), pp. 72–74.

Tanaka 1981: Tanaka, Michie. "Water and Sculpture." *Process: Architecture*, no. 24 (June 1981), pp. 100–06.

"Tanner Fountain, Cambridge, Massachusetts." *Process: Architecture*, no. 85 (Oct. 1989), pp. 94–99.

Jean Tinguely. Exh. cat., Musée d'Art et d'Histoire, Geneva, 1976.

Tomkins, Calvin. "The Garden Artist: Dan Kiley." *The New Yorker* 71 (16 Oct. 1995), pp. 136–47.

Treib, Marc. "Water: Design Vocabulary II." *Landscape Architecture* 77, no. 1 (Jan.–Feb. 1987), pp. 72–77.

Trulio, Matthew. "WET's Hydro-Technics." *Landscape Design*, no. 212 (July–Aug. 1992), pp. 16–18.

Tuan 1974: Tuan, Yi-Fu. *Topophilia: A Study in Environmental Perception, Attitudes and Values*. Englewood Cliffs, N.J., 1974.

Utz, Hildegard. "A Note on Ammannati's Apennine and on the Chronology of the Figures for his Fountain of Neptune." *Burlington Magazine* 115 (May 1973), pp. 295–300.

Vance, Mary A. *Fountains: A Bibliography 1960–1988*. Monticello, Ill., 1984.

Vial 1991: Vial, Marie-Paule. *Le Palais Longchamp, à la gloire de l'eau, des arts et des sciences*. Marseilles, 1991.

Violand-Hobi 1995: Violand-Hobi, Heidi E. *Jean Tinguely: Life and Work*. Munich and New York, 1995.

Walker, Peter. *Process: Architecture 118, Peter Walker, William Johnson and Partners, Art and Nature*. Tokyo, June 1994.

Walker, Peter, and Leah Levy. *Peter Walker: Minimalist Gardens*. Cambridge, Mass., 1997.

Walton 1986: Walton, Guy. *Louis XIV's Versailles*. Chicago, 1986.

Weber, Gerold. "Un livre d'esquisses inedit attribué à Tomaso de Francini (1571–1651)." *Bulletin de la société de l'histoire de l'art français* (1980), pp. 71–80.

Weber, Gerold. "Charles Le Brun's recueil de divers dessins de fontaines." *Munchner Jahrbuch der Bildenden Kunst*, ser. 3, vol. 32 (1981), pp. 157–181.

Weber 1985: Weber, Gerold. *Brunnen und Wasserkünste in Frankreich im Zeitalter von Louis XIV*. Worms, 1985.

Wiles [1933] 1975: Wiles, Bertha Harris. *The Fountains of Florentine Sculptors and Their Followers from Donatello to Bernini*. 1933, reprint, New York, 1975.

Wiles 1935: Wiles, Bertha Harris. *Fountains in Art*. Exh. cat., Fogg Art Museum, Harvard University, Cambridge, Mass., 1935.

Wolfe 1996: Wolfe, Gerard R. *Chicago In and Around the Loop: Walking Tours of Architecture and History*. New York, 1996.

Woodbridge 1986: Woodbridge, Kenneth. *Princely Gardens: The Origins and Development of the French Formal Style*. New York, 1986.

Woods, May. *Visions of Arcadia, European Gardens from Renaissance to Rococo*. London, 1996.

Wrede, Stuart, and William Howard Adams, eds. *Denatured Visions, Landscape and Culture in the Twentieth Century*. New York, 1988.

Wylson, Anthony. *Aquatecture: Architecture and Water*. London, 1986.

Yamada, Michiko. "Dan Kiley: Landscape Design II: In Step with Nature." *Process Architecture*, no. 108 (Feb. 1993).

Zim, Larry, Mel Lerner, and Herbert Rolfe. *The World of Tomorrow: The 1939 New York World's Fair*. New York, 1988.

Zinsser 1991: Zinsser, William. "'I Realized Her Tears Were Becoming Part of the Memorial' [Maya Lin]." *Smithsonian* 22, no. 6 (Sep. 1991), pp. 32–43.

Zion, Robert L. *Process: Architecture 94, Robert Zion: A Profile in Landscape Architecture*. Tokyo, Feb. 1991.

Zion and Breen 1963: Zion, Robert L., and Harold Breen. *New Parks for New York*. Exh. cat., Architectural League of New York and the Park Association of New York, New York, 1963.

Acknowledgments

Researching and gathering information has been somewhat like being a fountain pool gaining valuable substance and volume from both big and little drops of water, all from different sources. I owe enormous gratitude to many designers, colleagues, and friends, who, like a constant supply of revitalizing water, have sustained me with their splashes of stimulating insight, inspiration, advice, encouragement and support. Many were also highly instrumental in easing access to original works and documentation, or in significantly advancing the project to its realization. I am most grateful to all those who were very generous in sharing their expertise, time and resources. Ultimately, however, this book would not have been possible without the backing of Cooper-Hewitt, National Design Museum, Smithsonian Institution staff and resources, and for that I owe major thanks. To Dianne H. Pilgrim, director, and to Linda Dunne and Susan Yelavich, assistant directors, I extend appreciation for their support of the project. To all the generous funders sponsoring *Fountains: Splash and Spectacle*, I add my most sincere thanks.

Deepest gratitude goes to those most involved in the project, either during the beginning, middle, or final stages of realization. The Masters Program in the History of Decorative Arts, a joint program of Cooper-Hewitt, National Design Museum and the Parsons School of Design in New York City, has been a rewarding source for project assistants since 1993. I am particularly grateful to Margery Masinter and to Elizabeth Eustis for their remarkable efforts that became the basis of the bibliography, as well as for their initial lists of European and American fountains, designers, and works of art pertaining to fountains. I also acknowledge the contributions of Bridget Colman, Stacey Dunn, Kimberly Foster, and Susan Vicinelli, who provided crucial assistance at various stages.

The project benefitted from the energy and talents of two Mark Kaminski summer interns, an internship established to encourage promising young students in architecture or architectural history: Amy Hsieh (1994) and Benjamin Kim (1997). Volunteer intern Heather Barr (1994) capably researched fountains in film. I am indebted to Ana Luisa Dias Leite, who first arrived at the museum as a Fulbright fellow from Brazil, and who later became a volunteer project assistant providing encouraging feedback and creative suggestions as the project developed, in addition to augmenting research files.

In the critical stages of preparing this book and the accompanying exhibition, Jeannette Redensek has been a highly valued research associate who has collaborated on every important aspect. The project has been immeasurably strengthened by her keen intelligence, enterprising research skills, organizational talents, and her constant professionalism. She was an ideal partner for navigating the fascinating complexities of fountains history and design. I am exceedingly grateful for her vital role in the project's success.

I heartily thank all the authors of this book. I greatly appreciate their scholarly contribution and insight that substantially enhanced this publication. I particularly thank Kenneth Breisch, Andrew Scott Dolkart, Paula Deitz, Naomi Miller, and Marc Treib, who, over the course of many enthusiastic dialogues, made invaluable suggestions and provided key information that greatly enriched the book's content.

Maria Ann Conelli and Stephen Van Dyk were helpful in advising on the book's thematic approach at the earliest proposal stages. Stephen Astley, Bart Barlow, and Katherine Wentworth Rinne generously shared their expertise.

Behind every major project there is always a larger team providing necessary support in various aspects. I am grateful to my Cooper-Hewitt, National Design Museum colleagues. I extend most appreciative thanks to the Department of Drawings and Prints staff: Gail S. Davidson, Samantha Finch, Elizabeth Marcus, John Randall, and to our department volunteers, Dorothy U. Compagno, Madeline Greenberg, Phyllis Dearborn Massar, and Rolf Myller. I also thank former volunteer Ellin Liebman, and former interns India Leval, Chizu Makiyama, and Tanja Poppelreuter. I would especially like to acknowledge Jill Bloomer for masterminding a demanding photography request with grace and efficiency. I thank the following members of the staff for their contributions: Konstanze Bachmann, Dorothy Dunn, Janna Eggebeen, Laura James, James Kirk, Steven Langehough, Barbara Livenstein, Kerry Macintosh, Mei Mah, Lisa Mazzola, Jeff McCartney, Christine McKee, Barbara Miller, Caroline Mortimer, Gillian Moss, Katy Reed, Jen Roos, Cordelia Rose, Brent Rumage, Sheri Sandler, Lindsay Shapiro, Deborah Shinn, Larry Silver, Rona Simon, Lt. Dwight D. Stevenson and the security staff, Nerissa Tackett, Leonard Webers, Lois Woodyatt, and Egle Zygas.

I extend appreciative thanks to the staff of many European and American museums, libraries and other institutions for their helpful response to our requests pertaining to fountains. Among them are the American Academy in Rome; Art Institute of Chicago; Art Resource; Avery Architectural and Fine Arts Library, Columbia University; Belgian National Tourist Bureau; Canadian Centre for Architecture; Leo Castelli Gallery; Centre Georges Pompidou; Chicago Historical Society; Cincinnati Historical Society; City of Fountains Foundation, Kansas City; École Nationale Supérieure des Beaux-Arts; Esto; Fountain Society of the United Kingdom; Germanisches Nationalmuseum Nürnberg; The J. Paul Getty Museum; Harvard University Graduate School of Design, Francis Loeb Library Special Collections; Huntington Library; Kansas City Public Library; The Metropolitan Museum of Art, New York; Musée des Arts Décoratifs, Paris; Musée Carnavalet; Musée du Château at Versailles; Musée du Louvre, Département des Arts Graphiques; Musée d'Orsay; Museen der Stadt Nürnberg; Museum of the City of New York; Museum Jean Tinguely, Basel; The Museum of Modern Art, New York; National Building Museum, Washington, D.C.; National Gallery of Art, Washington, D.C.; National Monuments Record, Royal Commission on the Historical Monuments of England; Nationalmuseum, Stockholm; National Museum of American History, Smithsonian Institution, Washington D.C.; New York City Municipal Archives; New-York Historical Society; New York Public Library; The Isamu Noguchi Foundation; Oregon Historical Society, Portland; Pierpont Morgan Library; Project for Public Spaces, New York; Royal Institute of British Architects, London; Sächsische Landesbibliothek and Staatliche Kunstsammlung, Dresden; San Francisco Fine Arts Museums, Achenbach Foundation for Graphic Arts; Smithsonian Institution Libraries, Washington D.C. and New York; Stadtarchiv, Nuremberg; Swiss Tourism; Tate Gallery, London; University of California at Berkeley, Environmental Design Library; University of California at Los Angeles, Department of Architecture and Urban Design, Urban Innovations Group Archive; Victoria and Albert Museum; Wallraf-Richartz Museum, Cologne; WET Design; and The Wolfsonian Foundation.

I particularly thank those who were most helpful on behalf of *Fountains: Splash and Spectacle*: Cynthia Abramson, Bruce Altshuler, Pamela and Peter Ambrose, Dita Amory, Berge Aran, Theresa Bachand, Gordon Baldwin, Carmen Bambach, Eleanor Barefoot, Lydia Beauvais, Mirka Beneš, Barry Bergdoll, Mary Beth Betts, Catherine Bindman, Hilary Bischoff, Christian Bjone, Suzanne Boorsch, Joan Brigham, Emmanuele Brugerolles, David Burnhauser, Barbara Butts, Elizabeth and Charles Byrne, Bill Calloway, Maria Camoratto, Ulf Cederlöf, Julie Casemore, Richard Chaix, Alvin L. Clark, Jr., Virginia Clayton, Susan Cohen, Julia Converse, Mary Corliss, Shirley Crockett, Mary Daniels, Joan Davidson, Philip Davies, Mary Karen Delmont, Susan Delson, Linda J. Dillon, Robert E. Drake, Greg Dreicer, Sonia Edard, Margit Erb, Cinnia Finfer, Nancy Finlay, Ronald Lee Fleming, Bill Fontana, Merry Foresta, Tom Fox, Sharon Frost, Betsy Fryberger, Peter Fuhring, Mark Fuller, Jim Garland, Marie-Noële de Gary, Angela Giral, Bruno Girveau, Margaret Glover, Catherine Goguel, George Goldner, Marion Goodman Gallery, Margaret M. Grasselli, Howard Greenberg, Lawrence Halprin, Amy Hau, Bayanne Hauhart, Julia Henshaw, Charles Hind, Michele Horowitz, Richard Howard, Dorothée Imbert, Charles Isaacs, Annie Jacques, Pippa Johnson, Nicolas Joly, Claire Kahn, Ira Kahn, Dan Kany, Judith Keller, Jonathan Kuhn, Susan Lambert, Marianne Lamonaca, Jill Lever, Maya Lin, Gail Lloyd, Kathleen Luhrs, Elizabeth Lunning, Anne Lyden, Peter MacGill, Caroline Mathieu, Karen McCready, Elizabeth Miller, Evelyne Mock, Brigitte de Montclos, Joann Moser, Laura Muir, Dee Mullen, Luigi Mumford, Geneviève Musin, Mary Myers, Weston Naef, Dennis Nawrocki, Charles Newton, M. Nguyen, Wolfgang Nittnaus, Leslie Nolan, Carolyn Nott, Laurie Olin, Lillian Opsomer, Leslie Overstreet, Tricia Paik, Janet Parks, David Peyceré, Sally Pierce, John Pinto, Max Polonovski, Jos Poodt, Bill Raczko, Robert Rainwater, Arnaud Ramière de Fortanier, Wendy Wick Reaves, Marcia Reed, Robert J. Reeds, Françoise Reynaud, Margaret Richardson, Nancy Robertson, Andrew Robison, Joseph Rosas, Myra Rosenfeld, Arthur Ross, Susan Rossen, Jeffery Rudell, Shoji Sadao, Thelma Seear, Suzanne Sekey, Wendy Shadwell, Janet Skidmore, Michael Snodin, Kristin Spangenberg, Anne Spink, Miriam Stewart, Jeffery Stine, Michele Stone, Jesse Stovall, Louise Stover, Jerry Sully, Beryl Jean and Laurence M. Symmes, Athena Tacha, Selma Thomas, Moira Thunder, Mayumi Tsutakawa, Dan Tuttle, Julia Van Haaften, Françoise Viatte, Ann Volkwein, Roberta Waddell, Paul F. Walter, Wendy Walter, Guy Walton, Jennifer Watts, Uwe Westfehling, Bill Whitaker, John Willenbecher, Bill Wilson, Allan Wilson, James and Chris Wines, Stephen Wirtz, Wim de Wit, Robert Woodward, Mary K. Woolever, Stuart Wrede, David Wright, Elizabeth Wyckoff, Elyn Zimmerman, and Robert Zion. I also thank all the professional photographers whose work is illustrated in this book for kindly responding to my requests for fountains images.

Finally, I thank the London Thames and Hudson staff for expertly seeing this publication through to completion.

Marilyn Symmes, curator, Cooper-Hewitt, National Design Museum, Smithsonian Institution

Picture Credits

Frontispiece Photograph © Jane Lidz

2 Photograph © Bart Barlow

3 Cooper-Hewitt, National Design Museum, Smithsonian Institution. Art Resource, New York. Photograph Matt Flynn

Chapter 1

4 Cooper-Hewitt, National Design Museum Branch, Smithsonian Institution Libraries. Art Resource, New York. Photograph Matt Flynn

5 The J. Paul Getty Museum, Los Angeles, California

6 National Museum of American Art, Smithsonian Institution. Museum purchase from the Charles Isaacs Collection made possible in part by the Luisita L. and Franz H. Denghausen Endowment

7 Cooper-Hewitt, National Design Museum, Smithsonian Institution. Art Resource, New York. Photograph Matt Flynn

8 Photograph © Swiss Tourism/L. Degonda

9 Photograph © Balthazar Korab

10 Photograph © Hugh Palmer

11 Photograph © Steve Brady

12 Photograph © WET Design/Ira Kahn

13 Photograph © Jane Lidz. Originally published in *Water and Architecture*, by Charles W. Moore, photographs by Jane Lidz (Harry N. Abrams, Inc., Publishers, 1994)

14 Musée Carnavalet, Paris. © Photothèque des Musées de la Ville de Paris/Degraces

15 Courtesy of Leo Castelli Gallery

16 Photograph Erich Lessing/Art Resource, New York

17 Scala/Art Resource, New York

18 The Metropolitan Museum of Art. Harry G. Sperling Fund, 1973 (1973.265 recto)

19, 20 Cooper-Hewitt, National Design Museum, Smithsonian Institution. Art Resource, New York. Photographs Ken Pelka

21 Cooper-Hewitt, National Design Museum, Smithsonian Institution. Art Resource, New York. Photograph Matt Flynn

22 Cooper-Hewitt, National Design Museum, Smithsonian Institution. Art Resource, New York. Photograph Ken Pelka

23 Cooper-Hewitt, National Design Museum, Smithsonian Institution. Art Resource, New York. Photograph Matt Flynn

24–31 Cooper-Hewitt, National Design Museum Branch, Smithsonian Institution Libraries. Art Resource, New York. Photographs Matt Flynn

32–35 Courtesy of Time-Life, Inc. Photographs Bill Eppridge

36 Mark J. Millard Architectural Collection, © Board of Trustees, National Gallery of Art, Washington, D.C.

37 Graphische Sammlung, Museen der Stadt Nürnberg

38 Cooper-Hewitt, National Design Museum Branch, Smithsonian Institution Libraries. Art Resource, New York. Photograph Matt Flynn

39 Cooper-Hewitt, National Design Museum, Smithsonian Institution, Gift of the Port Royal Foundation, Inc. Art Resource, New York. Photograph Matt Flynn

40 Kupferstich-Kabinett der Staatlichen Kunstsammlungen Dresden

41 Photograph Erich Lessing/Art Resource, New York

42–44 Photographs © WET Design/Ira Kahn

45 Photograph courtesy of E. H. Butler Library, Buffalo State College/Paul Pasquarello

46 Photograph © Bart Barlow

47 Photograph SWA Group/Gerry Campbell

48 Photograph Peter Walker and Partners/Pamela Palmer

Chapter 2

49 Photograph François Bibal

50 Photograph H. Brooks Walker, National Geographic Society Image Collection

51 Print Collection, Miriam and Ira D. Wallach Division of Art, Prints and Photographs, The New York Public Library, Astor, Lenox and Tilden Foundations

52 Private collection, New York. Courtesy of Cooper-Hewitt, National Design Museum, Smithsonian Institution. Art Resource, New York. Photograph Matt Flynn

53 Cooper-Hewitt, National Design Museum Branch, Smithsonian Institution Libraries. Art Resource, New York. Photograph Matt Flynn

54 Film Stills Library, Museum of Modern Art, New York

55 Alinari/Art Resource, New York

56 [left] The Metropolitan Museum of Art, Harris Brisbane Dick Fund, 1949 (49.141)

57 [right] Victoria and Albert Museum, London. Photograph V&A Picture Library

58 Alinari/Art Resource, New York

59 National Gallery of Art, Washington, D.C. Mark J. Millard Architectural Collection, acquired with assistance from the Gwendolyn Cafritz Foundation

60 Paris, Musée du Louvre. © Photo RMN/ D. Arnaudet/G. Blot

61 Cooper-Hewitt, National Design Museum, Smithsonian Institution. Art Resource, New York. Photograph Matt Flynn

62 Paris, Musée Carnavalet. © Photothèque des Musées de la Ville de Paris/Briant

63 Photograph François Bibal

64 Private collection, New York. Courtesy of Cooper-Hewitt, National Design Museum, Smithsonian Institution. Art Resource, New York. Photograph Matt Flynn

65 Stephen Wirtz Gallery, San Francisco

66 Private collection, New York. Courtesy of Cooper-Hewitt, National Design Museum, Smithsonian Institution. Art Resource, New York. Photograph Matt Flynn

67 Cooper-Hewitt, National Design Museum, Smithsonian Institution. Art Resource, New York. Photograph Matt Flynn

68 Photograph François Bibal

69 Paris, Musée Carnavalet. © Photothèque des Musées de la Ville de Paris/Pierrain

70 Photograph Marilyn Symmes

71 Private collection, New York. Courtesy of Cooper-Hewitt, National Design Museum, Smithsonian Institution. Art Resource, New York. Photograph Matt Flynn

72 Photograph Barry Bergdoll

73 Victoria and Albert Museum, London. Photograph V&A Picture Library

74 Paris, Musée d'Orsay. © Photo RMN/B. Hatala

75 © Collection of The New-York Historical Society

76 Print Collection, Miriam and Ira D. Wallach Division of Art, Prints and Photographs, The New York Public Library, Astor, Lenox and Tilden Foundations

77, 78 Smithsonian Institution Libraries. Courtesy of Cooper-Hewitt, National Design Museum, Smithsonian Institution. Art Resource, New York. Photographs Matt Flynn

79, 80 Victoria and Albert Museum, London. Photographs V&A Picture Library

81 Photograph Philip Davies

82 Victoria and Albert Museum, London. Photograph V&A Picture Library

83 © National Monuments Record, Royal Commission on the Historical Monuments of England

84 Photography Collection, Miriam and Ira D. Wallace Division of Art, Prints and Photographs, The New York Public Library, Astor, Lenox and Tilden Foundations

85 Photograph Marilyn Symmes

86 Library of the Boston Atheneum

87 Oregon Historical Society, Portland (56862)

88 Oregon Historical Society, Portland (83843)

89 Cooper-Hewitt, National Design Museum Branch, Smithsonian Institution Libraries. Art Resource, New York. Photograph Matt Flynn

90 Photography Collection, Miriam and Ira D. Wallach Division of Art, Prints and Photographs, The New York Public Library, Astor, Lenox and Tilden Foundations

Chapter 3

91 Photograph © Jane Lidz

92 Musée Condé, Chantilly. Giraudon, courtesy of Naomi Miller

93 Allen Memorial Art Museum, Oberlin College, Ohio (R.T. Miller, Jr. Fund, 1952)

94 Photograph courtesy of Naomi Miller

95 National Gallery of Art, Washington, D.C. (Rosenwald Collection, 1943.3.376/PR)

96 National Gallery of Art, Washington, D.C. (Rosenwald Collection, 1943.3.1041, 1943.3.9327-29/PR)

97 Hauptamt für Hochbauwesen Nürnberg Bildstelle und Denkmalarchiv. Photograph courtesy of the Stadt Nürnberg Stadtarchiv, Bild-, Film-, und Tonarchiv

98 Biblioteca Estense, Modena, Italy (α.X.2.14 = Lat. 209, C.9r). Scala/Art Resource, New York

99 Vanni/Art Resource, New York

100 Photography Collection, Miriam and Ira D. Wallach Division of Art, Prints, and Photographs, The New York Public Library, Astor, Lenox and Tilden Foundations

101 Staatsarchiv des Kantons Bern. Photograph Frutig

102 Museen der Stadt Nürnberg, Graphische Sammlung

103 Hauptamt für Hochbauwesen Nürnberg Bildstelle und Denkmalsarchiv. Photograph Herrmann/ Hochbauamt, Stadt Nürnberg Stadtarchiv, Bild-, Film-, und Tonarchiv

104 Victoria and Albert Museum, London. Photograph V&A Picture Library

105 Archives of the City of Brussels. Photograph
J. J. Rousseau

106 Photograph Belgian National Tourist Office,
New York

107 Cooper-Hewitt, National Design Museum Branch,
Smithsonian Institution Libraries. Art Resource,
New York. Photograph Matt Flynn

108 Photograph Naomi Miller

109 Alinari/Art Resource, New York

110 Cooper-Hewitt, National Design Museum,
Smithsonian Institution. Art Resource, New York.
Photograph Ken Pelka

111 Hauptamt für Hochbauwesen Nürnberg Bildstelle
und Denkmalsarchiv. Photograph Hochbauamt, Stadt
Nürnberg Stadtarchiv, Bild-, Film-, und Tonarchiv

112 Photograph Naomi Miller

113 © Photograph Sandra Baker/Gamma Liaison
International

114 Erich Lessing/Art Resource, New York

115 Cooper-Hewitt, National Design Museum,
Smithsonian Institution. Art Resource, New York.
Photograph Ken Pelka

116 Cooper-Hewitt, National Design Museum,
Smithsonian Institution. Art Resource, New York.
Photograph Matt Flynn

117 National Gallery of Art, Washington, D.C.
(Ailsa Mellon Bruce Fund)

118 The J. Paul Getty Museum, Los Angeles,
California

119 National Gallery of Art, Washington, D.C.
(Rosenwald Collection, 1943.3.9520/GR)

120 The Pierpont Morgan Library, New York
(PML 373, ChLf1017)

121, 122 Alinari/Art Resource, New York

123 Cooper-Hewitt, National Design Museum Branch,
Smithsonian Institution Libraries. Art Resource,
New York. Photograph Matt Flynn

124 Photograph © Balthazar Korab

125 Aloe Plaza Commemorative Book, The Saint Louis
Art Museum, Gift of Howard Baer

126 Photograph © Collection of The New-York
Historical Society

127 Cooper-Hewitt, National Design Museum,
Smithsonian Institution. Art Resource, New York.
Photograph Matt Flynn

Chapter 4

128 Photograph © Marc Treib.

129 Scala/Art Resource, New York

130 Photograph Maria Ann Conelli

131 Cooper-Hewitt, National Design Museum,
Smithsonian Institution. Art Resource, New York.
Photograph Ken Pelka

132 Alinari/Art Resource, New York

133 Cooper-Hewitt, National Design Museum Branch,
Smithsonian Institution Libraries. Art Resources,
New York. Photograph Matt Flynn

134 Stockholm, Nationalmuseum, THC 1

135 Cooper-Hewitt, National Design Museum,
Smithonian Institution. Art Resource, New York.
Photograph Matt Flynn

136 Stockholm, Nationalmuseum, THC 7811

137, 138 Cooper-Hewitt, National Design Museum,
Smithsonian Institution. Art Resource, New York.
Photographs Matt Flynn

139 Bildarchiv Foto Marburg/Art Resource, New York

140 Cooper-Hewitt, National Design Museum,
Smithsonian Institution. Art Resource, New York.
Photograph Matt Flynn

141 Photograph © Étienne de Malglaive,
Gamma/Liaison International

142 Photograph © Michael Kenna, 1988, courtesy of
Stephen Wirtz Gallery

143 Photograph © Étienne de Malglaive,
Gamma/Liaison International

144 Cooper-Hewitt, National Design Museum Branch,
Smithsonian Institution Libraries. Art Resource,
New York. Photograph Matt Flynn

145 Victoria and Albert Museum, London. Photograph
V&A Picture Library

146 Bildarchiv Foto Marburg/Art Resource, New York

147 Cooper-Hewitt, National Design Museum,
Smithsonian Institution. Art Resource, New York.
Photograph Matt Flynn

148 Alinari/Art Resource, New York

149, 150 Musée du Louvre, Paris. © Photo
RMN/Michèle Bellot

151 National Gallery of Art, Washington, D.C.,
Mark J. Millard Architectural Collection, acquired with
assistance from the Morris and Gwendolyn Cafritz
Foundation (1985.61.107)

152 Photograph © 1995 Sandra Baker/Gamma Liaison
International

153 Cooper-Hewitt, National Design Museum,
Smithsonian Institution. Art Resource, New York.
Photograph Matt Flynn

154 Musée du Louvre, Paris. © Photo RMN

155 Wallraf-Richartz Museum, Cologne. Photograph ©
Rheinisches Bildarchiv

156 Photography Collection, Miriam and Ira D. Wallace
Division of Art, Prints and Photographs, The New York
Public Library, Astor, Lenox and Tilden Foundations

157 Wallraf-Richartz Museum, Cologne. Photograph ©
Rheinisches Bildarchiv

158 Cooper-Hewitt, National Design Museum,
Smithsonian Institution. Art Resource, New York.
Photograph Matt Flynn

159 Photograph François Bibal

160 Photograph © Bart Barlow

161 Photograph © Jane Lidz. Originally published in
Water and Architecture, by Charles W. Moore, photographs
by Jane Lidz (Harry N. Abrams, Inc., Publishers, 1994)

162 National Museum of American Art, Smithsonian
Institution. Bequest of Paul Manship

163 Photograph Arthur Lavine, courtesy of Chase
Manhattan Archives

164 Photograph Raymond Juschkus, courtesy of Chase
Manhattan Archives

165 Photograph Lawrence Halprin

166 Photograph SWA Group/Tom Fox

167 Photograph © Hugh Palmer

168 © National Monuments Record, Royal
Commission on the Historical Monuments of England

169 Cooper-Hewitt, National Design Museum Branch,
Smithsonian Institution Libraries. Art Resource, New
York. Photograph Matt Flynn

170 Photograph François Bibal

171 Photograph © 1995 Allan Philiba/Gamma Liaison
International

172 © National Monuments Record, Royal
Commission on the Historical Monuments of England

173 Photograph Niall Clutton/Arcaid, courtesy of Esto
Photographics, Inc.

Chapter 5

174 Photograph © WET Design/Ira Kahn

175, 176 Cooper-Hewitt, National Design Museum
Branch, Smithsonian Institution Libraries. Art Resource,
New York. Photographs Matt Flynn

177 Photograph © Sandra Baker/Gamma Liaison
International

178–80 Robert N. Dennis Collection of Stereoscopic
Views. Photography Collection, Miriam and Ira D.
Wallach Division of Art, Prints and Photographs, The
New York Public Library, Astor, Lenox and Tilden
Foundations

181, 182 Cooper-Hewitt, National Design Museum
Branch, Smithsonian Institution Libraries. Art Resource,
New York. Photographs Matt Flynn

183 Chicago Historical Society Prints and Photographs
Department (ICHi-17121)

184–90 Cooper-Hewitt, National Design Museum
Branch, Smithsonian Institution Libraries. Art Resource,
New York. Photographs Matt Flynn

191–93 Archives nationales/Institut français
d'architecture Archives d'architecture du XX siécle,
Paris – (AN/IFA)

194, 195 Cooper-Hewitt, National Design Museum
Branch, Smithsonian Institution Libraries. Art Resource,
New York. Photographs Matt Flynn

196, 197 Photographs © Museum of the City of New
York

198 Photography Collection, Miriam and Ira D.
Wallach Division of Art, Prints and Photographs, The
New York Public Library, Astor, Lenox and Tilden
Foundations

199 The Wurts Collection, Museum of the City of New
York. Photograph © Museum of the City of New York

200 Photograph © Museum of the City of New York

201 Private collection, New York. Photograph courtesy
of Cooper-Hewitt, National Design Museum,
Smithsonian Institution. Art Resource, New York.
Photograph Matt Flynn

202 Photograph Isamu Noguchi, courtesy of the Isamu
Noguchi Foundation, Inc.

203–07 Photographs © Bart Barlow

Chapter 6

208 © Photograph Robert O'Dea/Arcaid, courtesy of
Esto Photographics, Inc.

209 Cooper-Hewitt, National Design Museum Branch,
Smithsonian Institution Libraries. Art Resource, New
York. Photograph Matt Flynn

210 © National Monuments Record, Royal
Commission on the Historical Monuments of England

211 Mairie de Paris, Direction de l'Aménagement
Urbain et de la Construction. Photograph Guy Picard

212 Photograph Marilyn Symmes

213 Cooper-Hewitt, National Design Museum Branch,
Smithsonian Institution Libraries. Art Resource, New
York. Photograph Matt Flynn

214 Photograph © Balthazar Korab

215, 216 © Collection of The New-York Historical Society

217 Photograph Marilyn Symmes

218 Edward H. Bennett Collection, The Art Institute of Chicago. Photograph Chicago Aerial Photo Services, Inc.

219 Photograph © Peter J. Schulz/Gamma-Liaison International

220 Photograph Jack Denzer

221 Photograph courtesy of Maya Lin

222 Photograph © Adam Stoltman

223 Photograph © Elliott Erwitt/Magnum Photos, Inc., 1950

224–26 Photographs courtesy of Lawrence Halprin

227 Photograph Marilyn Symmes

228 Photograph Lawrence Halprin

Chapter 7

229 Photograph © Jane Lidz. Originally published in *Water and Architecture*, by Charles W. Moore, photographs by Jane Lidz (Harry N. Abrams, Inc., Publishers, 1994)

230 Photograph © Jane Lidz

231 Alinari/Art Resouce, New York

232 Scala/Art Resouce, New York

233 Photograph © Jane Lidz

234 Photograph Maria Ann Conelli

235 Cooper-Hewitt, National Design Museum Branch, Smithsonian Institution Libraries. Art Resource, New York. Photograph Matt Flynn

236 Scala/Art Resource, New York

237 Photograph Maria Ann Conelli

238 Photograph © Hugh Palmer

239 Erich Lessing/Art Resource, New York

240 Cooper-Hewitt, National Design Museum, Smithsonian Institution. Art Resource, New York. Photograph Matt Flynn

241 Print Collection, Miriam and Ira D. Wallach Division of Art, Prints and Photographs, The New York Public Library, Astor, Lenox and Tilden Foundations

242 Cooper-Hewitt, National Design Museum, Smithsonian Institution, Gift of Roger Selchow. Art Resource, New York. Photograph Ken Pelka

243 Cooper-Hewitt, National Design Museum, Smithsonian Institution, Gift of the Port Royal Foundation, Inc. Art Resource, New York. Photograph Ken Pelka

244 Photograph © Hugh Palmer

245 Photograph © Balthazar Korab

246 Photograph Joseph H. Bailey © National Geographic Society Image Collection

247–49 Photographs © WET Design/Ira Kahn

250 Photograph © Richard J. Korek

251 Photograph courtesy of The Mirage

252, 253 Drawings and Archives, Avery Architectural and Fine Arts Library, Columbia University

254 Ezra Stoller © Esto

255 Sächsische Landesbibliothek, Staats- und Universitätsbibliothek Dresden, Deutsche Fotothek/Thonig

256 Photograph Mary Randlett, courtesy of George Tsutakawa

257 Photograph Bruce Terami, courtesy of George Tsutakawa

258 Photograph © Tate Gallery Archive

259 Photograph Peer van der Kruis. Heeze NL/ courtesy of Museum Het Kruithuis, 's-Hertogenbosch

260 Photograph Leonardo Bezzola

261 Photograph Athena Tacha

262 Cooper-Hewitt, National Design Museum Branch, Smithsonian Institution Libraries. Art Resource, New York. Photograph Matt Flynn

263, 264 Photographs © Hugh Palmer

265 Museum Jean Tinguely, Basel

266–68 Photographs Leonardo Bezzola

269 Photograph © Jane Lidz. Originally published in *Water and Architecture*, by Charles W. Moore, photographs by Jane Lidz (Harry N. Abrams, Inc., Publishers, 1994)

Chapter 8

270 Photograph © Balthazar Korab

271 Photograph H. Brooks Walker, National Geographic Society Image Collection

272 Film Stills Library, Museum of Modern Art, New York

273, 274 Photographs © Marc Treib

275 Photograph courtesy of Urban Innovations Group Archives, University of California, Los Angeles

276, 277 Photographs © Balthazar Korab

278–80 Photographs courtesy of Robert Zion, Zion & Breen Associates

281, 282 Photographs courtesy of Lawrence Halprin

283 Photograph Oregon Historical Society Photographs Department, Portland (74432)

284 Photograph by Maude Dorr, Lawrence Halprin Archives

285 Photograph © Timothy Hursley

286 Photograph Jim Hallas, Lawrence Halprin Archives

287 Photograph © Richard Payne

288, 289 Photographs © Marc Treib

290–92 Photographs © Steve Brady

293 Photograph © WET Design/Ira Kahn

294, 295 Photographs © Jane Lidz

296 Photograph © Aaron Kiley

297 Photograph © Hugh Palmer

298 Photograph © Michael Moran, courtesy of Burton & Company

299 Photograph courtesy of Team Plan

300 Photograph © Xavier Testelin/Gamma Liaison International

301 Cooper-Hewitt, National Design Museum Branch, Smithsonian Institution Libraries. Art Resource, New York. Photograph Matt Flynn

302 © Leonard Freed/Magnum. Photograph courtesy of Howard Greenberg Gallery

Text Credits

p. 28 Charles Baudelaire, "The Fountain," from *Les Fleurs du Mal (The Flowers of Evil) and other poems*, trans. by Richard Howard. David R. Godine, Boston, 1982.

p. 33 Nicola Salvi (in his document on the Trevi Fountain's iconography), *c.* 1732, as translated by Hereward Lester Cooke in "The Documents Relating to the Trevi," *Art Bulletin* 33, 1956, pp. 149–73.

p. 59 Dante Alighieri, *Paradiso*, canto XXV, as translated by Arturo Vivante in *Italian Poetry. An Anthology*. Delphinium Press, Wellfleet, Mass., 1996.

p. 123 Johann Wolfgang Goethe, *Song of the Spirits over the Water*, 1779, as quoted in Ernst-Erik Pfannschmidt, *Fountains and Springs*, trans. by Diana Steinmetz. Universe Books, Inc., New York, 1969.

p. 137 Richard Wilbur, "A Baroque Wall-Fountain in the Villa Sciarra," from *New and Collected Poems*. Harcourt Brace Jovanovich, San Diego, New York, and London, 1989.

Index

Numerals in *italics* refer to captions to illustrations